Mediasphere Shanghai

Mediasphere

THE AESTHETICS OF

A STUDY OF THE WEATHERHEAD EAST ASIAN INSTITUTE

Shanghai

CULTURAL PRODUCTION

Alexander Des Forges

University of Hawai'i Press · Honolulu

© 2007 University of Hawai'i Press

Printed in the United States of America

12 11 10 09 08 07   6 5 4 3 2 1

Library of Congress Cataloging-in-Publication Data

Des Forges, Alexander Townsend.
   Mediasphere Shanghai : the aesthetics of cultural production / Alexander Des
Forges.
        p. cm. — (Studies of the Weatherhead East Asian Institute)
   Includes bibliographical references and index.
   ISBN 978-0-8248-3081-6 (alk. paper)
1. Shanghai (China)   I. Title.
   DS796.S24D47 2007
   700'.4251132—dc22

                                                                    2007010395

Studies of the Weatherhead East Asian Institute
Columbia University
The Weatherhead East Asian Institute is Columbia University's center for research, publication, and teaching on modern and contemporary Asia Pacific
regions. The Studies of the Weatherhead East Asian Institute were inaugurated in 1962 to bring to a wider public the results of significant new research
on modern and contemporary East Asia.

University of Hawai'i Press books are printed on acid-free
paper and meet the guidelines for permanence and durability
of the Council on Library Resources.

Designed by Paul Herr
Composited by Santos Barbasa of the University of Hawaii Press
Printed by The Maple-Vail Book Manufacturing Group

To my parents

Contents

Acknowledgments

This book focuses on the cultural production of a single city, but I have accumulated debts in many places while researching and writing it. I would especially like to thank my dissertation advisor, Perry Link, for his unflagging support and many helpful suggestions over the years. In Shanghai, I have benefited for almost a decade from the hospitality and advice of Yuan Jin, originally of the Shanghai Academy of Social Sciences and now at Fudan University.

At a time when I was just beginning work on this project, Ono Kazuko provided invaluable assistance in the form of affiliation with the Kyoto University Institute of the Humanities and many useful suggestions, for which I am very grateful. I would also like to thank Andrew Plaks, Susan Naquin, and Patrick Hanan for their willingness to read and comment on my work as it progressed, and Wang Jiquan at Fudan University and Kim Moon-Kyong of the Kyoto University Institute of the Humanities for taking the time to advise me on a number of hard-to-find sources. I am particularly grateful to Wei Shaochang for sharing stories of "old Shanghai," and for his gift of a photograph of the map on which figure 2 is based.

As this book took shape, it benefited greatly from comments and advice generously provided by David Wang, Rey Chow, and Dorothy Ko; I would like to thank them for their enthusiasm for this project. I am indebted to Madge Huntington at the Weatherhead East Asian Institute at Columbia University for her careful attention to questions of structure and wording; I would also like to thank Pamela Kelley, Ann Ludeman, and Terre Fisher of University of Hawai'i Press for their energy and impressive efficiency.

As a study of late-nineteenth- and early-twentieth-century cultural production, this book makes use of a variety of texts and images that were never intended to be collected and preserved, much less suffer the attention of later scholars. For this reason, I am indebted to the librarians and staff at the following institutions for carefully keeping the ephemera of previous centuries and for sharing them with me: Shanghai Library (especially Feng Jinniu and Zhu Junzhou), Shanghai Municipal Archives, Fudan University Library, Suzhou

University Library, Gest Library at Princeton University, Harvard-Yenching Library, Phillips Library, Peabody Essex Museum (especially Bruce MacLaren), the Österreichische Nationalbibliothek, Tōyō bunko, and the Kyoto University Institute of the Humanities Library.

The Pembroke Center for Teaching and Research on Women at Brown University provided a congenial and inspirational atmosphere for writing and revision in the form of a postdoctoral fellowship and a weekly seminar; I would like to thank Ellen Rooney and Elizabeth Weed, directors of the Center, for their commitment to challenging and wide-ranging conversations.

I owe a great deal to friends and colleagues who shared their responses to this project while it was a work in progress and suggested improvements. I would especially like to thank Yomi Braester, Chen Jianhua, Eileen Chow, Denise Davis, Megan Ferry, Poshek Fu, Joshua Goldstein, Alison Groppe, Michel Hockx, Hu Ying, Paize Keulemans, Brian Locke, Keith McMahon, Meng Yue, Daisy Ng, Pan Tianshu, Melinda Pirazzoli, Christopher Reed, Monique Roelofs, Carlos Rojas, David Rolston, Shen Ji, Tomoko Shiroyama, Ann Waltner, Ban Wang, Lingzhen Wang, Ellen Widmer, Catherine Yeh, and Paola Zamperini.

I am grateful for financial support from the Mellon Foundation, the Whiting Fellowship, the Fulbright-Hays program for doctoral dissertation research abroad, the Pembroke Center for Teaching and Research on Women at Brown University, and the office of the Dean of the College of Liberal Arts at the University of Massachusetts–Boston.

Earlier versions of parts of chapters 3 and 4 originally appeared in "Building Shanghai, One Page at a Time: The Aesthetics of Installment Fiction at the Turn of the Century," *Journal of Asian Studies* 62.3 (2003): 781–810. I am grateful for permission to include these portions here.

My colleagues at the University of Massachusetts–Boston have introduced me to the joys of teaching at an urban university and have provided valuable real-world wisdom. Many thanks to my parents, my sister and brother-in-law, and my parents-in-law for their interest and enthusiasm in this project over the years. Finally, I am indebted to my spouse, Terry Kawashima, who always inspires me to read closely, think carefully, and be sure to have a point. Her support and encouragement have been crucial to this book.

Conventions and Abbreviations

In the text, frequently mentioned novels are referred to by their translated titles. [For a list of the romanized titles as they are frequently cited in the notes, see page 185.]

Dreams of Shanghai Splendor	Sun Yusheng, *Haishang fanhua meng* (1898–1906)
Dreams of Shanghai Splendor, Continued	Sun Yusheng, *Xu Haishang Fanhua meng* (1915–1916)
Famous Courtesans Contending for Dominance	*Mengyou Shanghai mingji zhengfeng zhuan* (after 1904)
Hell in This World	Bi Yihong and Bao Tianxiao, *Renjian diyu* (1922–1924)
The Huangpu Tides	Zhu Shouju, *Xiepu chao* (1916–1921)
Lives of Shanghai Flowers	Han Bangqing, *Haishang hua liezhuan* (1892–1894)
Midnight	Mao Dun, *Ziye* (1933)
New Huangpu Tides	Zhu Shouju, *Xin Xiepu chao* (c. 1923)
New Shanghai	Lu Shi'e, *Xin Shanghai* (1909)
Romance on Hu River	Xu Qinfu, *Hujiang fengyue zhuan* (1921)
Shadows of Shanghai's Dusty Skies	Zou Tao, *Haishang chentian ying* (1896)
Shanghai Annals	Bao Tianxiao, *Shanghai chunqiu* (1924)
A Shanghai Swan's Traces in the Snow	Erchun jushi, *Haitian hong xueji* (1899)
Shanghai's Great Prospect Garden	Wumu shanren, *Haishang Daguan yuan* (1924)

Introduction

Et voilà Shanghaï!
—Tintin, *Le lotus bleu*

For twentieth- and twenty-first-century readers around the world, "Shanghai" is a name with real power, denoting the quintessence of modernity in East Asia, whether conceived of as glamorous and exciting, as corrupt and impoverishing, or as a complex synthesis of the good, the bad, and the ugly. How did the name Shanghai acquire this power? How did adventurers, refugees, and businessmen and women from across China and around the world know that Shanghai was the place they wanted to go? How did they learn what to expect when they arrived and how to become "Shanghai people" *(Szahaenin)*? I suggest that the answers to these questions can be found in part in the products of the Shanghai culture industry: the guidebooks, newspapers, novels, illustration collections, and films that portrayed Shanghai as a uniquely prosperous, fascinating, and dangerous city. These printed texts and images were among the city's most important industrial products from the second half of the nineteenth century into the first half of the twentieth; they made substantial profits for Shanghai publishers and film studios, advertised the city as a desirable destination wherever they were sold, and finally, conditioned the experiences of both visitors and residents through their specific visions of the city. It is this cultural production—in Chinese, Japanese, and a variety of European languages—that makes it possible for travelers from all over to arrive in the city with some variation of the words "So this is Shanghai!" on their lips, words that indicate not discovery but rather *recognition.*[1]

For readers of Shanghai fiction in particular, this recognition goes beyond the easily visible—the Bund skyline, the crowded streets and alleys, and the extremes of wealth and poverty—to encompass the subtler *aesthetic* forms through which Shanghai cultural production and social practice are organized. Four of these forms, which may be referred to more precisely as narrative tropes, stand out: (1) simultaneity: different things happening at the same time; (2) interruption: breaks in continuity; (3) mediation: a position between two sides that defines those sides as internally coherent and mutually exclusive entities; and (4) excess: the drive to expand without limit and consume without end. These forms give shape and meaning to the sensory and emotional overload—the bewildering array of sights, sounds, hopes, desires, and fears—that confronts individuals who come face-to-face with the city; they allow these individuals to impose a comprehensible and compelling order on that overload and convert a chaotic set of impressions into a coherent understanding of "what Shanghai is." In so doing, these forms constitute a conceptual foundation on which Shanghai's "social reality" is built, construct a frame through which the city can be perceived, and supply a template for the reader's own experiences there.

This book investigates the literary and visual dimensions of these four narrative tropes, as well as their social and material effects, with particular attention to the master genre in which they take concrete form—installment fiction set in Shanghai from the 1890s to the 1930s *(haishang xiaoshuo)*. In its narrative form (the way in which it tells its stories) and its mode of presentation (publication in regular installments), this serialized fiction provides both visitors and residents with a sense of what Shanghai is, and further, an imagination of *how* the city works and what it expects of individuals who find themselves there. This book aims to show how Shanghai fiction supplies not only the imagery that we now consider typical of the city, but more significantly, the very *form* through which the city could be experienced as a business and entertainment center, and imagined as the focal point of a mediasphere with national and transnational reach.

In addition, it will demonstrate the effects that the development of a Shanghai aesthetic—epitomized in installment fiction—has in the broader realm of twentieth-century Chinese cultural history, from the specific (inspiring the transformation of tabloid newspaper journalism at the beginning of the century) to the general (laying the temporal groundwork for the massive nostalgia industry that develops toward the century's end). Finally, this book suggests ways the tropes of simultaneity, interruption, mediation, and excess, among others, set the terms on which Shanghai is even now returning to cultural preeminence and transnational significance.

ॐ

Shanghai's role as site and inspiration for transnational literary and cultural production is well known. Works as varied as Yokomitsu Riichi's modernist installment fiction, *Shanghai* (1928–1929), von Sternberg's film *Shanghai Express* (1932), and Malraux's novel *La condition humaine* (1933) have for years been the subject of intense scholarly inquiry and debate.[2] More recently, Shanghai modernist fiction in Chinese from the 1930s and '40s has attracted a great deal of attention, as have turn-of-the-century guidebooks to the courtesan quarters.[3] Shanghai fiction in Chinese from the 1890s through the 1920s, by contrast, has received significantly less attention, most of it focused on *Haishang hua liezhuan* (Lives of Shanghai flowers), which began publication in installments in 1892, and appeared in a volume edition in 1894.[4]

But *Lives of Shanghai Flowers* was merely the starting point; installment fiction set in Shanghai took off in the mid-1890s and quickly became popular with contemporary readers. By the 1910s, these novels were understood by some authors to constitute a distinct type of long vernacular fiction: *haishang xiaoshuo* (Shanghai novels), characterized by obsessive attention to the contemporary, precision and accuracy in details of place and time, and a tightly woven and complex narrative structure that challenges conventional understandings of plot and storyline. These novels established Shanghai as the standard for urban sophistication against which other cities would be judged and inspired imitations set in locations across China.[5] Their influence is also clear in the better-known "traveling fiction" of the early twentieth century; just as Edo serves as the constant reference point that travelers in *Shank's Mare* cannot avoid talking about no matter where they travel in Japan, knowledge of Shanghai and its fiction is taken for granted in novels like *Ershi nian mudu zhi guai xianzhuang* (Strange happenings eyewitnessed over two decades, 1903–1910) and *Jiuwei gui* (The nine-tailed turtle, 1906–1910).[6] Even the hectic international peregrinations of the various characters in the best-selling *Niehai hua* (Flower in a sea of sin, 1903–1907, 1916) result in part from the author Zeng Pu's sense that it was necessary to go beyond the territory detailed so thoroughly in early Shanghai fiction.[7] As I argue in detail in the sixth chapter of this book, Shanghai novels published in installments in the late Qing and Republican era provided a necessary, though unacknowledged, grounding in form and content for the realist writer Mao Dun (who referred to *Lives of Shanghai Flowers* as a masterpiece of the "literary heritage") as well as for 1930s modernists such as Liu Na'ou, Mu Shiying, and Shi Zhecun.[8]

Shanghai novels continued to fascinate readers throughout the twentieth century, many of whom saw them almost as archaeological relics. In the late 1950s Hsia Tsi-an found several volumes in a hardware store in Seattle's Chinatown:

> They were wrapped up in paper, identified by titles written on with a brush, and stacked horizontally on the shelves. I wonder for how many years they had been left untouched—they were all covered with dust. The sight of these books makes me feel as if Chinese history stopped right there. I bought [*Xiepu chao* (The Huangpu tides), 1916–1921; *Haishang fanhua meng*

(Dreams of Shanghai splendor), 1898–1906; *Shanghai chunqiu* (Shanghai annals), 1924], and other exposé fiction of the early Republican era.

He began to read these novels, continued with *Lives of Shanghai Flowers,* and soon wrote to his brother that he had become interested in writing a study on "those Shanghai novels."[9]

Eileen Chang (Zhang Ailing), who began her own writing career in the 1940s, read Shanghai fiction as a child and singled out *Lives of Shanghai Flowers* and *The Huangpu Tides* for special mention as two of her favorite eight works of Chinese fiction, past and present. In the late 1970s she published a Mandarin translation of *Lives of Shanghai Flowers,* also in installments, and subsequently began work on an English translation, a revised version of which recently appeared in print.[10] Over the last two decades, late Qing and Republican-era Shanghai fiction has also served as inspiration for a wide variety of influential works, including Shanghai-centered short stories and essays by Wang Anyi, fiction set in Kuala Lumpur by the Malaysian Chinese writer Li Tianbao, and a cinematic experiment by the Taiwanese director Hou Hsiao-hsien (*Haishang hua*—Flowers of Shanghai, 1998).[11]

❧

This book begins with a question about the aesthetics of Shanghai installment fiction: how might the formal characteristics of Shanghai narrative give shape and coherence to Shanghai residents and visitors' sensory and emotional experiences of the city? Questions of form, however, cannot be limited to a realm of "pure aesthetics" that is separated from the social and material. They demand to be considered in conjunction with economic development, technological change, and political contestation for their full significance to reveal itself. What follows in this introduction is an outline of the theoretical grounds on which this book is based: the reasons why I believe formal and material concerns to be inextricably interrelated in the study of Shanghai installment fiction, how I understand these concerns to be related, and what specific types of connections between the aesthetic and the social this book will emphasize.

First, we address the question of cultural production, or the constitutive dimension of literary texts and illustrations. How could Shanghai fiction work to "construct" the city instead of merely reflecting it? How might the effects it had on its audiences take on a broader social importance? Second, this introduction demonstrates the significant implications of reading Shanghai fiction as a genre in its social and intellectual context, rather than as a succession of unconnected works. Third, by appropriating and redefining the concept of the "mediasphere," this introduction provides a theoretical basis for expressing the relationship between the formal and material qualities of Shanghai installment fiction on the one hand, and Shanghai's rapid rise to prominence as a national media center on the other. Finally, I locate this book in the broader context of Shanghai cultural history, explaining the differences in emphasis between my approach and existing paradigms in the field. The introduction concludes with a chronological account of the development of Shanghai fiction as a genre and an overview of the book as a whole.

Cultural Production

Until recently, scholars of late nineteenth- and early twentieth-century Chinese literature have tended to isolate literary texts as a particular category and understand them in one of three related ways: as reflections (of historical reality or individual experience), as expressions (of individual thoughts and feelings or universal artistic truths), or as symptoms (of the dilemmas of westernization, the contradictions of modernization, or the semicolonial predicament). In each of these cases, the literary text functions as a discrete object that is secondary to or derivative of the originary matrix or historical process against which it is defined, providing a concrete example of the kind of distinction between social "base" and cultural "superstructure" that Raymond Williams criticizes for its failure to grasp the significance of culture as a "constitutive social process."[12]

Indeed, according to Liang Qichao, one of the most famous theorists of fiction writing in Chinese in the twentieth century, there is another way of understanding literary texts: as fundamentally generative, producing effects on their reading public and society as a whole that should not be underestimated.

> Where did we Chinese people get the idea of holding scholars who took first place in the civil service examinations and prime ministers in high esteem? From fiction *(xiaoshuo)*. Where did our ideal of the talented scholar and the beauty come from? From fiction. Where did our thoughts of Robin Hood types and brigands come from? From fiction. . . . Has it ever been the case that these ideas were transmitted formally, like the master handing over the alms bowl to the disciple? And yet, from the butchers, cooks, peddlers, and messengers, old ladies, young girls, and boys, all the way up to those in the upper classes, those with talent and learning, every one holds at least one of these ideas dear. . . . This is because there are over a hundred works of fiction that have poisoned them directly or indirectly; it's that serious.[13]

Liang argues that fiction has the power to transform its readers and their attitudes fundamentally; he goes on to explain that even those members of society who do not read fiction are infected by it indirectly because the attitudes it produces are contagious. Liang's polemical assertions of the central significance of fiction are clearly a response to a specific set of historical circumstances and reveal an obsession with national reconstruction through literature that we may no longer share. But if we broaden the scope of these assertions to include other kinds of texts in addition to fiction, and allow that texts are not the sole agents of cultural production, but share the stage with many other factors, Liang's claims begin to remind us not only of certain Marxist reconsiderations of the distinction between base and superstructure, but also of more recent theories of the rise of nationalism.

Though he is writing eight decades after Liang Qichao, Benedict Anderson is also concerned with the question of nation formation—how is it that a *national* consciousness can be brought into being in a certain group of people? Anderson's answer, in part, is that the "imagined community" that is the nation depends on a new sense of simultaneity generated in the novel and the newspaper: ". . . these forms provided the technical means for 're-presenting' the *kind* of imagined community that is the nation."[14] The nation is not the only kind of "imagined community" possible. As Perry Link, Leo Lee, and Andrew Nathan first proposed more than two decades ago, and as numerous scholars have emphasized more recently, there is no aspect of cultural production in the late Qing and early Republican period that can compete with fiction and print journalism in forming communities of consumers, and it is no accident that profiles of the *xiao shimin* ("petty urbanite") class—whether in Shanghai or elsewhere in China—return so often to their reading habits as a central defining characteristic.[15] Literary address is clearly a powerful means of writing a variety of communities into existence.

呀

How exactly does cultural practice constitute social reality? How is it that we can speak of literary texts as producing specific social effects? As a heuristic device, it may be helpful to provisionally articulate three aspects of Shanghai installment fiction having three different—though ultimately related—effects on the metropolis and the reading public as a whole: (1) the text as mere object (produced in a factory, providing a return on someone's capital, paying someone else's wages, and creating a market for the machinery required to produce it); (2) the text as advertisement for the city (encouraging visitors from elsewhere in China); and finally, (3) the text as a narrative force that through its aesthetic characteristics structures the reader's experience of Shanghai as a city.

Shanghai's development as an industrial and commercial center in the late nineteenth and early twentieth centuries was due not only to international trade and the establishment of textile factories, but also in significant measure to the publishing and leisure industries. At the turn of the century, books and periodicals were among the most important industrial products that Shanghai had to offer—as had been the case in nineteenth-century New York—commanding an impressive share of foreign investment.[16] Christopher Reed estimates that approximately three hundred publishers and bookstores appeared in the Henan Road / Fuzhou Road area alone in the late nineteenth and early twentieth centuries; this publishing boom in turn created a new industrial niche, print machine shops, that would soon become one of the leading sectors of the Chinese domestic machine manufacturing industry, with a twenty-fold expansion between 1912 and 1932.[17] Even before we begin to consider Shanghai novels as participants in a symbolic economy, we must admit that as mere objects—stacks of printed sheets stitched between bindings, assembled in publishing houses equipped with domestically manufactured printing presses, and sold in stores—the novels were already an important element in Shanghai's economic development. I will pursue this discussion in detail in chapter 4.

Of course, people weren't buying fiction just to stack on a table as ornament or display on a bookshelf as a way to seem cultured. Books of fiction were purchased or rented to be read; novels set in Shanghai functioned as attractive presentations of an urban life of leisure. Shanghai fiction taught its readers to desire an "experience" that those readers had no idea they were missing and made the point that this object of desire could be obtained in a specific place—the city of Shanghai. Like newspapers and guidebooks, novels could explain Shanghai customs and practices to the reader, and typically included the names of the major streets and small alleys, fancy restaurants and lively teahouses, theaters and public parks that constitute one aspect of the urban "grid of reference" discussed in chapter 2.

The third aspect of these novels consists in their ability to organize the presentation of this kind of information in accordance with a particular kind of narrative aesthetic: in explaining to their readers what Shanghai was like, installment fiction in fact conditioned the experience their readers would have of the city—not only readers from elsewhere, but even those readers who had lived in Shanghai for years. Installment fiction helped shape readers' understanding of Shanghai by identifying certain phenomena as worthy of their attention, but also, and more significantly, by providing a concrete narrative logic and a specific aesthetic agenda according to which those phenomena could be put into a compelling and meaningful order.

As Gail Hershatter and Catherine Yeh have shown, turn-of-the-century

Shanghai newspapers and guidebooks did much to explain the city directly, addressing the reader in straightforward fashion.[18] Fiction did this as well, but it could also present the city in more subtle and contagious ways. In novels set in Shanghai, the narrator does occasionally speak directly to the reader about what it means to be there, but the strongest sense of the "Shanghai experience" emerges from a deeper textual level through certain recurring figures. For example, the trope of simultaneity, active at multiple levels, locates the reader in a broad chronologically regulated order; and the sense of near simultaneity between core and periphery assures him or her that Shanghai is at the leading edge of historical change, as we will see in chapter 3. Similarly, the repeated interruption and subsequent continuation of the narrative teaches readers a new mode of consumption, transforming the drive to reach the end of the novel or acquire a certain luxury item into a permanent state of desire that can never be fully satisfied (chapter 4). Mediation creates a sense of multiple coherent narrative lines within a complicated text, and likewise introduces and reinforces the mutually exclusive sets of identities (northern/southern, Western/Chinese, past/future) that constitute one of the major products of the Shanghai culture industry (chapters 1 and 5).

As Liang Qichao suggests, it is the indirectness of presentation in fictional texts that makes them in the end more productive and effective than texts with less vivid stories to tell.[19] If guidebooks and other reference works provide the "vocabulary" of the Shanghai experience for newcomers to the city, Shanghai fiction supplies the "grammar" of that experience both to visitors and to residents of the city: not only *what* a Shanghai person should know, but *how* he or she acts on that knowledge. It is through its narrative aesthetics—figures of simultaneity, interruption, mediation, and excess—that Shanghai fiction proposes a structure through which the reader's experience of the city can become meaningful. The very pervasiveness of these four tropes in Shanghai discourse of all genres from the 1930s forward, and the extent to which they have become natural, even necessary choices for cultural producers who aim to evoke the city, hints at the crucial role that Shanghai fiction played in defining the city beginning in the 1890s.

Existing scholarship on Shanghai literature tends to emphasize the social and political origins of its distinctive features, detailing the significant effects of the colonial project, international trade, and rapid industrialization on the city's cultural production. A great deal of productive research has been done by scholars who read literary texts primarily as a *result* of social processes. The aim of this book is not to deny the importance of economic development, technological change, and political struggle, but rather to take an alternative approach to Shanghai literary and cultural history by *also* emphasizing the active role that literary texts themselves have in processes of cultural production. How is it that visitors to Shanghai are convinced even before arriving that the city is the most up-to-the-minute and fashionable in China? Why does anyone want to visit in the first place? How do visitors and residents alike learn to spend to excess in support of the leisure industry, in striking contrast with conventional ideals of balanced consumption that knows its limits? How do they know what is "Western" and what is "Chinese"? Why does a sense of "interrupted history" contribute to the appeal Shanghai has again today for both tourists and investors? This book begins from the proposition that a consideration of literary texts as active participants in social processes, not merely passive onlookers or by-products, will help to provide answers to these questions.

Audiences

Who was reading these novels? To what extent can we identify an audience through which novels set in Shanghai participated in the broader cultural production of the city? Shanghai novels, especially those written in Wu dialect, have been dismissed by some scholars as a relatively minor phenomenon, with a readership that was strictly limited, but this characterization does not survive a careful look at turn-of-the-century publishing figures. As we will see later in this introduction and in the first chapter, the early Shanghai novels *Lives of Shanghai Flowers* and *Dreams of Shanghai Splendor,* which began to appear in the 1890s, were quite popular into the early 1910s; they were reprinted in numbers that rivaled the most popular May Fourth fiction of the 1920s and inspired both sequels and imitations around China. Though publication figures for the volume editions of Shanghai novels of the 1910s and 1920s are harder to ascertain, those works appeared first as daily installments in Shanghai newspapers with national circulation, ensuring a large potential audience. It has been noted that Mao Dun's *Ziye* (Midnight, 1933), his first novel set entirely in Shanghai, was surprisingly popular among readers who did not usually read fiction by May Fourth authors; clearly long-format representations of contemporary Shanghai were of more interest to early twentieth-century readers than many other topics chosen by May Fourth writers.[20] This suggests that (1) the dismissive attitude shown by advocates of "new literature" *(xin wenxue)* toward "old-style" fiction of this period was rooted as much in their anxieties about the limited popularity of works they championed as it was in the actual publication figures for Shanghai narratives; and (2) the definition of "readership" that these critics were working with excluded a great number (perhaps the majority) of actual readers, whose educational experience differed from their own.

How many people could read the novels, newspapers, urban sketches, and guidebooks that were rolling off Shanghai printing presses? The literacy rate in late nineteenth-century Shanghai itself was relatively high: roughly 60 percent of adult men and between 10 and 30 percent of adult women were able to read fairly simple texts.[21] (By way of comparison, mid-nineteenth-century England and Wales had literacy rates of just below 70 percent for men and just above 50 percent for women.)[22] We can infer from a number of sources (including newspaper editorials, urban sketches, and collections of lithographic illustrations) that by the 1890s women at a certain level of Shanghai society—and at least some men at every level—could and did read newspapers, *tanci* (narratives that consisted of both prose and verse portions), and novels.[23]

Evelyn Rawski's groundbreaking work on literacy in the Qing provides us with a point of departure for China as a whole: she concludes that basic literacy in the nineteenth century was between 30 and 45 percent for adult males and between 2 and 10 percent for adult females.[24] Literacy in urban areas was much higher, with some estimates of adult male literacy in Daoguang era (1821–1850) Guangzhou at 80 to 90 percent.[25] Books were not, on the whole, inexpensive, but circulating libraries made them available to those who could not otherwise have afforded them. One English observer in 1830s Guangzhou describes the libraries as follows:

> The librarian, with an assortment of books in two boxes, suspended from a bamboo laid across his shoulder, and with a little rattle in his hand to advertise his friends of his approach, sets off on his circuit, going from street to street, and from door to door. In this way he passes his whole time, and gains his livelihood. He loans his books, usually for a very short time and for a very small compensation. . . . The books thus circulated are chiefly novels, and sometimes those of a very bad character. The system, however, is a good one, and worthy the attention of the friends of useful knowledge. The librarian, whom I met at the door of the hong this afternoon, loaning books to the servants and coolies of the factories, said that his whole stock amounted to more than 2000 volumes. He had with him, however, not more than 300 volumes; the others being in the hands of his numerous customers.[26]

Though it could hardly have been the case that every person defined as having basic literacy was a frequent reader, mid- to late nineteenth-century accounts of circulating libraries name servants, factory workers, and coolies as their clients, and conclude that novels and other fiction were the most popular among borrowers; one novel set in Shanghai in the early twentieth century even refers to a library that specialized in "new fiction" *(xin xiaoshuo)*.[27]

Circulating libraries made fiction affordable to Qing-dynasty readers who otherwise might have gone without it by allowing them to rent instead of purchase. Installment publication served a similar purpose in a slightly different fashion for readers from the 1890s forward. As Perry Link has pointed out,

> When newspapers began serializing fiction, the device took on an economic logic for both readers and publishers. For readers, newspapers were—or at least seemed to be—a less expensive source of fiction than books and magazines . . . the total cost would not be different but the feeling of affordability would be present because each daily outlay seemed unimportantly small. And since there were, of course, many other good reasons for buying a newspaper, getting to read a novel could be viewed as a kind of bonus.[28]

In addition, the risk of wasting one's money on a novel that was uninteresting was significantly reduced. If the total cost of the novel was not much less when it was purchased in installments, one could be sure of spending the full price only on a narrative that was actually worth it; should the first installment or two prove uninspiring, there was no need to purchase the rest.

A basic prerequisite for cultural production is the effective distribution of the "means" of cultural production, whether texts, images, recorded sound, or film, to audiences who find them meaningful. The brief history of Shanghai fiction that follows later in this introduction provides more detail on the publication and distribution of Shanghai novels; chapter 1 discusses the question of readership for those novels that were written in Wu dialect. For now, I would like to suggest that it is likely that audiences for Shanghai fiction were broader and more diverse—in terms of geographical location, class, and gender—than is generally supposed.

Genre / Genealogy

What does it mean to read a group of texts as a genre? Recent theories of genre, rather than attempting to classify texts from disparate origins into a limited number of (logically deduced) universal categories, have tried instead to understand the appearance of specific generic traditions as historical processes. In the words of Hans Robert Jauss,

> Literary genres are to be understood not as *genera* (classes) in the logical senses, but rather as *groups* or *historical families*. As such, they cannot

be deduced or defined, but only historically determined, delimited, and described.[29]

In a related development, scholars have begun to emphasize the social dimensions of generic distinctions; Raymond Williams, among others, argues that genres should be seen as social constructions rather than as ideal types or sets of rules, and Fredric Jameson suggests that genres should be thought of more concretely as "literary institutions . . . social contracts between a writer and a specific public, whose function is to specify the proper use of a particular cultural artifact."[30] Instead of reifying an ahistorical definition of each genre, these theorists understand genres as sets of texts, readings, and rewritings that are open to growth and change.

In this book, the intention is to engage with this conception of genre and articulate a genealogy of the "historical family" that is Shanghai fiction from the 1890s through the 1930s, as well as its better-known "descendants" later in the twentieth century. This genealogy is not concerned with tracing a single dominant thread, nor in establishing a privileged moment of origin, but rather with showing the often-simultaneous progression of related texts over time; instead of focusing on issues of paternity and lineal transmission, it looks primarily at the relations between different members of several discontinuous generations of the textual family. Without postulating a grand metanarrative, this accounting will nonetheless reckon with the shifts, disruptions, and repetitions that authors of such metanarratives appropriate and reinterpret as evidence of the movement of History. Though it will identify concrete moments of dialectic reversal, my reading of these novels as a genre subscribes neither to a trope of continuous development nor to a dialectic governing the unfolding of the category as a whole; instead, it remains attentive to the contingency of the changes and disparities that allow us to differentiate one text from another. It is in this sense that I find Foucault's discussion of "genealogy" useful: although this accounting of Shanghai fiction is both more circumscribed and more concrete than Nietzsche's wide-ranging genealogy of morals, it shares that genealogy's interest in recording "the singularity of events outside of any monotonous finality . . . not in order to trace the gradual curve of their evolution but to isolate the different scenes where they engaged in different roles," as well as the related critique of searches for origin that presume "the existence of immobile forms that precede the external world of accident and succession."[31]

The basic criteria for membership in the historical family proposed here consist of the following: (1) publication in installments; and (2) narrative focus centered on the city of Shanghai.[32] In addition to these criteria, the related aesthetic figures I have already identified—simultaneity, interruption, mediation, excess—manifest themselves most concretely as problems to which these novels attempt to supply answers: how to manage a complex narrative structure with no single protagonist; how best to represent "nonstandard" speech in writing; how to make use of the distinctive features of the installment format; and how to bring a narrative that presents contemporary events to a satisfying conclusion, among others. Though different texts provide different—sometimes antithetical—answers to these questions, they all find them to be of real aesthetic significance.

There is already a genre in widespread scholarly use that includes several of the novels that I discuss in this book: *xiaxie xiaoshuo*—"depravity fiction," "courtesan fiction," or "novels about prostitutes"—originally formulated by Lu Xun in the early 1920s. Lu Xun suggested that this genre was best understood as a kind of "depraved" echo of *Honglou meng* (Dream of the red chamber) and organized the group of novels temporally through a change in attitudes towards the courtesan, from esteem and romanticization in early works like *Huayue hen* (Traces of the moon and flowers), to a "realistic" appraisal in *Lives of Shanghai Flowers,* to bitter condemnation and sensationalism in the early twentieth century.[33] Several of the earlier novels I discuss are considered by most scholars to belong to the *xiaxie* genre; as such, they have been read primarily as accounts of relationships between courtesans and their clients.[34] This generic classification has its strong points: if we read *xiaxie xiaoshuo* as a group, it becomes clear that the nineteenth century saw important developments in narrative form that established the conditions under which the first-person narratives so central to twentieth-century Chinese literature could appear.[35]

The selection of this single aspect of textual content to characterize the genre, however, implies an approach to fiction that is grounded in questions of morality. Given the overdetermination of the courtesan/prostitute as a figure in twentieth-century Chinese discourse that cries out for liberation and modernization, subsumption of Shanghai fiction under this generic rubric risks oversimplifying the complicated dynamics of power between women and men in the novels and suggests to the later reader graphic descriptions of sensual interaction that do not in fact appear.[36] Far from enacting voyeuristic sequences structured by the "male gaze," novels set in Shanghai present a milieu in which display and public humiliation are—with only the rarest exceptions—weapons wielded by *women* against men to great effect.[37] It is also worth noting that while the nineteenth-century European realist novel has far more than its share of courtesan types and outright prostitutes, scholars of those novels tend not to define them exclusively in terms of this aspect of their content.[38] In proposing to read novels set in Shanghai as a genre, my aim is not to invalidate "courtesan fiction" as a generic construct, but rather to supplement it by giving a more comprehensive and nuanced picture of the interaction between content, narrative form, and local social practice in fiction of the late nineteenth and early twentieth century.

What do we get from reading these works of installment fiction as a genre? The full answer to this question can be found only in the specific readings to follow, but it is possible here to hint at two immediate results of this approach to the texts. First, as we will see in chapter 3, each of these novels allegorically represents the structure of the genre as a whole in its individual narrative structure; just as no one narrative strand within an individual novel makes sense in isolation, each novel on its own is only one part of a larger representational project. The multiplicity of the narrative lines within each text figures the relationship of the novels as they appear in installments in different parts of the late nineteenth- and early twentieth-century mediasphere, reminding us that genre often must be read as a relation of simultaneity. The concept of genre allows a richer reading of texts and social practices in nineteenth- and twentieth-century Shanghai; in return, this reading calls our attention to a neglected dimension of the concept of genre.

Second, attention to the persistence of specific generic conventions, even as they are reproduced ironically, inverted, stretched, or reconceptualized, allows the reader to move beyond the dichotomy between "literary tradition" and "literary modernity" that invariably impoverishes the readings of texts in their specificity. Reading Shanghai fiction as a genre challenges paradigms that schematize the tensions and contradictions which constitute literature of this period as a confrontation between (Chinese) tradition and (Western) modernity.

In the late nineteenth and early twentieth centuries, Shanghai was often used by writers both Chinese and Western as a symbol of the complex cultural, political, and economic negotiations that have been referred to collectively as "modernization" or "westernization." Given a Victorian-era understanding of the movement of history as progress to a higher and more technologically sophisticated stage of development, free of undesirable practices and beliefs of the past, Shanghai's International Settlement, with its electric lights, running water, telephones, and "rationally" planned street system, filled out with buildings erected in the previous few decades, could well see itself as a "model community" more advanced than most cities in England, Western Europe, or the United States.[39] The first movie showings in Shanghai, for example, took place less than a year after the invention of cinematic technology in France. From the standpoint of Chinese writers, Shanghai was the stage where interaction with foreigners not only took place, but was illuminated by floodlights that cast such interaction elsewhere in China into relative darkness. From the point that this interaction was first seen as a teleological process aimed at the fundamental transformation of Chinese society and culture, Shanghai could only be identified as the locus of Chinese modernity.

Indeed, a preliminary inquiry into Shanghai texts and images from the 1860s forward leads us to many characteristics cited by scholars of Western modernity as typical of the modern experience: an atmosphere of detachment in which atomized (immigrant and in-migrant) subjects experience both freedom and bewildering rootlessness; an arena in which time itself seems to change its essential nature as human activity increases daily in speed and effect; a milieu in which the blank stare and the random stroll replace the oral/aural communion of yesteryear, in which even objects previously thought of as sacred repositories of wisdom (like books) or aura (works of art) are produced in factories and sold as mere commodities; and an urban environment in which the leisure industry is one of the foundations of the city's economic structure.[40] Shanghai fiction produces these "modern" effects over the course of its narrative even as it contests the same effects by subjecting them to implicit and explicit critique.

The majority of the narratives discussed in the early chapters of this book are generally considered to be "traditional" in form and content, whether they appeared in the 1890s or the 1920s. For this reason, reading them together with Mao Dun's novel *Midnight* and short stories by modernist authors of the 1930s (as I do in chapter 6) works across the division between the "modern" and the "not-yet-modernized." Grouping these apparently diverse texts together as a historical family disrupts the usual discourse of literary progress not only by juxtaposing "traditional" narratives with fiction whose "modernity" is above suspicion, but also by affiliating them specifically with Shanghai, generally understood as a locus of modernity. In addition, as we will see in chapter 7 and the epilogue, tracing Shanghai narrative's lines of descent through the twentieth century provides a clear accounting of the necessary interconnections between modernity and nostalgia.

My interest is not, however, in a recuperative project or an expansion of the modern canon; instead, I would like to suggest that attention to a single genre in its specific historicity provides an alternative to excessive reliance on the concept of "literary modernity" precisely because it enables us to read earlier fiction together with later realist and modernist efforts *without* on the one hand assuming a fundamental break between modern and premodern, or on the other postulating a monolithic "Chinese tradition" that continues without change.[41] The concreteness with which the genre can be delineated in its historical moment bridges the rhetorical gap between "the modern" and "what went before," and suggests the radical heterogeneity and variety concealed *within* these two reified categories. Thinking of genre as a kind of genealogy allows for close readings of multiple texts without forcing these readings to choose between serving as evidence for metanarratives of radical transformation or diagnoses of perpetual stagnation.

Mediasphere

The interrelatedness and simultaneity characteristic of Shanghai narratives asks us to read them as a genre, rather than each on its own. The aesthetic of regular interruption and consequent open-endedness joins with those characteristics to suggest that Shanghai fiction also traces the form of a much broader mode of textual and visual organization, the *mediasphere*. In this book, I make use of Régis Debray's neologism because I find his insistence on extending attention from "the visible system of the medium to the invisible macrosystem that gives it meaning" to be invaluable in the study of literary texts.[42] At the same time, I insist on particularizing the definition of the mediasphere and returning it to a more productive level of historical specificity. I understand the mediasphere to be a form of cultural production consisting of (1) a visual and textual field characterized by the drive to expand without limit; (2) the simultaneous and regular appearance of the wide range of cultural products that make up this field—fiction and nonfiction books, newspapers, magazines, illustrated collections, and eventually, recorded performances, film, and radio; and (3) frequent connections and references between these cultural products across boundaries between different texts, genres, and media.

Each of these aspects of the mediasphere appeared in isolation centuries before the rise of Shanghai as a cultural center. The drive toward unlimited expansion can be found in the aesthetics of oral storytelling and the written forms that claim to mimic it, as well as in the production and reproduction of morality books that have their own further propagation as an overriding message. Simultaneous or near-simultaneous textual production and consumption constituting a certain type of "imagined community" can be found in the triennial civil service examinations, with their attendant rituals and associated markets for up-to-date essay collections, and on a much more circumscribed level among the various small communities of readers of novels and *tanci* that were still in the process of composition. Longitudinal connections and references can be found in the many allusions so important in poetry and prose composition, as well as in the movement of figures, episodes, and characters back and forth between fiction and drama from the late Ming on. At the same time, the interaction between fiction and drama and the overlaps between the fields of ink painting, poetry, and calligraphy suggest ways in which productive exchange occurs not only between different genres, but even between different media, laying the groundwork for a new array of cultural products distinguished in part by the qualities understood to be characteristic of the *medium* in which they appear.

Although precedents for each of these aspects of late-nineteenth and early-twentieth-century Shanghai cultural production clearly existed, what is distinctive about the cultural production that is the focus of this book is the way in which these three aspects appear together in mutually reinforcing fashion—not simply as a new kind of industry or a national print market or a particular set of aesthetics or a mode of reading, but as all of these together—as a mediasphere. The dominance of a single city, Shanghai, within this field of textual and visual production is also unprecedented. Scholarship on Ming and Qing print culture suggests that prior to 1900, there were several regional publishing centers that divided the national market.[43] The rapid growth of the Shanghai publishing industry from the 1880s forward, by contrast, meant that by 1937 "an overwhelming 86 percent of all books published in China appeared under a Shanghai imprint."[44]

The importance of the mediasphere centered on Shanghai can be seen not only in material terms (the share of books printed and rapid development of a local economy based in part on publishing), but also in Shanghai's new status as a cultural center, and in the insistent discursive projection of Shanghai as the most significant meeting point between "the West" and "China."[45] Other treaty ports, such as Hankou and Tianjin, get proportionally far less attention for their "hybridity," and the extent to which Western missionaries circulated through the countryside, making converts even in remote villages, is often overlooked.[46] Shanghai becomes the focus of discourses of hybridity and interaction in part because its media had become so dominant at the national level. The paradoxical consequences of this include on the one hand, the willful disregard of certain aspects of the Western presence in the so-called "interior," and on the other, due to the emphasis on the Western presence in Shanghai, a mirror neglect of Shanghai cultural production not understood to relate in some form to "the West." Even as the concessions represented an attempt by local authorities to contain "foreign" influence in the nineteenth century by ceding it a defined space within the Shanghai area, so did "Shanghai" itself in the early twentieth-century imaginary represent a variety of discursive attempts to contain those "foreign influences" by allowing them more significance in our understanding of Shanghai than they deserve, and perhaps less significance elsewhere in China than is accurate.

Shanghai Paradigms

> Shanghai, not a colony, not even a concession, but a fortuitous aggregate of self-governing English Merchants.[47]

In his casual equation of the city as a whole with a particular minority of its residents, this British officer exemplifies the discourse of Shanghai as a city created out of nothing by European settlers, a discourse that arose in the second half of the nineteenth century through the conscious efforts of "Shanghailanders," English-speaking long-term residents of the city whose livelihoods were bound to the city itself and who could not easily relocate.[48] Two aspects of this discourse are most striking: first, the dramatic reversal that it represents from earlier English- and Chinese-language assessments of the city's development; and second, its quick spread and surprising persistence—though generally in weakened or altered form—more than a century later in the face of clear evidence contradicting its basic premises.

A wide variety of sources suggest the outlines of the historical archive that this Shanghailander rhetorical project aimed to erase. As early as the eighteenth century, trading concerns native to Ningbo began to relocate to Shanghai in the wake of its designation as the customs station charged with supervising all trade between the Yangtze River valley and the rest of the world; by 1814— three decades before Western merchants arrived—there was already a "Foreign Trade Street" (Yanghang jie) named for the offices of Chinese shipping companies that did regular business in markets as far away as Java, the Indian Ocean, and the Persian Gulf.[49] The decline of the Grand Canal in the early nineteenth century meant that grain shipments previously sent through Suzhou and Yangzhou on their way to the capital were now often transshipped through Shanghai instead, giving the local economy another important boost.[50] And indeed, early nineteenth-century European-language sources give us a picture of British envoys eager to establish Western trade through Shanghai precisely because they realized the extent of the domestic and foreign trade that *already* went through the city. One 1832 assessment refers to Shanghai as "the emporium of Nanking, and of the whole of Keängnan province; and as far as the native trade is concerned, perhaps the principal commercial city in the empire." According to another estimate, trade through Shanghai in the 1830s may well have been comparable to the level of trade through London during the same period.[51]

Late nineteenth-century attempts to rewrite the narrative of Shanghai's development and deny the city's economic significance prior to the Opium War were, however, quite successful. Even today, popular and scholarly texts tend to emphasize the role of European, American, and Japanese trade, direct investment, and military presence in stimulating Shanghai's growth between 1842 and 1937. Too often, we forget that the majority of trade through Shanghai prior to 1920 was domestic, not foreign, that some of the "Western" firms in Shanghai were part or even majority Chinese-owned, and that the city's rapid economic expansion over this hundred-year period owed a great deal as well to influxes of refugees from elsewhere in China and the associated surges in the value of Shanghai real estate.[52]

The Shanghailander rhetorical project—identification of the European presence as crucial to Shanghai's very existence as a prosperous city—has in fact been carried over with relatively little scrutiny into recent critical theorizing on the topic of Chinese "colonial modernity." We are told, for example, in an otherwise perceptive comparison of Shanghai and Hong Kong that Shanghai was "essentially created by Western colonialism"—an assessment with which Shanghailanders themselves would have eagerly concurred.[53] In asserting explicitly or implicitly that colonialism is the central determining factor in the formation of nineteenth- and early twentieth-century Shanghai society, scholars of "colonial modernity" likewise tend to attribute to diplomats, military personnel, expatriates, and settlers of European origin a degree of bureaucratic coordination that did not exist, a unity of interests that they did not have, and a level of cultural hegemony that they could not have achieved.[54]

It is true that the "colonial modernity" paradigm encourages a salutary reflexivity among today's scholars, and attends to certain of the unpleasant relations of power that undergirded important aspects of what is now often nostalgically recalled as "Old Shanghai." By calling into question optimistic narratives of Shanghai modernism and cosmopolitanism, it reminds us that Shanghai's current return to global prominence also has its price.[55] Yet as historians have recently begun to show, the colonial paradigm fails to address certain important complexities and contradictions, among them the prominent role of Chinese native-place organizations within the International Settlement and the French Concession;[56] the frequent conflicts of interest between settlement authorities in Shanghai and the foreign offices in the settlers' countries of origin;[57] the contingent and changeable nature of the International Settlement from its initial designation merely as a legal area of residence to its later relative political and legal autonomy, not only from Chinese authority, but also from European powers;[58] the power and wealth of trading families of Middle Eastern and South Asian origin;[59] and the arrival of large numbers of stateless and exiled Europeans in the 1920s and '30s.[60]

Clear parallels have been drawn between the Shanghai "concession" system and early nineteenth-century Qing administration attempts to contain and control Central Asian merchant activity in Xinjiang, and similarities have also been noted between the powers and responsibilities claimed by the French Concession and International Settlement administrations on the one hand, and those that native-place organizations—charged with the supervision of sojourners from other regions of China—customarily enjoyed on the other.[61] And as Pär Cassel has recently shown, even the famous Mixed Court, bulwark of the extraterritorial system in Shanghai, was modeled in large part on existing institutions originally designed to address Manchu-Han disputes under the Qing.[62] The fact that this "revisionist" trend has called into question even such well-worn symbols as the infamous sign in the Public Garden on the Bund suggests that we have no choice but to acknowledge the limits of the colonial paradigm.[63]

Indeed, what this historical scholarship suggests is precisely that binary distinctions between "China" and "the West" and between "colonial subject" and "colonizer"—so crucial both to the triumphalist narratives of modernization theory *and* to the critical responses to those narratives that focus on the colonial project and its results to the exclusion of all else—cannot be taken for granted, but themselves must be seen as motivated cultural products, historicized as the collective result of a variety of often contradictory self-definition projects. At the most abstract aesthetic level, as Shu-mei Shih has shown, even the Western modernism we think we know so well as an inspiration for 1920s and '30s Shanghai culture builds off specifically Chinese elements (not to mention the wealth of inspiration that it takes from other Asian and African cultures)[64]—it took a great deal of interpretive and pedagogical work in the early and mid-twentieth century to repress that essential hybridity and turn "modernism" into a recognizable symbol of a single, unitary "West." The interactions between "Western" and "Chinese" music in early twentieth-century Shanghai—from marching bands to folk songs, opera to jazz—are if anything even more nuanced and complex.[65]

Speaking more concretely about individuals and groups in nineteenth- and early twentieth-century Shanghai, we find that many do not fall easily on either side of the binary distinctions that modernization theory and its critics find essential. Examples include the Baghdadi, South Asian, or Southeast Asian merchants whose businesses counted as "British" and who received the same extraterritorial benefits in Shanghai, even though they were rarely considered part of "British society"; Koreans, Taiwanese, and even some Fujianese who registered as Japanese colonial citizens; stateless Russian and Jewish refugees, who had neither the economic nor the political power of other Europeans, but who outnumbered all other non-Chinese residents in Shanghai by the early 1930s;

and bicultural or "biracial" individuals such as the children of local "mixed" marriages, or new arrivals like the author Liu Na'ou, the exact nature of whose heritage was unclear to many of his contemporaries.[66]

&a

One of the aims of this book is to supplement existing paradigms of Shanghai cultural history. First, instead of beginning with the proposition that racial and cultural distinctions were invariably self-evident in late-Qing and Republican Shanghai, I investigate the extent to which distinctions between "China" and "the West," among others, were created and elaborated in the local Shanghai context. Instead of understanding Shanghai's "hybridity" as the natural result of two or more mutually exclusive cultural orders encountering each other, my aim is to demonstrate the importance of a concept of "hybridity" *(za)* as one of the crucial means for *constructing* local Shanghai interactions between individuals and groups as "encounters" between mutually exclusive others.

Second, this book balances attention to that aspect of Shanghai cultural production in which such distinctions were constantly foregrounded and inescapable with analysis of other aspects in which these distinctions become less relevant or operate in unexpected ways. It is precisely in the debate over the specifics of restricted access to the so-called Public Garden, for example, that it becomes clear what has been neglected in the study of Shanghai's public culture. Contrary to popular belief, the British-established Public Garden was not the first public park in Shanghai—Leisure Garden (Yu yuan) opened to the public in the space adjacent to the Temple of the City God in 1760, decades before the arrival of the first British envoy to the city.[67] Nor was the Public Garden of any interest to the majority of Shanghai cultural producers and consumers, despite its symbolic importance in the formation of Chinese nationalist rhetoric in the 1920s and '30s.[68] Chinese-owned parks such as Shen Garden (Shen yuan) and Zhang's Garden (Zhang yuan) were larger, better-attended, and far more spectacular than the Public Garden throughout the late nineteenth and early twentieth centuries. Indeed, it would have been truly bizarre if Shanghai residents had wanted to forsake the superior landscaping, entertainment possibilities, and general fashionability of the Chinese-owned parks for the dubious pleasure of a few benches and the company of Shanghailanders and seagulls. While Shen Garden offered a grand building, billiard tables, and a Western restaurant, and Zhang's Garden hosted visitors late into the night with firework displays, opera, and film screenings, the Public Garden closed each evening at dusk (fig. 1).[69]

The relative neglect of public parks like Zhang's Garden, Shen Garden, and Leisure Garden symbolizes a broader problem in the study of Shanghai cul-

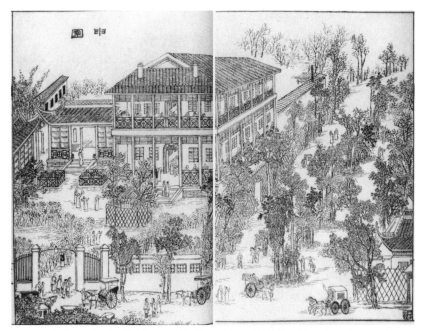

FIGURE 1 "Shen Garden." Lithographic illustration, 1884. *Shenjiang shengjing tu*, 2.27b–28a. Reproduction permission of Princeton University Library.

ture: to the extent that we focus exclusively on imperialist and semicolonial projects and the "native" responses to those projects, we allow a handful of Shanghailanders (backed up, to be sure, in moments of crisis by displays of imperialist military force) to set our research agenda; we are likely to overlook a wealth of cultural production in the process. If, as Jeffrey Wasserstrom has suggested, there are many "Old Shanghais," the role of the scholar of literature and culture should, like that of the historian, consist in part in comprehending the varieties of difference inherent in any "object of study."[70] This book aims not to dismiss or ignore the role of European technologies, ideologies, and financial and military capabilities as partial conditions of Shanghai cultural production, but rather to understand these aspects of Shanghai in a different perspective.

Shanghai Fiction: A Brief History

The first burst of Shanghai fiction appeared in the 1890s. In 1892 Han Bangqing published the first thirty chapters of *Haishang hua liezhuan* (Lives of Shanghai flowers) in his literary magazine *Haishang qishu* (Marvelous Shanghai writings); the full sixty-four chapter version appeared in eight volumes in 1894. Zou Tao's *Haishang chentian ying* (Shadows of Shanghai's dusty skies) followed close on the heels of *Lives of Shanghai Flowers;* it was published either in 1894 or 1896.[71] By the turn of the century, there were four more novels set in Shanghai: *Haishang mingji si da jin'gang qishu* (The four great courtesans of Shanghai: A marvelous account, 1898, probably one of Wu Jianren's earliest published works),[72] *Huoshao Shanghai Hongmiao yanyi* (A narrative of the burning of Shanghai's Red Temple),[73] *Haitian hong xueji* (A Shanghai swan's traces in the snow, published in installments in 1899 and possibly written by Li Boyuan), and *Haishang fengliu zhuan* (An account of Shanghai fashions, 1899).[74] Several of these novels were later reprinted by other publishers under slightly altered titles.[75]

Sun Yusheng's popular installment fiction *Haishang fanhua meng* (Dreams of Shanghai splendor), which appeared as a page-a-day newspaper supplement between 1898 and 1906, was the first blockbuster in the genre, selling almost as well as *Flower in a Sea of Sin* and *Yuli hun* (The jade pear spirit) would in the years to follow.[76] The significance of this novel in cities across China can be seen in the wave of imitations that sprang up in the late Qing, including *Suzhou fanhua meng* (Dreams of Suzhou splendor),[77] *Beijing fanhua meng* (Dreams of Beijing splendor),[78] *Beijing xin fanhua meng* (New dreams of Beijing splendor),[79] *Nianzai fanhua meng* (Twenty years' dream of splendor),[80] *Qizai fanhua meng* (Seven years' dream of splendor),[81] and *Xin fanhua meng* (New dreams of splendor).[82] Ironically, even *Lives of Shanghai Flowers* was reprinted in the late Guangxu era under the title *Zuixin Haishang fanhua meng* (Newest dreams of Shanghai splendor).[83] During this same period, *Lives of Shanghai Flowers* itself inspired no fewer than three sequels, one of which was written by Chen Diexian, who was to become a central figure in literary and publishing circles of the early twentieth century.[84]

The success of the specifically Shanghai novel encouraged the alteration of earlier novels—*Fengyue meng* (A dream of romance), a novel set in Yangzhou, was changed to refer to Shanghai instead, as we will see in chapter 1—and also inspired later authors. Most other novels with urban settings printed in this period included sections set in Shanghai, Wu Jianren's *Strange Happenings Eyewitnessed over Twenty Years* and *Hen hai* (Sea of regret), Li Boyuan's *Guanchang xianxing ji* (The bureaucrats), and Zeng Pu's *Flower in a Sea of Sin,* as well as many lesser-known and fragmentary political satires appearing between 1905 and 1910, among them.[85] The most famous of the "depravity novels," *The Nine-tailed Turtle,* which began to appear in installments in 1906, travels to Beijing, Tianjin, Suzhou, and Guangzhou as well as Shanghai, but responds specifically to *Lives of Shanghai Flowers, A Shanghai Swan's Traces in the Snow,* and *Dreams of Shanghai Splendor,* as suggested earlier in this introduction.[86] Urban novels of the first decade of the twentieth century that were city-specific but not set in Shanghai frequently acknowledged Shanghai as the premier metropolis and the Shanghai novel as their inspiration.[87] Shanghai was not the first city to be written in the Chinese novel, but it was the first to be *re*written, as each author told its story anew, and differently; by the end of the Qing, it had become a fundamental point of reference for urban fiction across China.[88]

Shanghai novels continued to appear into the Republican period, most notably Lu Shi'e's *Xin Shanghai* (New Shanghai, 1909); Zhu Shouju's *Xiepu chao* (The Huangpu tides, 1916–1921), a favorite of Eileen Chang's; *Hujiang fengyue zhuan* (Romance on Hu River, 1921), annotated by Xu Zhenya and his brother; Bi Yihong and Bao Tianxiao's *Renjian diyu* (Hell in this world, 1922–1924); and Xu Xiaotian's *Shanghai fengyue* (Shanghai romance, 1929).[89] From the late 1920s into the 1940s, authors of Shanghai fiction began to claim independence from earlier works in the genre and self-consciously ally themselves instead with theories of literary production and technique that they understood as foreign and different. Landmarks in this period include Mao Dun's *Ziye* (Midnight), published in 1933, and the short stories of Liu Na'ou, Shi Zhecun, and Mu Shiying, discussed in detail in chapter 6, but many others appeared that are not so well known, such as Lou Shiyi's *Shanghai kuangxiang qu* (Shanghai rhapsodies), Li Qingya's *Shanghai,* and Xu Xu's *Feng xiaoxiao* (The sound of the wind).[90]

Chapter Outline

Existing scholarship on Shanghai tends to explain the city's rise to prominence as the result of encounters between groups whose identities are fixed and mutually exclusive, between northerners and southerners, for example, or between Chinese people and Westerners. In the first chapter of this book, I take a different approach: instead of assuming the distinctions between these groups to be self-evident and invariant, I aim to show the extent to which these distinctions were themselves *products* of the Shanghai culture industry rather than its preconditions. Shanghai fiction makes extensive use of dialect writing, for example, but rarely includes specifically Shanghai vocabulary, expressions, or phonetic representations. Rather than constructing a single unified linguistic identity centered on Shanghai, these novels present a specific kind of stereotyped heterogeneity as characteristic of the city—Shanghai is the arena in which *Suzhou* dialect culture and the northern standard are defined against each other and in which they must struggle for dominance. Similarly, Shanghai novels work together with many other texts in Chinese and European languages to emphasize the differences between "Western" concession spaces and the "Chinese" southern city, moving discursively to make the distinctions between the two much more clear-cut and consistent than they ever were in practice.

Shanghai fiction takes pains to include precise references to markers of space and time. These references are unprecedented both in their accuracy and in their coherence, due in part, no doubt, to the frequent contestation of such markers in a rapidly industrializing and expanding city. At the same time, however, this obsessive attention to coherent systems of reference forms the most basic condition without which the narrative complexity and multiplicity characteristic of Shanghai installment fiction would not be possible. Most significantly, this attention foregrounds *referentiality* itself as a key narrative strategy—the practice of making intertextual references to the specific names, places, and moments that pervade the burgeoning field of Shanghai texts and images (guidebooks, newspapers, illustrated magazines, photograph albums, maps, lists, as well as other works of fiction). Although such a strategy may appear to resemble the realism that would become so popular in the May Fourth era, its aims and effects are radically different. Where realist fiction is animated both by an emancipatory mission and an ideological commitment to a pre-discursive Real that the text should reflect, works that concern themselves instead with referentiality aim for intertextual consistency and reciprocity, setting Shanghai fiction up as the master genre which is tied to all of the key points of reference in an ever-expanding discursive fabric.

In the third chapter, I show how the tropes of simultaneity and interruption that characterize Shanghai fiction from the 1890s through the 1930s combine with this expanding textual and visual field to sketch the outlines of a national mediasphere centered on Shanghai. At the formal level, Shanghai fiction is unrivaled in the number and complexity of its simultaneously progressing narrative lines; these narratives themselves, serialized concurrently in newspapers, magazines, or independent installments, were also consumed in rough simultaneity across China. In this sense, Shanghai serial narratives not only reinvent the lineal tropes of genre that had dominated fiction criticism to that point, but also represent a uniquely privileged means for the imagination of a national community of readers along the lines detailed by Benedict Anderson. Such simultaneity would not have been possible, however, without frequent interruption—of one episode by another, one narrative line by another, one type of narrative by another, and even "everyday life" by narrative and vice-versa. I argue that this aesthetic of interruption, which began in installment fiction, soon spread to newspapers, magazines, and other cultural products of the period. As the print culture analogue of cross-cutting and shot / reverse shot techniques in cinema, it established a new, more active mode of readership, and bound these readers ever more tightly to the mediasphere then under construction.

The best-known Shanghai novels had multiple extensions or sequels, appearing over a period of years; chapter 4 inquires into the sources and effects of the continuing hunger for more text that made these extensions and sequels profitable. Like night carriage-riding, another popular leisure pursuit in late Qing and early Republican Shanghai, the appeal of incessant novel reading lay in its transgression of aesthetic and moral restrictions and distinctions. The effects of this desire for more text are not insubstantial: First, the frequent sequels and extensions increasingly find their justification in an extensive rhetoric of rapid and unceasing social change, a rhetoric that eventually acquires a life of its own and comes to form one of the supports for the grand metanarrative of "Shanghai modernity." Second, as a commodity designed for leisure consumption, lengthy installment fiction was central to the Shanghai publishing industry, a key engine of the city's industrial development (as it had been in New York, Paris, and other cities). Finally, Shanghai narrative not only establishes the city as the ultimate tourist destination with its constant references to other urban leisure products and practices, but also—through the installment form itself—teaches the reader to conceive of consumption as an endless quest for more, rather than as a process that might reach a necessary limit, thereby helping to ensure that readers who do visit Shanghai will be reluctant to leave.

The fifth chapter emphasizes persons, or types of agency. What subjectivities are available in early twentieth-century Shanghai fiction? Who flourishes under the terms set in these narratives? First, quite evidently, brokers and middlemen. Close reading of Shanghai fiction shows not only that the broker is indispensable as a character in the plot, but also that he (occasionally she) is necessary to mediate among narrative lines themselves, bringing stories that otherwise would remain separate together. The brokers' paradox is to enable interaction and exchange between identities that they themselves have helped to define as radically separate. This move figures not only the social practice of the broker as an individual moving through Shanghai society, but also the place of the city itself between two sides ("China" and "the West") that it claims cannot communicate without its assistance. More generally, we see a concept of the *Szahaenin* (Shanghai person) take shape. With the exception of the foolish and the eccentric, newcomers to Shanghai are understood to quickly transform themselves into *Szahaenin,* a new kind of "native place" identity, which, through its very ease of acquisition, reconfigures the relationship between local identity and larger economic and political forces. It is my contention that the discourse of the *Szahaenin* as a unique identity—which continues to function as a powerful social force in China to this day—depends in large part not only on the characters and themes articulated in Shanghai installment fiction, but at an even more fundamental level on the very skills that this fiction requires of its readers and the aesthetic experiences it gives in return.

Chapter 6 investigates the ways in which the "Shanghai" produced in installment fiction from the 1890s to the 1930s serves as the irreducible ground for both realist and modernist novels and short stories of the 1930s by writers as diverse as Mao Dun, Liu Na'ou, and Shi Zhecun. Mao Dun makes use of this ground in his use of narrative structure and city space in *Midnight* (1933) and reflects on it critically in his analysis of the distinction between leisure and "serious" business. Modernist fiction, despite its many innovative aspects, is also conditioned from the start by formations of gender, language, and narrative structure that are first articulated in the earlier novels. In their presentation of the "modern girl," the city as an arena of polyglot cosmopolitan interaction, and the "stream of consciousness" as an expression of interior space, these short stories of the late 1920s and early 1930s make extensive use of figures and images produced and refined in earlier decades. Finally, while Mao Dun and the modernists develop novel approaches to ideological and psychological space respectively, these spaces retain important genetic connections to the concrete urban spaces produced in earlier texts.

The centrality of the nostalgic mode in post-1949 discourse on Shanghai is unmistakable: the late Qing and early Republican periods have been particularly inspirational to later journalists, historians, novelists, and filmmakers. The seventh chapter discusses a variety of efforts to come to terms with "old Shanghai," including Eileen Chang's *Lives of Shanghai Flowers* translation projects and commentary (1970s–1980s) and Hou Hsiao-hsien's fin-de-siècle cinematic experiment, *Flowers of Shanghai* (1998). My aim in this chapter is to detail first, the rhetoric and practice of recuperation common to many of these nostalgic looks back—rather than recreate the past, they attempt to remake it, supplementing its inadequacies; second, the transitivity of nostalgia (the way in which we are nostalgic for precisely that moment in the past that was in turn intensely preoccupied with an even earlier historical moment); and finally, the extent to which nostalgic attachment to the past depends in part on an equally powerful obsession with the contemporary moment. In this sense, chapter 7 establishes a nostalgic genealogy that reaches back to the very earliest moments of Shanghai cultural production and continues from that point forward to subtend its persistent fascination with the "new" and "contemporary."

Nostalgia is never merely a one-way street from our time back to the past;

it is also a call forward, a kind of address to the future. The epilogue inquires into the current obsession with "old Shanghai" and its link to Shanghai's rush to "regain" its former global prominence in the spheres of culture, trade, and finance. What role do the tropes and figures characteristic of Shanghai in the early twentieth century play in articulating the ideal of urban development toward which the city is working at the turn of the twenty-first century?

CHAPTER 1

Rhetorics of Territory, Mixture, and Displacement

Although Shanghai was only a county seat in the Qing administrative hierarchy, the city came to occupy a unique position in the Chinese literary and cultural imagination in the late nineteenth and early twentieth centuries. Looking back on this period, T. A. Hsia aptly likens Shanghai fiction to European writings about Paris and London.[1] From the works of Balzac and Hugo to those of Flaubert and Zola, from Dickens to Arthur Conan Doyle, Paris and London were seen as intoxicating and dangerous worlds apart, home to a "system of potentially unlimited energetic transformations and exchanges . . . an overheated circuit of power and signification."[2] Similar figures of unlimited circulation and frenetic exchange are central to our understanding of twentieth-century Shanghai; these figures appear in newspaper and magazine articles, illustrated periodicals, guidebooks, and movies, but most coherently and forcefully in Shanghai installment fiction.

Unlike Paris and London, however, Shanghai is generally understood as a city divided by the question of culture at its most basic level. On the face of it, the most striking characteristic of the city is the quick rise to prominence of the suburban regions settled by foreign merchants beginning in the 1840s and their eventual solidification over the course of eight decades into semicolonial extraterritorial spaces.[3] But despite the significance of these settlements, generally referred to as "concessions," scholars have tended to treat them as entities whose nature is self-evident and have neglected two critical questions: Who is conceding what to whom? And what are the connections between conceding and containment? This chapter addresses these questions through a detailed analysis of Shanghai's status as *territorial space*—a locus of cultural production in which the question, whom does this space *belong* to? cannot be considered apart from the question of how claimants to the space themselves are to be defined. As we will see in this chapter, what Shanghai produces for domestic consumption and global export is not just ordinary industrial goods such as bolts of cotton cloth, but a series of binary distinctions, the very terms on which identification of the claimants to this urban space—and, more generally, narratives of the city's history—depend. Shanghai serves as a factory of local, regional, and national identities.

❦

When late nineteenth-century Chinese readers first encountered fiction set in Shanghai, they were most likely struck immediately by the degree to which location is foregrounded. Unlike previous novels, Shanghai installment fiction advertises its setting in its title and at the beginning of the first chapter. Earlier long vernacular fiction, even works permeated with specific urban flavor like *Pinhua baojian* (A precious mirror for judging flowers) and *Fengyue meng* (A dream of romance), had titles that did not highlight a locale; by contrast, it was the rare Shanghai novel that did not include the words "hai," "haishang," or "Shanghai" in its title.[4] As Patrick Hanan has shown, *A Dream of Romance* strikes an innovative note in its mention of Yangzhou's popularity as a leisure center and its careful attention to local geographic detail;[5] Shanghai fiction would pick up on this urban emphasis and develop it still further in the following decades. The opening pages of Shanghai novels ordinarily focus on the rapid growth of the city's entertainment business, its importance as a tourist destination, and finally, the dangers that typical Shanghai leisure activities can pose; these points might be made either directly, as in the first chapter of *Lives of Shanghai Flowers,* or allegorically through descriptions of panoramic views of the Bund and accounts of arrival to the city by rail.[6]

From *Lives of Shanghai Flowers* to *Hubin shentan lu* (A record of master detectives on Shanghai's shores, 1928) the action takes place entirely or almost entirely in the concession areas and the southern city. In *A Shanghai Swan's Traces in the Snow,* the furthest that any of the characters travels is a one-hour steamboat ride down river; in *Lives of Shanghai Flowers* there is only a brief section of chapter 29 set in Zhao Puzhai's home near Suzhou. Even in novels such as *Dreams of Shanghai Splendor, Shadows of Shanghai's Dusty Skies,* and *The Four Great Courtesans of Shanghai: A Marvelous Account,* where the narrative begins in another city, the sections set elsewhere constitute only a small fraction of the whole, and the narrative changes character quite noticeably when it reaches Shanghai. In *The Huangpu Tides,* the narrator even makes a point of reminding us that he cannot tell us what happened to a character who flees the city, since he has left the scope of the narrative.[7] Well-known Shanghai landmarks, including restaurants, teahouses, theaters, and parks figure prominently, primarily as venues for action. Street and alley names cited can almost always be found on maps from the period and form a coherent matrix within which the characters move.

The reader is periodically reminded of Shanghai's singularity throughout these novels by remarks made by individual characters and by the narrator. Shanghai is a flourishing place, stimulating both young and old to excess; it is a place of rapid change, where it is hard to be sure what others are up to and what might happen next; part of it (the concession areas) is governed by unfamiliar regulations; and it is a haven for scoundrels and rascals of all persuasions. Furthermore, Shanghai has a transformative effect on visitors from other places: newcomers too often fall into bad habits characteristic of the city. For this reason, though it is not a problem to come and enjoy oneself briefly, if one does not have some kind of business to conduct it is vital to know when to leave.[8] Such comments work together with an unprecedentedly detailed and consistent iconography of urban space and time, innovative narrative rhythms, and a new level of intertextual connection—to be discussed in chapters 2, 3, and 4—to constitute an unusually powerful instance of symbolic production.

ॐ

Anne Querrien suggests that the significance of large cities grows out of the struggle between two distinct images of the urban center, the capital and the metropolis. The capital is a center of a cultural heritage and dominates a territory; the metropolis "is not a center and has no center," "has no identity to preserve," and begins with the slightest desire to exchange.[9] Were one to apply this distinction mechanically to late nineteenth- and early twentieth-century China, with Beijing as the capital and Shanghai as the metropolis, it would do little more than reproduce the *haipai* ("Shanghai style") and *jingpai* ("Capital style") paradigms established in the 1920s and early '30s with a view toward critiquing Shanghai literary production.[10] But read more subtly as a contrast between two different modes of production, the general administration and examination system on the one hand and trade and manufacturing on the other, the distinction reminds us that the important urban settings for previous vernacular fiction (Beijing, Nanjing, Suzhou, Hangzhou, and Yangzhou) were all at least regional seats of government and significant centers of literati culture, in addition to being important sites for economic exchange; they served as *both* "capital" and "metropolis," just as London and Paris did in the mid-nineteenth century.[11]

For this reason, fiction set in Shanghai represents an important departure: prior to the 1890s the city had no role as a center of elite cultural heritage, and it played only a small part in the overall Qing administrative scheme.[12] As late as 1876 Yuan Xiangfu identified Shanghai with cities that served primarily trade and manufacturing functions—Hankou, Zhuxian, Foshan, and

Jingdezhen—none of which was of much significance in the Qing administrative structure, and none of which had inspired fictional representations.[13] Christopher Prendergast argues that in nineteenth-century French literature, the view of Paris tended to shift in emphasis from city-as-capital to city-as-metropolis.[14] In this sense, the metropolis of Shanghai, based almost exclusively on the desire to exchange, not only differs from previous settings for Chinese vernacular fiction, but also stands as a hypothetical end toward which Paris and London moved through the nineteenth century. At the same time, however, it is evident that as "capitals" these cities retained claims to cultural centrality that Shanghai was in no position to make. Despite the intense focus on Shanghai as a unique location typical of texts and illustrations printed in the city, it is in the careful articulation of mutually exclusive identities affiliated with *other* locales that we will find the distinctive and most salient characteristic of Shanghai cultural production. Indeed, the very identity of the "Shanghai person" *(Szahaenin)* consists in part in his or her ability to mediate between these constructed "others," as we will see in detail in chapter 5. The present chapter focuses on two instances in which distinct and mutually exclusive identities are produced: the construction of a linguistic distinction between north China and the Wu dialect region, and the articulation of "Western" against "Chinese" in terms of ritual control and moral force.

Made in Shanghai

Wu and Northern Identities

From its earliest moments, Shanghai fiction played a key role in the production of a regional culture centered on another city: Suzhou. Han Bangqing, author of *Lives of Shanghai Flowers,* broke new ground by adapting conventions for representing Wu dialect speech that had grown up over centuries in poetry and prose-verse narratives *(tanci)* to represent nearly all dialogue in the novel. Although some local dialect expressions appear in earlier Chinese novels, no previous fiction had made as extensive use of a dialect so far removed from standard northern vernacular as *Lives of Shanghai Flowers*—so much so that the novel poses a real challenge to readers who are neither Wu dialect speakers nor familiar with the tradition of Wu dialect literature.[15] Han even invented a few transcriptions of his own, as he explains in his "Introductory Remarks":

> Suzhou local vernacular has many irregular characters that are used in prose-verse narratives. But they have been in use for a while and everyone knows

them, so I have made use of them. . . . Now some words have a sound but no written form, like the two words *wu* and *yao,* which Suzhou people *(Suren)* always run together as one sound when they are in a hurry; if I were to keep them as *wu* and *yao,* two separate characters, it would not be in accordance with the spirit of the situation. There was, however, no other character to stand for this sound, so I take *wu* and *yao* and write them together as one character. The reader should know that this *viao* character originally did not exist, but is formed by joining together two characters and reading them as one sound.[16]

This approach was soon imitated in other installment fiction set in Shanghai. Writing seven years later, the author of *A Shanghai Swan's Traces in the Snow* found no need to explain the use of these conventions, although the 1904 edition did include a list of common transcriptions of dialect expressions at the beginning as a concession to readers from other regions. Turn-of-the-century tabloid newspapers also took inspiration from this use of dialect to create the sense of a distinctive urban milieu. Several of these newspapers were available in major urban areas across China and featured columns describing the activities of Shanghai courtesans written primarily in Wu dialect. A handful of tabloids with more restricted circulation made even more extensive use of Wu dialect in columns and articles and included further serialized dialect literature like sequels to *Lives of Shanghai Flowers* as supplements.[17]

But one early Shanghai novel was written almost entirely in standard northern vernacular, Sun Yusheng's *Dreams of Shanghai Splendor.* In his *Tuixing lu biji* (Notes from the hut for retiring to enlightenment), Sun gives an account of his discussion of dialect writing with Han Bangqing, a conversation that began when the two authors traded works-in-progress on a boat trip from Beijing back to Shanghai:

I said to him, "[Your] book uses Wu dialect throughout; probably readers will not understand it too well. What's more, there are many words in Wu dialect that do not have written forms, when you write it must take lots of work. It would be better to change it into ordinary vernacular *(baihua)."* But Han replied, "When Cao Xueqin wrote *The Story of the Stone,* he used the dialect of the capital. Why can't my book use Wu dialect?" And he pointed to words in the manuscript that are spoken, but have no written forms, like *ven* and *viao.*[18] He said, "Even though I myself made up these characters, on that day when Cang Jie created characters, he probably also took [his own] meaning and made them.[19] What is wrong with such enlightened literary play? I myself act as the ancients and get a way to put a new face on things." I knew that he could not be persuaded and so did not raise the issue again. When the two books were published, one after the other . . . the Wu dialect was still all there [in *Lives of Shanghai Flowers*], making it very difficult for people from other provinces to read, so indeed his superior writing did not become very well-known. . . . I am sorry that Mr. Han wanted to write a book in Wu dialect, planting a single tree [with no companions]; that was in fact a great mistake, for Wu dialect is limited to one corner [of China], unlike the capital dialect which appears everywhere, and which people all know, so indeed this case cannot be compared to *The Story of the Stone*.[20]

Sun's anxiety about Han Bangqing's decision to write in Wu dialect seems quite natural: why exclude the majority of the reading public who are unwilling or unable to puzzle through novel transcriptions of an unfamiliar dialect? Most later critics echo this anxiety, certain that dialogue in Wu dialect must have doomed the novel to obscurity.[21]

Yet we know that Wu dialect prose-verse narratives circulated in large numbers during this period, and given the concentration of literate adults in the "one corner of China" that was the Jiangnan area, the audience for a Wu dialect novel was certainly a significant fraction of the potential audience across China.[22] A conservative estimate would place the number of literate adults in Shanghai, Suzhou, and the surrounding areas in the 1890s at close to half a million; adding those readers from Shaoxing, Ningbo, and other Wu dialect centers gives us a not inconsiderable portion of the 2 to 4 million Leo Lee and Andrew Nathan estimate for the readership in China as a whole during this period.[23] The potential literate audience for Wu dialect novels at this time probably equaled or surpassed English audiences of the late eighteenth and early nineteenth centuries—a crucial moment in the "rise" of the English novel—and even approached the numbers of Japanese readers in the late Edo period, also an era known for its flourishing vernacular fiction.[24] And as noted above, Shanghai novels written in Wu dialect in the 1890s were followed not only by Wu dialect sequels but also daily newspapers devoted to printing the day's events in dialect. When Shanghai booksellers met in 1905 to join in a boycott of American goods, they decided to publish pamphlets explaining the boycott in Wu dialect to reach audiences who did not read northern vernacular, suggesting that in certain circles the readership for novels that employed Wu dialect might well have been greater than the readership for fiction written in more standard language.[25] Clearly the potential market for Wu dialect fiction (and Wu dialect writing in general) was sizable.

And in fact Sun Yusheng's claim—repeated by later scholars—that *Lives of Shanghai Flowers* was not widely read is demonstrably false. Although *Lives of Shanghai Flowers* may not have sold as well as *Dreams of Shanghai Splendor,* one of the first true blockbusters, it inspired three sequels and went through no fewer than nine reprint editions in the first two decades after the first book edition appeared.[26] Reprint editions that retain all of the original Wu dialect dialogue continue to come out to this day, and seem to sell as well as Eileen Chang's late 1970s to early '80s version of the novel, in which the dialogue in Wu dialect is "translated" into Mandarin.[27]

ॐ

It is important to note that Sun and other critics of dialect fiction are writing in retrospect, at a time when Shanghai has become the acknowledged media center of the Chinese nation as a whole (*Notes from the Hut for Retiring to Enlightenment* was first published in 1925). The city had acquired that position by the late 1910s in part by relinquishing the possibility of providing its own coherent alternative to the national culture based on northern vernacular Chinese.[28] Indeed, the assumption that fiction (especially the novel) would serve as the vehicle of *national* salvation had become the foundation of early twentieth-century discourse on literature in Shanghai as elsewhere, and this emphasis on the novel's potential to literally produce a unified nation by creating national feeling among its readers left the dialect novel without adequate pretext for existence. When dialect speech did appear in a novel that aimed to renovate the nation as a whole, it had to be presented as distinctly secondary to the main business at hand. This was accomplished in the first decade of the twentieth century by restricting Wu dialect speech to courtesans, a restriction that began the removal of dialect from "serious" literary discourse.[29] By May Fourth, Wu dialect had been driven out of "literature's highest vehicle" and back into *tanci* and other forms lower in the new literary hierarchy; it would return in certain Shanghai fiction of the 1920s, but only to mark a specific nostalgic mode.

This development was by no means as inevitable as Sun Yusheng and most later literary scholars would have us believe: in nineteenth-century Japan, for instance, fiction written in Edo dialect played an important role in establishing that dialect as the national standard in the place of Kyoto dialect.[30] Indeed, the power that Edo fiction had to reconfigure patterns of written and spoken Japanese reminds us that dialect writing has a prescriptive as well as a descriptive dimension. Han Bangqing himself gives us a hint of this prescriptive dimension with his references to *Suren* (Suzhou people) and *Suzhou tubai* (Suzhou local vernacular) in the above quote. The dialogue in *Lives of Shanghai Flowers* is not in Wu dialect broadly defined, but rather—much more narrowly—in a certain standard variety of the dialect characteristic of Suzhou.

As T. A. Hsia has remarked with respect to *Lives of Shanghai Flowers,* "[s]ince the setting is Shanghai, a more realistic representation of the story would have included, besides the Soochow dialect, the dialects of Ningpo, Shanghai, P'u-tung, Northern Kiangsu, and Shantung."[31] A careful look at the dialogue in *Lives of Shanghai Flowers* shows, however, that for "there is none," Suzhou dialect *('mpe)* is used instead of turn-of-the-century Shanghai dialect *('mma),* with only two or three exceptions. The novel also uses *'næ,* a distinctively Suzhou expression, rather than *'nong,* Shanghai standard for the second person singular at the time.[32] And as Miyata Ichirō has shown, other pronouns, some indicative words, and expressive particles are characteristic of Suzhou dialect rather than the Shanghai dialect of that time.[33] *A Shanghai Swan's Traces in the Snow* makes use of the same conventions.[34] Instead of the careful "transcription" of everyday Shanghai usage that we might expect from *Lives of Shanghai Flowers, A Shanghai Swan's Traces in the Snow,* and other Shanghai fiction, their use of dialect writing constructs a normative linguistic identity centered elsewhere, in Suzhou.

As Christopher Prendergast reminds us in his discussion of the nineteenth-century French urban novel, stylistic differentiation between the characters' speech and the words of the narrator must not be ignored.[35] In all of the Shanghai novels that make use of Suzhou dialect in the dialogue, the descriptive portion of the text ("spoken" by the narrator) remains in the northern vernacular, a division of textual labor that sets up a literary distinction between the regional and the national standard.[36] What we find in early Shanghai fiction, then, is not a "pure" and self-contained articulation of Shanghai identity, but rather an abstracted Wu regional identity centered on Suzhou that is always already counterposed against a northern, "national" mode of speech and writing. And vice versa. In *Dreams of Shanghai Splendor,* which seems at first to be written entirely in the northern vernacular—even the dialogue portions—the narrator takes care to remind us regularly that the characters are "in fact" speaking in Suzhou dialect *(Subai),* even though the conventions for transcribing that dialect are not employed.[37] We can see that this is in fact the case, as characters confuse words that are homophones when given a Wu dialect pronunciation, but quite dissimilar in the northern pronunciation.[38]

It is this counterposition, this multivoicedness, that is characteristic of Shanghai cultural production. Instead of constructing a single unified linguistic identity centered on Shanghai, Shanghai fiction presents a specific kind of stereotyped heterogeneity as characteristic of the city—Shanghai is the arena in which Suzhou dialect culture and the northern standard are defined against each other and in which they must struggle for dominance.[39] Unlike the

Guangxu-era novel *Sanxia wuyi* (Three heroes and the righteous five), which includes a wide variety of dialect speech, only, as Paize Keulemans suggests, to subordinate it to standard Mandarin and reaffirm the central position of the capital, Shanghai fiction not only declines to give us specifically "Shanghai dialect," but further refuses to definitively privilege either Suzhou dialect or standard Mandarin.[40] It is no surprise that the term *za* (mixed, heterogeneous) frequently appears in Chinese accounts of Shanghai—it is precisely this insistence on heterogeneity and the mutual exclusivity of different groups that is the key product of the Shanghai culture industry.[41] Querrien sees heterogeneity as crucial to the function of the metropolis, "a membrane which allows communication between two or more milieus," based on the "desire to exchange."[42] This emphasis on exchange in conjunction with heterogeneity reminds us in turn of the formulation of exchange value in Marx's *Capital*: it is the value that the results of one's own labors have *for others*.[43] Similarly, it is Shanghai's production of identities of others ("Suzhou people," "northerners," and so on) not only for consumption within the city limits, but also, and perhaps most significantly, for consumption *elsewhere,* by Suzhou people and northerners themselves, that gives the city a crucial place in the twentieth-century cultural landscape.

By the turn of the century, printed material was one of the most important industrial exports from Shanghai to the rest of China.[44] In this way Shanghai began, as Raymond Williams wrote of nineteenth-century London, to produce and reproduce "the social reality of the nation as a whole," more than a decade before the May Fourth movement.[45] Even as texts produced in late nineteenth-century Shanghai present a fascinating urban milieu, they also standardize and literally mechanize the production of "Wu" as a regional identity centered on Suzhou, engendering at the same time a distinct sense of alienation from that identity through the slight geographic remove, and more importantly, through the very industrial quality of this production. Where earlier Wu dialect texts—especially prose-verse narratives—were written and copied by hand or occasionally printed by woodblock, Shanghai publishers moved quickly to print them on steam-driven lithographic and moveable-type presses. Where Wu dialect narratives in the early eighteenth and nineteenth centuries could address a community readership presumed to share certain regional cultural fundamentals, turn-of-the-twentieth-century Shanghai fiction containing portions in Wu dialect represents that culture in a sense as an *other*—not only to readers elsewhere in China, but even to Wu readers themselves.[46] Shanghai's claim to speak *for* other cultural centers in this way is integral to its emergence as a national media center.

"Chinese" and "Western" Identities

Writing in the 1920s, the author of one preface to *Xin Xiepu chao* (New Huangpu tides) compares Shanghai to the "marvelous grandeur of London, the splendor of Paris, the solemn dignity of Rome, and the sparkling beauty of New York," making a claim for Shanghai's membership in an elite club of world cities.[47] By this time, "Paris of the Orient" had also become a frequent epithet for Shanghai in English-language texts. In both of these cases, a special relationship between Shanghai and "Western" urban modernity is asserted. This kind of assertion has been understood by scholars analyzing 1930s Shanghai culture in two different ways: as a type of colonial mimicry of the metropolitan other that attempts to repress awareness of the city's own semicolonial conditions, or as a confident cosmopolitanism that takes that other as an equal.[48] In either case, however, it is presumed that we know how China and the West are defined; the complexity characteristic of Shanghai arises from the interaction between these two elements, sometimes with the addition of Japan as a third term.[49] It is not surprising that analysis of 1930s cultural production should take clear-cut distinctions between "China" and "the West" for granted, for a great deal of productive work had been done in Shanghai over the preceding century to establish and maintain the coherence and discreteness of these two identities. Without these efforts, it is doubtful that the China-West binary could ever have attained the clarity and intuitive feel that it now has, for as numerous historians of Shanghai have shown, regional and native-place affiliations often commanded stronger allegiance than a more abstract "Chinese" identity as late as the turn of the twentieth century; even the supposedly unproblematic designation of "British" in nineteenth- and early twentieth-century Shanghai could under certain circumstances include not only Scottish, Irish, and English individuals, but also Middle Eastern and South Asian merchants, not to mention ethnic Chinese businessmen from the Straits Settlement or Hong Kong.[50]

By the early twentieth century, it had become evident that Shanghai was the prime location for the production of "Wu regional culture," surpassing Suzhou in importance as a media and entertainment center even as Shanghai's products insisted on the identification of Suzhou as the standard of a certain kind of authenticity and refinement. But as Shanghai gained significance at the national level as a source of books, periodicals, newspapers, and illustrations, it became increasingly clear that another kind of identity production had been at work in the city all along: the elaboration and systematization of the dichotomy between "China" and "the West," a set of binary distinctions that has much in common with the nineteenth-century discourse on St.

Petersburg that distinguished "Russia" from "Europe." Nikolai Gogol wrote in 1836,

> It is difficult to seize the general expression of Petersburg. There is something similar to a European-American colony: just as little indigenous nationality, and just as much foreign confusion, which still has not fused into a compact mass. There are as many different nations in it as there are different strata of societies.[51]

This amalgamation is strikingly heterogeneous when compared with imperial centers like Paris, London, Moscow, or Beijing. As Yuri Lotman points out, the placement of St. Petersburg on the literal and figurative edge of Russian cultural space, complete with urban architecture modeled on that of Western Europe, ensured that it would signify the "complex interweaving of 'our own' and 'other people's.'"[52] This Petersburg is as preoccupied with the present moment as the city represented in Shanghai installment fiction; like Shanghai, it is also often figured as a sort of fantastic and feverish dream. And from the very year it was founded, St. Petersburg served as a manufacturing center not only for the weapons and battleships that Peter thought necessary to Russia's survival and expansion, but also of the very definitions "our own" and "other people's."

There are, of course, important differences. Petersburg was built as a projection of Russian imperial power; Shanghai's rapid expansion rested on domestic and international trade, tourism, opium, and the backs of refugees from turmoil elsewhere in China.[53] Petersburg was envisioned as a realization of the will of one ruler, as an "intentional city";[54] in stories by Gogol, poems by Pushkin, and novels by Dostoevsky, this will pervades structures of authority like the civil service bureaucracy and the police; it also reappears to terrify the populace in the guise of monuments like the Bronze Horseman, which become animated and move through literary texts in threatening fashion. The paranoia that characterizes many Petersburg texts of the nineteenth century found its match in the intense interest that the authorities took in those very texts and the power that censors had to insure that "inappropriate" texts would be expurgated or suppressed.[55]

This kind of paranoia is almost completely absent in Shanghai texts—and this absence is especially notable when we remember that the judicial-administrative structure (both formal and informal) plays a powerful and oppressive role in A Dream of Romance, a novel set in nineteenth-century Yangzhou and similar to early Shanghai installment fiction in several respects.[56] Shanghai, by contrast, could be understood only as a manifestation of the power inherent in the flow of commodities like silver, tea, and opium, and quite significantly, in the wild fluctuations in the value of real estate. Where St. Petersburg is distinguished by a despotic and totalizing bureaucratic mode, Shanghai's uniqueness lies in the contradictory imperatives that are imagined to drive competitive interaction among individuals and groups, and the very concreteness with which these interactions are given expression not only in print, but also in the physical environment itself: the streets, buildings, boundary markers, and so on. If the crucial struggles of Petersburg writing play themselves out in the psyches of troubled individuals, in Shanghai these struggles are literally marked out on the ground itself.

Lives of Shanghai Flowers begins by dropping the narrator in a specific named location loaded with metaphorical significance: the Lu Family Stone Bridge between the French Concession and the southern city, "the meeting point of Chinese and foreign spaces *(hua yang jiaojie)*."[57] This beginning alerts the reader to the significance that the complex space represented as the meeting of Chinese and foreign—Shanghai—enjoys not only in this novel, but in the entire genre of Shanghai fiction. Furthermore, it identifies *jie* as a key term in Shanghai discourse. *Jie* indicates marking out, separation without mixing, and by extension, the categories, spaces, and worlds resulting from these distinctions; it gains important resonance from its frequent use in Buddhist texts as a translation of the Sanskrit term *dhātu,* referring to things and matters each having their own characteristics.[58] Examples include not only *huajie* and *yangjie* (Chinese and foreign spaces, respectively), but also distinctions of occupation, class, or even literary genre (*piaojie*—the world of prostitution, *shangjie*—the commercial world, *xiaoshuo jie*—the world of fiction), and most intriguingly, *zujie* ("leased territory," now generally translated as "concession"). In other words, *jie* is particularly suggestive of attempts to mark out divisions in social space *and* subsequently naturalize such divisions. Lu Xun draws our attention to the contradictions involved in these attempts through his use of a pun on the word for "concession" in the title of one of his essay collections "Essays from a Pavilion in the 'Concessions'" *(Qiejie ting zawen).*[59] As Lu Xun suggests, and as numerous historians have demonstrated, the concessions were not fixed and well-delineated entities, but rather historical processes entailing complicated and intense movements of expansion that were contested on many fronts.[60]

Indeed, by the end of the nineteenth century, the construction and maintenance of symbolic boundaries between concession and non-concession areas of the city had become a pressing concern precisely to the extent that these boundaries lost their importance in the everyday practice of Shanghai residents. One could live in the southern city, work in the French Concession, and shop in the International Settlement, for example, crossing such boundaries as a matter of course; as early as 1860 Chinese residents were the overwhelming majority in all of the concession areas. In response, concession and settlement authorities undertook a variety of measures to ensure the distinctness of the concession areas vis-à-vis the rest of the city, including the obsessive maintenance of street surfaces, illumination of public spaces at night, attempts to suppress "undesirable" behavior in public, and so on.[61]

No less important than these practical measures were the rhetorical attempts to draw a clear distinction between one side and the other. The original center of the city, which remained under exclusive administrative control of the Qing, is often referred to by nineteenth- and twentieth-century writers in English as "the walled city," "the old city," or "the Chinese city."[62] By the 1920s this kind of rhetoric could be taken to its logical conclusion by a Shanghai resident of Western origin who refers to the southern city as "Chinatown," prompting his or her American visitor to rare depths of self-analysis: "It seemed strange to be invited by a Twenty-Years-in-China-Resident to go 'down to Chinatown' as though we were in San Francisco or New York."[63]

Inasmuch as each of these terms functions primarily in stark binary contrast with the adjectives "open," "modern," or "Western," applied explicitly or implicitly to the concession areas, each is of necessity incomplete. To refer to the "walled city" excludes the significant portion of the city that extended to the north, east, and south of the walls throughout the nineteenth century and into the twentieth.[64] To contrast the "old" city against the "modern" concession areas neglects the flourishing domestic trade and ties with South and Southeast Asia that characterized Shanghai before 1840 and do again today; if we recall the developmental trajectory that Christopher Prendergast identifies in nineteenth-century Paris, it becomes clear that cosmopolitan and metropolitan Shanghai represents in at least one sense the urban type toward which its "modern" European contemporaries moved. Finally, juxtaposition of an essentially "Chinese" space against a "Western" one erases the fundamental significance of Chinese consumers, residents, employers, proprietors, and investors in the concession areas and further ignores the extent to which such national or cultural distinctions constitute the specific *products* of a "colonial" city rather than the preconditions for its existence.[65] It is this last point, the question of how specifically Shanghai fiction articulates and refines such binary distinctions, that is the focus of the next section of this chapter.

ॐ

The southern half of Shanghai, the space under Qing administrative control, was also frequently contrasted with the northern concession areas in Chinese-language guidebooks, travel accounts, and newspaper articles throughout the late nineteenth and early twentieth centuries. In Shanghai installment fiction, this non-concession space could serve as neutral territory in the struggles among courtesans for clients. In the fourth chapter of *Lives of Shanghai Flowers,* for example, Wang Liansheng attempts to explain a three-day absence and deny that he has formed another liaison by claiming that he had been inside the city walls *(chengli)*.[66] On the one hand, the southern city represents a more serious and restrained lifestyle: when Du Shaomu first realizes in *Dreams of Shanghai Splendor* that he is spending too much time on questionable pursuits, he joins his more moderate friend Xie You'an and visits an old-fashioned acquaintance and several gardens in the section of the city within the walls.[67] On the other hand, the non-concession spaces lack the amenities common to the concession areas. In the seventieth chapter, Xie You'an, Du Shaomu, and others visit a friend who lives in the southern city to see the annual Ghost Festival procession. On their way out they are unfavorably impressed by packs of dogs and dark narrow streets, and there is a palpable sense of relief when they return to the relatively brightly lit streets of the concession area.[68] In an earlier chapter, Du Shaomu gets lost and works up quite a sweat trying to get to Also a Garden (Yeshi yuan), a garden located inside the city walls, and exclaims that the difference between the concession areas and the space inside the walls is like "the difference between heaven and hell."[69]

But to say that Chinese texts themselves cooperate in the production of East and West as distinct and mutually exclusive cultural entities, holding sway over distinct parts of the city, is not to suggest that they acquiesce in the specific relation of inequality that most Western writers attached to this dichotomy, despite Du Shaomu's frustrated exclamation. It is one of the hallmarks of most colonial and postcolonial scholarship that one "knows" who is the colonizer and who is colonized at the outset; this fundamental distinction is the precondition for all subsequent inquiries. But it is precisely this question that remains problematic in nineteenth-, and even, to a significant extent, early twentieth-century Shanghai.[70] It is important to note that the split between "native" and "foreign" urban spaces in Shanghai in fact lays claim to a specific and complicated history of interaction between "Chinese" imperial culture and "foreign" or *colonized* groups in other regions of the Qing, one example of which is the similar dual structure characteristic of cities on the northern and western frontiers.[71] When we remember that the term *zujie* did not originally suggest the entire apparatus of extraterritoriality that would later be attached to it, but merely the permission to rent houses in a particular area, that "unique" institutions like the Mixed Court had important precedents in previous centuries, and that by the time extraterritoriality reaches its full practical significance in the 1920s and '30s, stateless refugees and exiles from European countries far outnumber more privileged settlers from Britain, the United States, France, and Japan in the concession areas, it becomes clear that the dichotomy between "Chinese" and "foreign" in Shanghai may have assumed forms that postcolonial theory might struggle to imagine.[72]

Ritual vs. History

The claim of a radical disjunction between the English Settlement (centered on the intersection of Fourth Avenue and Stone Street) and the southern city (centered on Leisure Garden at the Temple of the City God) assumes just such a striking form in the last two chapters of *Dreams of Shanghai Splendor,* which present an ultimate unveiling of "truths" hidden behind all-too-attractive urban appearances. This unveiling takes the form of an itinerary that has been eight years in the making for readers of the novel in its installment form—the descent of the courtesan Yan Ruyu to her final judgment in the course of a walk from Fourth Avenue to the Temple of the City God.

Due to the hardships she has undergone and the reduced circumstances she has experienced after losing her hold on one of the male protagonists, Ruyu has by chapter 98 nearly lost her mind. Wandering down Fourth Avenue, she encounters a woman she feels once cheated her and confronts her. When the police patrol charged with keeping order in this area arrives from the west to take Ruyu into custody, she darts south into Zhaofu Alley, turns a corner, and then comes back out onto Stone Street heading south, leaving the police behind. Du Shaomu, her former patron, watches this entire scenario unfold from the second floor of one of the Fourth Avenue teahouses. Reflecting on the reasons for her problems, Du Shaomu goes out of the teahouse and lets himself follow her through the alleys, south across Yangjing Creek, through the French Concession, to the Old North Gate.

Confronted by the city wall, he considers returning to Fourth Avenue, but then thinks that he has spent so much time in courtesan houses he has not gotten a chance to see other places in Shanghai and further realizes that he has not been inside the city walls recently. He goes through the gate and walks down Center Street (Chuanxin jie), losing sight of Ruyu, who has turned off into a maze of side alleys. He enters Leisure Garden, at the Temple of the City God, and annoyed by the press of the crowds there wanders about for some time in search of a quiet place for tea. Finally he stops at a relatively deserted pavilion near the Nine Bend Bridge that features on its wall a couplet referring to transcendence of the illusory world, and settles in to watch the gaily dressed men and women from a distance. But the peaceful scene of children flying kites and playing with assorted toys is suddenly interrupted by the appearance of a noisy crowd of children surrounding a woman who is stark naked. The woman is Ruyu; her illness is now fully manifest, and she shouts and gestures, with the thumb and index finger on each hand brought together in the shape of a circle. Du Shaomu is mystified at first, but the wind carries the cries of the children over to him, and he realizes that they are chanting "Money! Money!" in mocking imitation of her.

The narrative project of *Dreams of Shanghai Splendor* is couched in terms of awakening the deluded to the illusory character of the urban pleasures in which they have lost themselves. Though it would be inappropriate to reduce a complex and multivoiced text to this dimension alone, this particular trajectory is motivated primarily by the drive to reveal a harsh original truth behind enticing urban (female) appearances. Du Shaomu first encounters Yan Ruyu at the end of chapter 14, when he becomes disillusioned with his original favorite, Wu Chuyun, who has betrayed him. But instead of awakening at this point, he transfers his desire for Chuyun directly onto Ruyu and becomes even more entangled. After Du Shaomu finally realizes the "falsity" of urban leisure culture in chapter 60, he no longer commits himself to any relationship with a courtesan, and almost simultaneously both Wu Chuyun and Yan Ruyu go into decline. Ruyu suffers terribly from syphilis and is caricatured in her encounters with male characters over the course of the next forty chapters; in chapter 99, her final descent and public humiliation are described in detail.

Ruyu's trajectory south across Zheng's Wooden Bridge recalls other trips down the "moral" slope in *Dreams of Shanghai Splendor* and other Shanghai novels, but the destination in this case is not the low-class establishments in the French Concession; it is instead the southern city that Du Shaomu previously described as "hell" compared to the "heaven" of the concession areas. Indeed, Yan Ruyu's deranged wanderings through the back alleys of the southern city, losing articles of clothing one by one and acquiring a mocking crowd of onlookers, represents a sort of hell in this world, a devastating retribution for her "sins." Perhaps even more disturbing, however, is the way in which this painful descent, ending with her confinement in an institution and subsequent death, is woven into the account of Du Shaomu's leisurely afternoon spent sightseeing in the same area, troubled only by excessive crowding. One character's movement to a higher level of detachment from the surroundings and deeper insight into the hazards of the city is predicated precisely on another character's simultaneous descent into extreme misery and abjection. Julia Kristeva defines abjection as "immoral, sinister, shady: a terror that dissembles, a hatred that smiles, a passion that uses the body for barter instead of inflaming it," words that have an uncanny resonance with the denunciations of courtesans and prostitutes found at certain points of *Dreams of Shanghai Splendor*.[73] But in Kristeva's understanding, abjection "beseeches and pulverizes the self" and disturbs identity, system, and order; here, by contrast, it is precisely abjection that grounds an enlightened order and affirms both identity and system.

In effect, the simultaneous presentation of these two characters' movements integrates two discourses that had appeared separately and in tension previously: the southern city as a refuge from the deceptions of the concession areas, and the southern city as a dirty, dangerous space. We find earlier in *Dreams of Shanghai Splendor* that retribution works most effectively *outside* the boundaries of the concessions. In chapter 56, Pan Shao'an has taken up residence just outside the French Concession to avoid paramours he has cheated; he is shot there by Deng Zitong in part because in this location they are subject to Qing authority rather than Western police. In chapter 57, Jia Fengchen—who swindles several of the main characters—dies in a house fire outside the concession area because there are fewer hydrants there and the firefighting operations are not as efficient. In both cases, the act of crossing out of the concession zone holds profound moral and narrative significance: the differences between concession and non-concession territories are constructed as central to the workings of retribution by this movement across a perceived border. The inseparability of "enlightenment" and abjection, of "just retribution" and monstrosity hinted at previously is here given explicit emphasis: the final hint of the monstrous aspect of retribution and the subsequent awakening is conveyed in the physical shock with which A Su, Jia Fengchen's former associate, reacts on meeting Yan Ruyu on Nine Bend Bridge—A Su stiffens, stares straight at people without reacting, and begins to shake uncontrollably.[74]

The mechanics of retribution function most efficiently, then, as a movement across difference between Municipal Council administration and Qing administration, suggesting a dynamic of exclusion and attraction between two fundamentally different spaces. To Western authors writing about Shanghai, the "walled city" stood (against the concession areas) for closed-mindedness and stubborn adherence to tradition. In Shanghai fiction, by contrast, the walls enclose a kind of moral-historical center, a repository of culture and a record of what has happened, in radical contrast to the "civilization" or technologized regime introduced from outside. The fundamental difference between the two spaces lies in their ordering principles. The concession areas are considered technologically advanced not only in the simple mechanical sense, but also, and more significantly, in the way their administrations marshal municipal employees (police, firemen, and others) to survey and control those areas. This administrative gaze misses few surface phenomena, enabling the apprehension of litterers and public nuisances as well as gamblers and more serious criminals. But in its very comprehensiveness, the technologized administrative structure loses control of the very space it lays claim to through a lack of discernment; it can see, but it does not finally understand what it sees. By the 1920s and '30s, officials in the Chinese police force frequently identified the concession areas as refuges for criminals;[75] as we can see here, the rhetoric of an insufficiently harsh extraterritorial juridical system appears already in Shanghai novels at the turn of the century. The technologized concession administration can also be seen as ritual administration, in both the generic sense and the pejorative sense.[76] Ritual involves repeated action in accordance with a set of defined rules that will eventually benefit the individual and the community more generally—this is the generic sense; in a less positive view, ritual can also refer to excessive concern with superficialities and appearances, regimentation, and a neglect of more serious and fundamental questions or problems. Chinese guidebooks, illustrated periodicals, and novels alike from this period marvel at the clean streets of the concessions, but find the arrest of individuals for littering and public urination to be a farce, given the serious crimes going on behind closed doors.[77] In their eyes, the social text is read by the Western Settlement authorities with too much attention to formal qualities and not enough to deeper meaning, producing a society that looks neat and well-organized on the surface, but is in fact repressive and unjust.

Since the judicial and administrative structure of the concessions is presented as fundamentally compromised in these novels, it is inevitable that concession authorities discipline criminals most effectively through exclusion and resignation, and relinquish judicial authority by acknowledging spatial and temporal limits.[78] Exclusion-as-judgment could be associated with concession space with particular ease, given both the racist dimensions of the colonial project and, conversely, the importance of the concession areas as a place of refuge in times of civil unrest. The southern city, especially that portion within the city walls, judges instead by attraction; here histories are uncovered and retraced, and both characters and readers are brought back to face the originary ground of Shanghai's prosperity, which had been masked by its displacement and the city's subsequent development. Public leisure culture in Shanghai begins with the dramatic opening of the Leisure Garden adjacent to the City God's Temple to the general public in 1760; more than a century later, this space proves to be the ground on which judgment is pronounced on that leisure culture. A similar itinerary, with its own associated sense of ironized redemption, appears several decades later in a novel by the Shanghai modernist Xu Xu: Shanghai is neither heaven nor hell, he writes, but "the journey from the gambling den to church."[79]

Following Du Shaomu, we find ourselves face-to-face with the narrative production of a significant binary opposition: a striking contrast between technological and ritual control in the concessions on the one hand and moral-historical force of the "walled city" on the other. What is fascinating about this discourse of difference is that it serves a specific narrative purpose as one part of a fictional product imagined, materialized, and sold as a commodity within a specific local, regional, and national context. Looking at the way the related contrasts between culture and civilization, technology and history, and, of course, "foreign" and "Chinese" are worked out in these novels and in other texts, we begin to understand how the oppositions we now think within were formed in part in fictional texts as a by-product of the narrative process. In the intervening century, these oppositions have been naturalized back in time and are now understood instead as the "historical" raw material that "fictional" process takes as a basis. As a territory, then, Shanghai has the ability not only to generate identities, but also to produce "historical fact."

Displacement

The reproduction and elaboration of these oppositions is not found in *Dreams of Shanghai Splendor* alone; another striking instance appears in the turn-of-the-century novel *Mengyou Shanghai mingji zhengfeng zhuan* (An account of a dream voyage to Shanghai: Famous courtesans contending for dominance), referred to here in abbreviated form as *Courtesans Contending for Dominance*. As noted in the introduction, the success of early Shanghai novels encouraged many imitators. In one case, rather than write a new work from scratch, an editor decided to alter portions of *A Dream of Romance* to change the setting from Yangzhou to Shanghai. The obvious first step was to change the title and the names of the main characters; in addition to *An Account of a Dream Voyage to Shanghai: Famous Courtesans Contending for Dominance*, the text was variously printed under the titles *Mingji zhengfeng zhuan* (An account of famous courtesans contending for dominance) and *Mengyou Shanghai zhengfeng zhuan* (An account of a dream voyage: Contending for dominance in Shanghai).[80] Fortunately for the editor, the text already included occasional remarks on Yangzhou; with the substitution of "Shanghai" for "Yangzhou" these would at least provide a hint of up-to-date flavor. Similarly, places, streets, and establishments could be given names that would be familiar to the Shanghai reader, although there are occasional slips.[81]

One of the most interesting substitutions takes place in a passage describing an opium box. In the original, the box, topped by a miniature lion with moveable eyes and tongue, could only have been manufactured in Shanghai; Yangzhou artisans could not have made something so complex. In the revised Shanghai version of the novel, appearing five decades later, such a box is beyond the capability of Shanghai artisans, and can only be imported from overseas.[82] The analogical relationship suggested by the substitution is the following:

> Shanghai : Yangzhou   (1848)
> the West : Shanghai   (1900)

Shanghai is to Yangzhou in 1848 as the West is to Shanghai at the turn of the century. So far, the changes in the text fit nicely with the standard metanarrative of Shanghai's development as "opening up to the West," and the conventional understanding of Shanghai as an intermediary between "China" and "the West." A second substitution some twenty chapters later, however, gives us a slightly different view of Shanghai's changing role over the course of the nineteenth century. The reference to Shanghai in this passage of *A Dream of Romance* is changed to Zhenjiang in *Courtesans Contending for Dominance,* leaving us with the following equivalence:

> Shanghai : Yangzhou   (1848)
> Zhenjiang : Shanghai   (1900)

This seems diametrically opposed to the identification of Shanghai with the West that took place twenty chapters earlier; the Shanghai of the middle of the century here translates into a turn-of-the-century city that was fast growing but still provincial.[83] Is this evidence of the hastiness or carelessness of the revision of *A Dream of Romance* into *Courtesans Contending for Dominance?* I would suggest the opposite, that these two substitutions appear contradictory only from a twentieth-century colonial or postcolonial vantage point. In the middle of the nineteenth century, Shanghai's flourishing economy and ties to the West still would not have meant that it was any less provincial, especially to a writer resident in a metropolis like Yangzhou; in this context, the selection of Zhenjiang (1900) to stand in for Shanghai (1848) is quite appropriate.[84] There is not only no contradiction between technological sophistication and rapid economic development on the one hand, and cultural "backwardness" on the other, but in fact a distinct logic to their conjunction, as suggested in the pages above.

Earlier in this chapter, I suggested that a key characteristic of Shanghai's cultural production is the manufacture of identities of and for *others*. At the same time, that cultural production also centers on a dynamic of substitution or displacement. In several senses, *Courtesans Contending for Dominance* is not an "authentic" Shanghai novel—as far as we know, it was never published in installments, and the traces of its Yangzhou origin are all too apparent to the careful reader. But in its unapologetic use of substitution, not only in the setting of the novel, but also in references to other locations within the text, *Courtesans Contending for Dominance* hits a note that is crucial to Shanghai fiction of this period at a number of different levels.

The narrative of Yan Ruyu's "return" to the southern city discussed previously in fact begins when another character, A Jin, is brought before the Mixed Court on charges of abusing Hua Haohao, a courtesan whom she owns together with a partner; the two owners are tortured until they confess. As part of their punishment, they are to be paraded around the Fourth Avenue area and publicly shamed for three days before being allowed to return to their original registered cities of residence.[85] After turning onto Fourth Avenue, A Jin stops on the steps of the "Door of Hope" (Jiliang suo) branch office to rest. This office for the "rehabilitation" of courtesans and prostitutes run by a foreign woman with Chinese assistants was responsible for bringing Hua Haohao's case to the attention of the Mixed Court. Here the crowd gets large enough to block off the entire street. Xie You'an, Du Shaomu, and several other characters, having heard about the procession, go to Great Prospect Teahouse (Daguan lou, at the intersection of Stone Street and Fourth Avenue) and claim seats upstairs for a better view of what is going on in the street below. Just as the police are beginning to move A Jin and her partner east down Fourth Avenue, a disheveled woman dashes out of the crowd and confronts A Jin. As the next chapter begins, we learn that this woman is none other than Yan Ruyu. She has mistaken A Jin for someone else she feels has cheated her and so confronts her. This is the point at which the narrative shifts to Yan Ruyu and her descent into the southern city discussed above.

The transfer from one stigmatized female character to another in front of the Door of Hope is highly symbolic. This institution, a joint Chinese-Western establishment located in the heart of the English Settlement, aims to give courtesans and prostitutes a means of transition into a new life, analogous to the passage to enlightenment the male characters/readers are supposed to experience as they read *Dreams of Shanghai Splendor* and other novels like it. But the narrative ultimately limits the Door of Hope to the role of a way station or point of transfer on the route back to the center of the southern city. (And of course Ruyu herself stands as a sign for transfer or substitution, since Du Shaomu's desire for Wu Chuyun is displaced onto Ruyu only after Chuyun cheats on him.) As the reader slides from A Jin to Yan Ruyu, from the center of the English Settlement to the center of the southern city, and is in the process reminded of Leisure Garden's historical significance, it becomes evident that Shanghai's rapid development is tied from its earliest moments to a specific kind of movement—displacement.

In other early twentieth-century Chinese fiction such as Wu Jianren's *Strange Happenings,* the narrative of Shanghai's origin depends on the rhetoric of Western impact discussed in the introduction—it is the advent of trade on Western ships that transforms a sleepy riverfront village into a booming metropolis.[86] This myth of origin was in fact found first in English-language texts written by Shanghailanders (European residents of Shanghai) and "China hands" in the second half of the nineteenth century; by the 1890s it had spread to many Chinese-language texts as well.[87] But Shanghai fiction offers such rhetoric in its opening pages only to later call it into question by emphasizing displacement *within* China—even within the Shanghai area—instead. The whole point of *Dreams of Shanghai Splendor* is to draw attention to what lurks *beyond* or *beneath* the surface of the myth; the rhetoric of "opening to the West" as origin so clearly articulated at the beginning of the novel is put into question as the narrative progresses, just as the attractive courtesans are later exposed as the miserable creatures that they "in fact" are.

What, then, is the historical significance of Leisure Garden? *Dreams of Shanghai Splendor* uses Ruyu's trajectory to reverse history, providing a thorough and penetrating response to "Western impact" rhetoric by presenting a genealogical inquiry into an earlier phase of public leisure culture in Shanghai. In 1760, in an innovative move, a group of local merchants purchased Leisure Garden—a landscaped space within the city walls—from the Pan family and donated it to the Shanghai City Temple. This became the first large public garden in Shanghai, to which admittance was evidently quite casual.[88] Near the end of the eighteenth century, the author Shen Fu, down on his luck, went to ask a friend in Shanghai for help. He was dressed so poorly that he did not dare to look for the friend at his office, but instead made an appointment to meet with him in Leisure Garden. By this point the "garden" was clearly open even to those who could not afford to dress well.[89] Writing in the 1840s, a Western observer noted that "Behind the [city] temple are what the people call tea-gardens; there is, however, very little that can be entitled to the appellation of a garden; but a few rocks and ponds, surrounded by houses for the accommodation of tea-drinkers who assemble there in great numbers."[90] Three decades later, Ge Yuanxu complained that the teahouses and shops in this space made it more like a market than a proper garden, and very noisy.[91] From the 1820s into the 1850s, this garden was the focal point of the Shanghai entertainment district, already a substantial part of the Shanghai area economy; smaller guilds and trade organizations also held their meetings there.[92]

Shanghai's leisure quarters moved north into the concession areas, however, when the southern city was attacked in the battles between rebel and Qing forces in the 1850s and 1860s.[93] The violent and contingent aspect of this displacement cannot be ignored: the City Temple and its grounds were at least partially destroyed three times in the mid-nineteenth century, once in the conflict between Small Sword rebels and Qing soldiers, and twice when the area was used as barracks for European soldiers during the Opium War and when Taiping forces drew near Shanghai.[94] By the late 1860s the entertainment district centered on Precious Virtue Street (Baoshan jie), the central stretch of Fifth Avenue in the English Settlement. By the start of the Guangxu period in 1875, the main establishments had moved another block to the north, relocating along Fourth Avenue.[95] The narrative in chapters 98 and 99 of *Dreams of Shanghai Splendor* reverses this movement, inscribing a return to the "origin." While the concession areas provide fertile space for the development of particular forms of leisure and entertainment, their ultimate source remains back in the southern city, the arena in which the revelation of their "true" nature takes place.

At this point, the reader pauses in his or her careful identification with Du Shaomu to realize that what has been revealed is not only the ugly truth hidden behind Yan Ruyu's smiling face, but also the very history of Shanghai's early development as a leisure center, a history that is usually masked or erased by the insistence that Shanghai owes its unique characteristics to the economic consequences of trade with Westerners. Like Du Shaomu, we realize only now how little thought we have given to the southern city, and how little time we have spent there. In a later novel, *New Shanghai*, this critique is made more explicitly, as a character who is knowledgeable about Shanghai history explains the formation of urban leisure culture in the southern city and its subsequent move north.[96]

Indeed, as we have seen in the introduction, substitution and displacement turn out to be key not only to understanding the development of Shanghai's entertainment world, but also the material and symbolic formation of the city as a whole, from the relocation of Ningbo-based traders to the city in the late eighteenth century to the shift in grain shipments to a coastal route in the early nineteenth century, which combined with the reorganization of the salt monopoly to shake Yangzhou's economic foundations even as it spurred Shanghai's rapid development—in Meng Yue's words, turning the Qing empire "inside out."[97] Over the course of the nineteenth century, civil unrest elsewhere in China, as well as in the Shanghai region, brought large numbers of refugees with varying resources to the city; as noted above, several of these instances of unrest also displaced a significant proportion of Shanghai leisure establishments from the vicinity of the Temple of the City God to the European settlements north of the city.[98] This logic of growth-through-displacement holds even in the most concrete details of the city's cultural life. The rise of Shanghai as a national theater center came as a direct result of government restrictions on theaters in Beijing and Suzhou; famous actors relocated to Shanghai in the 1860s and '70s, with the most enthusiastic of their audiences following them (even if only for short visits).[99]

Shanghai's attraction to displaced persons reached even further afield in the first half of the twentieth century, both domestically and internationally. In 1937 the population of the concession areas surged dramatically after the surrounding region fell to the Japanese army, providing yet again a major boost to Shanghai's economy, including the media and entertainment industry.[100] And since the peculiar territoriality of the concession areas allowed immigrants without visas to visit and settle there, Shanghai was, from the early 1920s onward, a relative haven for displaced and stateless persons from abroad, the largest groups of which were White Russian and Jewish refugees from Europe, as noted earlier.[101] The arrival of international refugees in particular highlights the ways in which the trope of displacement provides an important counterweight to discourses of colonialism and semicolonialism: just as the concessions reached the zenith of their autonomy and power vis-à-vis the Chinese government, the settlers of European and American origin who claimed the right to self-governing administration of these areas were increasingly outnumbered by refugees from Europe who lacked both political power and economic resources. According to some estimates, by 1934–1935 the White Russian and Jewish refugees in Shanghai numbered nearly 50,000; in these same years, the concessions had 20,242 Japanese residents, 9,225 British residents, 3,809 American residents, and 1,430 French residents.[102] Although the influx of European refugees in the 1920s and '30s did not materially alter the fundamental structures of power in the concession areas, it left lasting traces in the cultural production of the period.[103]

Finally, we may note that the very possibility of asserting that Shanghai began to thrive only on the arrival of Western merchants—a constant refrain in much of the writing on the city in all languages—depends on a shift in focus from the city center, which had been well represented in earlier works such as Yao Xie's manuscript "Kuhai hang" (Sailing a bitter sea, 1848) and Wang Tao's *Yingruan zazhi* (Random notes from the marshes, 1875), to the suburban farmlands to the north where Westerners were allowed to lease plots of land. If turn-of-the-century Shanghai texts had remained concerned with the southern

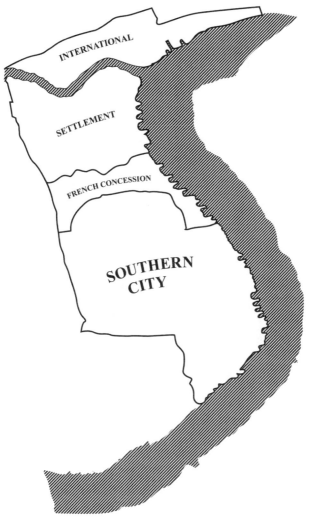

FIGURE 2 Schematic map of developed areas of Shanghai in 1895.
Based on "Xinzeng chongxiu Shanghai xiancheng xiang zujie dili
quantu."

city, Shanghai's development would not have seemed nearly so striking, nor so
atypical to tourists from other major Chinese cities. As late as 1895, for example, the southern city was comparable in size to the French and International
Settlements combined (fig. 2). Although nineteenth- and early twentieth-century population figures are not as detailed as one might wish, it seems likely that
a not insignificant portion of the long-term population growth in the French

Concession and the International Settlement before 1890 came at the expense of the southern city, and furthermore, that a fair amount of the growth in population of the concession areas between 1890 and 1920 came not so much from an increase in the population density of those original concession areas themselves as it did from their expansion to include a greater part of the rest of the city.[104] As Catherine Yeh and Zhu Weizheng point out, the northern city "eventually took over the name of Shanghai altogether in the public mind."[105] I would add that this takeover stemmed not only from the increased population density and prosperity of the core concession and settlement areas, but also from their expansion into surrounding urban areas, and most important of all, from the greater emphasis placed on the concession and settlement areas in a wide variety of Chinese-language texts.

So what caused this displacement of attention? It is evident that the new focus on the northern part of the city on the part of guidebook writers, memoirists, illustrators, photographers, and journalists was not unmotivated: Ge Yuanxu notes explicitly in the introductory remarks to his influential city guide *Huyou zaji* (Random notes on voyaging to Shanghai)—written in 1876—that he emphasizes the concession areas at the expense of the southern city because they contain the sights and activities that visiting merchants and officials, whether in Shanghai for business or pleasure or both, are interested in.[106] It is quite clear that many of the texts that write Shanghai's history are meant as "compasses" to attract and guide the uninitiated visitor; it is therefore imperative that these texts accentuate the features that would be perceived as unique to Shanghai and deemphasize or dismiss the parts that seem similar to other cities across China. This approach made a great deal of sense in the late nineteenth- and early twentieth-century market; it was in fact the concession areas that represented Shanghai's best claim to uniqueness in regional competition for tourists against established destinations such as Suzhou and Yangzhou, each of which had longer historical pedigrees and many more well-known tourist sites.

"Exotic" Westerners, their behavior, and their possessions proved quite profitable to local entrepreneurs from the earliest moments of the British presence in Shanghai. W. H. Medhurst and company, on their arrival to the city after the signing of the Treaty of Nanjing, at first availed themselves of the hospitality of a merchant named Yao, only to find he was charging local residents for the privilege of observing them in their rooms.[107] Strategies for exploiting interest in the exotic soon became on the one hand more subtle, and on the other, much broader in scope as "westernized" Chinese individuals, "westernized" architecture, and so on became objects of fascinated attention for recent arrivals from elsewhere in China; it is clear that the ability of certain Shanghai residents to profit from the interest readers and tourists had in the unfamiliar, the strange, and the new continued well into the early twentieth century.[108] This profitable business depended in part on the ability of Shanghai cultural producers to establish and maintain recognizable distinctions between the "familiar" and the "strange"; the contrasts that Shanghai installment fiction draws between the southern city and the concession areas constitute a key dimension of this broader "distinction maintenance" project.

ℬ

Prior to the Opium War, Shanghai was indeed a metropolis based on material production and exchange, including international trade. After the establishment of the concessions, the city also became a center of symbolic production—especially of distinctions between "self" and "other" or "Chinese" and "Western"—and a place of unusually marked consumption. This later transformation, paradoxically, is often identified by authors from the late nineteenth century forward as the *beginning* of substantial material production and exchange: the city is understood to flourish economically only after people begin writing about it as a distinctive and attractive location and so drawing visitors to it. The very persistence of this focus on symbolic production and consumption as measures of economic development and the related myth of Shanghai as a mere fishing village prior to the Opium War, show first, the importance of cultural production as both index and source of material prosperity; and second, the degree to which motivated cultural products—texts, illustrations, and paradigms—continue to structure retrospective attempts to grasp the "reality" of a given historical moment.

CHAPTER 2

From Street Names to Brand Names

The Grid of Reference

In 1892 Shanghai appears for the first time as a 360° panorama. Seen from the tower of Trinity Church through the lenses of photographers like Tomishige Rihei, the city is a collection of buildings organized into a grid by a system of streets and alleys (fig. 3).[1] This focus on the detail of the urban fabric constitutes a striking departure from Wang Tao's climb to the highest point in the southern city some three decades earlier; in his record of the trip, published in 1875, Wang took care to inform the reader that one could see for several *li,* but felt no need to provide any description of *what* could be seen.[2] The possibilities of photographic technology had seized the imagination of the Shanghai leisure class in the intervening years; Chinese-owned studios soon joined those run by Japanese and European photographers, and photographs of courtesans, local scenes, and examples of the colonial culture of display were widely available by the 1880s.[3] Perhaps the best-known late Qing photographer was Satō Denkichi, who owned a studio on Grand Avenue (Da malu, now Nanjing lu) that featured in both English- and Chinese-language guidebooks and sold a series of albums of Shanghai views, including sights such as the electric station, the water tower, the racing club, and the swimming pool.[4] Photographs of famous buildings, streets, and intersections portrayed Shanghai as a collection of locations, just as verses on Shanghai places had for more than one hundred years.[5]

Panoramic photography of the 1890s and early 1900s moved beyond this interest in individual locations and establishments; building on earlier Western and Chinese oil paintings of the Bund, the panorama integrated collections of specific places into a fantasy of "the city" as a legible whole, organized around a grid of representation, in the same way that Shanghai novels of this period brought multiple narrative lines together into a literary imagination of the city as a system of relations.[6] Indeed, the first Shanghai installment fiction appears in the same year as Tomishige's panoramic photograph and betrays a similar preoccupation with the urban grid. At its most obvious, we see this interest in the opening pages of *A Shanghai Swan's Traces in the Snow,* which

FIGURE 3 Detail of "Panoramic view of foreign section of Shanghai, China." Photograph, 1890s. C915.12 S528. Reproduction permission of Phillips Library, Peabody Essex Museum, Salem, Massachusetts.

likens the night vista of the Bund to a dragon stretched out along the river, but the city streets also structure Shanghai installment fiction at a deeper level.[7] Even a casual glance through the pages of any of these novels yields a profusion of well-known establishments, avenues, and *lilong* (alleys and lanes), all of which can also be found in guidebooks and newspapers and on maps from the period.

This city space is not a haphazard or formless jumble, but a system of relations between recognizable names that direct the reader to other types of representation: photographs, lithographic illustrations, maps, guidebooks, lists of city streets and establishments, and newspaper articles, among others. In addition, this attention to the structure of urban space is paired with the frequent mention of markers of time—hours of the day, days of the week, and days of the month—to form a grid of reference that is central not only to each of the novels individually, but also to the development of the genre as a whole, foregrounding *referentiality* as a key question. What do all of these names and markers refer to? And what effect does the internally consistent grid of reference that these names and markers constitute have on the reader?

The Map and the Calendar

The center of gravity in most Shanghai writing from the 1890s into the 1910s is Fourth Avenue (Si malu, now Fuzhou lu), an east-west thoroughfare in the English section of the International Settlement, along which many of the teahouses, restaurants, and theaters mentioned in the novels are located.[8] Fourth Avenue was at its most lively several blocks in from the Bund where it crossed Stone Street (Shi lu, now Fujian lu), an intersection that plays a key role in Yan Ruyu's downward trajectory discussed in the previous chapter (fig. 4).

A Shanghai Swan's Traces in the Snow also makes prominent use of this inter-section; the story begins in Ascending Peace Teahouse (Shengping lou), where the narrator comments that in this area "halls of song and houses of prostitu-tion are crowded together like scales on a fish or teeth on a comb," making it "an indescribable showcase of the new and different."[9] In early Shanghai fic-tion, courtesans of the highest rank (*changsan,* or *zasae* in Shanghai dialect) live for the most part within a block or two of this intersection. As one moves away from this point to the south (toward the French Concession) or to the west (toward the racetrack), "second-class" *(yao'er / yo'ni)* courtesans and the despised "independent prostitutes" or "wild chickens" *(yeji / 'iaji)* are more common.[10] The rock-bottom "flower smoke houses" *(huayanjian / hu'igei)* fre-quented by the servants of more prosperous characters are located even further south in the French Concession. Movement upward in the hierarchy is usu-ally accompanied by relocation to a better address: the second-class courtesan Zhang Huizhen starts out in Xiangchun Alley, west of the intersection between Fourth Avenue and Stone Street, then moves east to East Hexing Alley when she is promoted to the rank of first-class courtesan.[11] In later novels such as *The Huangpu Tides* (1916–1921), which have a more "domestic" emphasis, the primary loci of narrative activity shift to the Hongkou and Xinzha regions, to the north and west of the core of the old English Settlement. It is here that long-term couples and some families rent apartments and houses. Elgin Road, where Ni Junren shares a house with his concubine Wushuang, and near which Qian Ruhai rented a place for Ms. Shao (in Huaxing Lane), is close to the train sta-tion in the American section of the International Settlement, north of Suzhou Creek. Qian Ruhai and his wife, Ms. Xue, live in Xinzha; the Jias live nearby on Manpan Road.[12] Many locations are also to be found in the vicinity of Avenue Road (Aiwenyi lu, now Beijing xilu) and Carter Road (Kade lu, now Shimen erlu), both located northwest of the racetrack.

We can see already that the space in which Shanghai narratives unfold is not neutral or undifferentiated; it is instead a field charged with social meaning that is concretized in specific movements of characters across it in a way that is strongly reminiscent of Flaubert's *Éducation sentimentale.*[13] Indeed, the dis-tinctions are made so carefully in Shanghai fiction—as they are in guidebooks from the period—that even individual alleys or *lilong* often have a reputation. For example, Hong Shanqing is angered to learn that his sister and niece have moved into Qinghe Lane, which he sees as a den of iniquity; Qunyu Lane is identified as a good location; Baihua Alley and Jiu'an Alley are well-known for their courtesan houses.[14] Well over fifty *lilong* figure significantly in these nov-els, as well as a comparable number of shops, theaters, restaurants, teahouses, and parks, each identified by name.

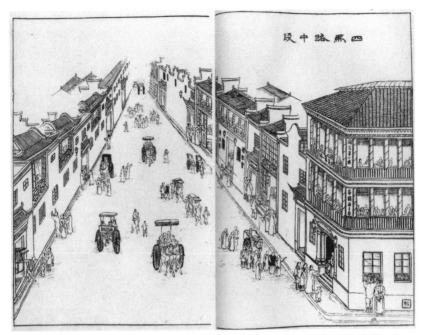

FIGURE 4 "Fourth Avenue Central Section." Lithographic illustration, 1884. *Shenjiang shengjing tu,* 2.37b–38a. Reproduction permission of Princeton University Library.

Shanghai novels are marked not only by the profusion with which specific *lilong* are cited as addresses and locations for action—this distinguishes them already from previous Chinese fiction—but also by the accurate and systematic representation of the spatial relationships that obtain between them. This is obvious as soon as any attempt is made to identify locations and follow narrative trajectories on a map from the period. The descriptions of individual locations as well as statements of the spatial relationship between any two or more locations are always consistent and agree with maps, street indexes, newspaper articles, and guidebooks.[15] We learn in *Lives of Shanghai Flowers,* for example, that Tong'an Alley accesses both Third Avenue and Fourth Avenue, that it is across from Gongyang Alley, and near East Hexing Alley; in *Dreams of Shanghai Splendor,* we find that Jiu'an Alley opens onto Stone Street and is near Zhaogui Alley, and so on.[16]

Why is there such concern for accuracy and coherence in the representation of urban space, as well as the careful evaluation of its various components? The periodic struggles between different groups over the exact boundaries of the concession spaces, the constant negotiation of the differences between concession and non-concession spaces, and even the question of how a "concession" might in fact be defined, discussed in the previous chapter, clearly encouraged close attention to spatial demarcation. In addition, the peculiar character of the *lilong* itself, an innovative mode of urban development, plays an important part. Large parcels of land originally laid out by concession authorities were leased by speculators in real estate (both foreign and Chinese), subdivided into smaller plots and developed as narrow alleys with rows of two-story houses and apartments; these alleys were given three- or four-character names with auspicious import that ended either in *li* (alley) or *fang* (lane).[17] While the broader city streets were lined with large stores, offices, restaurants, teahouses, and theaters, the *lilong* were a mix of commercial establishments and residences; they housed as much as 70 percent of the city's population in the late nineteenth and early twentieth century. The rest of the space in these alleys was taken up by courtesan houses, smaller stores, offices, *tanci* halls, rooms for short-term rental, and even, in some cases, schools and small factories.[18] Several publishers involved in the production of tabloid newspapers and Shanghai installment fiction had their printing houses and sales offices in these alleys.[19] As an involuted or intensified mode of development closely linked to the expansion of the original concession boundaries that took place at the same time, the *lilong* bore more than a passing resemblance to the Parisian arcades that Walter Benjamin took as a central organizing image in his project on the nineteenth-century European bourgeois consciousness, the *Passagen-Werk*.[20] Though these processes of expansion and intensified development are commented on directly in Shanghai novels only occasionally—such as in *Dreams of Shanghai Splendor* when Wu Chuyun returns to Shanghai after an absence of several years and is struck by the proliferation of new alleys and main streets—they form the distinct subtext against which these texts must be read.[21] This intensified urban development means that the "resolution" of Shanghai space was also constantly increasing; the finely grained space of Shanghai fiction incorporates this intensification into the very structure of its narrative.

※

The interest in accuracy and coherence was not, however, restricted to street names and establishments; the Shanghai novel is also remarkably precise in its representation of dates and times.[22] Shanghai installment fiction begins in 1892 with the narrator of *Lives of Shanghai Flowers* dreaming that he is falling through a sea of flowers, only to wake and recall the day's date as he lands in a heap on the Lu Family Stone Bridge. "He rubbed his eyes, regained his footing, and then remembered that today was the twelfth day of the second month. . . ."[23] References to specific dates and times persist throughout *Lives of Shanghai Flowers* and in every other example of the genre down to the late

1920s, giving a carefully measured chronological structure to each narrative as it unfolds. As I have shown elsewhere, although specific dates were often cited in earlier Chinese vernacular fiction, there was little sense that they needed to fit into a coherent temporal system; chronological discrepancies were frequently interpreted as deliberate signs on the part of the author to alert careful readers to another level of the text. In Shanghai novels, by contrast, the narrative frequently covers a shorter period of time, and references to dates and times are always precise and completely consistent, with no discrepancies.[24]

The effort required to maintain this level of detail and consistency alerts us to the importance of time in the text; moreover, it calls our attention to the close link between the spatial and temporal organization of the city.[25] The restricted spatial scope of the Shanghai novel makes a compressed timescale possible; unlike campaigns in *Sanguo zhi* (Three kingdoms) and *Shuihu zhuan* (The water margin), the journeys described in Shanghai novels from one alley in the concession area to another, to the Bund, or to Zhang's Garden take only a few minutes, or at most half an hour, by rickshaw or by carriage. Trips are often so short that they are made on foot. The relation between the specific narrative space of Shanghai and the special characteristic of Shanghai time is highlighted in these novels by the way time seems to change character altogether when characters move outside Shanghai, whether to outlying suburbs, to Suzhou, or even further afield. In *Dreams of Shanghai Splendor*, for example, the events of a single day in Shanghai may take a chapter or more to narrate, but Wu Chuyun's four-year odyssey from Wuxi to Suzhou to Tianjin takes up only fifteen pages; we begin to learn about her days in detail again only on her return to Shanghai.[26]

The concept of accurate public time would not have been a novelty to late Qing readers; the hours in a Chinese city were marked by horns, bell, drum, and neighborhood patrols as early as the Tang, and the *Zhouli* (Rites of the Zhou), a text dating to at least the Han, proposes that the hour be publicly displayed on wooden tablets. Private time had also been well kept and finely grained for centuries before the introduction of Western clocks and watches by means of water clocks and incense clocks.[27] Indeed, it is perhaps the relative ubiquity of the accepted systems of temporal indicators that allows most Qing novelists to treat the passage of time so casually. In striking contrast, the widespread installation of mechanical clocks in Shanghai residences and places of business, the tolling of the Customs House clock that could be heard through the city streets, as well as other peculiarities such as the British ritual cannon shot at noon each day afford the Shanghai novelist with a rich repertoire of new and different indicators of time.[28] Similarly, the introduction of a different calendrical system and the seven-day week defamiliarize the passage of time. By radically foregrounding the measures through which the passing hours, days, weeks, and months are announced and accounted for, these new and unaccustomed temporal indicators allow Shanghai installment fiction to dedicate itself just as obsessively to temporal consistency as to spatial coherence.[29]

Indeed, the two are related in Shanghai fiction at a fundamental level: the systematicity of grid and clock is not only inspired by the politics and peculiarities of colonial urban development, it is in fact *required* by the multiplicity of the narrative itself. Late Qing and Republican-era Shanghai novels are usually quite lengthy, even by the standards of Chinese long vernacular fiction. They have dozens of major characters and many overlapping storylines, and, in a tribute to the aesthetic principles outlined in commentaries to the better-known novels of the Ming and Qing, these narrative lines are woven together so closely that one episode does not come to a conclusion until several others have begun. Friends of the "author" of one Shanghai novel, *Shadows of Shanghai's Dusty Skies,* even suggest that he create a chart of characters before he starts writing, to avoid getting mixed up.[30] How can a reader, then, approach texts like these without becoming confused, especially when the reading in installments stretches over a period of months or even years?

In a mid-Qing novel like *Dream of the Red Chamber,* with many characters if fewer storylines than in Shanghai novels, the characters are organized in a consistent and detailed *genealogical* order that admits no imprecision or inaccuracy. The distinction between the Ningguo and Rongguo halves of the estate is that between elder and younger brother, and the residents of the special garden space are segregated as a generation apart from other members of the household. While the reader of *Dream of the Red Chamber* is never given a genealogical chart of the family relationships, it is a relatively simple task to produce one (whether consciously or subconsciously) as one reads. This well-ordered system helps the reader keep characters and episodes straight, and it must have seemed particularly appropriate in the eighteenth century, which saw a sustained rise in the social importance of lineages and genealogical discourse.[31]

Shanghai novels also deal with large numbers of characters, but in this case the different characters are usually friends, business associates, acquaintances, patrons, actors, courtesans, servants, and so on rather than blood relatives. For this reason, relations in Shanghai novels are concretized instead through reference to specific locations within a well-ordered spatial system. This multiplicity of characters moves through an unprecedentedly complex and challenging narrative structure, which we will examine in more detail in the next chapter.[32] Here I will note only that this structure can be resolved into multiple narrative threads that intersect at given points and then separate again, a type of organization in which simultaneous progression and coordination between what appear to be different threads is essential. Georg Simmel commented in 1900 that if the clocks of Berlin were to go awry, the city would cease to function; we may note that just as the transit system of a busy metropolitan area relies on the split-second accuracy of switches, signals, and connections to ensure its proper operation, Shanghai installment fiction, too, requires precise and consistent temporal progression to enable narrative movement from one story to another.[33]

Referentiality

In addition to providing us with a means of ordering complex narrative structures in the form of a reserve of systematic differentiations that are always available to the reader, these markers of time and place refer us elsewhere, beyond the bounds of the individual text. In their choice of recognizable locations, markers of time, and brand-name establishments, writers of Shanghai fiction call the reader's attention to the question of literary referentiality: What does it mean for a narrative to repeatedly point outside itself and send its readers off elsewhere? How does the system that organizes each individual text hook up with a broader intertextual or extratextual order?

It is no accident that contemporary theater, a genre of cultural production whose power derived in large part from its readiness to make references to events offstage, figures centrally in most Shanghai installment fiction. As Joshua Goldstein has shown, in the late Qing theater/teahouse, "social (audience) and representational (stage) spaces were approached as mutually permeable and continuous."[34] In the nineteenth-century European novel, the theater frequently provides the occasion and location for social interaction and narrative mixing that significantly advance the plot. Men in the audience fix their attention on women onstage; and women and men in the audience watch each other as well.[35] Public performance spaces in Shanghai fiction serve a similar function, with courtesans performing in "*tanci* halls" *(shuchang)* and in female theatrical troupes in hopes of gaining clients. But there is an important difference—both women *and* men on the Shanghai stage appear as targets of the audience's gaze.[36]

Most theaters in Guangxu period (1875–1908) Shanghai specialized in male troupes performing Peking opera, and in this case the gendered gaze was that of the courtesans, married women, and unmarried daughters of "proper" families in the audience; these women fetishized the male actors and conducted illicit affairs with them.[37] The attractive actor as competitor with the courtesan's "legitimate" client is a recurring theme, of which the most obvious example is Shen Xiaohong's relationship with a star who specializes in martial roles (Xiao Liu'er) in *Lives of Shanghai Flowers*, which leads her to neglect her client (Wang Liansheng) and eventually destroy her own standing in Shanghai society. Du Sujuan's affairs with actors figure as important subtext twice in *Dreams of Shanghai Splendor;* in the same novel, Xie You'an presents the dalliances of women (both courtesans and "proper") with actors to substantiate a narrative of general moral decline in Shanghai, explaining that a certain set of seats in some theaters has come to be denied to unaccompanied women because of their attempts to attract the attention of the actors on stage by tossing trinkets and otherwise making spectacles of themselves.[38] Even the advent of "civilized" or "enlightened" *(wenming)* reformist theater in the 1910s does nothing to reduce the appeal of actors to female characters, as we see in detail in *The Huangpu Tides.*[39]

The theater building was not only the literal site of interaction between the audience and those onstage (according to Meng Yue, "theatergoing operated as the focal point for a panoply of chaotic social events");[40] it also provided—in the form of the stage—an arena in which social interactions could be re-presented, both through the choice of familiar plays that could be understood to refer to contemporary events and, in an innovative development of the 1890s, by means of "new productions" *(xinxi)* that claimed to provide accounts of current Shanghai scandals.[41] Since these "new productions," which included notorious courtesans and Westerners as characters, drew much larger crowds than ordinary productions, managers of major theaters took care to schedule at least one every three or four months. One theater originally tried to put on a production titled *Sida jin'gang* (The four guardian spirits; referring to the four most famous courtesans in turn-of-the-century Shanghai) but it was immediately banned, so *Haishang fanhua zhaoxi* (Days and nights of Shanghai splendor), another topical production, was presented instead; in another theater, a production titled *Yeyou Xin malu* (Riding by carriage at night on New Avenue) chronicled common leisure pursuits and was welcomed enthusiastically.[42]

"New productions" that make explicit reference to contemporary news items appear as important plot devices within the pages of Shanghai fiction. In *Dreams of Shanghai Splendor,* for example, a satire presented at Red Cassia Theater (Dangui yuan) arouses the concern of Xie You'an: he fears that its subject matter—a man who squanders all of his resources and ends up pulling a rickshaw—may prove uncomfortable to his friend Tu Shaoxia, who met a similar fate and had only recently rehabilitated himself.[43] (Tu does indeed recognize himself in the figure of the wastrel, but is only grateful that he had better friends and so was able to eventually pull himself back together.) This theatrical re-presentation of social interactions could also take place outside theaters when female dramatic troupes *(mao'er xi)* set up a temporary stage and began to perform. In *Lives of Shanghai Flowers,* Shen Xiaohong is invited to Wang Liansheng's residence for the ceremony by which Wang will take Zhang Huizhen as his concubine. Xiaohong is embarrassed when one of the plays performed is *Kingfisher Screen Mountain,* a clear allusion to her betrayal of Wang.[44] This play alludes to Xiaohong's betrayal on two levels: first, the scene performed presents the story of an adulterous relationship and its consequences found originally in *The Water Margin;* and second, this very play is one in which Shen Xiaohong's lover, Xiao Liu'er, has earned his fame on the Shanghai stage, as we learned in the opening pages of chapter 30, where his stirring performance at Great Prospect Theater is described.[45] Theatrical presentations facilitate precisely those connections between viewer and viewed that excite the most severe moralistic condemnation, and at the same time obsessively revisit those connections, seeming to result in a doubling of the event. Yet in Shanghai installment fiction this doubling always involves repetition with a difference: either a past event is referred to but not retold fully, or the retelling is given a crucial ironic twist. In the former cases, we are told that a play or a scene is performed, but the performance itself is not described in detail;[46] the latter feature unexpected shifts or reversals of roles, for example, the identification of Xiao Liu'er—who is having an affair with Shen Xiaohong—with the heroic martial character Shi Xiu, who is *unjustly* accused of improper behavior by a woman who is in fact involved with a different man in *Kingfisher Screen Mountain.*

We must keep this slipperiness in mind as we consider what it means for a work of installment fiction to make clear references to individuals, texts, and events that seem to be located outside its own boundaries. Since the early twentieth century, there has been a strong tendency to read Shanghai fiction, especially *Lives of Shanghai Flowers,* as narrative that includes many "real" events and "real" people, as if these novels were best read as romans à clef. In his history of Chinese fiction, for example, Lu Xun cites an unsubstantiated account that characterizes *Lives of Shanghai Flowers* as a kind of blackmail, an attempt to extort money from a contemporary of the author named Zhao Puzhai. When the attempt failed, the author supposedly reacted by writing a conclusion that was unfavorable to Zhao and his family members.[47] Although a careful reading of *Lives of Shanghai Flowers* makes it quite clear that this could not have been the case, the profusion of precise time references, street names, well-known teahouses, restaurants, theaters, and so on, do suggest to the reader that these references index a specific contemporary social reality.[48] And indeed, champions of *Lives of Shanghai Flowers* (and other Shanghai fiction) have not only spent a fair amount of effort arguing that one or another individual was the "model" for a given character in the novel, they have also often cited the novel's "realistic" quality as one of its strong points.[49]

The intuitive appeal of such readings is easily explained. Once we establish that certain proper names (of streets, stores, teahouses, and theaters) can also be found in "nonfiction" sources (newspapers, guidebooks, and travel accounts), we are tempted to take the next step and find "sources" in the "real world" for the rest of the text. But since few readers of this fiction would have had the chance to meet the "real individual" that a character in the novel might appear to be based on, such references would rather recall the discursive construction of that person in newspaper articles, essays, and to a lesser extent, memoirs and local histories—not something truly extra-textual. As one author of verse collected in *Random Notes on Visiting Shanghai* points out, representation always precedes "actuality" even in social interaction: you visit courtesans based on their photographs, which are for sale in photography studios.[50] And despite the popular acclaim for the "truth" of such representations, authors of Shanghai fiction insist on a more skeptical attitude, especially toward articles published in newspapers: the motivatedness and "untrustworthiness" of newspaper writing is pointedly called to our attention as characters in the novels plant fake newspaper stories to deceive one another or the general public.[51]

The fascination with referentiality characteristic of Shanghai fiction therefore must not be confused with the realism that would become so important to Chinese literature in the Republican era: the privileged referent is not "social reality" as experienced by the authors and readers. Realism as a narrative strategy consists in a cathartic and emancipatory struggle to construct a better society through an accurate and thorough representation of an existing social reality that rests on a prediscursive base of power relations.[52] The figure of the mirror in motion, reflecting the world as it goes by, stands as an apt expression of the ideology animating realist writing. It is not that the realist writer does not exhibit selectivity and control—the mirror is in motion and reflects only what will fit in its frame—but for realist writers it is clear that the status of the image in the mirror can only be ontologically secondary to the original that it reflects.

When it comes to Shanghai fiction, the insufficiency of the reflective model is already hinted at by the twists put on the dramatic "recreation" of events that have actually been "experienced" elsewhere in the novel. The differences between realism and referentiality as narrative strategies become more evident once we look more closely at who exactly is telling the stories we are reading. In the early chapters of *Dreams of Shanghai Splendor,* for example, events are presented directly by the narrator as they happen. As the number of characters increases and the novel becomes more complex, however, narrative lines are more and more frequently suspended for brief periods while one character narrates a sequence of events that took place in a parallel story line but was never directly presented by the narrator. The emphasis shifts from a mimetic presentation of events in time and space to a diegetic presentation in which the role of intermediaries in the narrative process becomes increasingly significant.[53] This dynamic is taken even further in Lu Shi'e's *New Shanghai* (1909), in which the main characters themselves have no real adventures—they merely hear a great number of stories told by various narrators about things that happened to other individuals.[54]

Dreams of Shanghai Splendor frequently foregrounds the diegetic dimensions of its narratives: characters who tell others what happened elsewhere are said to speak "as though they had memorized a book and were reciting it"; and characters themselves borrow turns of phrase from narrators in earlier vernacular fiction and use them in ordinary discourse.[55] There is a fascination with other narrative genres that overlap with the novel itself: newspaper articles, song cycles, collected biographical accounts, dramatic productions, and even movies that relate directly or indirectly to the stories told in *Dreams of Shanghai Splendor* appear with more and more frequency within the text as the novel proceeds.[56] The doubling of the narrative in texts of other genres included or summarized within the narrative itself builds on the complicated dynamics of texts within texts established in earlier nineteenth-century courtesan novels like *A Dream of Romance, Traces of Flowers and the Moon,* and *Qinglou meng* (A Dream of the courtesans' quarter), but in this case the narrative, instead of representing itself as a duplicate or retelling of a single text in another genre or at another textual level, is itself actually fragmented and reinterpreted in many different kinds of texts.[57]

Indeed, where nineteenth-century courtesan fiction strove to replace the figure of the narrator who retells a story that is already known with the figure of an author who is presenting a true record of his own experiences or observations, *Dreams of Shanghai Splendor* turns things around and confronts us again with the potential that narrative has for intertextual connection. The references that appear so profusely throughout Shanghai fiction are not so much an attempt to ground the narrative in a shared social experience—after all, the majority of its readers would not have been from Shanghai—as they are links to a wide variety of other Shanghai-related cultural products, from newspaper stories to maps to photo albums, that were increasingly available in other cities across China from the 1890s forward. To the extent that specific place-names in Shanghai fiction were familiar to their readers, it is likely that these readers would have encountered those names first in other texts and images rather than in their perambulations around the city. Referentiality in this case is not merely one of the tools that realist writing has at its disposal to construct the "reality effect"; it is instead a narrative strategy in its own right that emphasizes—in the place of the mimetic relationship—the dialectic construction of a broad inter-textual network that crosses not only between one novel and another, but also between fiction, newspapers, guidebooks, maps, photo albums, song cycles, theatrical productions, and film.

Like the panorama, Shanghai fiction is intensely concerned with the rela-tionships between different points in space. At the same time, however, it em-phasizes *movement* through this grid of reference, and asks not only, how do these spaces relate to each other on a map? but also, what narrative functions might they serve? or how do they relate to each other as narrative elements? Roland Barthes defines a narrative sequence as a "logical succession" of car-dinal functions;[58] if we refuse to allow ourselves to be distracted by the use of proper names, but rather group the various locations named in Shanghai in-stallment fiction by type, it becomes clear that, with some exceptions, each type of location tends to be associated with a specific narrative function. Theaters are often arenas in which narratives of seduction begin; teahouses, by contrast, initiate accounts of fraud and trickery with fair regularity, whether as a location for plans to be hatched or a setting in which those plans can be set in motion. Where the theater constitutes a closed space where spectators are all looking at the performance or at each other, gazes in the teahouse are frequently di-rected outward as well, with clients leaning over balconies to watch the car-riages and pedestrians go by in the streets below, opening themselves up to a wider range of narrative possibilities. Parks serve as the arena for conflict and the frustration of desire, while Western restaurants provide a "private" haven in which various narrative sequences can be brought to a quiet conclusion, whether through negotiation or coercion. This suggests that the urban spaces represented in Shanghai novels can be understood to correspond to a narrative space governed by a distinct set of functions or operations.[59] This fiction con-structs not only a recognized layout of names, but also a recognized set of ways to behave in certain spaces.

In Barthes's discussion of the "reality effect," however, he notes the sig-nificance of "useless" details—touches geared to convince the reader of the narrative's authenticity precisely through their *resistance* to interpretation as functional components of a larger system. Barthes cites an example from a short story by Flaubert, in which a barometer appears atop a pile of boxes on a piano; unlike the gun on the wall that Chekhov claims must eventually be fired, this barometer plays no logical role in the unfolding of the plot. Through their very "meaninglessness," details such as these convince the reader of the "reality" of the story.[60] In the case of Shanghai fiction, by contrast, the importance of individual establishment or street names is not as details that are resistant to a coherent interpretive scheme, but rather as the crucial hints that allow the reader to *construct* such a scheme. Both the proper names of locations and the type of establishment each of these locations represents provide crucial footholds to the reader who is trying to piece together interrupted episodes into coherent narrative lines. While Barthes bases his analysis of narratives on texts that have relatively well-defined, often almost unitary plots, the situation in Shanghai novels is much more complex, posing serious challenges to the very idea of the coherent "narrative line." These challenges will be discussed in detail in the next chapter.

Two types of location epitomize the narrative complexity characteristic of Shanghai fiction: the courtesan house and the alley. In *Fin-de-siècle Splendor,* David Wang reads the courtesan house or house of prostitution in late Qing "depravity novels," particularly in *Lives of Shanghai Flowers,* as a space in which characters, qualities, and worlds presumed to be incompatible come into contact, rendering these establishments central to the new "public sphere" in Shanghai.[61] Similarly, Catherine Yeh understands courtesan houses in mid- to late-nineteenth-century Shanghai as the primary sites for social interaction.[62] Here I would like to extend this understanding of courtesan houses by focusing on their role as elements in the system of narrative lines that constitute the novels. The courtesan house serves a vital function within complicated narratives as a "switching station" from one story to another. Shorter episodes in Shanghai novels frequently begin in teahouses and end in restaurants, but shifts between longer-running narrative lines often take place at parties hosted by patrons at courtesan houses. These parties, ranging from elaborate banquets for up to sixteen patrons, down to intimate gatherings of four for mahjong, constitute the ideal circumstances under which the narrator can shift focus from one character to another in the most subtle fashion. Transitions are rendered less abrupt by having a number of different characters socialize together before moving on to the next development. Just as the party joins (or splits) narrative lines, the courtesan herself can work within the text either to bring patrons together as fellow guests or to create and manipulate conflict between two male characters, each of whom desires an exclusive relationship.

For both realism and roman à clef fiction, specific references are endpoints, closing off the text by grounding it in an extra-textual "real," whether that "real" is accessed through these references' resistance to interpretation, or conversely, through the apparent ease with which a fixed referent can be agreed upon for each reference.[63] In Shanghai fiction, by contrast, references open up channels and connections, even as the alleys *(lilong)* form an ever-intensifying network, thickening and tying together what was originally a more diffuse and sparse set of urban avenues. Alleys were not only sites for action, addresses where courtesans could be found, and spaces with specific reputations; most had at least two and sometimes three or four outlets onto main streets and could serve equally as thoroughfares, for those on foot or in a sedan chair. At the same time, the view from one second-story room across the alley into the second-story windows on the other side allows another dimension of interaction and observation, an alternate channel of communication that is presented as a novelty in lithographic illustrations from the period, and is quickly put into use in *Lives of Shanghai Flowers, The Huangpu Tides,* and other novels.[64] *Lilong* constitute a crucial type of space where frequent encounters occur between characters serving as vectors of different narrative lines.

Lilong literally connect the various urban spaces, make links between different narrative threads possible, and can even serve as metaphorical links between similar characters across textual boundaries. In *Dreams of Shanghai Splendor,* Wu Chuyun, one of the two most significant femmes fatales, resides first in East Shangren Alley (where two of the tougher characters in *Lives of Shanghai Flowers,* Wei Xiaxian and Huang Cuifeng live), and then in West Huifang Alley (where Shen Xiaohong, who has a destructive affair with an actor, lives in *Lives of Shanghai Flowers*). These locations, and Chuyun's move from the former to the latter, would have suggested to readers familiar with the earlier novel a specific reading both of Chuyun's "character" and of her eventual fate. At the same time, the use of specific alleys as a link between texts would remind the reader that characters in different novels were all circulating in the same circumscribed urban space and hint at the fundamental multiplicity of narrative lines not only within each novel, but also in the genre as a whole. The *lilong* figure the very workings of reference and suggest to the reader a mediasphere that is defined in part by an ever-thickening web of association.

Specific individual spaces serve as sites in the early Shanghai novels for identifiable types of narrative development; at the same time, these narratives construct a "Shanghai" composed of individual locations with specific and determinate relationships between them. Shanghai novels differ from most earlier vernacular fiction in that—as is the case for the panorama—it is precisely these *relationships* between spaces rather than the individual spaces themselves that constitute the real "setting" of the texts. Similarly, in the profusion of names, dates, times, and addresses we find in Shanghai fiction, it is not the referent per se that is the privileged endpoint—no matter where that referent is located—but rather the referential system of relations as a relatively coherent totality.

Conclusion

The reader of Shanghai fiction eventually acquires a grid of references charged with narrative significance, which will serve as context the next time he or she picks up a newspaper, flips through an illustrated periodical, or consults a list of popular restaurants in an attempt to decide where to eat when in Shanghai; the fiction organizes one's subsequent experience of the city itself. Indeed, the consistency and universal applicability of this grid—which one did not by any means need to be a Shanghai resident to appreciate—is one thread that helps to tie together an entire sphere of Shanghai-related discourse.[65]

In this way, it becomes possible to "read as a local" even before one arrives in Shanghai, because the fiction supplies the reader with a matrix in which to lodge disparate bits of information from a variety of sources, in a fashion analogous to Matteo Ricci's famed "memory palace" of an earlier era.[66] Fiction precodes the city in a way that is much more persuasive than the order that could be supplied by a guidebook or a map, however, for the simple reason that the logic of narrative compels the reader both to continually move forward and to assign a specific emotional significance to what could otherwise be a very dry collection of data. Consider, for example, the effects that the perusal of *Ulysses* has on one's experience of Dublin, or the construction of London in the minds of readers of Sherlock Holmes stories, or even Thomas Hardy's revival of "Wessex" in his fiction, a geographical designation that has now entered common usage as a name for the southwestern regions of England. The advantages that a narrative logic enjoys over a classificatory logic in engaging and affecting the reader will become even clearer in chapters 3 and 4.

At the same time, what we find in this emphasis on referentiality is a perpetual sliding, an unwillingness to close off meaning by identifying a single endpoint or final ground. Fiction, maps, guidebooks, photographs, newspapers, theatrical productions, and illustrated publications constitute a consistent, yet ever-expanding, network of references. This kind of referential system is particularly suitable for installment fiction, which, as we will see in chapter 4, makes unusually complex use of dynamics of conclusion and continuation. Referentiality also helps tie together a wide variety of cultural products in different parts of the mediasphere, many of which appear in "excerpted" form in the pages of Shanghai installment fiction as testimony to its self-imagination as a kind of master genre. Consistency within this textual and visual system confers an added legitimacy on each of the individual components; each repetition of a proper name within this system adds to its resonance and brings it one step closer to commercial apotheosis as a *brand name*.[67] It comes as no surprise, then, that frequent references to current establishments and brand names play a major role in the Edo-based installment fiction that was so popular in Japan roughly a century earlier, and was similarly concerned with questions of contemporaneity and referentiality. We will return to the question of the brand name in chapter 5, noting here only that this profusion of names, places, and times creates an infrastructure in which any number of narratives might be grounded, a grid of reference to which an open-ended and theoretically unlimited sphere of cultural production can be tied.

CHAPTER 3

Synchronized Reading

Installment Aesthetics and the Formation of the Mediasphere

The 1890s saw not only the introduction of panoramic photography, arranging Shanghai's buildings within a systematic grid of reference, but also a new focus on the urban crowd. The adoption of lithographic printing made cheap mass production of pages crammed with detailed images possible; in illustrations like Wu Youru's "Echuan huoqi" (fig. 5), the artist makes full use of lithography's potential to fill the page with a new level of exactness.[1] Earlier artistic representations of urban crowds, such as the Song dynasty handscroll *Qingming shanghe tu* (Spring festival on the river), were expensive rarities that could be appreciated only at the highest reaches of society.[2] In contrast, lithographic prints could be purchased for only slightly more than the usual woodblock illustration, despite their superior detail. These new urban images were produced to be distributed in large numbers, rather than to be concealed as unique treasures. To borrow an approach from Tony Bennett's essay on the "exhibitionary complex," we could say that the image of the urban crowd was no longer the exclusive property of the sovereign (or the elite classes), but had become a commodity available to many members of that same crowd.[3]

It is no coincidence that Shanghai installment fiction also begins on lithographic presses; both the periodical *Haishang qishu* (Wonderful Shanghai writings) and the first book edition of *Lives of Shanghai Flowers* were printed by the well-known Dianshi zhai (Dotting the Stone Press). Shanghai installment fiction overlaps with lithographic illustrations not only in its affordability—fiction on the installment plan representing a more economical approach to literary consumption—but also in its juxtaposition of an unprecedented number of characters and wealth of detail within the confines of the artistic work. Viewed from this angle, the multiple narrative lines characteristic of Shanghai fiction appear almost to explode out of the lithographic print, a story for each individual; conversely, the lithographic illustration can be understood to freeze the repeated comings together and fallings apart of

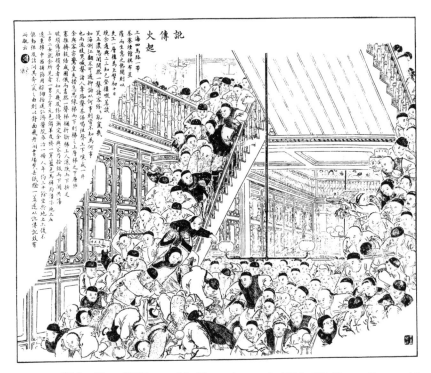

FIGURE 5 "False Alarm." Lithographic illustration, early 1890s. Wu Youru, *Fengsu zhi tushuo*, 2.20a. Reproduction permission of Harvard-Yenching Library.

individuals and storylines that constitute the Shanghai novel into a single moment.

But the aim of this chapter is to investigate precisely that dimension of Shanghai narrative that is *lost* in the lithographic illustration or the panoramic photograph, that cannot be exhausted in the visual representation of a single moment. In tracing the "explosion" of intersecting narrative lines in Shanghai fiction, this chapter asks how the complexity presented by illustrations of crowd scenes is sustained over the months, even years, it takes to finish reading a work of installment fiction. This temporal dimension is of particular significance since most Shanghai novels did not come out in volume editions until they had finished their run in installments, and so did not possess in their initial publication a clear identity as unitary objects.

Shanghai installment fiction is characterized by synchronic progression at multiple levels: narrative lines move forward together within each individual work; the works themselves are published concurrently; and readers consume them in a synchronized fashion (whether day by day, week by week, or month by month). As we will see in this chapter, this simultaneous progression depends in turn on constant crosscutting between elements and narratives, an aesthetic of continual interruption that would leave a lasting mark on other urban media such as the tabloid newspaper. At the same time, however, the constant movement from character to character and from storyline to storyline begins to suggest to the reader a new way of conceptualizing the structure of the literary work and a new understanding of his or her role in its production. It is precisely through these aesthetic characteristics that Shanghai installment fiction plays a central role in the imaginative production of the city as a desirable place to visit and a trendsetter for the rest of China. It is unique among cultural forms in this period in the effectiveness with which it employs these techniques to announce a new kind of literary product, to introduce a new readership to consume that product, and to signal, through its very form, the directions in which a new "national" arena of print and visual media would develop.

Simultaneity

As Benedict Anderson has shown, a sense of simultaneity was central to the imagination of national communities from the eighteenth to twentieth centuries. This sense was manufactured in part in the novel through the potential that the genre holds for multiple characters to be involved in different actions in different places *at the same time*.[4] As we have already noted, Shanghai fiction tends to be extremely complex: not only are many individuals doing different things simultaneously, but entire storylines (which may appear at any given moment to be quite separate, yet later turn out to be connected) progress simultaneously through the text. Han Bangqing himself finds this complexity to be a result of his innovative "techniques of interweaving and hidden flashes" (*chuancha cangshan zhi fa*).[5] Interweaving entails:

> One wave not yet having settled, another wave rises, sometimes linking together as many as ten waves, now east and now west, now north and now south, freely narrated without one episode ending, but in the whole work not a thread is left loose. The reader feels as though behind the text where there is no text there is still quite a bit more text; even though it is not clearly narrated, the reader can figure it out.[6]

"Interweaving" turns out to be one of the key formal characteristics of late nineteenth- and early twentieth-century Shanghai narrative; a good example occurs in chapters 3 and 4 of *Lives of Shanghai Flowers,* in which eight differ-ent episodes begin, without any of them coming to a conclusion. In these two chapters, the narrative follows a single character—Hong Shanqing, the mater-nal uncle of Zhao Puzhai, the young man from Suzhou with whom the novel begins—through a complex social and spatial itinerary around the English Settlement and introduces the reader to no fewer than five different constella-tions of characters.[7]

Such complexity is not restricted to the early chapters of Shanghai fic-tion. To better understand how it is sustained over a lengthy novel published in installments, we may turn to chapters 26 and 27 of *Lives of Shanghai Flowers,* roughly midway through the novel. In these chapters, the courtesan Lu Xiubao becomes more deeply involved with Shi Ruisheng, the rich young man she fa-vors over Zhao Puzhai; we learn that Su Guanxiang, a courtesan with close ties to the powerful Qi Yunsou, is in trouble with the Mixed Court; the petty fixer Zhuang Lifu attempts to get an introduction to Qi Yunsou in order to do business with him; Hong Shanqing, Chen Xiaoyun, Zhang Xiaocun, and others hold a gambling party; the miser Li Shifu is discovered by his steward Kuang Er to be patronizing a "low-class" prostitute; Kuang Er himself attempts to make progress with another woman of the same class; Li Shifu's nephew, Li Heting, gets involved with an illegal gambling ring; and Yao Jichun, an acquaintance of Li Heting's, manages to sneak away from his disapproving wife to spend time with the courtesan Wei Xiaxian. In addition, five of the eight narrative threads introduced in chapters 3 and 4 are still in progress, though they are only hinted at in these chapters. Although this is a particularly powerful example of the number of simultaneous storylines that can be covered in two nine-page chap-ters alone, this same characteristic interwoven structure and resulting sense of simultaneity persist in Shanghai installment fiction well into the Republican era.[8]

Complex interaction between multiple narrative threads did not begin with the Shanghai novel; it can be found to a limited degree in earlier long vernacular narratives, most notably in *Jin Ping Mei* and *Dream of the Red Chamber.*[9] Yet in the earlier novels, it is still a single protagonist or small group that forms a clearly identifiable narrative focus; the Shanghai serial narratives differ in that there is no single focal point, as the interaction *between* narrative threads constitutes the fundamental structure that governs the work as a whole. As we will see later in this chapter, this interaction itself is complex to the point of challenging the very integrity of the narrative line as a conceptual tool for reading the novel.

Furthermore, this distinctively multiple narrative structure joins with the installment format to initiate a new sense of *genre* as a relation of simultaneity.

Previous classics of vernacular fiction tended to have identifiable main plots and subplots, or else a succession of different episodes unfolding in different places: the sense of multiple narrative lines continually converging and diverging in a limited space was not so evident. Is it coincidence, then, that *Shuihu houzhuan* (Sequel to The water margin), *Xiyou bu* (Supplement to Journey to the west), and the entire franchise of *Dream of the Red Chamber* continuations appear only decades after each original is written, with each successor readily acknowledging the "priority" of the founding text?[10]

In contrast, narratives set in Shanghai are marked as a genre by simultaneity and multiplicity from their earliest moments: the usual language of influence—"earlier" and "later" texts, "model" and "imitation"—runs into serious trouble when we look at *Lives of Shanghai Flowers, A Shanghai Swan's Traces in the Snow, Dreams of Shanghai Splendor, The Huangpu Tides,* and other fiction published in installments. Unlike other narrative families in Chinese long vernacular fiction, in which a "patriarchal" text is understood to beget a more or less orderly generational succession of sequels and imitations, Shanghai novels appeared almost simultaneously and progressed synchronically as installment publications. Sun Yusheng, author of *Dreams of Shanghai Splendor,* wrote of meeting Han Bangqing for the first time in 1891, when both were in Beijing for the metropolitan examination.

> At once we were like old friends. After the examination, we went together back south on the China Merchants Steamship Company boat. It was a long voyage . . . and he showed me the unfinished draft of a novel . . . [with] twenty-four chapters. . . . At this time, I was in the midst of composing the first portion of *Dreams of Shanghai Splendor,* already having finished twenty-one chapters. On the boat, we exchanged manuscripts and read each other's work, delighting in comparing the two and finding that their roads were different but their destinations the same.[11]

This exchange of manuscripts suggests that even the "originary" *Lives of Shanghai Flowers,* first of the Shanghai novels to begin publication in installments in 1892, was already in dialogue with the yet to be published *Dreams of Shanghai Splendor.*

Sun Yusheng was also a good friend of Li Boyuan, the probable author of *A Shanghai Swan's Traces in the Snow,* and began printing a rival leisure paper, the *Xiaolin bao* (Forest of laughter daily), in the alley across from Li Boyuan's press.[12] *Dreams of Shanghai Splendor* began to appear in 1898, preceding the first installment of *A Shanghai Swan's Traces in the Snow* by approximately a year, but it continued for several years after *A Shanghai Swan* had finished. Wu

Jianren, to whom *The Four Great Courtesans of Shanghai: A Marvelous Account* (1898) is attributed, worked together with Sun Yusheng to edit the leisure paper *Caifeng bao* (Selected rumors daily); *The Four Great Courtesans of Shanghai* and several other early Shanghai novels were all published within a two-year span, and *The Nine-tailed Turtle* first appeared just as *Dreams of Shanghai Splendor* was coming to an end. This pattern of overlap and simultaneity, made possible by the installment format, recurs in the late 1910s and 1920s, with the contemporaneous publication in daily installments of *The Huangpu Tides, Shanghai Annals, Hell in This World,* and other lengthy narratives. By this time, even a single author might be responsible for the simultaneous production of a number of different works: in Lu Shi'e's *New Shanghai,* we meet a novelist whose drafts are scattered around his study in various stages of completion.[13] Finally, we find within Shanghai narratives not only the kinds of frequent references to certain key physical and temporal markers that we might expect from a group of narratives set within a single geographical grid of reference—albeit one that changes over time and according to the interests of different authors—but also more pointed and unique indicators of symbolic "exchange" between narratives, from the earliest moments of the genre down to novels of the 1920s and early '30s.[14]

In this sense, the multiple interactive narrative lines characteristic of an individual Shanghai novel allegorically present the more general structure of the genre, in which works overlap as they appear over time and represent the same urban space, referring to one another back and forth. Furthermore, this overlap hints at the way turn-of-the-century readers would have experienced each narrative as an element in the broader spectrum of textual consumption: the interwoven narrative lines within an individual text can stand as well for the mingled consumption of the narratives of many different types appearing simultaneously over a period of days or weeks in the late Qing mediasphere.

It is clear that the simultaneity inherent in this narrative complexity, together with the near-complete restriction of narrated action to the city of Shanghai and its immediate environs, holds enormous potential for the imagination of an urban community along the lines Benedict Anderson suggests for the nation-state as a whole. What is curious, however, is that Anderson restricts his analysis of the novel as a form to the potential multiplicity of narrative lines in the text, essentially ignoring the format in which many, if not most, nineteenth-century European novels appeared: installment publication. The one brief mention of serial fiction (in a footnote) is the exception that proves the rule. As fiction published in parts and in close association with daily papers (often *in* them), however, these installment narratives both represented simultaneity and were consumed simultaneously. In the case of Shanghai fiction, publication in installments made the novels literally contemporary with their readers, and also made one reader's initial experience with the text simultaneous with the first experiences of the majority of other readers. As such, that dimension of the imagined community that Anderson attributes to newspaper production and consumption—the "mass ceremony" of simultaneous readership—derives just as much from the production and consumption of installment fiction.[15]

Print editions of novels that constitute the premodern Chinese vernacular canon (the six "classic" novels and a handful of others) were widely available throughout the nineteenth century, but until the 1870s it was still quite common for long vernacular fiction to circulate exclusively in manuscript form for decades after completion. Close friends of the author might read the manuscript even as it was being written and offer comments and suggestions, but by the time a novel was printed and circulated in large numbers, such interaction between readers and author was often no longer possible. When turn-of-the-century fiction began to appear in small parts that arrived regularly, its very mode of presentation extended the sense of the open-ended text—which previously had been confined to the few friends among whom an author circulated his or her manuscript-in-progress—to a much broader audience.[16]

In addition, the association of a novel published in installments with the publisher of the newspaper or periodical in which it appeared meant that even the majority of readers who had no idea who the author was (pseudonyms were in use into the twentieth century) could still address him or her by mail. According to Sun Yusheng, it was in fact reader demand expressed in letters to the editor that caused *Dreams of Shanghai Splendor* to continue in daily serialization for so long and encouraged him to write an equally lengthy sequel.[17] In this sense, installment publication through an establishment with a fixed address radically expanded the group of readers who understood the author to exist in their own time, as their contemporary. This late-Qing interaction between author and readers constituted an important mediating instance between the small literary groups of the seventeenth and eighteenth centuries and the "roll-call fiction" and reader-completed narratives that become popular in the 1910s and '20s.[18] These exchanges would have been particularly vital in Shanghai, which was not only the setting of many of the early installment narratives, but also the city in which a sizable fraction of the readership resided, and where the overwhelming majority of installment series were published. If the complex narrative structures characteristic of Shanghai fiction imagine simultaneity by emphasizing multiple narrative lines, the publication of this fiction in installments in the late Qing and early Republican periods extends this simultaneity beyond the bounds of the individual text into the broader realm of cultural production, and further materializes it by regulating all readers' access to the texts according to a strict chronological standard.

An important qualification: for readers outside the immediate Shanghai area, the latter dimension is best understood not as simultaneity, but as "not-quite-simultaneity." Depending on the reader's distance from Shanghai and the reliability of the mail service, he or she would receive or purchase each installment anywhere from a few hours to a couple of weeks after it first reached its readers in Shanghai.[19] This suggests that sensitive readers outside Shanghai would have consumed fiction printed and delivered in daily installments with a certain double temporal consciousness: as often as they were assured of their complete engagement in the regular and inexorable forward movement of the narrative and their membership in a Shanghai-centered group of readers, they were also reminded of the delay that separated them from the "core" readership in Shanghai. For these out-of-town readers, whether in Nanjing or in Chengdu, the date at the head of the newspaper would not match the date on which the newspaper and its associated installment fiction was read. Such a dynamic of simultaneity and not-quite-simultaneity defines a readership community with at least two distinct tiers; or, to put it another way, helps to construct a national mediasphere whose central node is located in Shanghai. The trope of "modern" Shanghai leading the rest of a "backward" nation is not merely an abstract concept, but is reinforced even in these most "trivial" of details.

Interruption

We may be struck by the fact that certain turn-of-the-century Shanghai narratives, including *Dreams of Shanghai Splendor,* appeared in page-a-day installments that break off whenever the end of the page is reached, even if that break comes in the middle of the action. It has been suggested that this publication format results in episodic and disconnected writing, but this is not in fact the case.[20] If we look more closely, it becomes clear that *Lives of Shanghai Flowers*—published in 1892 in semimonthly, two-chapter installments—formally anticipates such frequent interruptions, and indeed makes use of similar breaks to structure the narrative aesthetically before they are at all "necessary." Instead of resolving an episode and beginning a new one every two chapters, *Lives of Shanghai Flowers* tells stories that are constantly interrupted *within* the two-chapter unit. This is the technique that Han Bangqing refers to as "hidden flashes" *(cangshan):*

Breaking into [a story] without warning, causing the reader to wonder and not be able to understand the reason [for plot developments], and then to urgently want to read on, but in the following passages abandoning [that matter] and narrating another; only when the other matter is finished then explaining the reason, but not explaining it completely—only when the whole matter finally comes out, does the reader know that in the preceding text there was not even half of a wasted character *(xianzi)*—this is the hidden flashes technique.[21]

The complexity of the narrative structure described, and the associated deferral of meaning, is echoed in the tortured syntax of this very description of the "hidden flashes" technique. This technique, which reminds one of Barthes's discussion of dystaxia, or intercut sequences in narrative, structures these texts at all levels.[22] Sometimes the information that the reader seeks is available within a paragraph or two, but other times it appears only dozens of chapters later. Repeated interruptions ensure that the necessary information will not be available immediately; most interrupted story lines do, however, pick up later on, and some continue for the entire length of the novel. The story of the love triangle consisting of the official Wang Liansheng, the first-class courtesan Shen Xiaohong, and her second-class rival Zhang Huizhen, for example, is told in roughly twelve stretches of narrative distributed evenly through *Lives of Shanghai Flowers;* most of these stretches are themselves interrupted by episodes dealing with other characters.

- Chapter 3: Here, early on, we learn only that Wang Liansheng's friend, Hong Shanqing thought he might be able to find Wang at the courtesan Shen Xiaohong's place, but he is not there. Neither is Shen Xiaohong; she is out riding in a carriage.[23]
- Chapter 4: Wang's steward comes with a message for Hong Shanqing, asking him to come to Zhang Huizhen's place in Xiangchun Alley; when Hong arrives he declines to help Wang purchase furniture for Huizhen's new place, because Shen Xiaohong would get angry at him. At this point, the reader can deduce that Wang is deceiving Xiaohong about his relationship with Huizhen.
- Chapter 9: Wang and Huizhen go to Bright Garden for the afternoon; they are seen by the actor Xiao Liu'er, and moments later Xiaohong arrives and attacks Huizhen.

ℐଚ

The tension continues over the next fifteen chapters, as Wang unsuccessfully attempts to break off relations with Shen Xiaohong.

ℐଚ

- Chapter 24: A seemingly innocent remark by Huizhen that Xiaohong cannot afford to let Wang go because she has many expenses leads Wang to ask Hong Shanqing about Xiaohong's financial situation. Hong will say only that she rides around in horse-drawn carriages, and that this habit is expensive.[24]
- Chapter 33: We (and Wang) finally learn that Xiaohong is having an affair with the actor Xiao Liu'er, and Wang decides to take Huizhen as his concubine. In the following chapter, Xiaohong is embarrassed at the banquet of celebration by the selection of a play that takes adultery as its subject, feeling that it has been chosen to refer to her affair with Xiao Liu'er.[25] Still, she tries to convince Wang to continue to support her.
- Chapter 54: Xiaohong's maid has given notice, and goes with a friend to Wang's house to ask for help in finding work. As they walk in, Wang's nephew rushes out, and they hear the sound of Wang beating Zhang Huizhen upstairs. Stunned, they withdraw to a teahouse to talk over what they have just seen and heard.[26]
- Chapter 56: Wang calls Shen Xiaohong to accompany him at a banquet.
- Chapter 57: It is finally explained that Huizhen was carrying on with Wang's nephew.[27] It is only at this point that most readers will realize that the performance of the play about an adulterous woman at the banquet in chapter 34 ends up being as much a reference to Zhang Huizhen's future betrayal as to Shen Xiaohong's past misconduct.

ℐଚ

The frequent interruptions characteristic of the "hidden flashes" technique turn out to be the necessary obverse of the simultaneity discussed above. Simultaneity within a given work of fiction is always generated in part through the reading process: since narrative itself can present events only in a linear sequence, flashbacks, reported action, terms like "meanwhile," and rapid cuts back and forth between storylines are necessary to persuade the reader to unfold multidimensional simultaneity out of a text that is in itself merely a sequence of words one after another. Shanghai installment fiction of the late Qing and early Republican eras makes particular use of the last of these techniques—frequent crosscutting between narrative lines—to convince the reader of the complexity of a city in which many different stories are in simultaneous progression.

ℛ

This aesthetic of continual interruption would have a profound impact on other genres and media operating in Shanghai in the first half of the twentieth century. By presenting readers of the early to mid-1890s with a narrative that shifts from one storyline to another and back again by authorial design, for example, *Lives of Shanghai Flowers* makes it possible for those same readers to accept breaks in the narrative in the years to come that result instead from the constraints of a particular mode of publication.[28] While critics like Qian Xinbo asserted that readers in the 1870s criticized the presentation of texts in installments, turn-of-the-century audiences had apparently become much more forgiving of this mode of presentation, even in its most obtrusive forms, as they flocked to serialized Shanghai fiction.[29] Stylistic innovation in this case paved the way for a change in the production and distribution of texts: the move from two-chapter installments published twice a month to page-by-page serialization on a daily basis.[30]

As I have shown elsewhere, the frequent inclination of critics to read Shanghai narratives as merely a series of anecdotes and disconnected episodes in imitation of journalistic style or as a result of the installment format is unwarranted.[31] But the insistence on the anecdotal and disconnected quality of newspaper writing by critics such as Liang Qichao is a useful reminder that Benedict Anderson's striking imagination of the newspaper *not* as a collection of discrete anecdotes, but rather as a form similar to the novel (with nations and individuals out of the news waiting their chance to rejoin the narrative at a later date) depends precisely on a willingness to read (and write) the newspaper as a multiplicity of simultaneously progressing narratives rather than as a mere collection of anecdotes.[32] Indeed, from the changes in format in cheap daily leisure newspapers *(xiaobao)* such as *Youxi bao* (Entertainment daily), *Xiaoxian bao* (Leisure daily), and *Shijie fanhua bao* (World splendor daily) in the early 1900s, it becomes clear that subsequent to the appearance of Shanghai novels printed in installments, publishers and readers did begin to see the function of the daily paper differently.

When these tabloid newspapers first began to appear in the 1890s, the news that they reported was entirely anecdotal in format: A encountered B in the Blue Lotus teahouse, and the following ensued. A typical article in the August 5, 1897 issue of *Entertainment Daily* tells the story of a cunning theft. The previous morning, a man in uniform with a Hunan accent called on a doctor who lived on East Street, just inside the Little Eastern Gate, to request medical attention for an old man several towns over. When the doctor objects to the distance, the caller replies that he has already reserved a small boat at Old Lock Bridge so they can make the journey together. Just as the boat passes New Lock on the way out of the city, the man in uniform announces that he has a brief errand to run and asks to borrow the doctor's umbrella:

> The doctor agreed to lend the umbrella, and had the boat tied up at a nearby teahouse to wait. How was he to know that the man in uniform was full of schemes and in fact headed straight for the doctor's house, where he claimed, "The doctor sent me because he will be away for several days. Since the weather is quite hot, he needs a change of clothes; he also asked for his ivory handled fan." The doctor's wife agreed to this and gave them to him, at which point he vanished without a trace. . . . [After waiting for quite a while], the doctor realized that he had been cheated, and he hurried back home, only to find that he had lost several tens of dollars in gowns and such. What was more, he had to pay the boat fare, and could only bewail his misfortune.[33]

End of story: there were no updates to come. Neither the doctor nor the man in uniform is identified by name; in most articles published in the 1890s individuals are identified merely by province or city of origin, and only occasionally is the reader even provided with the surname of the character in question.

By 1901, however, the Shanghai tabloid newspapers increasingly came to emphasize columns that identified courtesans, actors, and other individuals by full name, and gave fragmentary updates on their actions on a day-to-day basis. One example of such an update appeared in the November 30, 1901 edition of *World Splendor Daily*:

> Yesterday I saw Yang Feita. She said, "That Hong Baobao, I've already gotten rid of her! Now I've got someone on the way to Suzhou to get another [young woman]. She'll be a hundred thousand times better than Hong Baobao. Should be here by the end of the month. Please ask the gentlemen to stop by."[34]

It is presumed that the reader will be familiar with Yang Feita—literally, "the Consort's Couch," a madam's trade name—and will know that Hong Baobao used to be one of her courtesans, so no further explanation is offered. Another example, from the June 24, 1901 edition of the same newspaper:

> Last Saturday, I saw Lu Lanfen at Zhang's Garden, sitting near the right side of the door to Arcadia Hall. She was very proper, without a hint of dissipation, just like a lady. Just goes to show that proximity to vermilion leaves one

red, and nearness to ink leaves one black. Lu Lanfen hasn't been in the courtesans' quarter for six months and already has changed this much.[35]

In this case, it is expected that the reader will be familiar with the story of Lu Lanfen's recent marriage and move out of her courtesan house. Unlike the anecdote, which trades in part on the anonymity of the subject and is structured as an episode complete in and of itself, these updates are merely parts of stories that are in simultaneous progression, and have much less meaning for the reader who has not been following the columns over a period of weeks or months.[36]

Columns featuring this kind of gossip on the installment plan remained a staple of Shanghai leisure papers like *Jingbao* (Crystal three-daily) well into the 1930s.[37] When we remember that such gossip columns often appeared in close juxtaposition with installments of fictional narratives, that the two kinds of texts very likely drew from the same pool of readers, and finally, that the publishers of leisure papers themselves were often also authors of installment fiction, the significance of installment fiction as a formal inspiration for local journalism becomes evident. One Shanghai reader in 1931 confirms the continuing importance of Shanghai novels as a model for a certain aspect of the newspaper genre, explaining that he reads the scandal columns in the daily paper *as if* they were installments of *Dreams of Shanghai Splendor*.[38]

The significance of this transition from self-contained anecdotes to "fragmentary" updates on stories that run for weeks or months as a factor in the rapid expansion of readership of Shanghai leisure papers should not be underestimated. By moving from an anecdotal basis to a format in which even news items mimicked the installment fiction that sold alongside these tabloid papers, the papers could transform their readers from occasional casual consumers to "addicts" who required their daily fix in order not to lose track of what was going on. By the early 1900s, the most successful of these leisure papers sold in numbers rivaling established newspapers like *Shen bao*.[39] This, then, is the context in which the figure of the reader as a drinker craving his or her next chance to indulge first appears: for certain late Qing critics, the addictive quality of intermittent narrative—whether it was printed under the sign of fiction or of journalism—was a given.[40]

Like the newspaper, installment fiction of this era compels its readers not only through the interruption of one narrative line by another within the text, but also by the frequency and regularity with which it interrupts the reader's daily life and is in turn interrupted by that daily life. Scholars of European installment fiction frequently remark on its power to integrate the narrative into the rhythms of everyday life, and as Perry Link has noted, the "day's news" in early twentieth-century China could often find its way into the installment of fictional narrative that was published alongside it.[41] In the case of early Chinese installment fiction, it seems likely that this integration was experienced almost as a logical extension and intensification of the aesthetic of intercutting "busy" and "idle" (*mang* and *xian*) narrative lines in Ming and Qing fiction.[42] In Shanghai narratives from the 1890s through the 1920s, the increased complexity and rapidity of movement from one line to the next calls this dichotomy between episodes that move the overall plot forward and diversions that do not into question. Yet at the same time, the insertion of regular installments of the novel into the rhythm of daily (or monthly) life does invite the reader to understand the text metaphorically either as an exciting distraction from a boring daily existence or as a relaxing diversion from the stresses and cares of the day. It is no coincidence, surely, that this invitation comes at a time when Shanghai residents are increasingly and explicitly concerned with the question of leisure time and how to spend it (*xiaoxian*), and at a time when "diversion" has taken on new prominence in theories of literature.[43] In either case, this constant movement back and forth is not the mere reiteration of a convention, but the transposition of a textual aesthetic into a new "extratextual" dimension; it brings the world and the text together in a dystaxic or intercutting relationship, putting narrative lines inside and outside the text to a certain extent on equal footing.

In its power to involve the reader in the narrative(s) offered, this movement back and forth between storylines is not unlike the crosscutting technique in cinematic production. Film theorists have proposed that the formal characteristics of "classic" cinema (including crosscutting and shot / reverse shot techniques) work to "suture" or bind the viewer to the film and lead him or her to lose sight of its status as mere representation.[44] The operation of suture places the viewer within the imaginary space of the film, weaving him or her into the world it represents. In a similar fashion, the constant shuttling back and forth characteristic of early Chinese installment fiction—from narrative line to narrative line, from "fictional" narrative to "journalistic" narrative, and from narratives consumed to narratives "experienced"—joins with the referentiality analyzed in the previous chapter to bind the reader to the texts more firmly and regularly than before. What we are dealing with here is not a simple interaction between a reader and a single bounded work of fiction, but rather a complex arena of multiple imbricated narratives that surround the susceptible individual to the point of providing structure for his or her daily routine. It is in this sense, with our readers knitted in on all sides by narratives of different genres and *required* to take advantage of their simultaneous presentation in order to keep up, that we are justified in referring to an early twentieth-century Chinese mediasphere: simultaneity and interruption are two of its key figures.

The Task of the Reader

The prominence of the figures of simultaneity and interruption has important implications for the structure of the narrative line in the Shanghai novel. Like Roland Barthes, Gérard Genette, and other European critics who emphasize the importance of rhythmic change and delay in narrative, Chinese critics of long vernacular fiction prized slowdowns in narrative flow at moments of high tension.[45] In commentaries to classics such as *Jin Ping Mei* and *Dream of the Red Chamber,* this technique is praised as "idle strokes of the brush in the midst of busyness" *(mangzhong zhi xian bi),* in accordance with the theory that the literary text should develop in balanced fashion, alternating between extremes.[46] The *xian* ("idle" or "leisure") episodes for the most part do not move the main plot forward; they function instead as interludes, either maintaining the narrative tension or providing chances for the reader to cleanse his or her palate.

The Shanghai novel is different. "Individual" accounts are intercut and interwoven in such a fashion that it is impossible to separate them back out into self-sufficient "prior" narratives. The transition from one episode to another is frequently as abrupt as A leaving to see B, meeting C briefly by chance on the street, C then proceeding to a different destination, and so on. Most chapters contain at least one transition, and some have as many as five or six; in most cases transitions from one episode to the next occur before the first episode has come even to a provisional conclusion.[47] As one reads further, however, the fragmentary individual episodes seem to coalesce into a number of distinct and continuous narrative lines. Critics who approach these works with a conviction that a proper long narrative must be divided into a single main plot and a collection of less relevant subsidiary plots end by forcing the issue and reading the part for the whole.[48]

With this kind of semantic crowding, in which no one thread can be ultimately identified as central, and important revelations frequently are made about characters while they are "offstage," there are no real resting places for the reader. There are no idle words, and not even a single wasted character *(xianzi).*[49] Like Proust's *Remembrance of Things Past,* which nearly eliminated what Gérard Genette calls the "nondramatic summaries" that alternate with scenes of action in earlier French fiction, *Lives of Shanghai Flowers* inaugurated a new narrative style in its rejection of canonical rhythms.[50] This change initiated in the Shanghai novel consists of nothing less than a challenge to the integrity of the polarity between "busy" and "idle" at the level of the narrative line. Unlike the narrative shifts in *Dream of the Red Chamber* and *Jin Ping Mei,* where we know when we are moving from busy to idle and vice versa, movements from one line to another in Shanghai novels leave us unclear as to the relative importance of the storyline abandoned and the new storyline picked up.

A reader's initial impulse on being confronted with multiple characters and storylines in such a novel might be to attempt to prioritize: to privilege some narrative lines as central and pay less attention to other more peripheral lines. This hierarchizing approach has a precedent: in the critical discourse on Ming and Qing long vernacular fiction, the terms "host" *(zhu)* and "guest" *(bin)* were used both to create links and to differentiate between characters of primary and secondary importance, and by extension, between the plotlines in which those characters appeared.[51] Yet most Shanghai narratives frustrate attempts to make these differentiations.

In chapter 50 of *Lives of Shanghai Flowers,* for example, there is a moment in which the courtesan Sun Sulan worries that an approaching carriage may belong to her pursuer, the unpleasant Master Lai. It turns out instead that Third Master Shi and Zhao Erbao are in the carriage, and Sulan is relieved. Later, however, Erbao is forced to accommodate Master Lai because Third Master Shi has failed her; this confusion between the two carriages sounds a warning note more than ten chapters in advance. Similarly, in chapter 57, Hong Shanqing reveals that the courtesan Zhang Huizhen has threatened suicide in a fight with her patron; moments later, when Zhou Shuangyu is requested by a patron, Hong further reveals that Zhu Shuren will not marry Shuangyu as he had promised.[52] By the end of the novel, Shuangyu has attempted to force a double suicide to punish Zhu for his betrayal. As Han Bangqing points out in *"Haishang hua liezhuan liyan"* (Remarks on *Lives of Shanghai Flowers*), even the most desultory of conversations between characters is not mere chatter *(xianhua),* but rather carefully composed text *(wenzi),* hinting at developments to come.[53]

The blurring of the distinction between "host" and "guest," which radically challenges established reading strategies, confuses even the characters in the novel themselves. In the last quarter of *A Shanghai Swan's Traces in the Snow,* Xu Junmu considers himself (as we may well consider him to be) the host and Jiang Youchun the guest, as Xu attempts to court Miss Xiao.[54] But in the nineteenth chapter, Xu Junmu falls ill and disappears from the narrative, and by the end of the twentieth chapter, the reader finds that Jiang's relationship with the courtesan Gao Xianglan has been foregrounded to the extent that host and guest must be understood to have changed places.

ৡ৯

What kinds of problems do multistrand narratives create for theories of narrative? What challenges did Shanghai novels pose to their readers then, and continue to pose now? We may begin by noting that singularity of plot is basic to most Western theories of narrative, from the structuralist to the psychoanalytic. Gérard Genette's *Narrative Discourse,* for example, a rigorous and authoritative analysis of the categories and dynamics of narrative movement, reminds the reader with fair regularity not only of the perceived central significance of the single protagonist—or at least the single, well-defined storyline—in much of nineteenth-century European narrative, but also of the importance of the recognizable and unitary storyline to more general Formalist and Structuralist attempts to theorize narrative as a universal human phenomenon.[55]

Even in Peter Brooks's discussion of the novels of Dickens and Balzac, with their dozens of characters, we are told that plot must form an "intelligible whole," a single "goal-oriented" structure that drives the protagonist forward; a dominant dynamic of plot is individual ambition, which is "inherently totalizing." As is the case for Genette, it is of some importance to Brooks that a clear distinction be drawn between the "main plot" and possible "subplots," since the latter are mere detours, ways to ensure that the main plot remains on track to its singular destination. Plot, or the narrative line broadly defined, is "the thread of design, that makes narrative possible because finite and comprehensible."[56] By now we have moved beyond the particulars of the European novel; Brooks here is making the universal claim that this is how *all* stories work. Shanghai novels are particularly well-suited to expose the blindness of approaches based on this emphasis as they call sharply into question both the distinctions between narrative lines (or between "main plots" and "subplots") and those between the "host" and "guest" characters who populate them.

The emphasis on a main character and his or her story typical of European theories of narrative does have important and interesting resonance with one of the more significant concepts in Ming and Qing drama and fiction criticism, the "key" or central meaning of a work *(guanjian, tigang, zongzhi)* contained in a specific part (or parts) of the text. Closely related to this understanding of a unitary and accessible meaning is the structural term *zhu'nao,* or "controlling conception or feature," first discussed explicitly in Li Yu's (1611–?) drama criticism, where it anchored his definition of the shorter, more unified dramatic works he favored.[57]

But where Li Yu's idea of *zhu'nao* presumes that the key moment of a given text occurs only once, in Shanghai fiction such critical junctures are inherently multiple, and rather than serving as the undisputed crucial moments *within* individual narrative lines—Du Shaomu's realization of the emptiness of urban leisure, Tu Shaoxia's encounter with old friends after he has become a rickshaw puller, Zhao Erbao's decision to become a courtesan to pay off her and her brother's debts—they are instead the interstices where narrative strands are woven together and fray apart, in the chance encounters on the street, in parks, and in teahouses, but most of all, in the banquets that are hosted night after night in courtesan houses.[58] Each time we readers arrive at one of these parties, we must be ready to leave with a narrative line different from the one we arrived with, and there is little indication which it will be before it happens. But even this phrasing is imprecise, reifying the individual narrative lines as the invariant elements that make up the text. These moments, or interstices, are in fact the sites at which the "narrative line" is generated as a concept through the presentation of a selection from an array of possible alternatives.

৵৹

Writing about the "novel of plot," Fredric Jameson concludes that it lacks the potential to provide the reader with transformative insight, for he or she is too busy just trying to keep track of who has done what to whom.[59] I would suggest instead that although there is no single protagonist in these novels with whom the reader is assumed to identify and through whom the reader can reach an epiphany, the possibility of transformative insight cannot be dismissed. The reader of the Shanghai novel comes to a gradual realization about the nature of narrative space, the logical priority of *syuzhet* (the telling of the story) to *fabula* (the story told), and the central role of both contingency and the interpretive power of the reader in narrative structure. In Shanghai novels the system of narrative lines is brought to such a level of complexity that the reader is impelled to question the validity of the concept of a preexisting "narrative line" (or lines) within the text, independent of a specific reading process. The narrative lines *(fabula)* can be seen instead as (re)constructions performed by the reader on the basis of the text given *(syuzhet),* as the end product of the attempt to make sense of a baffling array of events and characters. It is in this revelation of the "narrative line" in the text as a contingent construction, a specific reading tied to the concrete conditions under which it is produced, rather than a characteristic objectively inherent in the text, that the Shanghai novel suggests a critique of the grounds on which both European and Chinese narratological enterprises have rested. It also points to a significant adaptation of the conventional "task of the reader" to a new literary form and to the social consequences adoption of this form would entail.

Yuri Lotman writes that each text contains an image of its ideal readership; as early as the seventeenth century, we find a clear image of the ideal reader both implicit in Chinese long vernacular fiction itself and explicitly delineated in commentaries to this fiction.[60] The reader is asked to focus intently on the text, allowing no detail to escape his or her attention. Seriousness of purpose is a prerequisite, as is the ability to appreciate subtle formal structures spread over pages or even chapters of the novel. Indeed, some commentators maintained as early as the seventeenth century that the skilled reader *creates* the text in the reading process; or at the very least, should read as if that were the case.[61]

Although there are fewer direct prescriptions for the reader in Shanghai fiction than in the classic Qing commentaries, novels set in Shanghai evidently presume the basic abilities first articulated more than two centuries earlier. Readers were expected to be able to follow many different characters through complicated series of events, actively construct continuing narrative lines out of the assembled fragments that constitute the text, look behind and think beyond the text itself, wait impatiently for new installments, and communicate with the author or publisher to indicate interest in continuations and sequels. The ideal reader would have mastery not only of the individual text, but also of other similar narratives running concurrently in other publications, reading the novels as a genre within the entirety of Shanghai print media; he or she is one for whom no effort on the part of the author to integrate the text into a broader urban discourse is wasted.

Despite the occasional hyperbole of Qing commentaries, this is not a reader who makes something out of *nothing*. As noted in the previous chapter, Shanghai fiction is characterized by a wealth of precise references—whether to markers of time, markers of space, types of behavior and narrative developments assumed to be typical of certain kinds of urban establishments, or other kinds of information from guidebooks and newspapers. It is the reader's task to work from these hints to develop the "fragmentary" storylines presented into a complex, but coherent and continuous narrative. Given the importance of simultaneity and interruption to Shanghai narratives, the reader's end product will likely depend not only on his or her reading of the text itself, but also on the careful integration of material from other texts in the genre, and other genres of texts that simultaneously compete for the reader's attention.

Indeed, the reader who is ready to decide for him or herself what is important and what is not is essential to the formation of the mediasphere. As detailed in the introduction, the mediasphere is a type of cultural production characterized by aspirations to comprehensiveness and omnipresence, an interest in defining the various genres of texts and images relationally rather than absolutely, and a commitment to complex interaction between cultural producers and consumers. The reader's willingness to go "afield" following references and looking for clues and information is crucial; he or she reads *across* the lines, calling not only textual but even generic boundaries into question. As suggested in chapter 2, this is in a sense the opposite of the roman-à-clef—instead of seeking to reduce the indeterminacy of the text by tethering its references to extratextual "known quantities," this reader opens the text out and assists in its drive to assert a near-universal relevance.

෴

In conclusion, installment fiction set in Shanghai from the 1890s into the 1920s has a distinctive aesthetic. This aesthetic centers on narrative multiplicity and complexity, incessant interruption, and constant challenges to conventional ideas of narrative continuity. It is an aesthetic that has specific social consequences. First, the imagination of a certain kind of narrative, generic, and lived simultaneity which, by remaining in tension with a sense of "not-quite-simultaneity," helps to establish Shanghai as the central locus of a mediasphere with national reach. Second, the spread of intercut narrative beyond the bounds of the novels themselves fires the expansion of a broad range of print media among the readers who soon would be known as *xiao shimin* ("petty urbanites") and requires those readers to turn their eyes toward Shanghai at least once a week, if not daily. Finally, the assumption that narrative "completeness" is the responsibility of these same readers: it is their task to read broadly, integrate across boundaries, and transcend the constraints of narrative line, text, and genre. Installment fiction set in Shanghai thereby provides a frame through which the city can be perceived as what "it is," and in its reach beyond Shanghai itself not only supplies the aesthetic grounding for a rapidly developing print mediasphere, but also serves as a metaphor that enables cultural producers to think of the national media to come: radio, film, and television, each with its own particular characteristics.

CHAPTER 4

Desire Industries

Constant Motion and Endless Narrative

> Those who are used to this can still keep their monkey-minds and
> horses-of-intention *(xinyuan yima)* under control; they can see
> through it and keep from being moved. But tourists and young
> men, when placed in this flower world, find it difficult to avoid let-
> ting their intent go wild and their minds be misled.
> —Fanhua meng, 1/3

Of all of the innovative and unprecedented features of *Lives of Shanghai Flowers,* surely the most disconcerting was its abrupt ending, leaving readers caught in a moment of high drama without any clear resolution. In the concluding chapters of the novel, Zhao Erbao (Zhao Puzhai's sister) has gone into debt to establish herself as a worthy match for Third Master Shi, a wealthy young man of good family, who leaves Shanghai at the end of the eighth month but promises to return in the tenth month to marry her. When it is heard months later that he has had a marriage arranged for him, Erbao has no choice but to take on the unappealing Master Lai as a patron. After an agonizing evening spent attempting to cater to his whims, at the end of which he loses his temper and has all the furnishings in her rooms destroyed, she sits down for a rest, only to hear a loud pounding at the door. Seven or eight servants enter to announce that Third Master Shi has been appointed the prefect of Yangzhou and instruct Erbao to hasten there to join him. She is overcome with joy, but suddenly sees Zhang Xiuying, the friend who accompanied her to Shanghai:

> Xiuying asked, "You're dressed so nicely, are you going out to ride in a
> carriage?" Erbao said, "No, Third Master Shi has asked me to go." Xiuying
> replied, "Don't be stupid! Third Master Shi died a long time ago, how could
> you not have known?"
> As soon as Erbao thought about it, it did seem that Third Master Shi
> was already dead. When she turned to ask his servants, she saw that they
> had changed into monstrous forms and were advancing to grab her. This

frightened Erbao into crying out, [at which point] she awoke with a start, her entire body covered with cold sweat, her heart pounding.[1]

The novel ends with these words; there is no gradual movement toward summation, no explanation, no moral pronouncements. And not only is Erbao's story left unresolved, so are most of the other stories in the text as well.

A similarly abrupt ending occurs in another early work, *A Shanghai Swan's Traces in the Snow*. Jiang Youchun spends the night talking with the courtesan Gao Xianglan, then lies down to take a nap. In a dream, he wanders into a garden full of trees with no leaves, though it is quite warm. All of a sudden, the trees sprout leaves and Jiang thinks to himself that he must be dreaming. Suddenly again, a fierce wind blows all the leaves back off the trees and Jiang is very surprised. The text ends at this point, after twenty chapters.[2] In both cases, the reader is rudely wrenched from a world that has grown familiar and left on his or her own to speculate on what might happen next. The contrast with earlier long vernacular fiction, which tended to reach a climax around two-thirds or three-fourths of the way through, and gradually wind down in the concluding chapters, is striking.[3]

Dreams of Shanghai Splendor, by contrast, offers a veritable surfeit of endings, followed by continuations. Where *Lives of Shanghai Flowers* claims to conclude by not concluding *(bu jie er jie)*, *Dreams of Shanghai Splendor* can be said to fail to conclude even as it concludes *(jie er bu jie).*[4] As originally planned, the work was to consist of sixty chapters, at which point the author promised that it would end rather than continuing on and on in the manner of inferior works. In the opening pages of the thirty-first chapter, the narrator explains:

> Now the first series has gotten to this point and suddenly stopped; each reader naturally must want to see what comes next, and the author also has no reason to stop and abandon this half-finished book. But recently, among the novels printed by booksellers, there invariably are those that fail to conclude with the first series and continue into a second series; failing to finish in the second series they continue into a third and a fourth series. When one reaches the third and fourth series the book still has not come to a conclusion, and the continuations add many superfluous elements, leading to a lack of connections between them. [This is] all due to the fact that the book has gone through several continuations, not all by the same hand. In this way a very good original book is made into something with a beginning and no ending, which is quite regrettable. . . . [I]n these last thirty chapters, the whole book will be wrapped up, and others will not be permitted to speculate wildly and come forth with continuations. If there is someone who enjoys writing

books, I can only direct him to write something different, because after these sixty chapters of *Dreams of Splendor* there will be no place to write more.[5]

According to this statement of intent, the sixty-chapter *Dreams of Shanghai Splendor* was to tie up all loose ends and leave no foothold from which another author could begin a sequel. The ideal of complete sufficiency, to which any additions would be superfluous—posed here in contradistinction to inferior serial works—clearly finds its roots in the aesthetics of vernacular narrative developed since the end of the Ming.

Professing to have been driven to compose a further continuation by his readers, however, Sun added a list of forty chapter headings for a third part of the work at the end of the sixtieth chapter; this "final" part appeared for the first time in book form in 1906, eight years after the first series had begun to appear in installments. Then, after a pause of nearly a decade, Sun began a sequel, which also ran to one hundred chapters in three series, titled *Xu Haishang fanhua meng* (Dreams of Shanghai splendor, continued).[6] Even this work did not exhaust the possibilities of the form, for he went on to write a number of other novels along similar lines in later years, which can be seen as more loosely related continuations of *Dreams of Shanghai Splendor* or as further variations on the theme of Shanghai life, in sum constituting an ambitious lifelong project that recalls Balzac's *Comédie humaine*.[7] The continuing appeal of the *Dreams of Shanghai Splendor* franchise is evident not only in the market for Sun's continuations and sequels, but also in the appearance of numerous imitations set as far afield as Beijing and Canton.[8]

ॐ

In a recent study of late Qing fiction, David Wang concludes that novels focusing on courtesans (most of which were set at least in part in Shanghai) "radically renewed the poetics of desire of traditional romantic and erotic fiction"; he goes on to draw on Lu Xun's comments on the genre to identify "excess" as a defining or normative characteristic of this "depravity fiction" *(xiaxie xiaoshuo)*. This excess occurs at three levels: (1) the stories themselves tell of individuals who have multiple romantic or erotic relationships; (2) the very mode in which the stories are told is excessive, either praising or condemning the individuals involved; and (3) the novels are often quite lengthy.[9] We may add that much of this fiction was published first in installments; desire therefore functions not only at the diegetic level to move characters within a single narrative line toward each other, but also as an extradiegetic dynamic that governs the reader's continued consumption of interwoven narrative lines that stretch into the future with no end in sight. *Dreams of Shanghai Splendor* exemplifies this excess in serial production, but even *Lives of Shanghai Flowers,* which has been mistakenly characterized by Hu Shi and other scholars as little-read, appeared in more than nine reprint editions and inspired at least three sequels in the two decades after it first appeared.[10] The popularity of both *Dreams of Shanghai Splendor* and *Lives of Shanghai Flowers* compares surprisingly favorably not only with that enjoyed by the best-known May Fourth writers in the 1920s, but even the largest best sellers such as *Flower in a Sea of Sin.*[11] Where does the persistent desire for an excess of text come from? How is this excess connected to publication in the installment format? Is there a contradiction between the abrupt endings of *Lives of Shanghai Flowers* and *A Shanghai Swan's Traces in the Snow's* on the one hand, and *Dreams of Shanghai Splendor's* repeated continuation on the other? How is the insatiable reader produced, and what are the consequences of his or her obsessive persistence for the city of Shanghai and its associated mediasphere?

Desire and Constraint

European critics of cheap fiction often likened it to a drug, whether alcohol or opium; at least one Chinese advocate of installment fiction found its appeal to constitute a form of addiction.[12] It is worth noting, however, that despite the widespread consumption of opium in turn-of-the-century Shanghai, the figure of the opium addict is of little significance within Shanghai installment fiction, and addiction to opium rarely ascends even to the level of plot device—in one case, a regular smoker of opium who visits Shanghai even comments that there's no need to smoke to pass the time, as the city itself is so fascinating.[13] Instead, in keeping with the phrase *yima* (the "horse-of–intention"), appearing in the epigraph that begins this chapter, which refers to a desire or will that one has difficulty controlling, the obsessive leisure practice that figures most prominently in much of Shanghai installment fiction is riding in horse-drawn carriages, especially at night *(ye mache).*[14] When horse-drawn carriages were first introduced, only some Westerners and the wealthiest Chinese merchants and literati could afford to ride in them, but by the 1890s, rental companies made the experience accessible to a much broader section of Shanghai society, with more than two thousand carriages available for rental by 1891.[15]

Horse-drawn carriages afforded not only a means of transportation from one point to another, but also a platform for display and observation, on which one could spend hours circling during the day or at night on Shanghai's lighted boulevards. We can see the prevalence of this circling by the way the narrator takes pains to inform readers when someone who has rented a carriage returns directly to his or her residence, or makes only one circuit instead of many.[16] A typical route might begin on Fourth Avenue, go west to Stone Street, north to Grand Avenue, east to the Bund, and then back south to Fourth Avenue; alternate routes could substitute Third Avenue for Grand Avenue, and Looking-to-Peace Street (Wangping jie) for the Bund, among other choices.[17] Men riding in carriages imitated the dress of actors (including narrow shoes and queues loosened so their hair hung freely over their shoulders), and women dressed like courtesans, in Western-style dresses, or in Japanese kimonos.[18] Unlike the sedan chair, which revealed only glimpses of the passenger, the carriage encouraged display on the part of its passengers, even as it enabled them to survey the scene through which they passed from an elevated vantage point rather than through the curtains of the sedan chair. On Fourth Avenue itself, there was a constant exchange of gazes between occupants of the carriages and customers on the balconies of the teahouses and restaurants.[19]

Even as one might circle the core of the English Settlement again and again to gaze and be gazed upon, an alternate itinerary away from this circuit sometimes proved equally attractive. Patrons and courtesans, courtesans and their lovers, and many others also rode west along Bubbling Well Road (the extension of Grand Avenue that led to Jing'an Temple and the more remote parks) to find relatively private suburban areas where their activities would *not* be observed.[20] Carriage-riding organized transgressive practices of display on the one hand and concealment on the other, with both imbricated in discourses of public sexuality and public leisure. This discursive entanglement extended to the figure of the carriage driver, who, if skillful, won a distinctive trade name among his peers and customers; like the actor, he represented a distinct masculinity that could interact with courtesans and prostitutes without paying for the privilege, in many cases receiving payment himself instead.[21] All of this caused a certain degree of alarm on the part of Chinese and International Settlement authorities, who responded by banning carriage-riding at night west of Mudwall Bridge.

As presented in *A Shanghai Swan's Traces in the Snow*, however, the Shanghai Municipal Council's attempts to stem the nighttime flow of carriage traffic to the suburban parks by posting policemen at Mudwall Bridge and in the parks are less than effective. In chapter 19 Gao Xianglan proposes Cao's Crossing (Caojia du) as an alternative less subject to supervision, and in chapter 20, a driver simply detours via Wang's Storehouse (Wangjia ku) and New Lock (Xinzha) to get to Fool's Garden. The one purpose that the police roadblock on Mudwall Bridge does serve in chapter 20 is as a tool in Gao Xianglan's attempt to run the carriage of a rival off the road.[22] Though the police barricade is aimed at thwarting inappropriate desire, that desire in turn appropriates the obstacle and uses it for its own purposes.

ॐ

A closer look at the rhetoric surrounding the repeated continuation of *Dreams of Shanghai Splendor* reveals a similar dynamic. The extensive serial production of this fiction coincides with a pointed critique of "endless" narratives; as noted above, the narrator himself has harsh words for those who keep on writing, making what was originally a well-structured work into a confusion of additions and elaborations. In the thirty-first chapter of *Dreams of Shanghai Splendor,* the narrator explains that he hopes to awaken readers from their illusions as soon as possible.[23] Yet we see that even as two of the main characters, Xie You'an and Du Shaomu, continually delay their return from dangerous Shanghai to calm Suzhou, the reader is understood to continue reading, and even demand more when the author threatens to bring the story to a close with Du Shaomu's enlightenment in chapter 60.[24] Like Du Shaomu, who is tricked into spending the night at a courtesan's house in chapter 71—even though by now he knows better—just because the courtesan promises to tell him the story of what happened to another character, we readers are hooked on the escapades of dubious characters and apparently communicate with the author to ask for more text.[25] Despite the narrator's best intentions, the novel turns out to be an endless labyrinth of desire.

How does this happen? As in the case of nighttime carriage rides, desire appropriates an "obstacle" to increase its own reach and intensity. In the previous chapter, I noted that the aesthetic of interruption characteristic of Shanghai installment fiction could inspire the reader to commit more intensely and thoroughly to the narrative (and even to the genre as a whole) because of the constant movement back and forth among a wide variety of what appear to be separate storylines. Here I would like to focus not so much on the obvious pleasures of moving rapidly from one thread to the next, but rather on the frustrations inherent in the sudden "truncation" of a narrative in which one has already begun to take an interest. Qian Xinbo of Shen Bao Press, one of the editors responsible for printing translated fiction in installments in the 1870s, faulted the installment method for leaving readers in suspense, unable to finish reading a text at will, and gave up on it for that reason.[26] Han Bangqing, writing about fifteen years later, found the particular merit of publishing in installments precisely in this supposed flaw.

> Someone said that in reading "The Tale of Duan Qianqing," one must wait
> for two months, won't that bother the reader? I say that it won't. When I have

time I read fiction, and whenever I reach a point that is strange and abrupt, I put the book down and do not read further, but instead thinking, how might it twist next, and how will it end? Having thought for days and not having come up with it, I continue reading and am suddenly enlightened. Isn't that great fun? Other times, I read to the halfway point, and predict that the twists and ending of the text should be thus and so, not guessing that the text to follow is in fact very different, then I am too happy; what dissatisfaction could there be?[27]

Han bases his defense of installment fiction on one of the generally acknowledged aesthetic criteria by which fiction had been judged for more than two centuries—the extent to which narrative time is extended or disrupted by insertion of other plotlines or descriptive prose to add suspense to the reading process.[28] In his view, installment publication is a mechanism that insures the reader will move slowly through the text and have ample opportunity to appreciate its subtleties.

Later authors went even further: the 1910 preface to *Beijing xin fanhua meng* (New dreams of Beijing splendor) approvingly likens the craving aroused by installment fiction to the thirst for wine experienced by a drinker; four years after that, Xu Zhenya argued that in the case of installment fiction *(baozhang xiaoshuo)*, "when one reads one page a day, stopping precisely at the right point, and then reflects at leisure, it will naturally have interest." If, by contrast, a reader spends an entire day to swallow a work of fiction in one gulp, the flavor is ruined, and he or she ends by losing any interest in reading the work again later.[29] Publication in installments is conceived of as a means to frustrate the reader's drive to finish immediately, a disciplining of that momentary drive into a permanent state of desire that borders on addiction. This stratagem of discipline-through-frustration is of course characteristic of narrative as a genre; at this historical moment, however, serial presentation is selected as the privileged agent which objectifies and externalizes this narrative property, thereby effecting this form of desire.

Most Ming and Qing vernacular fiction dealing with relationships between men and women thrives on the tension between the overarching moral message and the descriptive passages that at times work directly against that very message.[30] Fiction set in Shanghai in the late Qing adds an aesthetic dimension to make this dynamic more explicit and self-conscious; and publication in installments, with the attendant cravings and frustrations it arouses in readers, then represents a working-out of this moral and aesthetic dynamic in unmistakably material terms. Now it is not only the case that the reader "should not" read further, but in fact that he or she simply *cannot* read further—until the next installment appears. This is how the simple drive to the finish is transformed into the endless quest for more, how a relatively amorphous desire is given the precise and regular form of an addiction, the craving for one's "daily fix." To paraphrase Marx, the appearance of installment publication in conjunction with these specific moral and aesthetic "constraints" on narrative not only supplies text where it is needed; it also supplies a need for the text.[31]

૪ි

Readers apparently reacted strongly enough to the sudden ending of *Lives of Shanghai Flowers* that Han Bangqing felt it necessary to supply an afterword in which he responds to a visitor who asks for the chapters to follow the sixty-fourth. Han begins by stating emphatically that the novel is finished and that it is complete.[32] He goes on to explain the abrupt ending by referring to the way in which one enjoys wandering in the mountains, pausing for a rest when one gets tired, and taking pleasure in imagining the rest of the scenery out there.[33] The idea that the text should not be exhaustive, but instead leave room for the reader to produce meaning through the reading process is evident as early as the seventeenth century: Li Yu writes that "to lay everything out on the table is not as good as to cause people to imagine without end."[34] In this earlier understanding, the "text" *behind* the written text *(beimian wenzi)* gives the most pleasure when it is imagined rather than read, but the end of the written text still forms the final temporal boundary and remains a unifying moment. By the late nineteenth century the aesthetic valuation of incompleteness acquired a new dimension when the "text" *beyond* the final temporal boundary as well as the "text" behind the words themselves becomes an appropriate object of readers' imaginations.

But there is a sense in which Han's defense of the abrupt ending of the novel as a whole is disingenuous; when juxtaposed with his clear explanation of what the interruptions of the installment form can do to increase and sustain readers' involvement with the text quoted above, it seems that perhaps his afterword has not given us the whole story either. The visitor is clearly not satisfied with the mountain-climbing fable, and asks for further details on two of *Lives of Shanghai Flowers'* central characters. Han's response to this request is to stress that those stories (among others) are finished and nothing more can be said. But he does yield to the visitor's pressure and give a brief set of hints of what might happen to other characters in the future, suggesting that there might well be a sequel or continuation at some point. The visitor is disappointed not to get more at that very moment, but takes his leave, resigned to the frustrations of waiting.

As noted in the previous chapter, sequels to the best-known early and mid-Qing novels appeared only well after the original had acquired a certain degree of name recognition. What we find here in Han Bangqing's afterword is a new approach to the idea of continuation beyond the limits of the original: in arguing for the aesthetic value of abrupt endings, the author unexpectedly finds that his visitor has taken his previous claims about the virtues of the interrupted text that subsequently continues to heart. The more firmly he tells this visitor that the text has come to an end, the more persistent the visitor becomes. Just as the author manages to set up another barrier to the free flow of the narrative, the readers' "horses-of-intention" insist on finding a way around it. Even before the sequels to *Lives of Shanghai Flowers* and the continuations to *Dreams of Shanghai Splendor* begin to appear in print, then, we find that they are imagined as the logical side effects of the new aesthetic of interrupted narrative, understandable symptoms of the readers' commitment to the text.

Consequences

Discourses of Change

When the Crazy Immortal Who Warns About Dreams finished *Dreams of Shanghai Splendor,* buyers came in droves. It was reprinted four times and entirely sold out; this must be its textual fate. However, the situation in Shanghai changes day by day, and the splendor accordingly transforms itself, making it hard to exhaust in writing. So there were people who wrote to the Crazy Immortal to ask for a "concluding series," saying that the original ended too abruptly, and if a "concluding series" were written it would appropriately make up for what the previous text had failed to cover. The Crazy Immortal's interest was piqued; he laughed and agreed to do it.[35]

કર

Lives of Shanghai Flowers ends in a struggle between the author and reader as to whether there will be a continuation—a struggle that produces no immediate decision. In the case of *Dreams of Shanghai Splendor,* however, the reader wins easily. But as we can see from this explanation for the production of chapters 61 through 100, the narrator justifies the failure to bring the text to an immediate close not only by identifying the desire for its continuations among his readers, but also by finding the possibility (even the necessity) of continuations in the specific temporal characteristics of turn-of-the-century Shanghai, the "timeliness" that the city required of its representations.[36]

Readers' understanding of vernacular fiction in the Chinese context had always been dependent on the association between narrative and time, not only in that narratives take time to read, but also in that they are *timely*, or fundamentally connected to the times in which they appear, both in their subject matter and in the enjoyment that people derived from them. Changing times necessitated and produced new vernacular narratives that superseded their predecessors; the contrast that was often foremost in critics' minds was to classics of historical writing like *The Spring and Autumn Annals*, which owed its significance to its ability to transcend the passage of time.[37] But although timeliness was frequently invoked as a defining characteristic of vernacular fiction, novels claiming to tell stories set in the present were quite rare. With the exception of a set of "novels of current affairs" *(shishi xiaoshuo)* written at the end of the Ming, it was not until the middle of the nineteenth century that longer works began to identify themselves explicitly as representations of contemporary life.[38] *A Dream of Romance* (set in Yangzhou) is an early example; novels set in Shanghai that begin to appear four decades later in the 1890s develop this "contemporaneity" still further, with frequent references to dates, times, and ongoing stories in the newspapers and onstage.

୫ର

As if to persuade readers who might suspect that there is no real reason for the novel to continue, *Dreams of Shanghai Splendor* regularly notes the rapid change "characteristic" of Shanghai contemporaneity to reiterate the importance of this kind of timeliness. When Wu Chuyun returns from her stay in Tianjin, she is startled to find new streets and alleys in an area that were fields only three years before;[39] when Du Shaomu comes back to Shanghai he fails to recognize more than one or two names of currently popular courtesans—even the type of name that a courtesan might take has changed, with the new phenomenon of "special trademarks" *(shangbiao)*;[40] when Tu Shaoxia returns to the English Settlement for the first time in a while he is struck by the changes in dress and hairstyles for both men and women and new carriage decorations;[41] his friends have to explain to him why unaccompanied women are no longer allowed to sit in the seats nearest the stage.[42] Similarly, the three-series, hundred-chapter sequel *Dreams of Shanghai Splendor, Continued* (1915–1916) begins by noting that a decade has passed and circumstances have changed, so another book is called for to describe the "astonishing, amazing, ridiculous, pitiful, incensing, touching" events that the previous work did not cover.[43] Sequels and continuations to other Shanghai novels would continue to include such justifications in both specific and general terms well into the 1920s.[44]

In the opening pages of *Hubin shentan lu* (A record of master detectives on Shanghai's shores), published in 1928, we find an explicit reflection on Shanghai fiction conceived as an entire literary tradition grounded in the conviction that Shanghai is changing rapidly. The narrator concludes that though the earlier works in the genre record many significant Shanghai events, they seem out of date, whether written at the turn of the century or as recently as the early 1920s; it is time for more contemporary representations of the city.[45] It is now taken for granted that social change over time must inevitably inspire not only extensions of and sequels to original texts, but also extension of the genre as a whole through production of entirely new texts. Even radical changes in representational techniques or breaks with "tradition" may be recuperable to the category of Shanghai narrative if that genre is defined precisely by its mutability and ceaseless innovative drive.

Previous vernacular fiction spoke from a temporally unified subject position: criticism of or changes to the manuscript were usually based on the idea of a single superior ur-text, a concept that justified alterations to the "compromised" version of the text in current circulation.[46] The story narrated by the novel took time to unfold—and it takes time for the reader to consume it. But the novel itself is abstracted from the flow of history, a still moment of literary perfection mediating between two movements. In the focus on contemporaneity and the installment format we find in Shanghai fiction, this assumption slips away, to be replaced by a new sense of historicity in the genre, and even within individual texts. Over the very course of the writing and publication of these narratives in installments, times in Shanghai have changed sufficiently that the text must continue in order to remain timely. Unlike previous narrative representations of social conditions, which could be presented in finished form and maintain their validity for a significant duration, the serialized novel in Guangxu-era Shanghai represents itself as barely able to keep pace with changes in mores and customs. It claims to become a more open-ended and dynamic project with the aim not only of reproducing the qualities characteristic of a succession of individual historical moments, but also of tracing through its very form the changes in those qualities over time. It becomes possible to think of form literally *historically.*

But we may not want to subscribe without question to the causal relationship these texts propose, in which social change leads inexorably to formal development. Surely, the continued iteration of the formula "the times are changing faster than ever, things are new and different" is also always a means for the *production* of a Shanghai that is changing faster and faster over time, especially when read in conjunction with the increased attention to temporal markers and rapid shifts between narrative lines discussed in the previous two chapters. These representations are more crowded and complicated than previous vernacular narratives, instituting a new urban regime of "busy-ness" and hurriedness *(mang)*. It is difficult to separate this busy-ness (or business) from idleness (or leisure—*xian*), not only in the many occurrences and plot developments, but also in the very concreteness of lived urban "experience." Earlier long fiction could only rarely be confined to a single location; in the Shanghai novel, by contrast, many different narrative "lines" appear to develop in a single city, intensifying this sense of crowdedness and energetic potential. For this reason, we are justified in concluding that novels with an emphasis on timeliness are not mere reflections of the overheated times in which they appear, but also a significant factor in the acceleration of change; the fast pace of life in Shanghai in practice derives in part from these "fictional" representations.

In this way, Shanghai novels make their own distinctive contribution to the addictive rhetoric of "Shanghai modernity" that began as one component of guidebook and travel account discourse in the 1870s and would continue to intensify and spread through fiction, journalistic writing, advertising, paintings and prints, stage productions, intellectual discourse, radio broadcasts, and films until its apogee in the 1930s.[47] Before they even arrived in Shanghai, travelers from across China would have begun to prepare themselves for entry into a space of rapid change, thanks to the prevalence of this discourse. Serialized texts of the late Qing and Republican periods that seem to go on without cease make use of this discourse to explain their own persistence, and at the same time contribute to the future dominance and pervasiveness of this discourse through that very persistence.

The Leisure Industry

This is the problem with Shanghai's glamour: Once the place gets a name for itself, no matter what their age people all want to come to see and experience it.[48]

卐

Persistence is another word for a kind of productive repetition that can be almost industrial in character. It is already clear that Shanghai fiction invests the city as a whole with immense cultural energy, both positive and negative. Just as the horse-drawn carriages circulate again and again to put fashionable individuals on display, so the "endless" iteration of Shanghai fiction broadcasts a selective set of urban scenes in heavy rotation, putting Shanghai on display before a national audience. The rhetoric of excess so crucial to this display is of particular importance to one rapidly developing sector of the Shanghai-area economy—the leisure industry. When we compare the horse-carriage itineraries noted in Shanghai novels to maps coded by assessed or estimated property value, it becomes evident that these circuits passed by the most valuable real estate in the concession areas, suggesting that the itineraries of display related to the rising value of adjacent property in dialectic fashion.[49] Similarly, the ceaseless movement of readers through chapter after chapter focused largely on notable Shanghai leisure activities plays no small part in attracting increasing numbers of tourists to the city's parks, theaters, *tanci* halls, restaurants, and racetracks from the 1890s forward. It is no doubt for this reason that some later writers criticize certain Shanghai novels as "guidebooks to the world of prostitution" *(piaojie zhinan).*[50]

As Catherine Yeh has pointed out, the significance to Shanghai's economy of visitors from elsewhere in China and residents with leisure time to spend is indisputable.[51] Earlier texts often noted the importance of leisure activities associated with ritual practices such as temple attendance, festivals and parades, and pilgrimages: describing early nineteenth-century Yangzhou, the narrator of *A Dream of Romance* explains that people go to the temple "half to burn incense, and half to enjoy themselves."[52] In turn-of-the-century Shanghai texts, the emphasis shifts decidedly to the role that such leisure activities alone—independent of ritual pretext—can play in the symbolic and material economies of the city. Turn-of-the-century editorials in the tabloid papers *Entertainment Daily* and *Selected Rumors Daily,* for example, argued that courtesans and prostitutes were crucial to Shanghai's economic development; the latter went so far as to attribute a significant measure of Shanghai's prosperity, relative to Yangzhou and Zhenjiang, to a more permissive attitude toward prostitution on the part of the local authorities.[53] This point recurs frequently over the next two decades, as in the claim made in *The Nine-tailed Turtle* that Shanghai's economic success depends on the courtesan houses.[54]

Dean MacCannell has suggested that "the empirical and ideological expansion of modern society" is "intimately linked in diverse ways to modern mass leisure."[55] It is clear that in the late nineteenth and early twentieth centuries, the entertainment industry was a major engine of Shanghai's economic growth, attracting both short-term visitors and wealthy longer-term sojourners.[56] The cash spent by tourists from elsewhere in China and around the world moved quickly from the point of expenditure in theaters and courtesan houses to the trades directly dependent on the entertainment industry, and from there into the more general urban economy.[57] The tax revenues from houses of prostitution, opium dens, theaters, and other establishments were vital not only to concession administrations, but also to the Qing local bureaucracy.[58] It comes as no surprise, then, that although in the early 1850s the commercial center of Shanghai was still located inside the city walls, by the Tongzhi era (1862–1874), the economic center of gravity had shifted north to the English Settlement together with the leisure establishments; by 1897 Fourth Avenue was, according to one commentator, the most prosperous stretch of real estate in all of China.[59] Two decades later, one author notes that on Fourth Avenue "serious business premises are promiscuously intermixed with the giddy eating houses and places of entertainment, the one obviously helping the other to the mutual benefit of all concerned," and another credits the opening of a new theater, the New Stage (Xin wutai), in 1908, with sparking a revitalization of a neglected neighborhood and the return of business to the southern city.[60]

⁊ℨ

Crucial to this surge in the economic significance of leisure is a sense that free time is no longer just to be enjoyed, but rather something that must be actively *spent* through the consumption of commodities. "Since there is this [time for] rest, there is leisure; since there is leisure time, one must have a means of spending it."[61] From the 1880s forward, Shanghai residents and visitors could, to an unprecedented extent, turn to the products of print culture—books, newspapers, illustrated magazines, and so on—to find a means of spending their leisure time. As we have seen already, Shanghai novels play an important role in attracting tourists to Shanghai by cataloging the possible leisure activities available and by constructing a formal framework according to which a broader mediasphere could be imagined. But even when Shanghai installment fiction is treated most reductively, as a "mere" material commodity in isolation from its symbolic significance, its importance as a leisure product cannot be overlooked. The continued production of Shanghai narratives played an integral part in Shanghai's development as a publishing center; this publishing business was crucial to the development of Shanghai as a nineteenth- and early twentieth-century industrial metropolis, as it had been in Paris, London, and New York in earlier decades.[62]

Publishers had in fact been active in Shanghai for several centuries, and with the introduction of new printing technologies and the appearance of new kinds of texts that could be bought and sold in the 1870s, the city quickly became the media center of late Qing China.[63] One source claims a tenfold increase in publishers in the city and its suburbs—from fewer than ten to more than one hundred—between the 1860s and early 1890s.[64] As Christopher Reed has shown, one of the central factors in this boom was the adoption of lithographic printing technology, which had dramatic effects on the organization and business practices of printing houses, and on the image of the city as a cultural center.[65] In addition to its importance as a supplier of commodities—printed books—to meet public demand, this flourishing publishing industry in turn created a powerful demand for domestically produced printing presses, kick-starting a sector that would take a leadership role in the Chinese machine manufacturing industry for more than three decades.[66] By 1894 the publishing industry commanded 10 percent of foreign investment in Shanghai, a share larger than that of the Western medicine, food and drink, and cigarette industries put together.[67] This growth continued through the first three decades of the twentieth century: by the late 1930s Shanghai published more than 80 percent of China's books, and one publisher in Shanghai alone (Commercial Press) was publishing more titles than the *entire* publishing industry in the United States.[68]

Some of the growth in the Shanghai publishing industry in the late nineteenth and early twentieth centuries may be attributed to new reference works required by increased foreign trade; these included Shanghainese-Japanese dictionaries, collections of typical Chinese-English business letters, and even a bilingual edition of the Four Books.[69] Large-scale publishing projects became much more common, including a 1,500 copy run of the *Gujin tushu jicheng* (Complete collected illustrations and writings of the past and present) in 1,628 volumes, as did collections of illustrations by famous artists in the Shanghai area.[70]

But the majority of the increase occurred in two categories: first, books that helped one prepare for the civil service examinations, including standard reference works like *Peiwen yunfu* (Palace of rhymes) and the *Kangxi zidian* (Kangxi dictionary); and second, in leisure reading such as novels, *tanci,* travel accounts, and newspapers and other periodicals.[71] In the 1880s Kang Youwei asked Shanghai lithographers which books sold well; their answer was that the classics did not sell as well as collections of examination essays, and collections of examination essays did not sell as well as novels.[72] The novels printed in the 1870s, '80s, and '90s included most of the better-known works of the Ming and Qing, but also many manuscripts that had never or rarely been published before, such as *A Dream of Romance, Six Chapters from a Floating Life,* and Zhang Xinzhi's commentary to *Dream of the Red Chamber.*[73]

The striking development of the Shanghai publishing industry in the late nineteenth century can also be seen in the rapid increase in the publication of *tanci,* or prose-verse narratives, which had a readership that was probably broader than that enjoyed by almost any other form of leisure reading. *Tanci* were often written and read by women, and when turn-of-the-century authors better-known for their novels worried about how to reach a broad audience, they turned to the *tanci* form to make their points.[74] Shanghai publishers became dominant in this genre by the mid-1880s, producing cheap lithographic and lead-type editions.[75]

The cheapest form of leisure reading produced in Shanghai was the *xiaobao* (leisure paper or tabloid newspaper). Both the established daily *Shen bao* and the illustrated periodical *Dianshi zhai huabao* (Dotting the stone studio pictorial), printed in Shanghai, were available in major metropolitan areas across China by the 1880s.[76] The distribution of Shanghai periodicals elsewhere in China became even more profitable after the creation of the Chinese Imperial Post Office in 1896, and its decision in 1897 to allow lower rates for newspapers.[77] With this a new class of daily papers for leisure reading quickly appeared and flourished as an alternative to the established dailies. These leisure papers, or tabloids, focused on humorous stories and news from the Shanghai entertainment world, representing a new stage in the dissemination of images of Shanghai across China. Cheaper than the established papers at first—four to five cash per copy rather than eight to ten cash—these publications also included free inserts listing nightlife destinations and the names and addresses of first- and second-class courtesans in the English Settlement.[78] Though most of the readership was most likely concentrated in Shanghai and the Jiangnan area, we can see from the masthead of *Entertainment Daily* that it could be purchased in Beijing, Tianjin, Hankou, Hangzhou, Suzhou, Nanjing, Ningbo, and Songjiang in the months after it was founded, and by late 1898 it was available in twenty-four cities across China, as well as in Tokyo.[79] According to Naitō Konan, the ordinary *Entertainment Daily* print run dramatically surpassed that of *Shen bao* as early as 1899.[80] The years between 1897 and 1905 saw at least twenty other leisure papers appear; with one or two exceptions, they were published in Shanghai.[81] The success of these newspapers designed to help the reader spend leisure time enjoyably is attested to by the speed with which the more established papers like *Shen bao, Hu bao* (Shanghai times), and *Guowen bao* (National times) moved into the market with their own literary supplements.[82]

The leisure papers and literary supplements had close ties to Shanghai fiction from the very first, as we saw in the preceding chapter.[83] Shanghai fiction published in installments not only motivated readers to keep up with papers in which they appeared, but also provided the model according to which tabloid news could be written and read as a pattern of continuing stories rather than a collection of mutually unrelated anecdotes. After 1910 Shanghai fiction began to be serialized in the more "reputable" established newspapers available in major cities across China, such as *Xin Shen bao.*

Shanghai novels published in installments occupied a central place in Shanghai literary production from their first appearance in the 1890s for three reasons: first, they were written and set in Shanghai itself, unlike other fiction; second, as I have shown in detail in earlier chapters, they were characterized by a new and unprecedented aesthetic; and finally, they were closely tied to newspapers and periodical media, which also experienced explosive development in the Guangxu period (1875–1908). While they did not represent a sheer majority of volumes printed in Shanghai, they were significantly more popular than scholars have previously realized, and their crucial importance in the imagination of Shanghai as a trendsetting media center and in the selling of other media products meant that they commanded a significance in the leisure publishing market far beyond what their numbers alone might have suggested.

Consumption

Residents of Shanghai may well have seen the immoderation of installment production as an ironic commentary on the development of the city itself, in which the repeated continuation of narratives like *Dreams of Shanghai Splendor* transposes colonizing practice from city space to the mediasphere. Like the "concessions" of this period, the novel continues to enlarge its domain, each time insisting that this expansion will be the last.[84] For readers who have not yet made the trip to Shanghai, however, the text precedes the city: if, once entering the narrative, one is fascinated, and the morals that are evident to those who are enlightened are ignored in the unceasing quest for new experiences and stories about experiences, then the very form of the urban narrative teaches one how to relate to the city as an object of desire once one finally does arrive there. The eagerness with which one learns to anticipate each installment of Shanghai fiction that comes through the mail, and the certainty that missing one "update" is a matter of no small significance, find their parallel in the intensity with which one comes to look to Shanghai for the latest in everything—news, fashion, intellectual trends, health care, and education—because the latest in Shanghai is always "new" and "different." Here it is important to remember the close associations between Shanghai and opium consumption in the turn-of-the-century imagination. Just as the late nineteenth-century collection of aphorisms and verse *Yanhua* (Opium chats) notes that addiction to opium is not "natural," but must instead be learned over a period of time, the obsession with Shanghai does not spring fully formed into the minds of provincial youths; it must be carefully cultivated.[85] The cravings aroused by the narrative techniques characteristic of Shanghai fiction and by the installment format in which this fiction is presented provide a template for the reader's eventual engagement with the city itself.

The ceaseless iteration of installments—a flow of text broken only long enough to ensure that the reader is impatient for the next bit—teaches a new conception of consumption. Through their prohibitions and constraints on the drive to the end, moral and aesthetic regulations of access to the story in fact *restructure* and *sustain* readers' desire, which then demands in return ever more lengthy and involved narratives. Instead of a process that reaches natural limits and then stops, this new mode of leisure activity knows no boundaries and continues inexhaustibly and without limit. This kind of consumption was already hinted at in the *tanci* genre—which, as we have seen, became very much a "Shanghai product" in the late nineteenth century—with its seemingly endless descriptive portions and detailed digressions from the main plot. What Shanghai fiction does is institutionalize this potential limitlessness in its very mode of presentation, since there is always the possibility of another installment, or sequel, or other form of continuation, even if the author or narrator has pledged not even to consider it.

Expansion without limits, however, turns out to be the antithesis of the existing discourses of acceptable leisure consumption, which stressed balance, moderation, and reciprocity. In guidebooks, memoirs, and newspaper articles from this period, acceptable leisure-time activity consists in the reasonable expenditure of a portion of one's monetary resources in order on the one hand to restore one's spirit *(jingshen)* so that one is refreshed for the next day's work, and on the other, to help provide an income for the many urban residents whose livelihood depends on the leisure economy. What is not acceptable, according to these texts, is precisely excess, which threatens to unbalance the system and destroy one's own body through a vicious cycle of negative feedback.[86] This double discourse of leisure finds its most complete expression in guidebooks and memoirs of this period in discussions of opium; in newspaper articles, and especially in fiction, by contrast, it is mobile public exposure (in the positive *and* negative senses), that exemplifies this double discourse.

Most Shanghai novels refer at least in passing to carriage riding, but it is in *A Shanghai Swan's Traces in the Snow* that the speed of the carriage is thematized to the greatest extent, and the practice of nighttime carriage riding given the most narrative significance. Near the end of book, we find an account of Xu Junmu's failed attempts to become intimate with Miss Xiao, an unmarried young lady of a "proper" family, constructed in large part through reference to night carriage rides in the hottest months of summer. The repeated invocation of oppressive heat—an important figure of immoderation in earlier vernacular fiction like *Jin Ping Mei*—highlights excess implied by night carriage riding.[87] Toward the end of chapter 17, Xu Junmu and his friend Jiang Youchun become caught in an oscillation between downtown and the suburban parks, in an attempt to get closer to Miss Xiao and her friend, evening after evening as the heat continues.

Finally, on the second day of the seventh month, the courtesan Gao Xianglan, a mutual acquaintance, contacts the two men to say that she will be at Cassia Spirit Theater that night with Miss Xiao. After the performance, the women set off in their carriages, and Xu Junmu is ready to follow them—it is quite hot again even though it is night. At the last moment, however, he worries that rushing things might ruin his chances, so he and Jiang Youchun first do a circuit via Grand Avenue, Looking-to-Peace Street, and Fourth Avenue, only then proceeding to Gao Xianglan's place in Ankang Alley. Xianglan is not there, but her house faces onto the racetrack, from which the continuous sound of trotting hoofs can be heard, as people go around and around in carriages. Jiang is about to suggest going out to ride around themselves when Gao Xianglan returns alone. She explains that they had all been out riding and offers to arrange a meeting for the following night, since the weather will still be hot. The next day, however, Xu Junmu has taken ill with a fever and cannot go out. At this point, the focus of the narrative shifts to A You, Gao Xianglan's carriage driver, who is two-timing a woman who favors him.

More than any other fiction of this period, *A Shanghai Swan's Traces in the Snow* specializes in the evocation of ennui: the characters circle around and around, literally and figuratively, moving back and forth between frenetic arousal and alienated boredom. (Note Xianglan's exhilaration at giving chase to her rival Hua Yu and causing her carriage to crash into the police roadblock, a momentary distraction from the tedium of everyday life.)[88] In this, *A Shanghai Swan's Traces in the Snow* clearly anticipates the Shanghai characters and Shanghai movements that would become commonplace in realist and New Sensationist fiction from the late 1920s through the 1940s. More specifically, in its juxtaposition of excessive heat, sexual frustration, and movement around the city, it articulates a logic that Shi Zhecun, a modernist writer active three decades later, would use to structure his short story "Si xizi de shengyi" (Lucky Four's business). In this story, a rickshaw puller is tantalized by what he understands as advances from his female customer on a sweltering night, but ends in jail when he attempts to imitate the carriage drivers of earlier decades and his bolder contemporaries.[89] And indeed, this distracted circulation in *A Shanghai*

Swan's Traces in the Snow brings us back to the discourse of dangerous leisure found in Shanghai guidebooks and memoirs of the period. The dissipated life that can be spent only in such aimless movement continually wastes resources by releasing them into public circulation, allowing both one's finances and one's health to enter into destructive downward spirals. Like Xu Junmu, Gao Xianglan runs a fever the next day and is confined to her bed.[90]

༄

Circulation not only has the potential to harm an individual's health, it could also be the means through which he or she is publicly disgraced. The practice of repetitive public circulation and display as a means of constituting social space has a specific history in the eighteenth- and nineteenth-century Shanghai area (and more broadly, in late imperial Jiangnan). Neighborhoods organized themselves into units by cycling ritual responsibilities through various households over the years, and important festivals were marked by lavish processions that

FIGURE 6 "Brothel Servants and Prostitutes Paraded in the Street." Lithographic illustration, early 1890s. Wu Youru, *Fengsu zhi tushuo*, 2.21a. Reproduction permission of Harvard-Yenching Library.

helped to mark out neighborhood, village, and urban boundaries.[91] Operating on the same logic, but to different effect, it was common for the magistrate to order a ritual promenade of disgrace around the community for convicted wrongdoers, simultaneously defining the spatial and ethical limits of local society. To some, at least, this kind of public exposure was more to be feared than a whipping.[92] And as Wu Youru's illustration of a parade of disgraced prostitutes and brothel servants—complete with a caption that makes explicit reference to the general practice of riding around in carriages to show oneself off—makes clear, the parade of disgrace cannot be understood apart from its inverse, the culture of competitive public display and conspicuous consumption (fig. 6).

In the end, the figures of excess and consumption bring us to a close focus on the individual body and name *(shen* and *ming),* whether that individual is reading, smoking, drinking, gambling, getting whipped, or being paraded in front of a jeering crowd. The leisure activities so many are eager to engage in consume not only spare time and the money spent to purchase commodities; they even consume, eventually, the desiring body itself, laid low through fever, addiction, or destitution. Which individuals survive, and even prosper, in such a dangerous environment, and how? This is the question that the next chapter addresses.

CHAPTER 5

Brokers, Authors, "Shanghai People"

Given the centrality of broader structures such as the grid of reference, figures of simultaneity and interruption, and the dynamics of desire and excess to Shanghai installment fiction, what kinds of agency are available to the characters inside and outside the text? What subjectivities can an individual located in late nineteenth- and early twentieth-century Shanghai assume? How might Shanghai residents inoculate themselves against—and even profit from—the perils of excessive leisure consumption? The answers to these questions are not self-evident. The opium addict, for example, rarely appears as a figure of any consequence in Shanghai installment fiction, despite his or her ubiquity in certain other genres.[1] Three types that do flourish in the Shanghai novel are the broker, the entrepreneurial cultural producer (whether professional author or courtesan), and perhaps most significantly, the "Shanghai person" *(Szahaenin)*. Each of these types embodies the material and symbolic logics of text and context in the form of a single individual figure, presenting us with three chances to examine the processes of cultural production discussed previously within a more circumscribed arena. This chapter investigates the part that these types play in establishing Shanghai as a space "between" East and West, inventing a new kind of professionalism for Shanghai cultural producers, and reconfiguring the relationship between local identity and broader economic and political forces in twentieth-century China. In each case, we find that the actions and qualities brought together under a proper name to form a person or persons in the text set the terms under which social practice is conducted in the ensuing decades. These terms form a deep structure of Shanghai identity that, despite a period of relative obscurity from the 1950s into the 1970s, continues to play a central role in the rhetoric of the city down to the present day, as we will see in the epilogue.

Brokers

From the end of the second chapter of *Lives of Shanghai Flowers* to the middle of the fourth chapter, the narrative follows a single character, Hong Shanqing, as he moves around the International Settlement. Hong has been introduced already in the first chapter—he is the maternal uncle of Zhao Puzhai, the young man from Suzhou with whom the novel begins—but it is in the third and fourth chapters that his significance to the structure of the novel as a whole begins to reveal itself as he follows a complex social and spatial itinerary around the city. This itinerary begins when Hong Shanqing arrives at the Hall of Assembled Beauties, the courtesan house in Chessboard Street where his nephew, Zhao Puzhai, has become involved with the second-class courtesan Lu Xiubao. It continues through the rest of the afternoon and evening as Hong looks up friends, stops in to see his own "steady" courtesan, attempts to settle a business matter, attends several parties, and is introduced to more new characters.

The reader realizes sooner or later that a multiplicity of interwoven narratives is one of the salient characteristics of *Lives of Shanghai Flowers*, and that Hong Shanqing, as a mediating presence, is essential in his ability to bring different people, different classes, different occupations, and different narrative threads together.[2] Or, in light of the "narrative threads" discussion in chapter 3, we might better say that Hong Shanqing's appearances in the text represent occasions for the reader to define or redefine the different storylines to his or her own satisfaction. As I have reconstructed it elsewhere, Hong Shanqing's itinerary intersects with no fewer than five central narrative threads, as well as numerous others that progress simultaneously through the entire course of the novel.[3] The characters Hong Shanqing encounters range from high-ranking officials to petty functionaries and office managers, from high-class courtesans to servants, and from stewards of the powerful to his nephew from the suburbs of Suzhou. Of the most significant narrative elements in the novel, only the tender relationship between Tao Yufu and Li Shufang and the embarrassing mishaps of Li Shifu and Li Heting (uncle and nephew) are not introduced in this itinerary. On the one hand, Hong Shanqing's progress around town seems to bring disparate storylines together and raises the possibility that they may influence each other's development further over the course of the novel; on the other hand, however, we may note that the distances measured out by his steps and his moments in the back of a rickshaw serve just as vital a function in encouraging us to read these lines as *separate* entities.

৵৯

In the twelfth chapter of *Lives of Shanghai Flowers,* Hong Shanqing encounters another unofficial middleman, Tang Xiao'an, on the street; on comparing notes, the two realize that they are on remarkably similar errands for two different people and part laughing, leaving the reader with the sense that the streets of Shanghai are teeming with individuals on just this kind of errand.[4]

And indeed, the intermediary or "broker" frequently appears as an important character in Shanghai fiction. Any serious transactions must be conducted through a middleman: Hong Shanqing, Tang Xiao'an, Zhuang Lifu, and others in *Lives of Shanghai Flowers,* Tang Zhizhai and Lu Xiaoting in *A Shanghai Swan's Traces in the Snow,* Jia Fengchen and the most appropriately named Jing Yingzhi—"Managing it"—in *Dreams of Shanghai Splendor,* Du Minggan in *The Huangpu Tides,* and so on. These characters are expected to take a cut of any cash that changes hands as payment for their efforts, whether buying boat tickets, antiques, or a courtesan's contract; in some cases intermediaries make a living solely by arranging matters for wealthy Shanghai residents or visitors who are unable or unwilling to do so themselves. The social function of this intermediary is indeed paradoxical: his (in Shanghai novels they are almost exclusively male) profits result from bringing both sides in a deal together, and are therefore predicated on both sides remaining permanently alienated. He is simultaneously glue and wedge between the two parties.

Shanghai was—and remains today—almost invariably represented as a hybrid space, in which "Chinese" and "Western," *hua* and *yang,* could be found *together* in close contact or in combination; as we have seen already in the first chapter, the city is understood as the intermediary enabling interaction between distinct cultures or civilizations. But it is rarely noted that the interests of an intermediary—to the extent that the manifold interests of Shanghai residents can be seen in concert and as a sort of unity—are always as much in the "original" separation of two sides as they are in the eventual mediated contact between them. A memorable literary example of this separation appears in the second and third chapters of *Flower in a Sea of Sin,* when the protagonist Jin Wenqing, having just won highest honors in the civil service examination, stops through Shanghai and learns—apparently for the first time—of the importance of the world outside China and outside the texts he has spent his life studying. The lasting impression left in the reader's mind is of a unique city in which certain unusual Chinese people can speak foreign languages and certain unusual foreigners can speak Chinese.[5] By insisting on mutual incomprehensibility between "Chinese people" and "foreigners" in general as normative, this early segment not only prepares the reader for the misunderstandings and mishaps that will follow in the novel, but also suggests that without skilled brokers and talented intermediaries, no interaction whatsoever is possible.

The best-known Shanghai brokers are the compradors who brought Western and Chinese establishments together even as they assured both sides that an intermediary was indispensable, often growing immensely wealthy in the process.[6] In the 1920s and '30s Shanghai also became known as the place where difficult high-level negotiations between political factions could be conducted.[7] And from the 1850s to the 1950s, mediation was central to the workings of everyday life and small-scale businesses in Shanghai, from the foreign citizens in whose names leases were nominally registered (serving as intermediaries between the Municipal Council and the actual Chinese leaseholders) to the "second landlords" (er fangdong) who divided up rental properties and sublet them (serving as intermediaries between many tenants and the original landlord) to the designated mediators active in local teahouses.[8]

Given the prevalence of these kinds of mediation, it becomes clear that reading the binary cultural distinctions between "Chinese" and "Western" as specific *products* of Shanghai and other treaty ports is an important supplement to the conventional understanding of these same cultural distinctions as the originary conditions under which the treaty-port system took shape. It is for this reason that although "brokers" and intermediaries appear in much vernacular fiction of the Ming and Qing, it is only in the Shanghai novel that (1) the broker becomes one of the central characters, and (2) mediation as such continually constitutes and reconstitutes the relationships by which the narrative structure as a whole works itself out; as we saw in chapter 3, the distinctions between narrative lines are not inherent in the text, but must be actively constructed in the reading process.

Indeed, if we return to the term *jie* (territory, space, world) that plays so important a role in the discursive construction of Shanghai urban space, by indicating spaces that are demarcated or separated, it will come as no surprise that this character, contains within it a second character, also romanized as *jie*, which means, among other things, "to separate, to be sandwiched between, to border on, to bridge or connect," and even "to serve as a social intermediary for two men in a fashion similar to a matchmaker between a man and a woman."[9] This kind of mediation, so important as a livelihood to certain Shanghai residents, becomes increasingly significant to the city as a whole, to the extent that Shanghai fiction often seems to deliberately undervalue the importance of mediation between "Chinese" / "Western" conducted by the city's nearest competitors in that regard, Hong Kong and Japan.[10]

When we look carefully at the text of *Lives of Shanghai Flowers*, we realize that just as Hong Shanqing's social position in the text is that of an intermediary, his *textual function* is that of a broker between narrative lines. Aside from his ineffectual attempts to return his relatives to Suzhou, his character takes little significant action and undergoes no emotional struggles or development; as Eileen Chang points out in her commentary to the novel, even his association with the courtesan Zhou Shuangzhu nearly disappears when Wang Liansheng leaves Shanghai and Hong has no further need to accompany him socially and host banquets.[11] His own narrated experience is the empty center that—through mediation—enables the complex organization of the rest of the text.[12] Such mediation is crucial not only to the particular structure of Shanghai installment fiction, which consists of narrative lines that are discrete only to the extent that we read them as discrete with the help of brokers like Hong Shanqing, but also to the myths of "China" and "the West" that become so powerful in the late Qing. Just as the profusion of narrative elements can be retrospectively strung into a series of coherent interwoven narrative lines, so can the confusion of practices, texts, and concepts characteristic of late Qing and Republican Shanghai be organized into coherent and nearly mutually exclusive categories of East and West with the interested assistance of an intermediary who stands to benefit from this very exclusivity.

ક৯

The formal and thematic construction of individuals like Hong Shanqing as brokers in early Shanghai installment fiction corresponds indirectly to the massive mediation projects undertaken between "China" and "the West" by translators, educators, musicians, and compradors in Shanghai and elsewhere, from bilingual editions of the Four Books to translation and textbook series, from jazz recordings to joint-venture companies.[13] By the 1920s and '30s, the complex narrative structure central to Shanghai fiction expands to address this distinction as a question of literary aesthetics. The author of fiction, like so many journalists, editors, translators, and teachers in "new-style" schools of this same period, takes up the role of broker between two constructed literary heritages, "native" and "foreign."[14]

It is perhaps self-evident that May Fourth writers and critics like Mao Dun can be understood as intellectual brokers, deriving a great deal of their authority from their ability first, to represent a relatively coherent set of "Western" literary techniques, approaches, and standards in Chinese, and second, to judge works produced by Chinese authors according to these imported standards. But as Perry Link and Rey Chow have shown, authors of novels stereotyped as "Mandarin Duck and Butterfly" or "old-style" fiction also had an important role in the textual construction and interpretation of "the West," and of new phenomena within China.[15] Where Mao Dun and other May Fourth and modernist writers enthusiastically displayed their techniques as new and radically different, downplaying any connections with previous Chinese fiction, Shanghai novelists of the 1920s and '30s focus the reader's attention on continuities they see between their works and earlier Chinese texts. If Mao Dun and the New Sensationists presented themselves as middlemen who could unite foreign literary techniques and the domestic object of representation (Shanghai) through a revolution in literary practice, writers of Shanghai installment fiction like Zhu Shouju *(The Huangpu Tides)* and Bao Tianxiao *(Shanghai Annals)* imply through their approach an ability to bring together both "foreign" and "native" literary techniques *within* existing aesthetic frameworks. In both cases, Shanghai serves as the space in which East and West are constructed against each other, and Shanghai texts are a crucial site for the production of "Chinese literary tradition" and "literary modernity." While the role of broker sits awkwardly on Mao Dun and other May Fourth critics' shoulders, authors of Shanghai fiction in particular step into Hong Shanqing's shoes with great ease.

Scholars of modern Chinese literature frequently follow May Fourth critics in their assessment of European and Chinese narrative techniques as fundamentally different, and to a certain extent incompatible. It should come as no surprise that such differentiation can be found in many of the literary works written by those same May Fourth critics, as they were at pains to distance their own production from a "tradition" that they understood as reified and monolithic. But other fiction from this period resists attempts to constitute radically exclusive categories of narrative technique. Shanghai novels of the 1920s include narrative techniques adapted from European and Japanese literature, yet at the same time they retain devices, like couplet chapter headings and the chapter-ending advice to turn to the next chapter to see how things develop, that are characteristic of much Chinese long vernacular fiction from the seventeenth century forward.[16]

In *Huangpu Tides* (1916–1921), characters' inner voices begin to appear in detail that was unprecedented in Shanghai fiction; *Shanghai Annals* (1922–1924) expands on this development and employs the broad narrative strokes characteristic of French and English nineteenth-century realist novels to great effect in the opening chapters. And in prefaces to *Hell in this World* (1922–1924) and *Waves in a Sea of People* (1926), we find references to "realism" *(xieshi)* that would not seem out of place in the writings of contemporary May Fourth critics. But these elements of the discourse and practice of "realist" fiction share the page with allusions to the mirror of Qin and the burning rhinoceros horn of Wen Jiao, images drawn from *Xijing zaji* (Random notes from the Western Capital), a collection of accounts from the Han dynasty, and the *Jinshu* (Official history of the Jin dynasty), respectively, and previously deployed to sanction different representational orders aimed at different kinds of enlightenment.[17] In effect, the reader is treated to a virtuoso display of cross-cultural parallelism, in which the author juxtaposes literary techniques and ideologies of different origins with a view to highlighting their differences, only to step forward as an individual uniquely qualified to bring the two sides together in a harmonious and profitable relationship.

A similar dynamic appears in the very language of the text. Nineteenth-and early twentieth-century Chinese "vernacular" fiction often contained a significant quantity of text in more literary language, setting up an opposition between simple conversation or narrative of action presented in the vernacular, and more "refined" speech and lengthier descriptive portions, presented in a more literary style. Early Shanghai novels like *Lives of Shanghai Flowers* and *A Shanghai Swan's Traces in the Snow* reconfigure this split by distinguishing between the voice of the narrator (in relatively refined vernacular) and reported speech (in dialect). As noted in the first chapter, this split was crucial to Shanghai's self-definition vis-à-vis Suzhou regional culture on the one hand and a "national" vernacular on the other. Since this heterogeneity is fundamental to the city's image as metropolis, it comes as no surprise that the multiplicity of linguistic registers persists in Shanghai fiction of the 1920s and '30s such as *Shanghai Annals* and *Hell in This World*. While many advocates of "new literature" *(xin wenxue)* strove to produce texts in a uniform, westernized vernacular, writers of Shanghai fiction continued to employ a range of expression: at first, the combination of vernacular and literary, and then, increasingly, a combination in which westernized vernacular replaces the literary language.

A concrete logic of substitution is at work here: where previously literary and vernacular language had been yoked together to draw the narrative cart, now "new-style" or westernized vernacular on the one hand and "old-style" vernacular on the other are juxtaposed to the same end. The substitution works well in part because the westernized vernacular has taken on a social function and prestige similar to that of the literary language in the previous centuries.[18] The implication of such a substitution—especially when made with no effort on the part of the author to alert readers to it—is that this new "mixture" can and should be read the way the older "mixtures" were. That is, *not* as a refractory and arbitrary combination of two discrete essences, but rather as an integration of parts that are distinct but nevertheless belong together—in fact, can be fully understood as distinct only when seen in juxtaposition in the work of a skilled intermediary.

The overall effect in *Hell in This World* and other novels of the 1920s, then, is not of jarring and incongruous contrasts between "traditional" and "modern," but of narratives that present themselves as heterogeneous in composition yet internally consistent, implying a genealogy of literary techniques that integrates elements from different technologies of representation, specific contributions from other "Chinese" genres, and, finally, strategies and tactics found first in other "national" literary traditions. Images, techniques, and figures from other media, other genres, and other countries obtain work permits allowing them employment alongside "natives" in the Shanghai novel with remarkable speed and a minimum of fuss. It was this attempt at a smooth integration of specific techniques of "foreign" origin into literature written in Chinese that irritated May Fourth critics most about the majority of texts produced in the 1910s and 1920s; rather than confronting society as a whole with Western literary theories and techniques, Shanghai novelists, among other writers of the 1920s, staged a textual reconciliation, demonstrating that the adaptation of new techniques did not necessarily imply wholesale and immediate social transformation. Shen Yanbing (Mao Dun) is characteristically blunt in his criticism of works that ally formal innovation with "old" content, writing in "Women you shenme yichan?" (What heritage do we have?) that "old-style" fiction that is changed only superficially through the addition of a "new-style" preface and punctuation has the potential to shake the self-assurance of advocates of literary reform and endanger their capacity to discover truly new literary territory.[19] Works that confused "Western" and "Chinese," "old" and "new," had the potential to challenge the very definition of "new literature" as a unitary, knowable, practicable (or even desirable) phenomenon. Instead of the hobbled and clichéd decadence that Shen wanted to see in "Chinese literature," the openness to selective innovation found in Shanghai novels of the 1920s constructs "Chinese literature" as dynamic and ready to accept techniques seen as unusual or different as a matter of course, revealing both the contingency and the limitations of "wholesale westernization" as a literary strategy and scholarly trope. Shanghai is the privileged space in which this development of a literary tradition in Chinese can work itself out, and the newly professional Shanghai authors are the intermediaries ideally placed to lend a helping hand.

The Business of Cultural Entrepreneurship

The professional author arrives in Shanghai fiction in 1909, in the first chapter of *New Shanghai*. When Li Meibo, one of the main characters, shows up unexpectedly at the narrator's house on the opening page, the narrator is *editing a novel* that he has written. And this is not his only work of fiction; when Li enters the narrator's study, he catches sight of two completed manuscripts, which he leafs through with great interest: *A Stylish Circuit Intendant* and *New Flower in the Sea of Sin*. Manuscripts showing up within novels is nothing new; their mysterious appearance is a technique first used in *Dream of the Red Chamber* and elaborated upon in the best-known novels about courtesans through the nineteenth century, producing the author as a recognizable fictional character decades before writers of fiction gained widespread social attention.[20] But each of these previous cases subscribed to the ideology of the novel as a masterpiece, a singular outpouring of all the emotions, perceptions, and experiences that one uniquely qualified individual had gained in the course of a lifetime—each author could be expected to have only one book in him (or her). Even as late as Wu Jianren's *Strange Happenings Eyewitnessed over Twenty Years* (1903–1910), the narrative is meant to be the complete recollections of one individual, to be shared with those who can respond to it appropriately.

Dreams of Shanghai Splendor, by contrast, suggests a certain multiplicity, not only in the numerous narrative voices and the frequent extensions of the narrative, but also in the reproduction of narrative content in a variety of different genres, as noted in chapter 2. This multiplicity takes the logical next step in *New Shanghai,* in which at least four manuscripts make their appearance, we are told of twenty more that the narrator has had published, and it is strongly implied that the narrator derives at least part of his living from writing these works.[21] In the final chapter, he reveals his most recent project to Li Meibo and Shen Yifan, the very two characters around which he has organized his newest work, *New Shanghai.* Inasmuch as *New Shanghai* shows us novel writing as a routine practice in a specific social context, rather than as a heartfelt life task that aims to transcend the ages, it presents the readers with an image of the *professional* writer of fiction. There is an interesting parallel here with the transformation of the painter's sketchbook *(huagao)* from trade secret to widely available commodity in the preceding three decades; by the turn of the century artists had already moved to stake their claim to fame through the early publication of something that had in previous generations been a carefully guarded secret.[22] In the writer's case, the very possibility of a professional routine—repeated composition of narratives, some running simultaneously—depends on both the ideology of the changing times and the conception of genre as a space of simultaneity discussed in the previous two chapters.

This image of the professional writer is not, however, without its stresses and strains. Michel Hockx has shown that writers' self-definition in the 1920s often involved distinctive "position-taking"—advocates of "new literature" defined themselves against "old-style" literature, whether written in classical Chinese or in the vernacular.[23] In the 1910s, we see a similar process unfolding at a much more basic level. Rather than establishing oneself as the advocate of one type of vernacular fiction and critic of another, as was common in the 1920s, writers of fiction in the 1910s found it necessary first to establish the legitimacy of the very category "professional writer of fiction."

Early in the first chapter of *Xin Shanghai,* the reader is abruptly introduced to a newspaperman who is obnoxiously self-important, ignorant, and always out for himself. Even his table manners are bad—he is not only greedy, but also omnivorous, and the narrator feels called upon to describe his gluttony in excessive and satirical detail. This caricature is no accident. The earliest writers of Shanghai novels were also newspapermen, working as columnists, reporters, editors, and in the case of Han Bangqing, Li Boyuan, and Wu Jianren, as publishers as well. We can see the importance of this link not only in the publication of fiction in installments alongside or within newspapers and the widely held perception that the daily news could serve as a source for novelistic inspiration, but also in the effect that the narrative structure first implemented in Shanghai novels had on the format organizing gossip columns in the newspapers.

By the early 1920s, however, the professional writer of fiction, or editor of a literary magazine, had become quite distinct from the newspaper editor or reporter. The year 1909 represents a key moment in this process of disassociation; at this point, vernacular fiction was still associated primarily with newspapers, even as fiction magazines began to appear as a separate genre.[24] Though authors of vernacular fiction and newspapermen might already have started to think of themselves as members of separate professions, the distinction would most likely have been unclear to the reading public, and the vernacular fiction these authors produced was not yet welcome in the better-known fiction magazines such as *Xiaoshuo yuebao* (Fiction monthly).[25] In his appetite for everything (barely leaving bones on the plate) this newspaperman represents not only a type of social conduct to be disdained, but also, more significantly, an approach to literary production that must be relegated to a subordinate position for the professional writer of fiction to emerge as a separate, respectable category.[26]

Given that vernacular fiction was considered a commodity frequently characterized by inferior aesthetic quality, not only by readers and critics, but even by authors themselves, it was of vital importance to writers of fiction in this period to establish themselves not as indiscriminate collectors and recyclers of anecdotes, but rather as producers of texts with aesthetic and moral value.[27] At the same time, it is a newspaperman who is assigned to tell us that the narrator should be considered "a great novelist" (*da xiaoshuo jia*), pointing to tensions inherent in this attempt to assert a distinction that audiences will begin to accept only in the years to come.[28] In this effort, it is almost irrelevant that, as I have shown elsewhere, most vernacular fiction set in Shanghai was in fact well-crafted and carefully organized in such a way as to maximize the narrative's ability to involve the reader; it was the public perception of it as hastily produced that needed to be countered.[29]

The appearance of this professional writer and his products in 1909 is not simply an issue of aesthetic quality or professional pride, but also a question of profit, coming as it did in close conjunction with the institution of a copyright regime that defined written narratives, among other products, as intellectual property; standardized payment to authors for their manuscripts quickly ensued.[30] Within a few years, authors like Xu Zhenya began to take legal action against unauthorized printings of their works, and by the middle of the 1920s, the professional imagined in *Xin Shanghai* would begin to command the allegiance of a national audience.

Unlike Han Bangqing, Sun Yusheng, and Li Boyuan, who wrote novels and had them printed in periodical or daily publications that they themselves produced, authors of the 1920s were either freelance or contractual employees who answered to the new owner of the means of production, a publisher who was not a writer, but was solely responsible for managing his own or another's investment. As Perry Link notes, after the unprecedented popularity of *The Jade Pear Spirit* in the early years of the Republic, "commercialization of fiction escalated from supplying public demand to creating, stimulating, and coaxing it."[31] But the fruits of this stimulated demand were not always monopolized by the publisher. First, authors were generally under contract to supply only a given amount of prose daily or weekly to a newspaper publisher; once their quota was filled, they were free to spend the rest of their time writing for other publishers or attempting publishing ventures on their own.[32] Second, the savvy author of a serialized novel had at least one tactic to ensure that profits could be shared to some extent. Zhu Shouju, the author of *The Huangpu Tides*, retained the copyright to the work as a whole for himself, and had only the first ninety-odd chapters serialized in *New Shen bao*—readers who wanted to find out how the novel ended had no choice but to buy the entire hundred-chapter volume edition when it came out from Xinmin tushuguan.[33] Here we find evidence of authorial control over the text as commodity in social practice echoing the authorial control represented *within* the text more than a decade earlier in *New Shanghai*.

The constant negotiations between the cultural producer and the proprietor/investor characteristic of literature and journalism during this period call our attention to parallels between the professional writer and the courtesan; what belongs to the boss and what to the courtesan is frequently an issue both in Shanghai fiction, and in other documents connected more directly with the practice of prostitution.[34] The identification between literatus and courtesan was a centuries-old trope by this point, conveniently available for use by late nineteenth-century Shanghai intellectuals like Wang Tao who felt underappreciated; Catherine Yeh and Ellen Widmer have investigated the complicated dynamics of courtesans who wrote and educated men who wrote about them, and have demonstrated the centrality of these dynamics to turn-of-the-century Shanghai literary culture.[35] Here I would like to focus exclusively on a key quality of Shanghai installment fiction that brings this identification between courtesan and author to a new level. If we think back to the deceit employed by the courtesan Liu Xianxian mentioned in the previous chapter—in which she gets Du Shaomu to come to her place and pay for a banquet in response to her promise to tell him what happened to another character—it also becomes clear that the enterprise of the courtesan is similar to that of the author of install-ment fiction, in that she uses constraints, interruptions, and delays to sustain her client's interest—to attempt to ensure that he is never satisfied with what he is able to attain, but is always asking for more.[36] Although Shanghai actors and carriage drivers take a more ad hoc approach, a similar dynamic governs their relationships-for-pay with female patrons.

Brand names *(biaoji* or *hao)* were in widespread use in China by at least the early years of the Qing dynasty for medicine, silk, tea, and other commodities.[37] In the first decade of the twentieth century, Shanghai courtesans begin to give themselves special names referred to as "trademarks" or "brand names" *(te-bie shangbiao)* to set themselves apart from their competitors.[38] *New Shanghai* works in a similar fashion to open up a space within which the name of the professional writer can function as a brand name—a function that publish-ers, and later authors like Zhang Henshui, could systematize and exploit to sell novel after novel on the basis of the popularity of previous fiction printed un-der the name of that writer.[39] The early appearance of the professional author as a figure in Shanghai fiction should come as no surprise. The very utility of a brand-name author lies in the fact that there are audiences who are convinced (or have been persuaded) that yet another installment of the same thing (or something similar from the same source) is desirable; the professional author depends in large part on a readership that is always ready to buy the next por-tion of his or her literary production on the basis of those portions that they have already consumed. In this sense, the figure of the professional author of fiction is a consequence of the turn-of-the-century efflorescence of installment fiction and the dynamic of desire and excess discussed in the previous chapter. Even if the professional author does not technically publish in installments, his or her continued success as a professional grows out of a particular mode of literary consumption that has everything to do with the endless quest for more, and very little to do with the drive to finish a text once and for all.

Szahaenin

As a broker and a profitable operator, Hong Shanqing stands in for Shanghai authors. But he is also a specific instance of one of the most striking prod-ucts of the Shanghai novel—the "Shanghai person" *(Szahaenin / Shanghairen)*.

Always on top of the situation, sometimes treacherous and scheming, usually on the make, and well adapted to life in the bewildering big city, "Shanghai people" dominate these novels even though they are rarely identified as such explicitly. Of all the local and regional identities in early twentieth-century China, that of the Shanghai person is distinctive, perhaps even unique, in one respect. Other native-place identities were typically acquired at birth and could not subsequently change; one's native-place identity was tied to the place where one's father, grandfather, or ancestor of a more remote generation was born. Should a family happen to relocate from one city to another, or from one region to another, any shift in native-place identity would most likely occur only generations later. In striking contrast, one could become a Shanghai person in the first half of the twentieth century solely on the basis of one's *own* years of experience in the city, even while retaining the native-place identity affiliated with another city.

The following assessment clearly expresses both Shanghai's particularity and its paradoxical ability to reframe the entire question of local identity:

> Of all the metropolises in all the countries in the world, the one whose citizens are strongest in the ability to assimilate is Shanghai. No matter where a person is from, once he or she reaches Shanghai, he or she cannot avoid three habits: following the trends of the times, devoting attention to luxury, and esteeming slipperiness. If this does not happen, he or she probably cannot become a true Shanghai person *(Szahaenin)*.[40]

The writer begins by noting that Shanghai people assimilate most quickly, but in the very next sentence moves to a slightly different assertion—that people from *elsewhere* tend to change dramatically as soon as they arrive in Shanghai. Even as they retain their original native-place identities, people from elsewhere qualify themselves as authentic "Shanghai people" merely by the speed with which they assimilate. Conversely, the readiness with which they are considered "Shanghai people" attests to the power of the city to transform newcomers. The relative ease with which Shanghai identity could be acquired, and the fact that it functions as a kind of overlay, added onto one's native-place identity rather than replacing it, raise two important questions: How can Shanghai identity be defined, since it so different from other regional identities? And how, concretely, is one transformed into a "Shanghai person"?

Deprived of place of birth (or ancestors' place of birth) as a criterion, writers concerned with defining Shanghainese identity resort to experiential, behavioral, and psychological attributes of the individual. Trendiness, slipperiness, cosmopolitanism, pragmatism, sophistication, astuteness, and opportunistic attention to detail are a few of the related attributes assigned to the Shanghai personality. These attributes are not inborn, but are rather understood to be the near-inevitable result of exposure to the specific Shanghai environment. Writers often traced the transformation of an individual into a "Shanghai person" to the acquisition of distinctively Shanghai habits or customs, a process that ordinarily took less than a year.[41]

What are the distinctive features of the Shanghai environment that effect such a transformation? What habits have the power to remake an individual's lifestyle, attitude toward money, indeed, his or her entire moral outlook? In a recent book on everyday life in early twentieth-century Shanghai, Hanchao Lu explains the Shanghai identity as an effect of the highly commercialized environment of the city from the late nineteenth century on, a regime of commodification and exchange that reaches from the banks and trading houses on the Bund to the commercial establishments and lively market in sublet spaces in the back alleys across the city.[42] Wu Fuhui offers a similar explanation, tracing the source of Shanghai attitudes and practices not only to increased commercialization, but also to the culture and traditions of eastern Jiangnan.[43] But claims that a certain "historical reality," whether economic base or cultural heritage, constitutes the ground or origin of social practice must also consider the very terms according to which that "historical reality" has been constructed, and the specific formal qualities of the texts and practices in which that construction takes place. This is particularly true given Shanghai's crucial importance in the industrial production of local, regional, and national identities in early twentieth-century China, as noted in chapter 1. Our perception of Shanghai as a highly commercial environment in fact depends on texts and oral accounts, which themselves are subject to generic conventions. Even the definition of the "petty urbanite" residents seen as typical of Shanghai, the *xiao shimin,* depends not primarily on their occupations, but rather on the kinds of housing they occupied and, significantly, on the kinds of books and magazines they read—a clear example of a social group constructed in part as an audience for a specific genre of texts.[44]

And indeed, we can locate the origin of Shanghainese "identity" in part by seconding Liang Qichao's assertion, cited in the introduction, that fiction has the ability to create and alter patterns of thought and behavior. At the thematic level, it is quite clear that Shanghai novels construct the "Shanghai person" for the reader; these novels excuse behavior that may be perceived as immoral or heartless not only by presenting models of ruthlessness and deception as characters, but also, and more significantly, by shifting the responsibility for one's actions onto the city environment as a whole. In emphasizing the latest in fashionable dress and leisure occupations, as well as the ever-changing character of the city, these novels give a sense of Shanghai as a place where time moves faster and faster and residents of the city have no choice but to rush to keep up. If we go beyond the thematic to look at the way in which the texts are put together, the centrality of the "Shanghai experience" with its transformative potential becomes even more evident: the very narrative structure of novels set in Shanghai encourages us to think of the city as a fast-moving marketplace in which all is for sale and everything is negotiable. Surely the rapidly shifting narrative lines and schemes for getting ahead that are so important in many of the Shanghai novels must have contributed to the definition of Shanghai residents as busy people moving ceaselessly about town and making contacts. Furthermore, the emphasis on mediation as fundamental to cultural interaction, narrative structure, and even socializing among friends and acquaintances inevitably casts human relations in Shanghai as mercenary—for mediation is most recognizable as such when it involves fungible quantities, whether these are quantities of cash, real estate, stocks, or favors.

Shanghai novels not only represent the city as a nexus of feverish exchange and rapid movement, they also contain within themselves the image of an ideal reader who will be at home in that atmosphere.[45] In chapters 1 and 2, we saw that these novels suggest a way of reading as a local—not only by mastering the dialect, but also by knowing where the various locations cited fit into the more general economic, moral, and cultural hierarchies structuring the city. Furthermore, as noted in chapter 3, the complexity of each individual narrative requires the reader to pay careful attention while reading and to invest his or her energy wisely, since many stretches of narrative have meanings that become evident only much later in the reading process. The genre as a whole asks the reader to keep up-to-date on a variety of narratives progressing simultaneously in different periodical publications, suggesting that a command of the contemporary mediasphere as a whole will provide the reader the most enjoyment. As a result, the careful reader of the text learns not only Shanghai content (names of places, tricks and traps to avoid), but also Shanghai vocabulary (the right words to use so as not to remind everyone that one is a recent arrival), and finally a way of relating to one's surroundings as an apparently confusing environment that in fact will render significant rewards to the individual who keeps track of everything that is going on.[46] Building on the image of the ideal reader presented in commentaries to the better-known works of fiction and drama in the Ming and Qing, Shanghai novels expect this diligent reader to take on situations in which key information is missing or concealed, and work them to his or her own benefit; this productive consumer is of course analogous to the "Shanghai person" making his or her way through the crowded city.[47] The ideal reader of the Shanghai novel is well on his or her way to becoming a "Shanghai person" in every respect; the importance of this mode of "naturalization" can easily be imagined in a city with a consistently high proportion of residents who came from elsewhere.[48]

ఇ

The picture of relatively easy assimilation to the culture of the city that we find in most Shanghai fiction differs dramatically from the conclusions that most historians of the city draw. Indeed, one of the difficult questions faced by social historians of the city is how a Shanghai identity could develop in the first place, given the important differences in place of origin, dialect, class status, and occupation, among residents of the metropolitan area.[49] Discrimination against "Subei people" beginning in the first decade of the twentieth century is only the most striking of these divisions.[50] Furthermore, how could the Shanghai identity then become so coherent as to play a powerful and consistent cultural role in the Jiangnan region, as well as elsewhere in China? Bryna Goodman writes that

> Aside from common residence in the city, it is difficult to pinpoint specifically urban practices which might provide the basis for the formation of Shanghai identity, prior to the development of a Shanghai municipal government in 1927.[51]

Although overstated, this assessment does remind us of the real significance that literary texts and artistic performances must have had in the construction of Shanghai identity, for there is no doubt that "Shanghai people" were recognized as such long before 1927.

Recently, the question of Shanghai identity has been addressed from a variety of perspectives: Laura McDaniel has detailed the ways in which the exclusionary policies of Shanghai storytelling guilds contributed to a local identity that was in part linguistic; Catherine Yeh has investigated guidebooks and maps of the city, tracing the boundaries of Shanghai space; and Christopher Reed and Leo Lee have emphasized the role of textbook and reference work publishers in establishing Shanghai as a center of high culture.[52] Vernacular fiction had wider, and in some cases, more enthusiastic audiences than local storytellers, mapmakers, and textbook authors, suggesting the significant role fiction would also have played in the construction of a Shanghai identity. Installment fiction's crucial contribution consisted of the following: it provided a detailed image of the *Szahaenin,* suggested that newcomers to Shanghai could become *Szahaenin* with relative ease, and as a literary form yielded the greatest enjoyment to readers who possess the skills supposed to be characteristic of this *Szahaenin.*

The discrepancy between Shanghai fiction and retrospective narratives written by professional historians is due in no small part to the productive orientations of historians' source material: native-place association records, guild histories, oral accounts of discriminatory practices, and other materials consulted by historians of the city frequently aim through their very form to construct specific regional identities as inescapably determinative of individual experience in the city. As such, these sources are also likely to provide only a partial account of the complexities of identity politics in late nineteenth- and early twentieth-century Shanghai. To ask whether the representation of social interaction in Shanghai fiction is "faithful" to the turn-of-the-century social "reality" is, in fact, almost beside the point. With certain important exceptions, the urban environment has been relatively thorough in its transformation and re-identification of newcomers from the middle of the nineteenth century to the present day. Whether Shanghai novels give us a representation that corresponds to specific details of social practice at the turn of the century as recorded in other genres of source material is perhaps less important than their ability to articulate the terms on which contemporary and subsequent generations, no matter what their "origin," could aspire to become known as Shanghai people.

CHAPTER 6

Marxists and Modern Girls

Shanghai Fiction and the 1930s

The preceding chapters have argued that Shanghai installment fiction plays a crucial role in Shanghai cultural production from the 1890s forward and suggest that this fiction articulates the terms on which the city would be understood in the decades to come. Most scholarship on Shanghai literary production draws a clear distinction, however, between realist and modernist fiction of the 1930s and '40s and earlier Shanghai narratives. Realist and modernist authors are understood to work primarily in a transnational mode, referencing Japanese and European precedents rather than earlier literature in Chinese. This chapter analyzes Mao Dun's classic realist novel *Ziye* (Midnight, 1933) and several short stories by modernists such as Liu Na'ou and Shi Zhecun with the following questions in mind: How valid is the distinction between Shanghai fiction that is counted as *xin wenxue* (new literature) and Shanghai fiction that is stigmatized as *jiu wenxue* (old literature)? To what extent does our understanding of realist and modernist fiction as radically different from earlier works unquestioningly reproduce the value structure set up by May Fourth critics in the 1920s? And finally, what might we gain by reading works of the 1930s together with their predecessors?

It might seem difficult to link *Midnight,* a novel written by Shen Yanbing under the pen name Mao Dun, with the Shanghai fiction discussed in the preceding chapters. Shen Yanbing was the editor assigned in the early 1920s to steer *Xiaoshuo yuebao* (Fiction monthly) away from "Mandarin Duck and Butterfly" fiction toward the "new literature" advocated by May Fourth critics and activists. It is evident from the criticism leveled at the Chinese fictional tradition and what were understood to be its contemporary practitioners (including most authors of 1920s Shanghai novels) in the pages of *Fiction Monthly* and *Wenxue xunkan* (Literature ten-daily) that Shen Yanbing, like other advocates of "new literature," aimed at nothing less than a revolution in Chinese literary practice.[1] Shen himself was a well-known translator and authority on European theories of realism and naturalism by the late 1920s. Clearly, when he set himself the task of writing *Midnight* under the name Mao Dun, the narrative was meant to be a completely different kind of text from earlier Shanghai fiction; it was intended to have more in common with the works of Zola and Tolstoy than with those of the "geniuses of the foreign mall" *(yangchang caizi)* like Zhu Shouju, Sun Yusheng, and Bao Tianxiao.

Critics have tended to take Shen Yanbing/Mao Dun at his word, and with a very few exceptions have characterized *Midnight* either as heir to the nineteenth-century European realist or naturalist novel or as one of the founding texts in the Chinese school of Socialist Realism.[2] Yet neither the former analysis of the novel, based in large part on Shen Yanbing's articles on European literary theory published in the 1920s, nor the latter conception of it, owing much to Mao Dun's late 1930s and post-Yan'an reinterpretive moves, alone can do justice to the complexity of the text. A closer look at the way this narrative is constructed reveals the extent to which alternative genres and heritages make a place for themselves in a literary practice dominated by the theoretical discourse of realism.

❦

Midnight begins, as many Shanghai novels before it did, with the entry of a "naive" outsider into urban society and his experience of sights, smells, sounds, and speeds that he could not even have imagined previously. From the opening words of the novel, it is clear that we readers, unlike the outsider, are in familiar territory:

> The sun had just sunk below the horizon and a gentle breeze caressed one's face. . . . Under a sunset-mottled sky, the towering framework of Garden Bridge was mantled in a gathering mist. Whenever a tram passed over the bridge, the overhead cable suspended below the top of the steel frame threw off bright, greenish sparks. Looking east, one could see the warehouses on the waterfront of Pudong like huge monsters crouching in the gloom, their lights twinkling like countless tiny eyes. To the west, one saw with a shock of wonder on the roof of a building a gigantic neon sign in flaming red and phosphorescent green: *LIGHT, HEAT, POWER.*
>
> At this time—on this perfect May evening—three 1930-model Citroëns crossed the Garden Bridge like a flash of lightning, turned westward, and headed straight along North Suzhou Road.[3]

Wu Sunfu, a Shanghai industrialist, his sister, and his brother-in-law are in these Citroëns. They have brought Wu's father to Shanghai to avoid conflict in the region of his hometown—bringing up the theme of Shanghai as refuge once again—and the older man is scandalized by the Shanghai scenes that he witnesses for the first time on the way from the dock to his son's mansion off Bubbling Well Road (Nanjing xilu). Bright lights, loud sounds, and open displays of female sexuality are chief among the disturbing stimuli, just as they had been in writings about Shanghai for more than a century, and the shift from carriages to automobiles seems not to have changed the basic character of Shanghai streets and avenues.[4] Marston Anderson notes that the metaphors of "fever and reckless transmission" are central to the construction of both the speculative and sexual economies in Mao Dun's Shanghai;[5] this theme of the metropolis as overheated and overstimulating, endowed with endless potential to seduce both visitors and residents, recalls the dynamics of excess and consumption analyzed in chapter 4. *Midnight* inherits this earlier conception of Shanghai and constantly returns to the trope of desire and seduction in its reconstruction of the city along similar textual lines. As is the case in the earlier novels, the supposed intent is to demystify the city and enlighten readers so that they may avoid its snares and illusions; but again, as in so much earlier "didactic" narrative, the detailed catalogue of temptations interferes with the stated aim.

As the text progresses, the narrator's attention shifts from one character to another, following A to meet B, then B to meet C, then D, then back to A again. The focus shifts from one group to another or from one character to another in almost every one of the nineteen chapters, and in some chapters the focus shifts as many as six or seven times.[6] The overall structuring principle of *Midnight*, a novel that attempts to present a panoramic picture of Shanghai in the early 1930s, is thus remarkably similar to that governing *Lives of Shanghai Flowers, A Shanghai Swan's Traces in the Snow, The Huangpu Tides,* and other earlier Shanghai fiction. In the process, a number of different groups of individuals are portrayed as each strand of the narrative develops, and events important to an individual are as likely to happen when he or she is "offstage" as when he or she is the explicit subject of the narrative. As readers, we find out about these developments either directly, through comments by other characters, or indirectly, by piecing together clues that appear later in the text, often pages or whole chapters later. It is only in the closing pages of chapter 18, for example, that Zhao Botao's plan to manipulate the rules governing the stock market and ensure his triumph over Wu Sunfu is revealed. Furthermore, unlike in the European fiction that Mao Dun admired, the information is given to the reader not by Zhao Botao himself, nor by the narrator, but only in conversations between other characters, after the fact. Just as in the earlier Shanghai narratives, it is often impossible to tell when a character is first introduced whether he or she will play a central or peripheral role in the narrative; at the same time, it is frequently difficult for the first-time reader to resolve the various plot developments and shifting alliances. Like many other Shanghai novels, *Midnight* encourages a hermeneutic style of reading that continues to refer back to earlier portions of the text even as it moves forward; such a strategy is less necessary in reading Mao Dun's earlier works. As a result, at least one 1930s critic found *Midnight* to be the "best organized" of Mao Dun's long fiction.[7]

In addition, *Midnight* is extremely topical, concerned with the immediate present and the closest moments of the past. David Wang and Jaroslav Průšek have found Mao Dun's writing in general to be obsessed with the contemporary; in writing a novel about Shanghai—which he originally intended to publish in installments—Mao Dun finally encountered a generic tradition in which such "up-to-dateness" was a defining concern.[8] Up-to-dateness is conveyed in two ways: first, as in the earliest Shanghai novels, the trendiest destinations, commodities, and practices are frequently invoked, like the 1930 model Citroën that makes recurring appearances throughout the novel;[9] second, as first seen in *The Huangpu Tides,* specific political and military developments on the contemporary national and international stages have a direct impact on individual characters.

Finally, the ending of *Midnight,* with its unresolved tone and central character attempting to deny the fate assigned to him or her, echoes the final sentences of *Lives of Shanghai Flowers* and *A Shanghai Swan's Traces in the Snow.* Where Zhao Erbao dreams of a marriage to Third Master Shi, only to have the dream turn to a nightmare and wake up, in *Midnight* Wu Sunfu, financially ruined beyond his worst expectations, suggests to his wife that they go on a vacation—her reaction reminds us that here too, disappointment may await him. Just as in *Lives of Shanghai Flowers* and *A Shanghai Swan's Traces in the Snow,* the many different storylines that constitute the text are for the most part left unresolved; the text ends without concluding *(bujie er jie).* Will Lin Peishan marry Colonel Lei? Will the general strike succeed? Has Zhao Botao succeeded in establishing his own primacy in the Shanghai financial sector, or is he also overextended and ready to fall?

৵৹

In sum, *Midnight* is built on a solid foundation of Shanghai narrative conventions, from the novel's thematic focus on contemporary city life and the problematics of desire and demystification, to its structure constituted by rapidly shifting narrative lines, to its sudden ending, in which important narrative threads are left unresolved. Why is it that Mao Dun's debt to previous Shanghai novels, clearly substantial, has not yet been recognized? This question can be approached from two angles: first, by a relatively narrow inquiry into the char-

acter of realism as a narrative strategy and its reification in the Chinese context; and second, through a broader cultural and ideological critique of the
discourse of modernity (especially "Chinese modernity") initiated by writers of
the May Fourth generation and reproduced by Chinese and Western scholars
of Chinese literature.

Despite praising *Lives of Shanghai Flowers* as a masterpiece, Mao Dun
claims that it does not have anything to offer in terms of literary technique.[10]
Writing in the 1920s, (as Shen Yanbing) he advocated realism or naturalism,
and was highly critical of the descriptive techniques and narrative structure
that he considered characteristic of Chinese fiction.[11] From the late 1930s on,
he campaigned for what would become known as Socialist Realism. In a talk
given in 1939, Mao Dun claimed that he had wanted to give a fuller account
of the activities of revolutionary characters in *Midnight* and make them the
real focus of the book, but had been prevented from doing so by the threat
of censorship by the Nationalist Government.[12] The attempt to present one's
own work in a different light by putting the blame for "omissions" on censor-
ing authorities, while quite possibly either entirely honest or an unconscious
reassessment, may also have been an expedient measure, given the changed
political situation. Nevertheless, these two modes of assessment have conditioned the study of Mao Dun's literary production, inasmuch as most scholars build their readings of *Midnight* and other works on the firm conviction
that an author must be treated as a privileged interpreter of his or her own
works.

But there is also a concern specific to realist fiction as a genre. As Marston
Anderson has pointed out, realist texts tend to derive their authority from the
claim to represent mimetically the world in which we live; intrinsic to this claim
is a hostile attitude toward earlier texts and a declaration of independence from
received tradition, which might constrain or distort an "objective" representation of reality.[13] To the extent that Mao Dun considered himself a realist (or
naturalist) writer, he was bound not to call attention to formal inspirations
drawn from texts that he dismissed as "traditional." Similarly, when scholars
employ "realism" as an analytic category without subjecting the category itself
to analysis or questioning its usefulness in the case of *Midnight,* they too are
bound to overlook similarities in style and content between earlier works in
Chinese and Mao Dun's fiction.

Mao Dun did frequently cite Tolstoy and Zola, among other European authors, as sources of inspiration for his own writing, which has led scholars to
focus on European literary texts in an effort to identify themes and narrative
techniques that Mao Dun might have appropriated for his own use. These references to European authors might seem to contradict the characterization of

realist fiction proposed above; I would suggest, however, that rather than citing the novels written by Tolstoy and Zola as straightforward textual sources for his own works, Mao Dun read these authors as *theorists* of the writing process. We can find in the articles published in *Fiction Monthly* and elsewhere a fascination with Tolstoy and Zola connected directly to their social and cultural function as Russian and French intellectuals and activists. When Shen Yanbing writes that Tolstoy is the founding intellect of the modern era, there is a clear desire on his part to take Tolstoy's *person* as a model for action; this desire is hardly concealed by his immediate acknowledgment that he is very different from Tolstoy.[14] While Shen Yanbing / Mao Dun might not have been comfortable recognizing the degree to which his own images of Shanghai and narrative structure were derived from earlier Shanghai novels, especially those he characterized as "Mandarin Duck and Butterfly fiction," since Tolstoy and Zola could be understood to operate as advocates of methods of writing rather than merely as writers, their influence could be relocated to the originary stage in which the genre (realism / naturalism) is selected, rather than remaining inconveniently evident as constraints on the "objective" reflection of reality undertaken once realism was selected as the operative method.

For this reason, scholars have been able to articulate quite clearly European influences on Shen Yanbing's *theory* of literary production.[15] Yet when it comes to finding narrative techniques and images in *Midnight* that can be traced back to specific European sources, their efforts are much less conclusive. In *Milestones in Sino-Western Literary Confrontation,* Marián Gálik strives to show that *Midnight* is indebted to Tolstoy's *War and Peace,* Zola's *L'Argent,* and H. A. Guerber's *Myths of the Norsemen.*[16] But while critics suggested early on that Zola's novel was an important source for Mao Dun's depiction of stock market conspiracies, Mao Dun himself claimed that he had not yet read *L'Argent* when he wrote *Midnight.*[17] Furthermore, two crucial pieces of textual evidence that Gálik cites to show that Mao Dun had Norse myths in mind while he was writing *Midnight* are explained in a completely different fashion in Mao Dun's *Wo zouguo de daolu* (The road I have walked).[18] While Mao Dun's assertions are not a priori more believable than Gálik's, it is clear that the potential borrowings from Zola and Norse myths are fundamentally less significant than the thematic material and organizational techniques drawn from previous Shanghai fiction discussed earlier in this chapter. In Mao Dun's writings, then, we find a division of labor: European texts could provide a posture and an overall ideology of literary production, but the actual practice—the construction of the narrative—is taken in large part from earlier Shanghai narratives written in Chinese. Such an unacknowledged division of labor may also have caused anxiety in other writers of the May Fourth generation.[19]

ℰ𝔞

The specific differences between *Midnight* and earlier Shanghai narratives are in some cases even more compelling evidence for the value of a close comparative reading than the similarities discussed above. Most of the events narrated in *Midnight,* for example, differ significantly from those found in late Qing and early Republican Shanghai novels. In the earlier novels, parties, banquets, and other forms of mixed-gender socializing are the occasions for a majority of narrative developments. In *Midnight,* by contrast, with the exception of two instances in which a "woman of society" *(shehui zhi hua)* is included in a situation that involves business discussion, the largest portion of the narrative is given over to formal and informal business meetings between men; the second dominant theme is the conflict between men and women on strike and the factory bosses. The distinction between business and pleasure is sharply demarcated in *Midnight,* with two notable exceptions, one highlighting the power of Zhao Botao and suggesting his eventual triumph, and the other emphasizing the futility of Wu Sunfu's attempts to resist Zhao.[20]

The shift in focus from leisure to business is also evident in the schemes various characters essay to enrich themselves. In earlier Shanghai novels, the most complex and treacherous schemes often centered on gambling—the novice, befriended by scam artists, does well at first, but soon loses nearly everything. The wiser characters see through the plot at this point (if they had not done so even earlier), but some fools persist in the attempt to recoup their losses *(fanben).* This invariably involves very high stakes and almost as invariably results in the mark going deeply into debt. The creation of a stock market in Shanghai added another arena in which such swindles could be conducted—the parallel between playing the market and gambling is noted already in *The Huangpu Tides.*[21] In *Midnight* this parallel is developed more fully: schemes to defraud the unaware are perpetrated primarily in the stock market and usually involve government bonds. Those who are certain of good news (political or military) buy government bonds, and those who are convinced that the news will be bad sell the bonds they own and even borrow bonds from others to sell short. Speculators like Zhao Botao, who have connections in the government and with armies on both sides of the civil war, are well positioned to profit from the ignorance of ordinary speculators. Indeed, they are not above bribing soldiers at the front to throw battles in order to affect the value of government bonds on specific dates of their choosing.

The atmosphere on the floor of the stock exchange reminds the reader of the tense situations in which thousands of taels change hands in earlier gambling matches.[22] In Feng Yunqing, the rural landlord who arrives in Shanghai and promptly makes unwise investments, we find Mao Dun's equivalent of Jin Zifu and others in *Lives of Shanghai Flowers* and *Dreams of Shanghai Splendor,* who risk fortunes assembled over the course of a generation or more at the gaming table or at cricket fights.[23] Hit with unfavorable developments on the bond market, Feng Yunqing attempts to *fanben,* win back his stake; but by the end of the novel it is clear, though never explicitly stated, that he has lost again, and is now completely bankrupt.[24]

On looking back at earlier Shanghai fiction, one might be inclined to wonder when any of the male characters finds the time to do any work; unlike Wu Sunfu and other captains of industry in *Midnight,* they are not to be found closeted with their associates in boardrooms and clubs, but rather at parties held in courtesan houses and banquets at famous restaurants. But upon closer inspection, it becomes evident that these social occasions serve as an important arena not only for gossip and flirting, but also for negotiating business deals and displaying accumulated cultural capital. The narrator of *The Nine-tailed Turtle* remarks that although Shanghai is the central port for trade between China and the rest of the world, the city's economy depends in large part on expenditures undertaken in courtesan houses.[25] One character in *A Shanghai Swan's Traces in the Snow* goes even further, exclaiming, "If you don't invite a courtesan along in Shanghai, it's impossible to get any business done."[26] As we have seen in chapter 4, the particular genius of these earlier works lies in the way they reveal the extent to which "business" and "pleasure" are inextricably linked, and often even indistinguishable to the unskilled observer; even courtesan houses were occasionally run with a sort of employee stock option plan.[27] It is for this reason that naive visitors to Shanghai like Zhao Puzhai in *Lives of Shanghai Flowers* and Du Shaomu in *Dreams of Shanghai Splendor* are easily drawn in both by the pleasures available and by the possibility of earning a profit in Shanghai; their downfall comes when they are unable to apprehend the "true" nature of the relationships between business and pleasure, between earning and spending. As Hong Shanqing admonishes his nephew Zhao Puzhai, if one is not in Shanghai for business reasons, it is dangerous to stay too long. In chapter 13 of *Dreams of Shanghai Splendor,* Du Shaomu puts together a plan to invest in the creation of a new publishing house at some expense to himself; in truth this is just a cover story to convince his well-meaning friends to let him stay longer in Shanghai and continue "wasting" his time and money in leisure pursuits—in effect, he spends his own money just to have the chance to spend more of it, with no return in sight.[28] Du Shaomu and Zhao Puzhai continually maintain that their aim is to arrange their own business deals in Shanghai and get rich; but their plans never materialize, and they remain unaware until it is almost (in one case) and entirely (in the other) too late that their own expenditures are merely giving others the chance to profit greatly.

In *Midnight,* a novel informed by Marxist conceptions of historical development, the focus is not on leisure-time activities, but on the ways in which this lifestyle can be "supported"; the struggles between classes in society are as important as struggles between individuals within or across class lines. Having seen the city of Shanghai represented in this way, we can return to earlier Shanghai novels with a new set of questions. *Midnight* makes explicit the class tensions that serve as a subtext to much of the narrative in *Lives of Shanghai Flowers* and *The Huangpu Tides* (among others), and directs our attention to the function of exploitation attempted and contested as an organizing theme. In *Midnight* the paradigmatic opposition is between the rich factory owner and the impoverished female factory workers, many (women) arrayed against one (man); in earlier fiction, by contrast, we realize that the exploitative relations are individualized, and the typical relationships emphasized are that between a courtesan and her madam, that between a courtesan and her client, and that between a maid and her boss (usually female). *Midnight* also reminds us that

FIGURE 7 Female workers at a silk filature. Lithographic illustration, 1884. *Shenjiang shengjing tu,* 2.49b–50a. Reproduction permission of Princeton University Library.

in focusing on maids, entertainers, and prostitutes as representative of working women, these earlier Shanghai novels tell only half of the story of patriarchal exploitation. Female factory workers were featured in illustrated publications as early as the 1880s and played leading roles in the overwhelming majority of strikes in Shanghai's factories during the 1890s and early 1900s, but these working women are almost entirely absent in Shanghai novels before *Midnight* (fig. 7).[29]

Mao Dun's emphasis on work rather than, or in isolation from, play calls our attention to certain omissions that are fundamental to earlier representations of the city. So is Mao Dun's approach more comprehensive or panoramic, giving us a broader picture of the reality of Shanghai? This is a conclusion often reached by scholars of modern Chinese literature, but *Midnight* does not encompass the earlier works completely and move beyond them; it stands rather as a supplement to them, making up their lack, but prevented by this same logic from offering a "comprehensive" view itself.[30] The same reciprocal partiality is also apparent in Mao Dun's critiques of contemporary urban culture; in "Dushi wenxue" (Metropolitan literature), an essay published in 1933, he maintains that Shanghai's development is only apparent, as it consists merely of increased consumption and not increased production.[31] In nineteenth-century Shanghai guidebooks, by contrast, the link between leisure expenditure and urban development was treated in sophisticated fashion; and most Shanghai novels of the 1890s through 1920s, as noted above, find business and pleasure so thoroughly imbricated as to be inseparable.[32] It is this subtlety that Mao Dun's analysis misses; he neglects the complicated interaction between consumption and production so central to the late nineteenth- and early twentieth-century Shanghai economy in order to show most clearly the economic "base" on which he understands a superstructure of culture or leisure practices to be erected. As we have seen in chapter 4, however, a significant sector of the Chinese machine manufacturing industry in the 1920s and '30s formed as a direct response to the flourishing Shanghai publishing industry, which in turn was built on a "base" that consisted in large part of the demand for leisure reading.[33] Like other May Fourth writers and critics, Mao Dun could not bring himself to consider leisure "serious" business, whether as a part of the urban economy or as motivation for quality literature; this is, in its own way, a reading of Shanghai that is just as naive as the misconceptions that Zhao Puzhai and Du Shaomu bring with them.[34]

৵৯

The thematic construction of Shanghai as a place is quite significant in *Midnight*, as it had been in previous Shanghai novels. In the earlier narratives, there is also an intense concern with the accurate and precise construction of narrative *space:* specific locations are cited, the reader is frequently informed of the exact route by which a character moves from one point to another, and characters themselves are frequently individuated in part through reference to their location in the geography of late Qing and Republican-era Shanghai. Specific locations continue to carry semantic and cultural weight in *Midnight;* in chapter 18, young people indulge themselves at the Rio Rita Park, as men and women had at Zhang's Garden and Fool's Garden at the turn of the century. Furthermore, two of the defining sequences in *Midnight* are narrated in close detail as they move in opposed directions down Nanking Road (Grand Avenue). In the first chapter, Wu Sunfu's father is taken by car from the north shore of Suzhou Creek across the Garden Bridge, down the Bund and then west on Nanking Road. Reaching the end of the road at the intersection with Tibet Road (Xizang lu), the automobiles continue west along Bubbling Well Road and eventually turn off on a side street. In the ninth chapter, demonstrators planning to commemorate May 30th begin to gather around the intersection of Tibet Road and Nanking Road, and set off east down Nanking Road with the aim of marching to the Bund and then north along Szechwan Road (Sichuan lu).[35] Reading this opposition in terms of Qing theories of vernacular fiction, we cannot dismiss this "opposition at a distance" as mere coincidence.[36] It is clear that specific locations matter in this novel too; where in the previous novels Fourth Avenue was the theater of display, in *Midnight* that function shifts three blocks north to Nanking Road (Grand Avenue), continuing the historical and narrative trend of displacement to the north noted in chapter 1. Nanking Road is the stage on which the narrator introduces Mr. Wu and the reader to the Shanghai cityscape; it is also the focal point of political displays by students and workers for the benefit of other Shanghai residents—political displays which in this case are ultimately addressed to the reader, with the hope of converting him or her to a politicized understanding of the contemporary situation.

But apart from these striking narrative sequences, identifiable locations are relatively rare in *Midnight.* In the central conflict between Wu Sunfu and other industrialists on the one hand, and between Wu and striking workers and communist organizers on the other, specificity of location is apparently no longer of significance. In chapters 13 through 16, for example, tense negotiations and confrontations take place at the factories, at the mansions of the industrialists, and in the slum area in which the workers live. In previous Shanghai novels, the exact geographical relationships between these three locations would have been quite explicit—it would even have been possible that a factory, a mansion, and a slum area could be located to particular blocks on a city map from the period, and likely that the reader would be given some sense of how to get from one location to the others. In *Midnight,* by contrast, we are left without much of a clue. Instead of specific addresses, we are given locations that have almost become typical rather than individual: The Factory, The Slum, and The Owner's Mansion. The primary system of reference is no longer geographical, but explicitly ideological, and the reader is appealed to not as a Shanghai resident or potential visitor but as a participant in the political conflict over China's future. This, of course, is one logical politicized extension of the increasing representation of Shanghai as "typical" of Chinese society as a whole that appears in narratives published in the 1920s like *Romance on Hu River* and *Shanghai Annals.*[37] The political space—a set of multiple arenas for conflict, tied to a set of narratives of what "the nation" needs to do, whether policy proposals or political lines—is designed to be detachable from its site of origin so that it can be mapped onto configurations developing in other cities and towns throughout the nation, itself a broader space in which the same policy proposals and political lines can struggle. The set of political stands is organized in a fashion that is analogous to the urban space analyzed in chapters 1 and 2 above: from the point of view of the narrator and the individual characters, there are moral valences to the set as a whole, as well as boundaries defining the set into discrete elements; those moral valences and boundaries are in turn materialized through the voyages of specific individuals from one point to another (political conversion experiences).[38] A similar transposition of the narrative dynamic into a more abstract and "universal" register is also key to the appropriation of Shanghai space by the modernist writers of this same period, as we will see in the second half of this chapter.

Modernist Literature: From the "Modern Girl" to Stream of Consciousness

Just as Mao Dun was beginning to convert "Shanghai" into an ideological space, other writers like Liu Na'ou, Shi Zhecun, and Mu Shiying were working to transform it into a psychological space. The modernist or "Shanghai-style" *(haipai)* shorter fiction that flourished from the late 1920s into the early 1940s differed in many ways from Mao Dun's *Midnight:* in the conception of the social function of literary texts, in the literary techniques used to create the texts, and finally in the choice of European and Japanese models the authors claimed as inspiration. But "Shanghai" as chronotope, a semantic field simultaneously spatial and temporal, still constitutes not only the condition under which the texts can be produced, but also the ultimate referent, the object that they are all in some way bound to depict.[39] Over the last two decades scholars have become especially interested in this modernist fiction and poetry, written and published for the most part in Shanghai; the fiction in particular is often referred to as "new sensationist" *(xin ganjue pai)* to emphasize its affiliation with the Japanese *shin kankaku ha* of the 1920s and early 1930s. Short stories written by Liu Na'ou, Mu Shiying, Shi Zhecun, Ye Lingfeng, and others are seen to reflect a new "modern" metropolis—a Shanghai of fast cars, bright lights, and newly independent women, where European and American influences have penetrated the urban culture to the extent that French and English words are scattered through stories set in the city, and urban narratives must display a new concern with the passage of time and with the inner or psychological life of their characters.[40] In their often persuasive attempts to mark off modernist fiction as a distinct phenomenon characteristic of the 1930s and 1940s, many scholars offer a set of stark distinctions between fiction of this period and narratives from the turn of the century, the 1910s, and even the early 1920s. Earlier fiction concerns itself primarily with space; modernist fiction is interested exclusively in time. Earlier fiction is journalistic and anecdotal, while the writers of modernist texts are storytellers who cause the reader to experience shock rather than merely reading about it.[41] Wu Fuhui goes so far as to liken the leisure culture of the late Qing, which grounds the earlier narratives, to "a beautifully adorned dead body that stinks," but comments that the leisure culture of the late 1920s and early 1930s, by contrast, is "enthusiastic, takes joy in life, and is full of energy."[42]

The simplicity of the binary terms in which these contrasts are staged is arresting. In suggesting that the earlier works represent a smooth continuation of a consistent tradition, while the later texts stage a rupture with and departure from that tradition that is absolutely without precedent, this approach reproduces the split between contemporary literature and all that went before that was central to May Fourth claims for texts in the early 1920s. In a recent critical reconsideration of the politics involved in modernist writing of the 1930s, Shu-mei Shih demonstrates the extent to which these texts rely on a bifurcation between metropolitan (Western and Japanese) texts and semicolonial practice in Shanghai—the former is valorized and the latter repressed. Yet even in this incisive and detailed critique, the "modern" and hybrid texts of the late 1920s and 1930s are contrasted implicitly with a tradition lacking in critical potential that can only be subverted.[43]

Such distinctions were not always so clear to writers at the time. Shen Congwen and Lu Xun, for example, identified the *haipai* or "Shanghai style" of the 1930s with the Mandarin Duck and Butterfly fiction of the 1910s and '20s, tracing a genealogy of "depraved" urban leisure texts back past May Fourth.[44] Writing in 1931, Zhou Leshan explained that he read the scandal columns of the newspaper as though they were installments of *Dreams of Shanghai Splendor,* showing that this work remained the standard against which a certain style of urban representation could be judged.[45] At a more "refined" level, Eileen Chang, considered one of the brightest stars of the modern/modernist canon, made clear her admiration for both *Lives of Shanghai Flowers* and *The Huangpu Tides,* ranking them as two of her favorite eight works of Chinese literature, and asserted that in writing *Lives of Shanghai Flowers* Han Bangqing "transcended his era and his cultural heritage" to produce a work that was "thoroughly modern and international." She even took Lu Xun and Hu Shi's assessment of *Lives of Shanghai Flowers'* style as "plain and natural" *(pingdan er jin ziran)* as a standard for her own writing.[46] Wu Fuhui argues that Eileen Chang, together with certain other writers of the 1940s, represents a special case in that, once "modern" writing of the 1930s had triumphed over "old-style" writing, later writers could return to "tradition" and selectively adapt techniques and tropes from it.[47] But this clear distinction between "modern" and "traditional" does not always hold up under close readings of the texts in question. As we shall see below, the connections between the Shanghai fiction discussed in the first five chapters of this book and the writings of Liu Na'ou, Shi Zhecun, and Mu Shiying are quite significant.

೪ৡ

This is not to say that those writers publishing in *Xiandai* (Les contemporains), *Wugui lieche* (Trackless trolley), and other literary magazines of the 1930s were not doing anything different. Indeed, as Yingjin Zhang has pointed out, they introduced new descriptive codes, defamiliarizing the cityscape by ignoring or reversing "logical" conventions of narrative description.[48] The very object of the narrator's gaze changes: as Shu-mei Shih explains, the commercialized cityscape itself is aestheticized and eroticized, appropriated as a scene worth describing in detail; the city is often also anthropomorphized with startling effect.[49] Although most scholars have focused on conventions taken from French and Japanese texts and Hollywood cinema, modernist writers also appropriated images and techniques from German film of the 1920s showing a particular fondness for the metropolitan decadence of Berlin and the films of UFA (Universumfilm Aktien Gesellschaft).[50] The resulting cosmopolitan look could be as bold as the cover of Liu Na'ou's *Dushi fengjing xian,* which presented the reader with the title in French *(Scène),* with floodlight beams shining from the "c" and each of the two "e"s in exactly the same way that floodlight beams shone from the "o" and the "e" in the advertising poster created by Mark Fleiss for Fritz Lang's 1928 silent film *Spione* (Spies) (figs. 8 and 9).

FIGURE 8 *Dushi fengjing xian* (Scène). Jacket illustration, 1929. Courtesy of Yomi Braester.

But beginning at the most superficial thematic level, we find immediate commonalities between modernist writings about the city and earlier Shanghai fiction: the city is presented as a space of movement or flow, bright lights, fast cars or carriages, consumption and excessive expenditure; everything is temporary at best, exhaustion follows on the heels of overstimulation, and the city is as dangerous as it is pleasurable.[51] Moving on to the authors and their theory and practice of literary production, we find them now as before preoccupied with finding means of representation that are adequate to the changing times, writing in gendered public spaces—then courtesan houses, now dance halls—about the nightlife found in those same places, exploring the literary dimensions of "intoxication" and its narrative effects, and understanding literature primarily as a form of leisure or entertainment (differing in this from the May Fourth writers).[52] Newspaper articles could serve as source material and as a format that lent itself to ironic reproduction; and even the periodicals that would eventually publish modernist writing often got their start as vehicles for Mandarin Duck and Butterfly fiction in the mid-to-late 1920s and continued to publish diverse texts through the 1930s.[53] Furthermore, if the development of modernist urban fiction from the late 1920s into the 1940s is juxtaposed with the changes in Shanghai installment fiction over the period 1890 to 1925, we see similar generic movement from the "public" to the "domestic." The carriage riding and teahouse carousing in *A Shanghai Swan's Traces in the Snow* contrasts with the plotlines in *The Huangpu Tides* that unfold for the most part inside private apartments; in related fashion, the hectic circulation of characters in Liu Na'ou and Mu Shiying's work in the 1930s is replaced by Eileen Chang and Yu Qie's more subtle focus on the everyday in the 1940s.[54] These similarities in theme, mode of publication, and generic development call for a reading of modernist fiction with specific reference to Shanghai installment fiction. In this section, I will focus in particular on three fields considered fundamental to modernist writing: gender—specifically the figure of the "modern girl"; language—the use of "foreign" vocabulary and grammatical structures; and interiority—stream-of-consciousness writing.

The Modern Girl

Scholars writing on the Shanghai modernists have been impressed by the "new woman" who appears in their fiction—a "product of the modern times" *(jindai de chanwu)* who enjoys speed and power and is both frank and sexually aggressive to an extent not found in most May Fourth fiction. This "new woman"—or "modern girl"—returns the male gaze and refuses to allow herself to be constituted as a passive object; instead she asserts her own autonomy and consciously or unconsciously poses a direct challenge to male authority and self-control.[55] The narrator in Mu Shiying's "Bei dangzuo xiaoqianpin de nanzi" (Men taken as leisure items) says to a female acquaintance, "Rongzi, what a modern girl, thriving on stimulation and speed! You are a mixture of *jazz*, machinery, speed, urban culture, American flavor, modern beauty," and Ye Lingfeng even represents the "modern girl" as a sports car.[56] (English words appearing in the original texts are given in italics.) One such "modern girl" criticizes a man who is interested in her for his slowness:

> Oh, you're really such a little kid. Who asked you to be so clumsy? Eating ice-cream, going for a walk, what a waste of time. Don't you know that *love-making* should be done in a car with the wind blowing by? There's green shady space for that outside the city. Hey, I've never spent more than three hours with a *gentleman*. This is an exception, you know.[57]

As Yingjin Zhang points out, however open the woman may be at first, these scenarios almost all end in the same way: "the unknown woman eventually vanishes from the exclusively male field of vision," reminding one of Benjamin's concept of "love at last sight" as a particularly urban delight.[58]

ℬ

Where does this "new woman" or "modern girl" come from? How does she relate to the historical and literary context in which she appears, 1930s Shanghai? Shu-mei Shih investigates the dynamics of the "modern girl" and her interactions with male characters and concludes that she is closely linked to Shanghai's semicolonial status. The identity of the "modern girl" is "ambivalent . . . no longer 'essentially' Chinese," owing a great deal instead to the image of the Hollywood actress, the women portrayed in the fiction of French writers like Paul Morand, and the "westernized *moga* [modern girl]" from Japan; this ambivalent identity, in turn, gives her a "surprising degree of autonomy and agency."[59] This transnational genealogy is quite convincing, but there is one more element that is of central significance. When the Shanghai reader encountered women who like to ride out to suburban areas for rendezvous, he or she would certainly have been reminded of Wu Chuyun and Du Sujuan in *Dreams of Shanghai Splendor*, Shen Xiaohong in *Lives of Shanghai Flowers*, Jiang Qiuyan and Hua Yu in *A Shanghai Swan's Traces in the Snow*, and so on. When the reader met women who enjoy speed for its own sake, Gao Xianglan and her friends (unmarried daughters of "proper" families), who tear around at top speed in hired carriages in *A Shanghai Swan's Traces in the Snow*, must have come to mind. When the woman in "Reqing zhi gu" (Passionate to the bone) suddenly demands cash from a man who has romanticized her, most readers would probably have thought back to the delicate dynamics of attraction and expenditure that govern so many of the relationships in Shanghai novels from the 1890s right up through the 1920s, from *Lives of Shanghai Flowers* to *Haishang huo diyu* (Living hell in Shanghai, 1929).[60] Indeed, for sheer verbal and physical aggressiveness, the "modern girl" would be hard pressed to match Du Sujuan, Xu Xingyun, Shen Xiaohong, and Wei Xiaxian, to name only a few of the most notorious female characters from late-Qing and early Republican-era fiction.[61]

The woman who invites pursuit but cannot be caught is a well-known modern trope; as such, we might expect her to differ strikingly from the women in turn-of-the-century Chinese fiction.[62] But a close reading of turn-of-the-century Shanghai novels reveals that the elusive woman was there as well: in *Lives of Shanghai Flowers* Zhao Puzhai thinks that he has secured the right to a relationship with Lu Xiubao, only to find that she has negotiated the sale of her virginity to another man; in *A Shanghai Swan's Traces in the Snow* Yan Huasheng and Xu Junmu are frustrated in their pursuit of women who at first seem interested; in *Dreams of Shanghai Splendor* and *The Huangpu Tides* courtesans opt out of "steady relationships" at will and wives may well abscond after marriage with all objects of value in the house.[63] There is an entire genre of fraudulent seduction in earlier fiction known as the "Immortal's Leap" *(xianren tiao),* in which a woman seems at first very interested in a man she encounters on the street; once the man is lured into her room and has taken off his clothes, the woman surreptitiously signals her "husband," and this partner in the swindle batters down the door and proceeds to extort a ransom from the naked man in return for not taking the case to court.[64] In modernist fiction, as in earlier novels, the reader is also drawn into the trap with the image of the accessible woman, and then frustrated at the last moment when the narrator does not follow through, showing that the "immortal's leap" functions just as well as narrative technique as it does as moneymaking scam. My aim here is not to contest the significance of changes in women's status as social practice in the first half of the twentieth century, but rather to indicate that the representations of unattainable and autonomous women that form a staple of modernist short fiction of the 1930s sold well to Shanghai readers in part because these readers had literally grown up on representations that were quite similar.

As Hu Ying has shown, May Fourth writers and critics reinforce the validity of their discourse of the "new woman"—a woman who is educated and to a certain extent able to think for herself—by critiquing or dismissing the received image of an educated woman, the *cainü.*[65] Similarly, I would argue, Shanghai writers in the 1930s found it necessary to highlight the "foreignness" and "modernity" of their creations—referring to them repeatedly as "products of the modern age" or "products of the metropolis," describing their physiques in terms perceived as "Western," giving them obtrusively "cosmopolitan" tastes in literature and music—in order to differentiate them from the women in earlier texts that they in fact resemble in important ways.[66] And indeed, a fascinating counterpoint to the discourse of the "modern girl" can be found in the retroactive construction of the "medieval maiden" *(zhongshiji sheng chunü)*, who appears in Mu Shiying's 1935 collection *Sheng chunü de ganqing* (Passions of the saintly maiden) and inspires a corresponding "medieval" male chivalry in Xu Xu's "Yinglun de wu" (England fog, 1947). While the "medieval maiden" may appear to be a conservative or reactionary impulse, deeply rooted in tradition—Wu Fuhui sees her figure as an attempt by modern writers to revive a certain "old-fashioned" or "rural" type from the past—I would suggest instead that she is just as much a "product of modern times" as the "modern girl."[67] No return to a perceived past is ever complete; in this case the very term itself, "medieval maiden," a Chinese product based on an imported word that in the source language already insists on its distance from the era to which it refers, clearly places the entire representational project under the sign of irony. The figuration by Chinese writers of "their own past" in terms borrowed from a "modern" European attempt to imagine its own genesis and development reminds us that for any reader who encounters modernist writers before reading urban fiction from previous decades, the earlier fiction may well "naturally" be located within a discourse of literary modernization that is colonial in origin and effect even as it may claim to question the colonial project.

Hybridity and Language

The choice of the linguistic field (or fields) in which a narrative unfolds is of crucial importance. Word choice, grammatical structure, inclusion or exclusion of regional idioms, differentiation between voices by class, and even the literal means by which the words are represented (the precise choice of a system of symbols to be printed on the page) are the axes according to which the linguistic field(s) of a narrative are constructed. In the first chapter, we saw that the early Shanghai novels were marked by a dispute over whether Chinese characters could be used in a way that differed from the northern standard (which had been the norm for earlier novels) to represent a specific regional linguistic identity. The very efficacy of this mode of written representation to constitute a regional literature with hundreds of thousands of readers elicited fierce condemnation and assertions of illegibility from authors and critics writing from a "national" position. By the late 1920s, the proposition that literature should properly be national was sufficiently entrenched that the viability of regional writing could be conveniently forgotten; in works by Mao Dun and modernist writers, there is almost no trace of "dialect literature." What does appear in the writings of the New Sensationists, however, is an idiom that strives toward the international and the transnational, rather than the national. This distinctive idiom consists of two primary elements: the inclusion of European words in the text written using the roman alphabet, and the introduction of unfamiliar grammatical structures that are, or seem to be, of foreign origin.

From the kinds of words written in the roman alphabet we can get a sense of their place within the modernist texts: "saxophone," "jazz," "carnal intoxication," "say it with flowers," "Riviera," "Venus," "ma chérie," "sportive," and so on.[68] The use of these words is often symptomatic: they operate from a privileged position in the text and convey a specific effect. In Ye Lingfeng's "Liuxing xing de ganmao" (A contagious cold, 1933), the narrator explains how he met a young woman named Zhenzi. He is looking into the window display at a bookstore that sells foreign books when a woman next to him suddenly reads one of the titles out loud, *Men without Women.* The narrator notes that her tone is challenging, and he responds by reversing the order of the words in the title to *Women without Men.* They flirt for a moment or two, she offers him her business card, and he invites her to cocoa. The Hemingway title—read aloud in the original English and reversed, sparks a "modern" romantic entanglement.[69] Words in English and French work in many of these stories as narrative catalysts—they are just as productive in this sense as theater and teahouse scenes were in earlier fiction; in other stories they serve as more subtle indicators of what is going on, even if the words themselves are not "responsible" for what ensues.[70]

In addition to the strategic use of words in the roman alphabet, modernist texts were known for their unusual sentence structure, ranging from very short sentences to very long ones, and intentionally "disjointed" syntax.[71] Critics of Liu Na'ou and Mu Shiying's style of writing found it to be "un-Chinese" (either Japanese or Western in feel), thereby reproducing Liu Na'ou's original characterization of Japanese New Sensationist writing as un-Japanese in flavor, carrying even in its country of origin "the aura of importation."[72] Liu Na'ou is a particularly important figure in this respect. He was educated in part in Japan and came to Shanghai to study French at Aurora University (Zhendan daxue).[73] Shi Zhecun once commented that Liu Na'ou originally wrote Chinese as though he were writing Japanese, which might suggest a certain correlation between Liu's ability to speak Chinese and his ability to write it; in other words, that the "Japanese influences" one can find in his writing reflected his own command of the Chinese language as a whole.[74] Yet another source notes that Liu had a genius for learning spoken dialects and could converse fluently not only in Mandarin and Shanghai dialect, but also in Cantonese, and even Xiamen dialect.[75] Since this fluency in dialect speech is not reproduced in his fiction, however, we may suppose that Liu Na'ou drew a clear distinction between oral conversation and literary composition, and that his "Japanese-influenced" written style was a deliberate choice; this alienation of the oral from the written suggests an avenue for the critical consideration of the "foreign" in the language of Shanghai modernist texts.

It might at first seem that the modernist idiom is a natural reflection of the polyglot Shanghai environment, an expression in writing of the "Yangjing bang" heteroglossia that characterized everyday spoken interaction in the city. An advertisement for *Scène* that appeared in 1930 recommends Liu Na'ou's syntax, word choice, and selection of topics in the following words: "The freshness of his style is unprecedented and best reflects our times."[76] As Wu Fuhui and Yu Xingmin, among others, have pointed out, a distinct dialect of English known as "Yangjing bang English" (after the creek that formed the southern boundary of the English Settlement) began to develop in the mid-nineteenth century and had its own vocabulary, grammar, and elaborate conventions by the beginning of the twentieth century. Yao Gonghe, writing in the 1910s, describes it as "a special kind of language, neither Chinese nor Western, that everyone in Shanghai knows."[77] While this language was no one's mother tongue and was considered corrupted and ungrammatical by educated Chinese and foreigners alike, it was indispensable to the city's daily functioning. Many expressions that originated as Yangjing bang English persist in Shanghai dialect vocabulary to this day, and Zhang Zhen has recently adapted "Yangjing bang" as a figure for the cultural production of early twentieth-century Shanghai in general, as a more nuanced alternative to the conventional designation *haipai* (Shanghai style).[78] The modernist idiom of the late 1920s and early 1930s was not, however, a simple reproduction of this linguistic interaction in written form; even the use of Yangjing bang spoken language as a metaphor for modernist writing can be misleading. The relationship between the everyday words spoken on the street and the language used by writers like Liu Na'ou, Mu Shiying, and Shi Zhecun is in fact dialectical; the latter specifically erases the former, literally writing it out of existence as it reaches instead toward a different cosmopolitan ideal.[79]

Yangjing bang English was not merely a spoken language; there were two distinct ways in which it was transcribed. Just as Suzhou and Shanghai dialect texts were written both in Chinese characters and in romanized form, so could Shanghai residents choose to represent Yangjing bang English either by appropriating standard characters for new phonetic uses, or through a new written syllabic system based on elements of certain Chinese characters that was used to transcribe Yangjing bang English phonetically.[80] But these kinds of written representation are nowhere to be found in modernist writings. The vocabulary and grammatical structures peculiar to Yangjing bang English are suppressed, as are the characteristic features of Shanghai dialect itself; they are replaced in these texts by English and French words in the roman alphabet and grammatical structures heavily influenced by written Japanese, English, and French (which had a much more limited audience than phonetic appropriations and Yangjing bang grammar would have had). Woven into the very fabric of these texts is a denial of Shanghai's generative capacities both as a regional city and as a specifically hybrid place; in their place is a claim to an elitist transnational space. Is it an accident that modernist fiction should gain newly appreciative audiences now, in an age fascinated again with the international, the transnational, and "globalization"?

As I have shown in the first chapter, the politics of "nonstandard" writing form an important dimension of earlier Shanghai novels like *Lives of Shanghai Flowers, A Shanghai Swan's Traces in the Snow,* and *Romance on Hu River,* helping to construct the regional audience as a social group and also to position Shanghai as a *national* media center, able to mediate the regionalisms of north and south. Similarly, the use of words and grammatical structures perceived as "purely foreign" by Liu Na'ou, Mu Shiying, and others appealed to a specific audience of readers who defined themselves in part by their relation to "the West." Shu-mei Shih identifies a general "strategy of bifurcation" through which these authors attempted to separate metropolitan culture (desirable) from colonial (local) culture (undesirable) and "self-consciously sought *not* to take the colonial reality into consideration." As Shi Zhecun remarked in an interview with Shih in 1990:

> As for myself, I was influenced by the texts of Western culture rather than Shanghai's colonial culture. Colonial influence was limited to those Shanghai writers who did not know Western languages, hence when they wrote modernist fiction they often gave themselves away.[81]

This general bifurcation must have been an important motivation for the repression of actual Shanghai dialect and Yangjing bang English in the works of Shanghai modernist writers—note the emphasis Shi placed on the knowledge of Western languages. The suppression of the local polyglot speech even as the claim is made that it is represented has a further history specific to Shanghai: in earlier Shanghai fiction, the adoption of conventional standards for the writing of Wu dialect speech in effect erased the many other dialects heard in Shanghai at the time, including Shanghai local dialect, Pudong dialect, and Ningbo dialect, not to mention Yangjing bang English. In both cases, the move away from a national standard language—toward a regional standard in one case, toward a transnational ideal in the other—yields significant aesthetic benefits for the reader who is appropriately prepared. But these texts do not, ultimately, provide a representation of Shanghai "reality" that is more "true" than even the works that are least linguistically adventurous. To the extent that the coherent and mutually exclusive linguistic identities produced in these texts find ready audiences, the full specificity and complexity of the territory in which they are produced is denied.

Narrative "Flow"

Like *Midnight* and all the Shanghai novels before it, modernist fiction in the 1930s was fascinated with the narrative production of specific urban spaces. Locations—whether racetracks, theaters, dance halls, or parks—are referred to by name, and protagonists are frequently portrayed in motion along carefully laid-out itineraries through the metropolis, reinforcing or challenging economic, moral, and semantic hierarchies.[82] Rather than rehearse these external spatial markers and itineraries at length, this final section explores the ways in which an urban space is transformed into space that is "fundamentally interior," the individual consciousness. Yingjin Zhang identifies "flow" as a key characteristic of modernist urban fiction—not only the flow of time, but also the movement of city crowds, traffic, and even the protagonist's stream of consciousness.[83] This sense of flow and circulation of course recalls the discourse of productive and dangerous leisure found in Shanghai texts as early as the 1870s, in which time, money, even one's very spirit can melt away, joining into a general movement that can be healthful or destructive depending on one's point of view.[84] The sense of rapid flow that one may take away from these texts is, however, a construction that is made possible only through the persistent inclusion of its "opposite"—stops, breaks, and sudden shifts.

Shi Zhecun's story "Zai Bali da xiyuan" (At the Paris Cinema) is a prime example of the discontinuities inherent in this rapid "flow"; it begins with a jump straight into the consciousness of the narrator and keeps up the dizzying pace for more than ten pages:

> What, is she actually shoving forward to buy the tickets herself? This puts me
> to shame, isn't this guy looking at me, this bald-headed Russian? This woman
> also has her eyes fixed squarely on my face! Yes, and this guy puffing on a
> cigar, he's looking at me now as well. They're all looking at me. Well, all right,
> I know what they're thinking. They're a little bit contemptuous of me, no,
> more than that, I think they are actually sneering at me. I don't know why on
> earth she had to insist on buying the tickets? . . . Surely she must know what
> an awkward spot this puts me in? I am a man, a gentleman—and whoever
> saw a man escort a lady (a "lady" of whatever degree) to the cinema, and the

lady going up to buy the tickets? Never; I've never seen such a thing. My face feels hot, it's probably gone very red. Isn't there a mirror around here? If there is one, I'll look at myself in it. Oh! This guy is actually laughing openly at me! How dare you mock me? Surely you must have seen her lunge suddenly toward the ticket window. I couldn't stop her, how could I? I wasn't prepared for this, who could have anticipated such a thing? Oh, I can't take it, I want to turn around and go out the door, let me just stand outside on the steps for a while.[85]

The story continues in this vein, with each of the woman's occasional brief comments or gestures setting off lengthy and absurd reflection by the male narrator in a new and different direction. It is important to note that the flow in these stories is not continuous and unidirectional.[86] The stream of consciousness is for the most part punctuated, as there is no time for prolonged reveries. Breaks in the flow come in two varieties. First, the outside world suddenly impinges on the narrator's psychological state, as, for example, when T interrupts H's walk with a "modern woman" in Liu Na'ou's "Liangge shijian de bu ganzheng zhe" (Two who weren't in tune with time), or when a woman the narrator is accompanying suddenly announces that the rain has stopped in Shi's "Meiyu zhi xi" (One rainy evening).[87] A second, and more significant, kind of break or change in direction comes when the narrator him or herself switches from one theme to another, abruptly changing mental trajectories while maintaining complete self-absorption. These breaks may occur more than once in the same sentence—I find six in the paragraph quoted above. They are in fact the elements that in the aggregate give the reader a sense of flow, whether smooth or turbulent, from one topic to the next to the next. No thought is ever fully complete, because the next has always begun to claim the protagonist's attention before the last can come to an end.

Indeed, we find in these texts some of the same rapid and disorienting narrative shifts, and the same demand for hermeneutic reading to decode what is going on, that was characteristic of even the earliest Shanghai novels. Abrupt breaks in the narrative appeared first as a deliberate aesthetic in *Lives of Shanghai Flowers*, then as a quality enforced by page-a-day serialization at the turn of the century, and now they return as an aesthetic choice. The difference lies in the projection of the metropolitan landscape and its consequent narrative mode onto the subjectivity of the urban characters. While narratives continue to move briskly about Shanghai in the external narrative portions, they also jump about within the characters' minds, progressing in fits and starts, always interrupted and subject to delay and misdirection. The ending of "At the Paris Cinema," like many other stories of this period, is abrupt, with the narrator informing us that the woman took her own taxi rather than allowing him to accompany her. But just as we are ready to conclude that she will never want to see him again, he tells us that she asked him to meet tomorrow to go to Fanwangdu Park. The train of thought moves from one track to the next, and final destinations are often hinted at but rarely, if ever, reached. Resolution is provided not by a neat tying up of all the different narrative threads that the reader is busy piecing together, but rather by a sudden end to the text itself.

By emphasizing psychological interiority as a field within which narrative could move, or to put it slightly differently, by constructing subjectivity as a space within which a story could be told, Shi Zhecun and Liu Na'ou elaborated upon the internal monologues that began to appear in May Fourth fiction of the early 1920s. This elaboration consists of a narrative inversion of urban space, bringing us back to *Lives of Shanghai Flowers* and its successors, which write the city as a space of narrative "lines" as early as the 1890s in a fashion precisely analogous to later stream-of-consciousness narrative. Again in the 1930s, the dynamics of delay, displacement, juxtaposition, and sudden termination determine the very structure of the Shanghai narrative. The modernist representation of an individual character's consciousness in these stories depends on a folding over of the established cityscape and its vectors of (interrupted) movement around an empty center; the space created within this fold becomes a privileged "interior consciousness" that is dynamically structured as a narrative arena.[88] Yet the importance of this fold in modernist writing of the 1930s reminds us that the interiorization of the cityscape was anticipated in nineteenth-century guidebooks as well as in most of the early Shanghai novels, through the location of Shanghai within a dream.[89] There is a dream sequence early in *Dreams of Shanghai Splendor* that prefigures the arc of the narrative as a whole; *Shadows of Shanghai's Dusty Skies* locates the possibility of its own genesis in a dream; one character ends *A Shanghai Swan's Traces in the Snow* just as he wakes from a dream; and in *Lives of Shanghai Flowers,* the narrative begins with a dream by the narrator and ends with Zhao Erbao's sudden awakening from a nightmare.[90] In the latter two cases, the narrative cannot proceed beyond this moment of waking, leaving the reader with the impression that all that has gone before is nothing but a dream; the representation of the city is bounded in the end by the limits of an individual's consciousness.

Conclusion

Mu Shiying's "Shanghai de hubuwu" (Shanghai foxtrot, 1934) also ends with an awakening, but here the blast of factory horns startles the entire city, not just a single individual ("Shanghai has woken up!")[91] In this story we find a special variety of the narrative movement discussed above; as pointed out by Leo Lee, part of the story is constructed in circular fashion.[92] In addition to the dynamics of return created through the repetition, with slight alterations, of several paragraphs at the heart of the story, more concrete evocations of circular movement appear in words and phrases scattered through the text, a circularity and repetition that Yingjin Zhang ties to a new temporalization of urban narrative.[93] This temporal circularity reminds us in turn of the endless circuits in carriages around town that form such an important part of the narrative in earlier Shanghai novels. Repetition and return are not only dynamics of interiority, but also movements that inscribe semantic, ethical, and ritual boundaries in urban space. This attention to "external" ritual and ethical boundaries re-surfaces in "Shanghai Foxtrot," where the incessant circularity of the text is tied closely to an incestuous relationship between a young man and his stepmother (the text informs us that "legally" *(zai falü shang)* she is his father's wife, even though, given her age, she should be the father's daughter-in-law).[94] Two terms mediate—go between—circular motion and ethical/ritual inscription in this story. The first is the form of the music itself *(xuanlü)*. Through its codified order *(lü)*, musical form refers back to ritual and the "legal" relationship between the father and stepmother; through the first character of the compound, *xuan,* as well as through the frequent juxtaposition of *xuanlü* in this story with words like *rao,* the figure of the music is indissolubly bound to circular motion. It is only while dancing the waltz—that is, moving around to music—that one is able to make certain declarations of emotion that are privileged, yet also ritual. Secondly, and more abstractly, the word *xunli* (pilgrimage, or tour of inspection) is introduced by the narrator to refer to three moments: gambling, an encounter with wild chicken prostitutes on the street, and the dance hall.[95] Again, not only does the concept of the pilgrimage or tour at the abstract level (a departure, a voyage to a destination, a return—a sequence frequently repeated over time) render these moments circular, so does the specific composition of the term—the first character, *xun,* signifying circular movement while the second character, *li,* refers the reader to any number of discourses of ethical/ritual production.[96]

This movement around—*xun*—figures as well in the term for Settlement and Concession police, *xunbu,* linking the senses of ritual production in "Shanghai Foxtrot" to the obsessive walking of the beat and the technologized administrative regime of the concessions. No matter how seductive it may be, this circulation and inscription ultimately proves futile. The police are unable to penetrate the surface of the city, the merrymakers dancing in nightclubs or riding around in carriages at night wake up pale and hungover, and Yan

Ruyu wanders, gesturing madly with her thumb and forefinger in the shape of a circle, reminding us of her life spent in the failed pursuit of wealth.

࿇

Midnight, Scène, "Shanghai Foxtrot," and other similar works are generally agreed to be "modern"; *Lives of Shanghai Flowers* and other Shanghai install-ment fiction, from *Dreams of Shanghai Splendor* to *The Huangpu Tides* and beyond, are often thought to exist on the far side of the divide between the modern and "tradition." Yet we see already in the 1890s and early 1900s, at a moment when "the modern" as such is not yet an explicit intellectual concern, that its supposed symptoms inhabit the very form of the earlier fiction: ever-increasing speed, complexity, and expansion; rapid and disorienting movement from one interrupted narrative to another; the domestication of desire into something approaching addiction; and the contrast between radical simulta-neity and the feeling of always somehow being a step behind. Together with the parallels and connections drawn in this chapter, these symptoms suggest that categorical distinctions between one set of narratives and the other owe as much to the rhetoric of cultural modernity and its need to distance self from "other" as they do to close readings of the texts in question.

Given the repression of the "past" that constitutes the modernist project, a neat genealogy of influence confined to the texts—text A acting on text A' and text B acting on text B'—is generally not an option.[97] Instead, this book looks more broadly to the dialectic between text and social practice, in which earlier works establish the necessary conditions for production of later works—con-ditions that may be reified into individual components such as "readers' tastes and expectations," "urban textual traditions," "author's interests and moti-vations," "capacity of the Shanghai print industry," and even "what tourists do when they come to the big city." (Of course, the very distinction between "text" and "social practice" is highly variable and must also be historicized; it is presented here as a heuristic device or a kind of shorthand.) Insofar as "1930s Shanghai" was a historical moment produced in part by Shanghai in-stallment fiction of the 1890s through the 1930s as I have suggested in chapters 1 through 5, we can argue for an intensely mediated but nonetheless relevant connection in addition to any intertextual links that would satisfy a more re-strictive reading.

My aim has not been to argue for the "modernity" of the Shanghai novel as a genre, nor to imply on the other hand that timeless qualities of a static and reified Chinese urban culture persist in certain genres of Chinese litera-ture throughout time. I am, rather, interested in demonstrating that even as "Shanghai" was radically transposed into ideological or psychological textual effects in the work of Mao Dun and the New Sensationists respectively, the associated narrative complex continues to function, and the city itself continues to be understood as a "fast, noisy, vibrating whirlpool that draws everybody under its spell."[98] My intention is not to redraw the line marking the "onset of literary modernity," but rather to suggest that any such line can only be a post hoc construction by a certain reader in his or her specific moment, no more valid in its linearity and simplicity than the filiations through time and lines of descent that it cuts across and works to deny.

CHAPTER 7

Lineages of the Contemporary and the Nostalgic

In a hardware store in Chinatown which also sells radios and watches I found some old books. These were all published thirty or forty years ago. They were wrapped up in paper, identified by titles written on with a brush, and stacked horizontally on the shelves. I wonder for how many years they had been left untouched—they were all covered with dust. The sight of these books [*Dreams of Shanghai Splendor* and *The Huangpu Tides,* among others] makes me feel as if Chinese history stopped right there.
—T. A. Hsia, Seattle, July 4, 1959*

T. A. Hsia's diasporic literary archaeology highlights a persistent trope in the reception of Shanghai installment fiction from the May Fourth era forward: we must "excavate" or otherwise rescue texts that have fallen into obscurity and brush off the layers of dust that stand between them and later audiences. Whether this dusting takes the form of an enthusiastic preface to a 1920s reprint edition, a letter to one's brother teaching in the United States, a "translation" of dialect portions into standard Mandarin in the 1970s and English in the years to follow, or imaginative adaptations of the form to new locales and the content to new forms and new technologies at the turn of the twenty-first century, it cannot be avoided. Insistent on their contemporaneity at the moment that they first appear, these texts are now enjoyed primarily in a mode that is intensely nostalgic.

It would be a mistake, however, to suppose that this nostalgic mode is exclusively backward-looking, repetitive, and unproductive. As Svetlana Boym points out, nostalgia can be prospective as well as retrospective.[1] This chapter examines the return of Wu dialect writing in the 1920s and its significance for May Fourth writers and critics, Eileen Chang's attempts to find new audiences for *Lives of Shanghai Flowers* in the 1970s and '80s, and Hou Hsiao-hsien's cinematic experiment, *Haishang hua* (Flowers of Shanghai, 1998), aiming to sketch out an analytic of nostalgia that takes into account the significance of transitivity, repetition, and nostalgia's complex relationship with the contemporary. Specifically, this chapter investigates the conditions under which the nostalgic look back becomes anticipatory and the concrete aesthetic characteristics through which this shift is articulated.

Dialects and Gardens

As noted in chapter 1, dialogue in Wu dialect was introduced in Han Bangqing's 1892 novel *Lives of Shanghai Flowers,* and was soon taken up by other writers of Shanghai fiction. From his preface to *Lives of Shanghai Flowers,* it is clear that Han Bangqing saw the use of Suzhou vernacular in a novel as an important innovation. Use of the vernacular is completely logical, and even necessary to the work, but Han compares it playfully to Cang Jie's mythical invention of writing to emphasize its lack of precedent. The use of Suzhou vernacular also combines with new approaches to the scope of the novel, the presentation of city space and time, and a narrative aesthetic of interruption, making it an integral part of an endeavor that is presented as fundamentally and self-consciously new. Fifteen years later, in *The Nine-tailed Turtle,* this set of associations remained important; the fashionable and up-to-date courtesans who speak in Wu dialect, while their "country cousins" in other cities make do with the northern vernacular. By the 1910s, however, Wu dialect dialogue had fallen into almost complete disuse; it does not appear in any of the notable works of the period—*New Shanghai, Dreams of Shanghai Splendor Continued,* or *The Huangpu Tides.*

When dialogue in Wu dialect reappeared a decade later in Xu Qinfu's *Hujiang fengyue zhuan* (Romance on Hu River, 1921), it was part of a very different complex of associated characteristics. To begin with, the title of this novel refers to Shanghai as "Hu," which no previous Shanghai novel had done. This usage was common in guidebooks and travel writing of the 1870s to 1890s, but by the early 1900s, it had yielded to the more straightforward "Shanghai." Instead of giving the title a "new" flavor, then, this new usage points the reader backwards, linking the title with late nineteenth-century guidebooks rather than with the other Shanghai novels that appeared in the 1910s and 1920s. The rest of the title, "a tale of wind and moon" (*fengyue zhuan*), reinforces the archaism with its evocation of "romantic" evening scenes, preparing us for a novel that deliberately distances itself from the contemporary city. *Romance on Hu River*'s choice of narrative technique further strengthens the nostalgic sense: a close look at the texture of the narrative reveals more commonalities with earlier works in the genre like *Lives of Shanghai Flowers* and *A Shanghai Swan's Traces in the Snow* than with the roughly contemporaneous *The Huangpu Tides.* At the same time, however, there is a slight difference in its presentation of dialogue in dialect. While all dialogue in earlier Shanghai fiction was given in Wu dialect, *Romance on Hu River* marks the gender distinctions that had since become associated with dialect. It uses Wu dialect for all dialogue between men and women, and among women themselves, while using northern vernacular to represent the voices of male characters speaking among themselves.[2]

Romance on Hu River seems to have attracted enough reader interest that Xu Qinfu decided to arrange a major reprint edition of *Lives of Shanghai Flowers* just one year later through the same publisher (Qinghua shuju); Xu also wrote a preface for the reprint. It was this reprint edition that quickly caught the attention of two key May Fourth critics, Hu Shi and Liu Fu, leading in turn to the well-known 1926 Yadong tushuguan reprint of *Lives of Shanghai Flowers,* with their prefaces attached. Xu's nostalgic project therefore resulted not only in an evocation of the mood of previous works, but eventually, in the literal resurrection of the first example of the genre in reprint form, with the enthusiastic backing of two prominent intellectuals.

⁊ə

Lives of Shanghai Flowers' return to print in the early 1920s was greeted with excitement by Liu Fu and Hu Shi because these writers had already given some thought to the question of how exactly a new Chinese literary language, and more broadly, a new literature, could be created. Liu Fu was among the foremost advocates of "folk" and "regional" culture(s) as a crucial source of material for the construction of a new, vital language, and *Lives of Shanghai Flowers,* which he praised as "a representative work of Wu dialect literature," fit into this project nicely.[3] Though less consistently committed to "folk" culture than Liu Fu, Hu Shi was also enthusiastic about the role he envisioned for *Lives of Shanghai Flowers* in the construction of a new literature, ending remarks titled "*Lives of Shanghai Flowers* is the first masterpiece of Wu dialect literature" with the following words:

> We take the publication of this reedited version of *Lives of Shanghai Flowers* very seriously. We hope that the reappearance of this innovative work . . . will win the attention of writers who speak Wu dialect and that they will continue to develop this already mature trend toward Wu dialect literature. If this masterpiece of dialect literature can inspire writers from other areas to create a variety of such literatures, and if these literatures continue to provide China's New Literature with new material, new blood, and new life, then Han [Bangqing] and his *Lives of Shanghai Flowers* truly can be said to have given a new appearance to Chinese literature.[4]

One cannot fail to notice that the word "new" appears no fewer than five times in the last two clauses of the last sentence. The stated aim here of reprinting *Lives of Shanghai Flowers* is to give writers a second chance to join in an innovative project—a project that will, Hu Shi supposes, play a crucial role in the May Fourth era.

ဖြ

If Hu Shi and Liu Fu's prefaces to the 1926 reprint edition reveal a firm conviction that *Lives of Shanghai Flowers* deserved readers' attention and could enrich the new vernacular literature that was just starting to be written, Eileen Chang's preface and postface to her "translation" of this work into Mandarin—first printed in installments in the late 1970s and then in a volume edition in 1983—take a much more pessimistic view. Citing Hu Shi's designation of *Lives of Shanghai Flowers* as the "first masterpiece of Wu dialect literature," Chang goes on to identify it also as the last. She claims that it had disappeared from sight by the early Republican period, to be revived briefly in the 1922 and 1926 reprint editions, but by the late 1970s these editions had become extremely rare. In an attempt to remedy what she understands to be the sad neglect of the original 1890s editions and the 1920s reprints, Chang translates all the Wu dialect of the original into Mandarin. Her hope is that easing access to the work for readers outside the Wu dialect region will allow it to escape its bittersweet reputation as a "lost masterpiece."[5] She is none too optimistic, however, writing in the postface of her fear that "readers will for a third time abandon *Shanghai Flowers.*"[6]

Integral to the nostalgic lineage as Eileen Chang understands it is the sense that if *Lives of Shanghai Flowers* can be brought back from oblivion, it will be through the assistance of a related or supplementary text. The publication of *Romance on Hu River* broke ground for Xu Qinfu's reprint of *Lives of Shanghai Flowers;* similarly, it was Hu Shi's preface to the novel, reprinted in his collected works, that inspired a teenage Eileen Chang to go in search of the reprint edition in which it originally appeared.[7] Chang's translation can be understood to serve a similar purpose; in addition to keeping the novel in print in altered form, it may engage some readers intensely enough that they will decide to seek out the original, Wu dialect and all. The importance of Eileen Chang's own popularity in reviving interest in *Lives of Shanghai Flowers* in the 1980s and early 1990s Taiwan and Hong Kong cannot be ignored; as "Eileen Chang fever" swept through these audiences, the reissue of *Lives of Shanghai Flowers* in an Eileen Chang translation, in contexts such as the *Zhang Ailing quanji* (Collected works of Eileen Chang), was of real significance. Just as Hu Shi's preface had introduced Chang to the work in the 1930s, it is highly likely that the success of her serialized "translation" in the late 1970s and early 1980s influenced Guiguan's decision to reprint the Yadong tushuguan edition in 1983. As we will see later in this chapter, Chang's version of *Lives of Shanghai Flowers* becomes a crucial step toward Chu T'ien-wen and Hou Hsiao-hsien's 1998 film version of the novel.

As I have shown previously, however, Hu Shi, Liu Fu, and Eileen Chang radically underestimated the degree to which *Lives of Shanghai Flowers* and other Wu dialect fiction was popular not only in the 1890s, but even into the 1910s and '20s. *Lives of Shanghai Flowers* inspired multiple reprint editions, sequels, and enthusiastic mentions in prefaces to other Shanghai fiction during this period. *Lives of Shanghai Flowers* may not have reached the levels of popularity enjoyed by *Flower in a Sea of Sin* or *Jade Pear Spirit*, the two best-selling original novels in the early twentieth century, but it continued to circulate among a broader set of readers all too often overlooked or discounted by May Fourth-era intellectuals well into the 1930s.[8] Furthermore, as shown in the previous chapter, Shanghai installment fiction served as an important, though unacknowledged, ground for *Midnight* and New Sensationist fiction. Finally, although *Lives of Shanghai Flowers* and other Shanghai fiction most likely did not enjoy wide circulation in the People's Republic in the 1950s, '60s, and '70s, the 1983 Guiguan reprint edition was actually preceded by a February 1982 Renmin wenxue chubanshe reprint of the original 1894 volume edition of the novel, as part of the "Zhongguo xiaoshuo shiliao congshu" (Collectanea of materials for the history of Chinese fiction) project. This 30,000 copy reprinting, most certainly not inspired by *Lives of Shanghai Flowers'* importance to Eileen Chang, was followed three years later by a 100,000 copy run, as well as by numerous others over the last two decades. As I noted in chapter 1, it is in fact likely that reprints of the original Wu dialect version of the novel now sell at least as well as Eileen Chang's translated version, despite the fame of the latter.

ℰℛ

Novels of the 1920s hark back to *Lives of Shanghai Flowers* not only in the renewed use of Wu dialect, but also, in the case of Wumu shanren's *Haishang Daguan yuan* (Shanghai's Great Prospect Garden, 1924), in a return to the private garden as a privileged kind of quasi-urban space. *Shanghai's Great Prospect Garden* is perhaps the most unusual Shanghai narrative of the 1920s: it tells the story of a foreign merchant named "Hantong" and his Chinese wife, their cooperative effort to become rich, and the garden that she built with some of the proceeds. In the preface and opening pages, there is concern with the ontological status of the story itself that brings the reader back to courtesan fiction of the mid-nineteenth century, with its playful use of dreams and myths as framing devices.[9] The story is related to a young man in installments by a mysterious older man: each night, when the young man falls asleep, the old man appears and takes up where he left off the previous night. The narrator, in turn, copies down each dream installment the next morning, accumulating a sizable manuscript almost without noticing it. It is this manuscript, revised and edited, that is offered to the reader. In this *telling* in installments, which replaces *publication* in installments, *Shanghai's Great Prospect Garden* recalls *Traces of Flowers and the Moon,* a courtesan novel published more than four decades earlier that foregrounded the circumstances under which its story was told in parts, thereby functioning as a kind of substrate to the phenomenon of installment publication.[10]

Wu Guilong, among others, has pointed out the extensive parallels between this novel and the story of real estate and opium dealers Silas Hardoon (1847–1931) and his wife that can be reconstructed from contemporary historical sources.[11] At the same time, *Shanghai's Great Prospect Garden* refers the reader back to an extensive lineage of garden narratives, including most prominently *Dream of the Red Chamber* and *Shadows of Shanghai's Dusty Skies,* and, to a lesser extent, the garden section in *Lives of Shanghai Flowers.* More than any other novel set in Shanghai in the late Qing and Republican periods, *Shanghai's Great Prospect Garden* rejects the relational space and the urban street system, focusing instead on a smaller and more clearly demarcated space of wonder in a way that recalls Ying-shih Yü's analysis of the "two worlds" in *Dream of the Red Chamber.*[12]

What we will discover, however, is that this representation of the garden as spatially and temporally removed from the rest of the city is also an attempt to recuperate the earlier narratives, to supplement what they lacked. Like the discourses glorifying courtesans of yesteryear that also flourished in the 1920s, it is no coincidence that this narrative, in contrast to other Shanghai fiction, is explicitly set in the past.[13] *Shanghai's Great Prospect Garden* is in fact a clear attempt to reconstruct the figure of the garden in Shanghai fiction, just as other texts aim to rework the language or the subject matter of Shanghai fiction.

To understand this reconstruction project, we must take a closer look at the different kinds of public and semipublic spaces known as *yuan* (gardens or parks) in late nineteenth- and early twentieth-century Shanghai. As pointed out in the introduction, the infamous Public Garden on the Bund was in fact one of the less important parks in the city. It does not register in any significant way in Shanghai fiction, whose typical park scenes include Shen Xiaohong's violent attack on Zhang Huizhen in Bright Garden, and the showdown between the carriage drivers and actors summoned by rival courtesans in Zhang's Garden, in which the importance of conflict as spectacle is revealed.[14] Parks like Zhang's Garden and Fool's Garden had stages on which male and female theatrical troupes performed, and fireworks displays often drew large crowds as well;[15] but the greatest show to be seen consisted of the "real" theatrics and figurative fireworks resulting from frustrated desire. The park was a prime locus of spectacular conflict due to its character as space both "public" and "private," with a guaranteed audience. Like the late twentieth-century American shopping mall, parks were privately owned and run as profitable businesses, and their owners had an incentive to maintain a certain degree of order by hiring park attendants and calling on the police when necessary. Physical conflicts in the park were less likely to result in substantial property damage than those that took place in a courtesan house; at the same time, the certainty that *excessive* violence would be quickly controlled by foreign policemen may well have made parks a preferred arena for confrontations engaged within understood limits and according to unspoken rules of conduct. In this connection, it is also worth noting that although rallies and political meetings held in parks do not appear in Shanghai fiction, these spaces nonetheless were key venues for early twentieth-century protest activities, as Meng Yue has shown in detail.[16]

ℬ

Despite the general emphasis on spaces open to all who could pay the entrance fees, more secluded gardens also have an important function in the Shanghai novel. The garden, unlike the park, is often posed as a refuge from the exigencies of life in the public world, both as a refined spot to escape the "vulgar" *(su)* commodity culture assumed to be characteristic of Shanghai and as a literal refuge for courtesans and their lovers who are threatened by some person outside the garden walls. This dual sense of the garden as refuge and space charged with romantic potential clearly draws heavily on the image of the garden in *Mudan ting* (Peony pavilion) and *Dream of the Red Chamber,* and it also reflects the rhetorical erasure of the garden's commercial aspects typical of other Ming and Qing texts. Yet it is noteworthy that the presentation of gardens in early Shanghai novels is frequently, if not primarily, ironic.[17]

Xu's Garden (Xu yuan), known for its flower displays, is one such garden. In the final chapter of *Dreams of Shanghai Splendor,* the farewell banquet for Zhen Minshi, the idealized scholar who is versed in both Chinese and Western learning, guests happen to notice Wen Miaoxiang, a "reformed" courtesan, who is dressed soberly and quietly enjoying the sights with her new husband.[18] In chapter 46 of the same novel, Xie You'an uses the occasion of a chrysanthemum contest held at Xu's Garden to form a poetry society, in an attempt to spend his leisure time in a more refined fashion. Only the more poetically inclined of his friends are invited, and they tour the garden at a leisurely pace, enjoying the sights and then writing poems about the chrysanthemums in an evident reference to the chrysanthemum poetry-writing scene in *Dream of the Red Chamber*. Yet this brief moment of calm does not last: its interruption is played for laughs as word comes that Qian Shouyu, their bumbling traveling companion from Suzhou, has gotten himself into trouble with gamblers in Hongkou.

In fact the reader is never allowed to forget the outside world against which these garden spaces are constituted. Also a Garden (Yeshi yuan) appears early in *Dreams of Shanghai Splendor* as one of the "less worldly locations" *(qingjing zhi di)* that Du Shaomu is taken to by Xie You'an in an attempt to distract him from his involvement with Wu Chuyun.[19] But by chapter 19 Du is using it as a safe haven in which to discuss strategy with Jing Yingzhi as they plan their retaliation against Pan Shao'an, who has made fools of them both by carrying on with their "steady" courtesans. It is also in chapter 19 that we learn that until recently Also a Garden had been a lively space for urban recreation: before the civil disorder of the 1850s and 1860s courtesan houses were located nearby and the crowds there resembled those now to be found in Zhang's Garden. After the courtesan houses moved to the concessions, Also a Garden was essentially deserted for a few years, but in the mid-Tongzhi period (the late 1860s) a doubleblossomed lotus bloomed in the pond, attracting large numbers of sightseers. After that Also a Garden gradually regained its popularity. The Daoist in charge of upkeep began to sell tea to supplement his salary and was doing quite well until a local official petitioned to have the operation shut down on the grounds that such a refined location should not resemble a collection of teahouses at a market. With the prohibition against selling tea in effect, the garden is again nearly deserted.[20]

As we have seen in chapter 1, *Dreams of Shanghai Splendor* cites the rhetoric of Shanghai's "foreign origin" in its opening pages, only to challenge that very rhetoric in its closing chapters. Similarly, the novel aims to enlighten us about the nature of public and private spaces in Shanghai, setting up an opposition between the chaos and noise of public parks and the quiet of secluded gardens only to question its validity by revealing the extent to which gardens were sites of struggle and of the active assertion of the literati ideal by exclusion, rather than locations with an unbroken tradition of "refined" elite activities.[21]

The private garden that commands the most textual attention in early Shanghai novels is Qi Yunsou's Bamboo Hat Garden on Bubbling Well Road, which appears in *Lives of Shanghai Flowers*. In this family-owned garden we find rockeries, ponds, refined architecture, poetry circles and intellectual riddles, sworn sisterhoods, and even little actresses, reminding the reader inevitably of the garden in *Dream of the Red Chamber*.[22] It seems a world apart from the downtown atmosphere that prevails in the city proper; one merchant asks with evident apprehension about what is expected of him when he receives an invitation to a gathering there: will he have to compose poetry?[23] The garden is a space in which young lovers can express their attachment to each other, as well as a place for courtesans pursued by unpleasant clients to hide. For this reason, critics have tended to see the garden portions of *Lives of Shanghai Flowers* as inferior or even extraneous to the greater part of the novel set in the city streets.[24] A common objection is that these portions represent a stereotyped vision of the garden drawn from *Dream of the Red Chamber* and other earlier works; they are filled with idealized portrayals of the author's heroes and do not fit with the tone of the work as a whole.

Yet to read the garden as an idealized refuge and to take its denizens as wish-fulfilling projections is to ignore the pervasive irony that inflects any claim that this space might make to transcend the pettiness of the world outside its walls. It is notable that though the garden is frequently offered as a haven (e.g., in chapter 41, to Zhu Shuren and the courtesan Zhou Shuangyu; in chapters 43 and 44, to the sensitive young man Tao Yufu; in chapters 45 and 50, to Yao Wenjun and Sun Sulan, respectively, both courtesans in tough situations), the two actresses who actually live there see no future for themselves and wish that they could leave.[25] Although the garden is the crucial arena for the development of two apparently ideal relationships (between Zhu Shuren and Zhou Shuangyu, and between Shi Tianran and Zhao Puzhai's sister Erbao), one of these liaisons ends in acrimony and an attempted double suicide and the other in the desertion of Erbao, who is then left with no choice but to accommodate the very same undesirable client that other courtesans avoid by fleeing to the garden. In view of these dismal developments, Qi Yunsou's claim to be "Master of Romance" rings hollow, and even this apparently romantic and refined space is shown to operate on the same fundamental principles as the world outside.

જી

For later authors and critics, Shanghai garden spaces offer an important point of entry for their own distinctive contributions to the field of Shanghai narrative. *Shanghai's Great Prospect Garden,* for example, rewrites earlier Shanghai fiction by shrinking the focus of the story to the garden itself and casting the garden in an almost utopian light as a privileged arena for the kind of imperial East-West cosmopolitanism that Meng Yue identifies in eighteenth-century Yangzhou gardens.[26] The concerns and conflicts that could not be kept out of "private" gardens in earlier Shanghai fiction are here excluded much more effectively.

While the author of Shanghai's *Great Prospect Garden* attempts to rescue *Lives of Shanghai Flowers* and *Shadows of Shanghai's Dusty Skies* by recovering the "private" garden and making it a more positive, less problematic space,

Eileen Chang tries instead to improve *Lives of Shanghai Flowers* by ridding it of the majority of its garden sections. In addition to translating the dialogue from Wu dialect into Mandarin, Chang responds to criticisms of the garden scenes in the second half of the novel as self-indulgent and uninteresting by condensing the nine chapters that include garden scenes into five, eliminating many of the party games, poetry competitions, and other garden pursuits.[27] Chang made similar deletions in her draft translation into English, most of which Eva Hung decided to follow in her revision of the draft for publication.[28] Though these decisions to improve on or rework earlier fiction seem to move in opposite directions, their motivation is similar: a sense that past texts cannot simply be brought back and expected to flourish naturally. Their revival requires extensive assistance, whether that assistance consists of radical thematic reworking, translation of dialogue, or enthusiastic prefaces and postfaces.[29] In this context, later writers and critics' insistence on *Lives of Shanghai Flowers*' "unpopularity" becomes more understandable—unless the work is somehow "lost" to begin with, the archaeological labors of digging through layers of sediment, dust removal, restoration, interpretation, and even alteration are rather less urgently needed to "save" it.

Transitivity

Crucial to later critics' understanding of *Lives of Shanghai Flowers* as an appropriate subject of restorative literary archaeology is their isolation of the novel from the broader context of Shanghai fiction. But as I suggested in chapter 3, the Shanghai novel, more than most other types of fiction, acquires a deeper resonance when it is read as a genre, rather than as one or another work in isolation. The 1920s revival of *Lives of Shanghai Flowers,* when understood in its generic context, turns out to be not so much the miraculous recovery of a long-lost unique work of art as it is an example of the broader tendency of works in this genre to vary periodically in the volume of their production. To understand this context, one must look beyond reprint editions of earlier fiction and retrospective works like *Romance on Hu River* and *Shanghai's Great Prospect Garden* to inquire into the more general dynamics of Shanghai fiction in the 1910s and '20s.

We may begin with the prefaces to the volume edition of Zhu Shouju's *The Huangpu Tides,* which appeared in May of 1921 (the same year as Xu Qinfu's nostalgic *Romance on Hu River*), after five years of serialization in *New Shen bao.*[30] Specific mention of late Qing Shanghai novels as a genre—and the first use of the phrase "Shanghai fiction" *(haishang xiaoshuo)*—comes in two of the four prefaces to this novel, which, like *Lives of Shanghai Flowers*, was a favorite of Eileen Chang's.[31] Like earlier Shanghai narratives, *The Huangpu Tides* deals at great length with the social interaction between men and women and the rise and fall of individuals and families; two of the three prefaces to the book edition of this title relate it explicitly to earlier Shanghai novels.

The second preface claims that *The Huangpu Tides* will be remembered together with Sun Yusheng's *Dreams of Shanghai Splendor*.[32] The third preface goes into more detail, beginning with praise for *Dream of the Red Chamber*'s capacity to "present that which is real through that which is imagined" and proceeding to critique recent attempts to represent Shanghai:

> In recent years, there have been many new Shanghai novels. But they are mired in description of the [outward] forms of society, and their "great skill" in carving [i.e., writing] is like adding mud to one already in the muck.... Should one seek novels that can present what is real through what is imagined, descend into the depths and venture into unusual and dangerous literary territory, they will be hard to find.
>
> In the Qing period, a book called *A Shanghai Swan's Traces in the Snow* appeared in Shanghai; although it was also a romantic work, its milieu was constructed with subtle phrases, and the writing can enter into the limitless, pass through, and come out again; [the author] is really a master of sketching in outline. *Lives of Shanghai Flowers* also uses Suzhou dialect to effect; these novels are a good example of the wonder of similar artistry producing different works. I would say that these are both among the best students of *Dream of the Red Chamber* and are fit to contend competitively in the world of fiction.[33]

The aesthetic lineage is established: the "realism" of *Dream of the Red Chamber* finds its echo a century later in Shanghai novels of the 1890s. These original and masterly works are, however, succeeded in the ensuing years by imitations that are merely ornamental. The stage is set for a literary restoration.

> Now my friend Dream-teller of Shanghai has written *The Huangpu Tides*, and at the time of publication requested a preface from me. I'm not very perceptive, but I have seen rather much of the origins of the world of fiction, and I can boast that of the new novels that have come out in recent years here in Shanghai, there is none that I have not seen, so I can probably make subtle distinctions that others cannot,[34] read them and know their flavor. Now Dream-teller's book is without a doubt superior in the art of sketching in outline [as was *Lives of Shanghai Flowers*], and in the loose and easy move-

ments of the brush and subtle evocations of the milieu, I feel it significantly surpasses *A Shanghai Swan's Traces in the Snow.*[35]

The title *The Huangpu Tides* refers the reader back to Li Hanqiu's *Guangling chao* (Tides of Guangling), a lengthy serialized work set in Yangzhou that began to appear in 1909. This reference deepens the resonance between *The Huangpu Tides* and the first wave of Shanghai fiction, which may well have been inspired in part by the 1883 publication of *A Dream of Romance,* also set in Yangzhou.[36] But the prefaces to *The Huangpu Tides,* rather than identifying it with *Tides of Guangling,* instead locate it within a genre exemplified by the Shanghai novels *Lives of Shanghai Flowers, Dreams of Shanghai Splendor,* and *A Shanghai Swan's Traces in the Snow.* This lineage, which is claimed to have stylistic affiliations with *Dream of the Red Chamber,* is the context against which *The Huangpu Tides* is to be read.

What else is missing from this lineage besides *Tides of Guangling?* First, the so-called "novels of exposure" *(qianze xiaoshuo),* many of which include at least a few chapters set in Shanghai and were widely popular in the first decade of the twentieth century. This is not so surprising, however, because despite Shanghai's significance in early twentieth-century Chinese cultural production, these novels are primarily travel narratives; they spend an immense amount of time and energy moving from one city to another, one region or another, or even abroad. Second, and more striking, is the absence of *New Shanghai,* the most obvious representative of Shanghai fiction from the decade 1905–1914. If we look carefully at the lineage constructed in the 1921 prefaces to *The Huangpu Tides,* it becomes clear that the continuity it traces between *Dream of the Red Chamber* (late eighteenth century), *Lives of Shanghai Flowers, Dreams of Shanghai Splendor,* and *A Shanghai Swan's Traces in the Snow* (1890s), and *The Huangpu Tides* (1916–1921) is a continuity structured around significant temporal gaps—we could even call them interruptions.

Within months of the publication of *The Huangpu Tides* in a volume edition and the appearance of *Romance on Hu River,* other narratives set in Shanghai began to come out. These included *Renjian diyu* (Hell in this world, 1922–1924), *Shanghai chunqiu* (Shanghai annals, 1924), *Haishang ranxi lu* (A record of [things seen by the light of] a burning rhinoceros horn in Shanghai, 1925), *Renhai chao* (Waves in a sea of people, 1926?), and *Shanghai fengyue* (Shanghai romance, 1929). Each of these works manifests distinct characteristics, but when read together, it becomes evident that all continue to elaborate the discursive field that is Shanghai narrative. Similar novels continued to appear into the 1930s, constituting a significant fraction of the "Shanghai-style" *(haipai)* literature of this period. It is clear from comments made in the prefaces and introductions to these works that daily publication in installments of a few hundred words was still the norm; preoccupation with Shanghai urban space, complex narrative structures composed of multiple intersecting story lines, and the strategic retelling of events from earlier in the narrative or repackaging them in a different generic form or different medium, whether newspaper story, stage play, or movie, continued to mark these novels as they did earlier Shanghai narratives.[37]

It is also worth noting that publication of *The Huangpu Tides* in installments began shortly after Sun Yusheng's sequel to *Dreams of Shanghai Splendor (Dreams of Shanghai Splendor, Continued)* appeared in 1915–1916. If we think back to *Romance on Hu River* (published in 1921) and *Shanghai's Great Prospect Garden* (published in 1924), it becomes clear that the late 1910s and '20s mark on the one hand a nostalgic revival that refers us to the most popular works of the 1890s and early 1900s, along with new interest in producing sequels to those works, and on the other a burst of new production that was focused on the contemporary city. This juxtaposition is no accident.

In chapter 3, we looked at Shanghai fiction synchronically, in terms of simultaneity. Here I would like to shift to a diachronic analysis, which emphasizes not so much the relationship between novels that appear at roughly the same time, as the overall dynamic of a genre in which groups of texts appear in bursts—action, followed by a lull, followed again by action. Based on what we have seen so far, 1894 to 1905 would qualify as an active period, 1906 to 1914 is relatively quiet, and then Shanghai installment fiction returns to the market in 1915 with Sun Yusheng's sequel to *Dreams of Shanghai Splendor*. To continue with the archaeological metaphor, we can return to Hsia's discovery of Shanghai fiction stacked on shelves in Seattle to imagine their temporal sedimentation—regular deposits of layer after layer of cultural production.

There are significant parallels between this pattern and the discourse of the "vanishing courtesan" identified by Gail Hershatter in a wealth of 1920s Shanghai guidebooks and newspapers. This discourse returns obsessively to the idea that the last quarter of the nineteenth century was the "golden age" of the Shanghai courtesan, lamenting the disappearance of the true courtesan and her replacement by the streetwalker.[38] In both Shanghai installment fiction and Shanghai "non-fiction" writings about courtesans the 1880s and 1890s constitute an originary moment of sorts, which texts of the 1920s and '30s seek to extend, duplicate, or recapture. In addition to generating new texts, this nostalgic project is productive in two senses: it makes earlier texts available to a broader audience in reprint editions as noted above, and it also lays the foundation for the "old Shanghai" discourse that persists to this day. The period idealized in the 1990s and 2000s as an object of nostalgia—"old Shanghai"—is the 1920s and 1930s, the very moment at which *Romance on Hu River, Shanghai's Great Prospect Garden,* and other Shanghai texts began to look back to the 1880s and 1890s as a golden age.[39] This double movement is central to the kind of lineage construction that the writers of the prefaces to *The Huangpu Tides* undertake. A lineage is constructed or perpetuated at any moment through a repayment to the past of the debt that one hopes to incur from the future. The fact that we now look back to precisely the time when nostalgic discourses about an even earlier era flourished suggests not only that this transitivity may be one of the determining characteristics of nostalgia, but also that the object of nostalgia is not, ultimately, a particular time or place, but rather that sensation of nostalgia itself.

Cinema

Movies began to be shown in Shanghai teahouses in 1896, within a year of the invention of the medium, and just two years after publication of the volume edition of *Lives of Shanghai Flowers.* Almost immediately, film crept into Shanghai fiction: in the fifty-ninth chapter of *Dreams of Shanghai Splendor,* which appeared in installment form in May or June of 1903, several of the male characters watch a short film set in a courtesan house like the ones that they patronize on a more or less regular basis. In 1908 a 250-seat theater dedicated to showing movies opened in Hongkou, and theaters continued to open through the 1910s and 1920s; in 1930 the city had over thirty theaters, and the leading fan newspaper claimed a national circulation of one million.[40] By then, attending films had begun to challenge reading fiction for dominance as a popular means of spending leisure time among Shanghai residents; cinematic techniques also began to play an inspirational role for writers of Shanghai fiction like Liu Na'ou and Mu Shiying in the late 1920s and early 1930s.[41]

At the same time, we may want to consider cross-medium influences in the other direction. As Zhang Zhen suggests, the effects of the serial mode of production characteristic of the 1920s Shanghai culture industry can be seen quite clearly in films of the period.[42] Other effects may go against our intuitive sense of how film and written narrative interact, but are significant nonetheless. For example, we find a variety of features in Shanghai installment fiction of the 1920s like *Hell in This World* that seem to derive from film narrative: opening with a panoramic description of a station scene, zooming in for a closer look at two individuals who will figure prominently in the narrative, focusing closely on gestures and facial expressions, and finally concerning itself with the question of "female subjectivity." Certainly, some of these features incorporate techniques that would have been familiar from the movies that more Shanghai residents watched each year. But the relationship between new technologies of cultural production and stylistic change is never simple, and features characteristic of classic Hollywood cinema were not all present in movies of the 1910s and early 1920s. Insofar as these same features occurring in *Hell in This World* derive from specifically *literary* developments over the previous three decades, or even the previous century, we may also see this work and its predecessors as literary participants in the production of a "cinematic" mode of narrative. That mode, presented not only in groundbreaking films, but also in certain images, written texts, and dramatic presentations, provides a conceptual frame through which spectators can watch movies as narratives and which teaches them to expect precisely those qualities from later films; cinematic technology and production techniques hasten to address those expectations as they continue to develop.

The interior monologues found in *Hell in This World*, for example, do not draw on contemporary cinematic technique so much as anticipate its development. Films with sound were several years in the future, and voice-overs would come even later; texts like *Hell in This World* helped to establish a narrative practice and an interest in certain aspects of that practice that would in turn set specific tasks for cinematic narrative as it continued to develop. Similarly, in chapter 40 of *The Huangpu Tides*, we find an early description of "cinematic" spectatorship—an audience sitting quietly in a darkened second story room, watching the antics across the alley, in a room whose occupants have forgotten to draw the curtain—that most likely *precedes* the introduction of the darkened theater in which spectators are enjoined to remain silent.[43] This complexity puts us on notice that we may not want to rush to assert media specificity as an absolute determinant of form and content and suggests that the relationship between technological development and change in cultural production and consumption is not a one-way street, but is always fundamentally dialectic.

ℬ

A "courtesan film" first appeared in the pages of a Shanghai novel in 1903. What happens when *Lives of Shanghai Flowers* finally appears on movie screens ninety-five years later—in Hou Hsiao-hsien's film version, *Flowers of Shanghai* (1998)?[44] To audiences unfamiliar with Shanghai fiction, the dreamy and sumptuous spectacle presented in Hou's film may seem perfect as a visual representation of a narrative set in "decadent Shanghai" of the 1890s. For readers who are accustomed to reading Shanghai installment fiction, however, it comes as a shock; our expectations of the late-Qing city have been conditioned by a quick-moving, rapidly shifting, and thoroughly interwoven set of stories, in which dramatic public actions are as significant as the more slowly paced private moments that the film picks up on. The film, by contrast, has been generally understood as a slow procession of tableaus, with little apparent connection to lead the viewer from one scene to the next.[45] Given that infidelity is a constant theme in Shanghai fiction, it is perhaps no accident that *betrayal* springs to mind as the first characterization of what we are seeing on screen.

Generally speaking, the differences between novel and film fit nicely into a familiar series of binary oppositions: tradition/modernity, interior/exterior, decadence/energy, and so on. In a striking twist on the usual teleology of cultural forms, however, it is the 1998 film that feels "antique" and the century-old novel that feels "modern." Where the novel is a riot of colorful and strong-willed men and women moving freely through a fascinating urban space, the film gives us a very different picture. Many of the women in the written narrative use strong language and do not hesitate at violence when it serves their purposes, abusing the men in their lives and other women unlucky enough to get in the way both verbally and physically. In the film, however, these scenes are deliberately suppressed—the courtesan Shen Xiaohong's attack on her rival, Zhang Huizhen, for example, an early high point in the novel (chapter 9), gets only a passing mention in the form of gossip retold in the film, despite the fact that the rivalry between these two courtesans has been selected as one of the central narrative threads and given greater emphasis than it received in the novel. There is a single exception to this general rule when the courtesan Zhou Shuangyu confronts her young client, Zhu Shuren, about his broken vow to marry her and attempts to force him into a double love suicide. But even this exception is rendered in a low-key and played-out manner that is absolutely incompatible with everything we have previously learned about Zhou Shuangyu's fiery personality. Instead of screaming at him when he fails to drink the opium-laced wine, she merely whines, and the crucial moment when she manages to take physical control and force a portion of the dose down his throat is obscured from the camera by the curtains of her bed. In this case and others, the representation of courtesan women in turn-of-the-century Shanghai owes far more to late twentieth-century images of passive and exoticized "traditional" femininity than to the turn-of-the-century novel that the film purports to present on screen.

Even as the film shifts the balance of power heavily toward the male characters, it narrows the focus of the story down to the indoor interactions between courtesans and their clients. Gone are the mad races around the city in carriages, the noisy operas that provided the perfect cover for assignations, the physical confrontations in parks, and the very texture of the streets themselves.

These outdoor activities are crucial in the novel, since, as we have seen, many of the rapid switches from one narrative line to the next take place when one character encounters another by chance on the street or in a teahouse, theater, or other public location. In the movie, however, everything takes place indoors, and the rooms are isolated enough from the "outside world" that it is possible to come out of the film believing that all the action takes place in a single giant house of prostitution, instead of in many different establishments spread across the city.[46] The sense of wide-open exchanges, frenzied movement, and infinite potential that is key to Shanghai fiction—and central to the imagination of Shanghai as the vital hub of a new, fast-moving mediasphere—is completely gone.[47]

Although the stifling atmosphere of *Flowers of Shanghai* is highly evocative, it in fact refers primarily to a Shanghai retrospectively constructed by a number of authors in the Republican period, most notably in works like Eileen Chang's "Qingcheng zhi lian" (Love in a fallen city) and "Jinsuo ji" (The golden cangue). Here we see that the transitivity characteristic of nostalgia is not always perfect; the "original" referent can, unsurprisingly, be occluded by the temporal intermediary. In this case, the other intermediary is Eileen Chang's translation of *Lives of Shanghai Flowers* into Mandarin, and more important even than the text itself, her preface, postface, and explanatory notes.[48] Hou Hsiao-hsien and Chu T'ien-wen have not only worked back through Eileen Chang's translation to access the earlier works—maintaining in the process some parts of her explanatory apparatus of commentary, which frame the events unfolding onscreen as distant and requiring an intermediary to render them comprehensible—they have also extrapolated one dimension of Chang's own creative work to its logical extreme. The entire mise-en-scène of the film reminds one of nothing so much as the oppressive settings against which Eileen Chang's own characters will struggle in the decades to come.

୧ଏ

Yet despite our sense of betrayal, there is a fundamental kinship between the written narrative and the movie: not in *what* they say to the reader or spectator, but rather in *how* they say it. Barbara Johnson suggests that translation must ultimately aim to be faithful neither to the letter nor the spirit of the original, but rather to the struggle between the two that is specific to that original.[49] While the content and style of *Flowers of Shanghai* differs radically from that of *Lives of Shanghai Flowers,* there is a certain complementarity between the two in the difficulties they give their consumers—in the struggle between the reader or viewer's desire for a coherent and comprehensive narrative and the obstacles placed in the way of that desire.

One of the defining characteristics of *Lives of Shanghai Flowers* is its ability to frustrate the expectations that readers bring to it; the novel makes such frequent and rapid shifts from one character to another that it is up to the reader to decide how each individual narrative line is defined. This continual interruption that constitutes the text then ends abruptly in mid-story, itself interrupted, leaves its readers frustrated and expecting more. Hou Hsiao-hsien's film frustrates the viewer, but in a different way; as Xu Gang points out, frequent cuts in the narrative would in fact be too familiar to late twentieth-century movie audiences to constitute much of an obstacle.[50] In reading Shanghai fiction, the reader frequently feels that the narrative focus slides too easily from one storyline to the next; it does not attach securely enough to any individual character, location, or narrative thread. In the film, by contrast, the viewer's frustration results from just the opposite, a camera that is *too* securely attached, unwilling to cut from shot to shot—there are fewer than forty shots in the entire film, and the average shot lasts over three minutes—and disinclined in most of these shots to move beyond the four walls within which a given scene begins. Early in the film, there is a disturbance in the street outside, but the camera refuses to budge—we are left watching people leave the room and then return discussing what they have seen. In the novel, such a disturbance would have been an appropriate pretext for the narrative to rush off with another person encountered by chance in the street, leaving us wondering what happened after we left; here instead, we never get a clear picture of what happened outside to begin with. This kind of restraint, obscuring the spectators' vision, constitutes a dominant principle in the cinematography of *Flowers of Shanghai,* as we have noticed already in the struggle between Zhou Shuangyu and Zhu Shuren. Even at the key moment where Wang Liansheng (played by Tony Leung), discovers that the courtesan Shen Xiaohong is cheating on him with an actor, the viewer is given only the slightest glimpse of a pair of men's shoes underneath a screen as an indication of what Wang Liansheng has seen. It quickly becomes clear that an optic of restrained movement can be just as challenging as one of excessive movement.

To the extent that Hou's film is a nostalgic reconstruction of "old Shanghai," it runs drastically counter to the spirit of the work it purports to interpret and seems to constitute an extreme example in the lineage of attempts to resurrect *Lives of Shanghai Flowers* by altering it. Yet at the moments when the nostalgic look and the nostalgic detail are pushed too far, overloaded, and overdone, and especially at the moments where the viewer may chafe at the formal cinematographic restrictions imposed on the narrative, the fin-de-siècle film *Flowers of*

Shanghai betrays its kinship with the frustrating narrative that dates from the end of the previous century.[51] Film and novel differ in the sets of conventions that they push to their limit and beyond, but in this transcendent gesture they are quite similar.

In this context, it is worth considering Walter Benjamin's "Task of the Translator," a polemic against the concept of translation as a rendering of meaning from one language into another.[52] Benjamin argues that a translation should not seek to reproduce the original, but rather to complement it, likening the translation and the original to fragments of a broken vessel that can be fitted back together.[53] Two assertions are woven together in this key passage: first, translation is not a mimetic project in which fidelity is the issue, rather it is an attempt at supplementation, filling a lack, with the ultimate aim of redemption. Second, this supplementation acts not in the realm of meaning, but rather in the way that meaning is brought forth—the mode of signification in the original. In this sense, it is in fact to be expected that if the novel frustrates its readers by moving too quickly around the city, the film will frustrate its viewers by remaining stuck in one room each scene, moving with the slowness of molasses. The "mode of signification" is none other than a challenge to the constraints associated with the chosen mode of production, specifically, the limitations apparently inherent in the medium.

In the case of the novel, the mode of production in question is publication in installments. For audiences in 1890s Shanghai, the initial publication of the novel in two chapter installments may well have been a stumbling block. Turn-of-the-century critics criticized the installment method for keeping readers in suspense, unable to read through the entire text at their leisure. Han Bangqing, on the other hand, found the particular merit of publishing in installments precisely in this frustration of the reader's drive to finish immediately. The parallel technology in Hou Hsiao-hsien's film is less explicitly delineated, but nonetheless unmistakable. In forsaking the rules governing more conventional film-making—eye-line matches, shot/reverse shot composition—and emphasizing instead long takes with slow movement around the room, often from a slightly higher vantage point than in Hou's previous films, with key actions and scenes obscured or missing, the cinematography in this film comes to remind one unmistakably of an automated surveillance camera operating within strictly fixed parameters.[54] *Flowers of Shanghai* seizes the conflict over the appropriate framing of action that Sergei Eisenstein understands as a clash between the "director's logic" and the "logic of the object" and heightens it to the extent that the viewer tends to sympathize with the latter, to the point of imagining a logic that is merely suggested into existence.[55] This is in fact analogous to the restraints placed on the reader of installment fiction that Han Bangqing delights in, for the very reason that they force the reader to become a full participant in the process of aesthetic production.

Historicizing the reception of these two cultural products brings us to the question of the two modes within which they are produced: nostalgia, in the case of the film, and contemporaneity, in the case of the novel. The reciprocity and complementarity between texts in different languages for Benjamin indicates kinship at a more fundamental level—between languages themselves, each of which exhibits a yearning for complementation and fulfillment. It shouldn't come as a surprise, then, that the nostalgic and contemporary modes of cultural production are similarly complementary. It is not only that the two set each other off when they themselves are contemporaries, but also that nostalgic works attempt to reconstruct only those periods that have already identified themselves as worthy of such attention. In the previous section of this chapter, I suggested that nostalgia takes as its object the nostalgic feeling of an earlier era—that a historical moment can ensure its lasting influence by paying tribute to an earlier moment—but this is not the whole story.

Another important means of accomplishing this kind of identification is through the production of texts and images at *that* time set in *that* present, the one that later will be recreated—in other words, through the insistent *contemporaneity* of the earlier period. And since writing about the present constitutes a call that awaits a response from future generations, any work that aspires to contemporaneity itself achieves its full effect for later audiences only when it is juxtaposed with a nostalgic recollection also produced for those later audiences.[56] It is not until we see Hou Hsiao-hsien's movie at the end of the twentieth century that we begin to realize the radical contemporaneity that Han Bangqing's novel showed its late-nineteenth-century readers. This fuller understanding of *Lives of Shanghai Flowers* comes in part from the similarities between novel and film—the delays of installment fiction resembling slow-paced scenes in the movie, the restraint of the "surveillance camera" aesthetic recalling the refusal in the novel to give any account of the characters' interior life—but even more from the differences between the two.

Epilogue

Shanghai 2000

In an article written soon after the appearance of the film *Flowers of Shanghai,* Xudong Zhang suggests that we should understand Shanghai nostalgia in the 1990s as a kind of defense mechanism, "a sentimental Chinese response to a global ideology" that functions as a means to "absorb a socioeconomic shock."[1] Linking the work of Eileen Chang and Wang Anyi to dynamics of socioeconomic change and questions of class identity clearly opens up productive avenues for analysis; in this concluding chapter, however, instead of emphasizing the reactive qualities of Shanghai nostalgia, I would like to return to the question of how tropes and figures—often understood as merely formal qualities—can work to determine material social development, and ask, how do the aesthetic characteristics specific to Shanghai nostalgia themselves contribute to the renewed social, cultural, and economic significance of the city since the early 1990s? Ackbar Abbas writes that "in Shanghai, the past allows the present to pursue the future"; if, as Svetlana Boym also suggests, nostalgia and progress can be inextricably linked, what role might the tropes and figures of Shanghai fiction play in reestablishing the city as a focal point in the twenty-first-century Chinese cultural imaginary?[2]

Increased consumption of Shanghai-related commodities is perhaps the most basic instance of nostalgia's constructive capabilities. As they did in the late nineteenth and early twentieth centuries, Shanghai texts and images at the turn of the twenty-first century provide a steady stream of income to cultural producers located in or near the city and at the same time sell a particular conception of the city to potential visitors from elsewhere in China and around the world. Once these visitors arrive, there is no shortage of Shanghai establishments to provide commodified experiences of the "old" city, from the Peace Hotel to the shops around Leisure Garden to coffeehouses along Huaihai lu (formerly Avenue Joffré).[3] Two of these projects are most striking for their careful self-presentation as ideal examples of hybridity between past and future: the Shanghai Art Museum and the shopping/restaurant development in the Xintiandi area, which takes as its slogan "Where yesterday meets tomorrow in Shanghai today."[4] The Shanghai Art Museum inhabits the old Shanghai

Racetrack clubhouse, for nearly five decades after 1949 the main building of the Shanghai Library. Xintiandi has been built out of the *shikumen* homes lining several alleys adjacent to the founding site of the Chinese Communist Party. In each case, a structure charged with historical significance has been reworked as an establishment that emphasizes the present and future; these ventures are clearly aware that their success will depend in part on the frisson that visitors experience upon standing astride the gap between past and future that they claim to be uniquely qualified to mediate.

Here we can sense the renewed importance of the figures of "betweenness" and mediation discussed in detail in chapters 1 and 5: Shanghai poses itself now not only as the privileged intermediary between "China" and "the West," but also as the best place in which to integrate globalization past and globalization future into a coherent narrative.[5] This self-presentation certainly does not go uncontested, but to the extent that it succeeds, it does so through extensive reference to an array of Shanghai tropes that are no less effective for having been largely suppressed in mainland cultural discourse for over three decades. The *Szahaenin*, having spent some years diminished to a collection of personality traits, preferences in cuisine, and a mode of dialect speech, reemerges on the national stage as the extremely capable and fashionable "hero" of a capitalist and media-saturated future, though not, to be sure, without his or her own weaknesses and less admirable qualities. This reemergence spans a wide range of genres and media, from the glossy illustrated book *Yuedu haipai nü* (Reading the Shanghai-style woman), written by "Jenny"; to the chatty "Ala Szahaenin" (We Shanghai people) radio show on Dongfang guangbo tai (Eastern broadcast station); to the serious *Xin Shanghairen* (New Shanghai people), a volume resulting from a think-tank conference attended by prominent local academics in the humanities.[6] While works aimed at popular audiences tend to essentialize *Szahaenin* according to established stereotypes (clever, fashionable, mercenary, and so on), the more academic works, with a few exceptions, tend to temper these essentializations only by supplementing them with an insistent "in-migrant transformation" discourse. Once again, it is suggested that those from outside Shanghai can themselves aspire to heroic stature if they relocate to the city and master the new referential system, thereby transforming themselves into *Szahaenin*.[7]

This renewed version of Shanghai identity overlaps in certain crucial ways with the near-ubiquitous media image of the "successful individual" (*chenggong renshi*) analyzed by Wang Xiaoming.[8] The "successful individual" is fully at home in the excess that characterizes the city today—unequalled numbers of construction cranes, skyrocketing real estate values, luxury hotels, boutiques, and restaurants, and the tallest structure in China, not to mention the world's fastest train, which runs between the city and Pudong International Airport. Michelle Huang traces the correspondences between this rapid urban development and the problematic "global city" model, reminding us that for every individual who comes to Shanghai and succeeds, there are many more whose presence is acknowledged only infrequently, and who have no chance to establish themselves as legal urban residents—the migrant laborers who build the new infrastructure and skyscrapers, without which the new managerial and professional class would have nowhere to live and work.[9] In the early twentieth century, the *Szahaenin* began to define him or herself in part against a constructed Subei identity; the "successful individual" or "new Shanghai person" at the turn of the twenty-first century is even more dependent on an exploited "floating population" *(liudong renkou)* whose efforts support his or her enjoyable lifestyle. Under these circumstances, it comes as no surprise that Shanghai nostalgia also expresses "approval of the present" and "confidence about the future." As Hanchao Lu has pointed out, this nostalgia represents a specifically political endorsement of a particular approach to global capitalism and its commercial culture that is understood to have been dominant in Shanghai of the 1930s.[10]

ℰ∂

The idea of nostalgic return to an earlier time is predicated on a perceived break between then and now; as Shu-mei Shih notes of cultural history written under the sign of nostalgia, "It is as if Chinese modernity, as a construct that is always defined along the lines of westernization, can only exist in spurts, without historical continuity."[11] Similarly, T. A. Hsia writes that encountering Shanghai fiction in 1950s Seattle made him feel "as if Chinese history stopped right there."[12] Different genres of cultural production mark this interruption in different ways. In Xu Xixian and Xu Jianrong's photo album comparing Shanghai locations from the early 1970s to the early 1990s with those same locations in the present (2004), the demarcation between past and present is established through layout and use of color (past on even-numbered pages in black and white, present facing past on the following odd-numbered pages, in color).[13] Temporal change is represented not as a continuity, but as a sudden transition from one disconnected moment to the next. The 2004 images are still recent, but it is not hard to imagine a time when they too will seem to cry out for new records of the present to face the past that they have become. As we have seen, it is the very fact of interruption, the abruptness with which Shanghai installment narratives break off, that generates a constant and powerful desire to continue reading. Looking back from the twenty-first century, it becomes evident that History can also be constructed as a continuity of desire that is the dialectical product of ceaseless interruption. As Deleuze and Guattari put it, "Far from being the opposite of continuity, the break or interruption conditions this continuity: it presupposes or defines what it cuts into as an ideal continuity."[14]

Indeed, even as fictional episodes are interrupted within each installment of a Shanghai novel, even as the overall narrative is interrupted by the installment form, even as the progress of the novel is interrupted by pauses between series or before a sequel, even as the development of the genre as a whole is interrupted by intermittent gaps in fictional production, so Shanghai's development itself appears to have been interrupted by three decades of "socialist neglect" and restrictions on in-migration from the mid-1950s to the mid-1980s, only to surge forth even more energetically in the 1990s and 2000s, as if someone had suggested *"reculer pour mieux sauter"* as a strategy of urban development. The failure of "permanent revolution" as a motivating discourse in the long term (as seen in the Great Leap Forward and the Great Proletarian Cultural Revolution) suggests, conversely, that attempts to force an ideal and unbroken continuity may be doomed to defeat.

The important point here is not that socialist industrialization failed Shanghai in the 1950s, '60s, and '70s—as Xudong Zhang indicates, there is good evidence that by some measures the city benefited a great deal and in fact grew faster during these years than it would in the 1980s[15]—but rather that it failed to capture the city's imagination, just as the significance of Shanghai's material production and international shipping trade prior to 1840 was overshadowed in the minds of both residents and visitors by the burst in symbolic production and consumption that characterized the city from the 1880s into the 1930s.[16]

The Shanghai culture industry rose to prominence in the 1880s and '90s, creating a national mediasphere as it transcended older centers of print and image production like Beijing, Suzhou, Yangzhou, and Nanjing. This dominant position in the realm of cultural production was lost in the 1950s as Hong Kong emerged and Beijing reemerged as cultural centers in their own right.[17] What we see in Shanghai *again* in the 1990s is the transformation of a prosperous but relatively "uninspiring" trade and manufacturing center into a city that profits from its service, entertainment, and culture industries to command a central position in both national and global imaginaries. The rhetoric of Shanghai only now "recovering" its past glory after decades of neglect and stagnation depends not only on the centrality of the culture industry to both the "appearance" and the "reality" of material prosperity, but also on the aesthetic of interruption and the associated increase in desire characteristic of Shanghai installment fiction. Shanghai people at the turn of the twenty-first century, we are told, are eager to get on with the next installment of a story that they understand to be open-ended and unending.

Notes

The following novels are frequently referred to and cited in their abbreviated form in the notes (short title, chapter/page number):

Chentian ying	Zou Tao, *Haishang chentian ying* Shadows of Shanghai's dusty skies (1896)
Daguan yuan	Wumu shanren, *Haishang Daguan yuan* Shanghai's Great Prospect Garden (1924)
Fanhua meng	Sun Yusheng, *Haishang fanhua meng* Dreams of Shanghai splendor (1898–1906)
Fengyue zhuan	Xu Qinfu, *Hujiang fengyue zhuan* Romance on Hu River (1921)
Haishang hua	Han Bangqing, *Haishang hua liezhuan* Lives of Shanghai flowers (1892–1894)
Haitian hong	Erchun jushi, *Haitian hong xueji* A Shanghai swan's traces in the snow (1899)
Renjian diyu	Bi Yihong and Bao Tianxiao, *Renjian diyu* Hell in this world (1922–1924)
Shanghai chunqiu	Bao Tianxiao, *Shanghai chunqiu* Shanghai annals (1924)
Xiepu chao	Zhu Shouju, *Xiepu chao* The Huangpu tides (1916–1921)
Xin Shanghai	Lu Shi'e, *Xin Shanghai* New Shanghai (1909)
Xin Xiepu chao	Zhu Shouju, *Xin Xiepu chao* New Huangpu tides (c. 1923)
[Xu] Fanhua meng	Sun Yusheng, *Xu Haishang fanhua meng* Dreams of Shanghai splendor, continued (1915–1916)

Zhengfeng zhuan   *Mengyou Shanghai mingji zhengfeng zhuan*
                          A dream voyage to Shanghai: Famous courtesans
                          contending for dominance (after 1904)

Ziye   Mao Dun, *Ziye*
                          Midnight (1933)

Introduction

1. "For most people, the very word 'Shanghai' provoked excitement, stimulated the imagination, and raised hopes. 'So this is Shanghai!' was a usual exclamation of newcomers, both foreign and the Chinese." Hanchao Lu, *Beyond the Neon Lights: Everyday Shanghai in the Early Twentieth Century*, p. 48.

2. Less well-studied, but also significant are pulp works like *Shanghai: City for Sale* and *Shanghai: Paradise of Adventurers* (Robert Bickers, "Shanghailanders: The Formation and Identity of the British Settler Community in Shanghai, 1843–1937," *Past and Present* 159 [May 1998]: 200–201); illustrated installment publications like Hergé's *Les aventures de Tintin: le lotus bleu,* first published in a volume edition in 1936; and publications in European languages other than English and French. According to Marcia Ristaino, Shanghai was probably the single largest Russian-language publishing center in exile in the 1930s (*Port of Last Resort: The Diaspora Communities of Shanghai,* pp. 83–84).

3. Li Oufan, "Zhongguo xiandai xiaoshuo de xianqu zhe," *Lien-ho wen-hsüeh* 3.12: 8–14; Yan Jiayan, "Xin ganjue pai zhuyao zuojia," *Lien-ho wen-hsüeh* 3.12: 15–19; Heinrich Fruehauf, "Urban Exoticism in Modern and Contemporary Chinese Literature," in *From May Fourth to June Fourth: Fiction and Film in Twentieth-Century China;* ed. Ellen Widmer and David Wang; Yomi Braester, "Shanghai's Economy of the Spectacle: The Shanghai Race Club in Liu Na'ou's and Mu Shiying's Stories," *Modern Chinese Literature* 9 (1995): 39–58; Wu Fuhui, *Dushi xuanliu zhong de haipai xiaoshuo;* Yingjin Zhang, *The City in Modern Chinese Literature and Film: Configurations of Space, Time, and Gender;* Leo Ou-fan Lee, *Shanghai Modern: The Flowering of a New Urban Culture in China, 1930–1945;* Li Jin, *Haipai xiaoshuo yu xiandai dushi wenhua;* Shu-mei Shih, "Gender, Race, and Semicolonialism: Liu Na'ou's Urban Shanghai Landscape," *Journal of Asian Studies* 55.4 (1996): 934–956, and *The Lure of the Modern: Writing Modernism in Semicolonial China,* 1917–1937; Peng Hsiao-yen, *Haishang shuo qingyu: cong Zhang Ziping dao Liu Na'ou.*

On courtesan guidebooks and sketches, and other related texts, see Catherine Yeh, "The Life-Style of Four *Wenren* in Late Qing Shanghai," *Harvard Journal of Asiatic Studies* 57.2 (1997): 419–470, "Reinventing Ritual: Late Qing Handbooks on Proper Customer Behavior in Shanghai Courtesan Houses," *Late Imperial China* 29.2 (1998): 1–63, "Creating the Urban Beauty: The Shanghai Courtesan in Late Qing Illustrations" in *Writing Materiality in China,* ed. Judith Zeitlin and Lydia Liu, and *Shanghai Love: Courtesans, Intellectuals, and Entertainment Culture, 1850–1910;* Gail Hershatter, *Dangerous Pleasures: Prostitution and Modernity in Twentieth-Century Shanghai;* Paola Zamperini, "On Their Dress They Wore a Body: Fashion and Identity in Late-Qing Shanghai," *positions* 11.2 (2003): 301–330; Ellen Widmer, "Inflecting Gender: Zhan Kai / Siqi Zhai's 'New Novels' and Courtesan Sketches," *Nannü* 6.1 (2004): 136–168.

4. See especially David Der-wei Wang, *Fin-de-siècle Splendor: Repressed Modernities of Late Qing Fiction, 1848–1911,* pp. 81–114; Chen Bohai and Yuan Jin, eds. *Shanghai jindai wenxue shi,* pp. 224–379; Yuan Jin, *Yuanyang hudie pai,* pp. 1–40; Keith McMahon,

"Fleecing the Male Customer in Shanghai Brothels of the 1890s," *Late Imperial China* 23.2 (2002): 1–32.

5. Alexander Des Forges, "Street Talk and Alley Stories: Tangled Narratives of Shanghai from 'Lives of Shanghai Flowers' (1892) to 'Midnight' (1933)," pp. 77–78, 111–112.

6. Especially in *Jiuwei gui*, Shanghai fiction is taken as a model, and Shanghai itself is presupposed as the standard against which all other major cities visited by the protagonist will be judged. For a clear example of the former, compare chapters 61 through 63 of *Haishang fanhua meng* with chapters 2 and 3 of *Jiuwei gui*; for examples of the latter, see Zhang Chunfan, *Jiuwei gui*, pp. 2, 7, 11, 1009, 1010–1012, 1024. When Zhang Qiugu encounters Jin Yuelan soon after his arrival in Suzhou, he explains to his companion that he knew her previously in Shanghai (obviously before the beginning of the narrative). Zhang, *Jiuwei gui*, 19. See also Wu Jianren, *Ershi nian mudu zhi guai xianzhuang*, and Paola Zamperini's discussion of Hu Baoyu's visit to Beijing, chronicled in *Jiuwei hu*. Zamperini, "On Their Dress They Wore a Body," pp. 305–306.

7. Zeng Pu, "Xiugai hou yao shuo de jiju hua," originally printed in 1934; reprinted in *Niehai hua ziliao*, ed. Wei Shaochang, pp. 128–129.

8. Mao Dun, "Women you shenme yichan?" reprinted in *Huaxiazi*, p. 137. The other "masterpieces" mentioned in this passage are *Honglou meng*, *Shuihu zhuan*, *Xiyou ji*, and *Rulin waishi*.

9. T. A. Hsia, "Novel and Romance: Hsia Tsi-an on Chinese Popular Literature," trans. Dennis Hu, *Chinese Literature: Essays, Articles, Reviews* 2.2: 231–232.

10. Zhu Shouju, *Xiepu chao* (1916–1921; reprint, Shanghai guji chubanshe, 1991), introduction, p. 3. Hereafter references to this edition will cite only the title. See also Zhang Ailing, "Yi Hu Shizhi," in *Zhang kan*, pp. 141–154. Eileen Chang's Mandarin version of *Haishang hua* was published as a two-volume edition by Huangguan in 1983; the English version, revised by Eva Hung, was published in 2005 by Columbia University Press as *The Sing-Song Girls of Shanghai*.

11. Wang Anyi, *Xunzhao Shanghai*; see especially "Haishang fanhua meng." Alison Groppe references *Haishang hua liezhuan* in her analysis of Li's *Zhoufu lianhuan zhi*, in "Not Made in China: Inventing Local Identities in Contemporary Malaysian Chinese Fiction." A discussion of Hou Hsiao-hsien's film appears in chapter 7 of this book.

12. Williams, *Marxism and Literature*, pp. 19, 153–154.

13. Liang Qichao, "Lun xiaoshuo yu qunzhi zhi guanxi," reprinted in A Ying, *Wan Qing wenxue congchao*, vol. 2, p. 18; this translation based in part on Gek Nai Cheng's translation in *Modern Chinese Literary Thought: Writings on Literature, 1893–1945*, ed. Kirk Denton, p. 79.

14. Benedict Anderson, *Imagined Communities: Reflections on the Origin and Spread of Nationalism*, p. 25.

15. Perry Link, *Mandarin Ducks and Butterflies: Popular Fiction in Early Twentieth-Century Chinese Cities*, 5ff, 189–190; Leo Ou-fan Lee and Andrew Nathan, "The Beginnings of Mass Culture: Journalism and Fiction in the Late Ch'ing and Beyond," in *Popu-*

lar Culture in Late Imperial China, ed. David Johnson et al.; Wen-hsin Yeh, "Progressive Journalism and Shanghai's Petty Urbanites: Zou Taofen and the Shenghuo Enterprise, 1926–1945," in *Shanghai Sojourners,* ed. Frederic E. Wakeman Jr. and Wen-hsin Yeh; Lu, *Beyond the Neon Lights,* pp. 61–64; Lee, *Shanghai Modern,* especially chapters 1 through 4; Haiyan Lee, "All the Feelings That Are Fit to Print: The Community of Sentiment and the Literary Public Sphere in China, 1900–1918." *Modern China* 27.3 (2001): 291–327.

16. Yuan Jin, *Yuanyang hudie pai,* p. 34; Stuart Blumin, "George G. Foster and the Emerging Metropolis," in *New York by Gas-Light and Other Urban Sketches,* 11ff.

17. Christopher Reed, *Gutenberg in Shanghai: Chinese Print Capitalism,* 1876–1937, pp. 17, 128–160, especially p. 155.

18. See Yeh, "The Life-Style of Four *Wenren,*" "Reinventing Ritual," "Creating the Urban Beauty," and *Shanghai Love;* Hershatter, *Dangerous Pleasures.*

19. A Ying, *Wan Qing wenxue congchao,* vol. 2, pp. 16–17; Denton, *Modern Chinese Literary Thought,* p. 76.

20. In its first three months, *Ziye* was reprinted four times; the first five editions totaled 23,000 copies—this many for a work of "serious fiction" was still rare in the early 1930s. Mao Dun, *Wo zouguo de daolu,* vol. 2, pp. 122–123. As we will see in chapter 1, however, it is quite likely that there were more than 20,000 copies of *Haishang hua* in print as early as the first decade of the twentieth century.

21. Yuan Jin, *Zhongguo wenxue guannian de jindai bianqe,* p. 36. See William Rowe, *Hankow: Conflict and Community in a Chinese City,* pp. 23–27 for a discussion of urban literacy in nineteenth-century Hankou.

22. Richard Altick, *The English Common Reader: A Social History of the Mass Reading Public,* 1800–1900, p. 171.

23. See, for example, the *Youxi bao* statement of purpose, *Youxi bao* no. 63, p. 1. According to Huang Shiquan, writing in 1883, "The majority of women of good families in Shanghai can read and write." Huang, *Songnan mengying lu,* p. 102. As Dorothy Ko has shown in *Teachers of the Inner Chambers: Women and Culture in Seventeenth-Century China,* women were reading and writing far more than previous scholarship had imagined as early as the late Ming. In illustrated collections of Shanghai scenes like Wu Youru's *Haishang baiyan tu* (first printed c. 1891; reprinted in *Wu Youru hua bao*), the female reader is an important figure; women often spend leisure time reading or writing. See pp. 1.4a, 1.16b, 1.17b, 2.3a, 2.4b, 2.5a, 2.9b, 2.18a, 2.20b, and also *Xinji Haishang qinglou tuji,* 2.11a, 2.24a.

24. Rawski, *Education and Popular Literacy in Ch'ing China,* p. 23.

25. Rawski, *Education and Popular Literacy in Ch'ing China,* pp. 11–12, 17.

26. *The Chinese Repository,* vol. 4, p. 190.

27. Rawski, *Education and Popular Literacy,* pp. 11–12. See also an article in *The Celestial Empire* (June 12, 1896, p. 605)—which classifies Chinese audiences into three distinct groups: literati; artisans and businessmen; and laborers, small shopkeepers, and so on—and Meir Shahar's analysis of the turn-of-the-century Beijing rental market in *Crazy Ji: Chinese Religion and Popular Literature,* pp. 124–129, 271. The novel is Lu Shi'e's *Xin Shanghai,* 9/40.

28. Link, *Mandarin Ducks and Butterflies*, p. 151.

29. Jauss, *Toward an Aesthetic of Reception*, p. 80.

30. Williams, *Marxism and Literature*, pp. 184–185. Frederic Jameson, *The Political Unconscious: Narrative as a Socially Symbolic Act*, p. 106. In an otherwise perceptive discussion of the role of genre in twentieth-century literary criticism, Jameson does, however, slip into an overly simple dichotomy between the "fixed" forms of previous genres and the generic "process" that he sees as characteristic of the European (and American) novel of the late nineteenth and early twentieth centuries. *The Political Unconscious*, pp. 151, 185.

31. Michel Foucault, "Nietzsche, Genealogy, History," in *Michel Foucault: Aesthetics, Method, Epistemology*, ed. James Faubion, pp. 369, 371. In this essay, Foucault contrasts the quest for an origin *(Ursprung)* against the preferred tracing of descent *(Herkunft)*: "to follow the complex course of descent is to maintain passing events in their proper dispersion; it is to identify the minute deviations—or conversely, the complete reversals—the errors, the false appraisals, and the faulty calculations that give birth to those things which continue to exist and have value for us" (p. 374).

32. Of these two criteria, the former is the more flexible: there are several novels that I read as members of the genre that were intended for installment publication, but ultimately appeared only in volume editions (e.g., Mao Dun's *Ziye*) or which formally incorporate this mode through the *telling* of the narrative in installments even as they were first published in volume editions (e.g., Wumu shanren's *Haishang Daguan yuan*).

33. Lu Xun, *Zhongguo xiaoshuo shi lüe*, pp. 211–222. See also Lu Hsun, *A Brief History of Chinese Fiction*, pp. 319–355. As novels of the nineteenth century become better-known, there have been challenges to Lu Xun's typology; see, for example, Patrick Hanan, "*Fengyue meng* and the Courtesan Novel," *Harvard Journal of Asiatic Studies* 58.2 (1998): 345–372.

34. Huang Lin, *Jindai wenxue piping shi*, pp. 526–537; Guo Yanli, *Zhongguo jindai wenxue fazhan shi*; Wang, *Fin-de-siècle Splendor*, pp. 91–99; Keith McMahon, "Fleecing the Male Customer"; Yeh, *Shanghai Love*, especially chapter 6. Cf. A Ying's approach to this question in *Wan Qing xiaoshuo shi*.

35. Wang, *Fin-de-siècle Splendor*, pp. 53–116; see also Alexander Des Forges, "From Source Texts to 'Reality Observed': The Creation of the 'Author' in Nineteenth-Century Chinese Vernacular Fiction." Although these developments are particularly prominent in courtesan fiction, they are found as well in certain other nineteenth-century novels: see Patrick Hanan, *Chinese Fiction of the Nineteenth and Early Twentieth Centuries*, pp. 9–32.

36. As David Wang notes, *Haishang hua* is filled with "amazingly ordinary" characters; sensual descriptions are not significant in the novel. *Fin-de-siècle Splendor*, p. 91. The same is true of the other novels discussed in this book, with the exception of *Jiuwei gui* and Mao Dun's *Ziye*. See also McMahon, "Fleecing the Male Customer."

37. See, for example, the importance of (western) restaurants in Shanghai fiction as preferred neutral locations for men attempting to work out disputes with women;

restaurants were much more private than teahouses. Des Forges, "Street Talk and Alley Stories," pp. 137–138.

38. For a discussion of courtesans in the work of Balzac, see Albert Béguin, *Balzac visionnaire: propositions*, pp. 151–179.

39. Linda Cooke Johnson, *Shanghai: From Market Town to Treaty Port, 1074–1858*, p. 343; Robert Bickers, *Britain in China: Community, Culture, and Colonialism 1900–1949*, pp. 85–86, quoting a recruit to the Shanghai Municipal Police in 1919: "Shanghai is the best city that I have seen and will leave any English town 100 years behind—that's not exaggerated. It is the most cosmopolitan city of the world bar none and the finest city of the Far East."

40. Georg Simmel, "The Metropolis and Mental Life," reprinted in *Classic Essays in the Culture of Cities*, ed. Richard Sennett, 47–60; Christopher Prendergast, *Paris and the Nineteenth Century*, passim; Walter Benjamin, "The Work of Art in the Age of Mechanical Reproduction," *Illuminations:* 217–251; Dean MacCannell, *The Tourist: A New Theory of the Leisure Class*, p. 3.

41. For a more detailed discussion of the rhetoric of modernity in the field of Chinese literature, see Alexander Des Forges, "The Rhetorics of Modernity and the Logics of the Fetish," in *Contested Modernities in Chinese Literature*, ed. Charles Laughlin. See also Bryna Goodman's critique of the "colonial modernity" paradigm in "Improvisations on a Semicolonial Theme, or, How to Read Multiethnic Participation in the 1893 Shanghai Jubilee," *Journal of Asian Studies* 59.4 (2000): 916–921.

42. Régis Debray, *Media Manifestos*, trans. Eric Rauth, p. 33. "When as literary critics we study the nineteenth-century novel or the *feuilleton*, how often do we think about the Stanhope press, the penny newspaper, the national network of schooling, and the railroads that all supported the demand for this literary form?" (pp. 33–34). Note that in the Shanghai case we can speak of the converse as well: popular literary forms literally creating the demand for domestically manufactured printing presses. See Reed, *Gutenberg in Shanghai*, pp. 128–160.

43. See, among others, Lucille Chia, *Printing for Profit: The Commercial Publishers of Jianyang, Fujian (11th to 17th Centuries)*; Timothy Brook, *The Confusions of Pleasure: Commerce and Culture in Ming China*; Kai-wing Chow, "Writing for Success: Printing, Examinations, and Intellectual Change in Late Ming China," *Late Imperial China* 17.1 (1996): 120–157; Ellen Widmer, "The Huanduzhai of Hangzhou and Suzhou: A Study in Seventeenth-Century Publishing," *Harvard Journal of Asiatic Studies* 36 (1996): 77–122; Cynthia J. Brokaw, "Commercial Publishing in Late Imperial China: The Zou and Ma Family Businesses of Sibao, Fujian," *Late Imperial China* 17.1 (1996): 49–92.

44. Reed, *Gutenberg in Shanghai*, p. 207; see also p. 8.

45. On the connection between new publishing practices and Shanghai's rise in cultural status, see Reed, *Gutenberg in Shanghai*, p. 90.

46. Albert Feuerwerker has estimated that by 1919, only six percent of China's 1,704 counties were completely lacking in missionary presence. Cited in Bickers, *Britain in China*, p. 69.

47. A British officer, 1884; in Ristaino, *Port of Last Resort*, p. 7.

48. "Shanghailanders appropriated 'Shanghai' for themselves. The phenomenal growth of the port and later its industries were portrayed as solely their creation. . . . Like the Boers in South Africa or the Deliaan planters in Sumatra, they saw themselves as having moved into 'empty' lands." Bickers, "Shanghailanders," p. 199. See also Bickers, *Britain in China*, pp. 14–15.

49. Susan Mann Jones, "The Ningpo *Pang* and Financial Power at Shanghai," in *The Chinese City between Two Worlds*, ed. Mark Elvin and G. W. Skinner, especially p. 74; Wu Guifang, *Songgu mantan*, pp. 109–111, 161; Yang Guangfu, *Songnan yuefu*, pp. 170, 172; Johnson, *Shanghai: From Market Town to Treaty Port*, pp. 160–162, 165, 183. As John Orchard put it, "Shanghai was a great trading center long before the foreigner brought in his security. The port would have continued to develop economically if the foreigner had heeded the wishes of the Chinese and remained in Canton." "Shanghai," *The Geographical Review* 26.1 (1936): 10–11.

50. Johnson, *Shanghai: From Market Town to Treaty Port*, pp. 163–164. By this time there were already 3,000 or more ocean-going boats engaged in regular trade between Shanghai, Tianjin, and other North China ports. Dai An'gang, "Shanghai yu wan Qing caoyun biange," in *Shanghai yanjiu luncong* 2, pp. 51–56.

51. Karl Gutzlaff and Hugh Lindsey visited Shanghai in 1832; this quote is taken from Gutzlaff, "Journal of a Residence in Siam, and of a Voyage along the Coast of China to Mantchou Tartary," in *The Chinese Repository* 2nd edition, vol. 1, 125f. John E. Orchard notes that "[Lindsey] was so impressed by the number of junks in the harbor that he had the entries counted and found that in seven days some 400 junks ranging in size from 100 to 400 tons passed Woosung bound for Shanghai. If this record was characteristic of the entire year and not of the month of July alone, when Lindsey visited Shanghai, the city was one of the large ports of the world and compared favorably with London." (p. 6). See also references to other early British accounts of Shanghai on pages 5, 6, and 23–24. Orchard, "Shanghai," *The Geographical Review* 26.1 (1936): 1–31. Cf. Rhoads Murphey, *Shanghai: Key to Modern China*, pp. 59, 221n.

52. On trade through Shanghai, see Murphey, *Shanghai: Key to Modern China*, pp. 116–132. On Chinese ownership of "British" real estate and significant proportions of shares in "British" corporations, and the diversity of individuals who could claim "British" identity under a variety of circumstances, see Murphey, *Shanghai: Key to Modern China*, p. 6, Bickers, *Britain in China*, p. 13, and Chiara Betta, "Marginal Westerners in Shanghai: The Baghdadi Jewish Community, 1845–1931," in *New Frontiers: Imperialism's New Communities in East Asia, 1842–1953*, ed. Robert Bickers and Christian Henriot, pp. 43–45. For the role of refugees from elsewhere in China in Shanghai's economic development, see J. W. Maclellan, *The Story of Shanghai: From the Opening of the Port to Foreign Trade*, pp. 47–57; Wang Tao, *Yingruan zazhi*, p. 115; *Youxi bao* no. 695, pp. 1–2; Murphey, *Shanghai: Key to Modern China*, pp. 10–11.

53. Ackbar Abbas, "Cosmopolitan De-scriptions: Shanghai and Hong Kong," *Public Culture* 12.3: 769–786.

54. See, for example, Tani Barlow's discussion of "colonial modernity," and her critique of Fairbank's account of the "treaty port system," in which she suggests that Fairbank is inappropriately resistant to understanding Shanghai on colonial terms. "Colonialism's Career in Postwar China Studies," in *Formations of Colonial Modernity in East Asia,* ed. Tani Barlow, p. 392.

55. For a succinct discussion of the inequities inherent in Shanghai's current boom, see Tsung-yi Michelle Huang, *Walking between Slums and Skyscrapers: Illusions of Open Space in Hong Kong, Tokyo, and Shanghai,* pp. 99–136.

56. See Bryna Goodman, *Native Place, City, and Nation: Regional Networks and Identities in Shanghai, 1853–1937,* pp. 125–137; Goodman, "Improvisations on a Semi-colonial Theme"; and Johnson, *Shanghai: From Market Town to Treaty Port.*

57. Bickers, "Shanghailanders"; Nicholas Clifford, *The Spoilt Children of Empire: Westerners in Shanghai and the Chinese Revolution of the 1920s;* Ristaino, *Port of Last Resort;* Bickers, *Britain in China;* Bickers and Henriot, *New Frontiers.* "Throughout the period 1843–1937, the foreigners at Shanghai pressed the Chinese authorities for an extension of their own administrative powers and the area of the two foreign settlements. In this endeavor they found lukewarm support or outright opposition from the foreign diplomatic representatives at Peking and from the foreign offices in the home countries. . . . The complex political and economic structure of modern Shanghai was erected primarily on the precedents resulting from bluff, maneuver, and *force majeure* of the assertive foreign residents of the city." Murphey, *Shanghai: Key to Modern China,* p. 24; see also pp. 15–17.

58. See, for example, the wording in the Treaty of Nanjing itself, reprinted in *Treaties between the Empire of China and Foreign Powers,* ed. William Frederick Mayers, p. 1. The Shanghai Municipal Council began as a committee charged only with maintenance of local roads and jetties; as Robert Bickers writes, "[t]he government of the International Settlement was a complicated affair, an accretion of precedent over thin legal foundations." Bickers, "Shanghailanders," pp. 166, 168, 172–174, 180–181. See also Goodman, "Improvisations on a Semicolonial Theme," p. 889. The formation of the French Concession was if anything even more contingent and ambiguous, as detailed in Johnson, *Shanghai: From Market Town to Treaty Port,* p. 247. By the 1920s, as Bickers points out, "The SMC [Shanghai Municipal Council], however, was constitutionally responsible only to its electorate, and not to any direct consular or diplomatic authority (unlike its French neighbour). Shanghailanders were fond of reminding themselves, and the world of this fact. Exactly who the SMC was answerable to always remained unclear." *Britain in China,* p. 127.

59. Ristaino, *Port of Last Resort;* Betta, "Marginal Westerners"; Claude Markovits, "Indian Communities in China, c. 1842–1949," in *New Frontiers,* ed. Bickers and Henriot, pp. 55–74.

60. Ristaino, *Port of Last Resort.*

61. Indeed, Linda Cooke Johnson concludes that the International Settlement was in the early decades virtually indistinguishable from the kind of arrangement that sojourning groups from other areas *within* China enjoyed in Shanghai, from the pro-

cedures through which the land was acquired, facilities for recreation set up, goods bought and sold, to the legal rights and responsibilities of the concession authorities to deal with "their own people." Johnson, *Shanghai: From Market Town to Treaty Port*, pp. 202–206. "In many ways, then, the British Settlement was the near equivalent of the other 'outsider' guilds at Shanghai. The 'Yingguo huiguan,' or British guild, fitted neatly into the preexisting Chinese mercantile system. In Chinese documents, the reference is to the *yiguan* ('barbarians' *[hui]guan*). Compared with the memberships of some of the *huiguan*, which ran into the thousands, the Westerners' small numbers made them considerably less of a nuisance. In the multiethnic environment of the suburbs of Shanghai, they were just another set of outside sojourners *(wailai)*, if a little more 'outside' *(wai)* than those from the farther parts of China" (p. 206). See also pp. 185–186, 189–192, 247, 265–266, 322–323. As Joseph Fletcher has pointed out, an approach similar to the Shanghai "concessions" had already been taken by the Qing government toward Muslim merchants on the northwest frontier beginning in 1835, involving in that case as well armed confrontation leading eventually to agreements on extraterritoriality, "most-favored-nation" treatment, and the institution of more direct trade relationships. Fletcher, "The Heyday of the Ch'ing Order in Mongolia, Sinkiang, and Tibet," in *The Cambridge History of China*, ed. Denis Twitchett and John K. Fairbank, vol. 10, pp. 360–395, especially 375–385. It is likely that this precedent was in the minds of officials in charge of coming to terms with the British in the 1840s and 1850s. Ristaino, *Port of Last Resort*, p. 7

62. "[I]t is clear that when the Qing government tried to accommodate Western demands of extraterritorial rights and involvement in legal affairs, it did so with very clear precedents in mind. Especially in the case of Shanghai, it is evident that the Mixed Court was as much a Qing institution as it was a foreign implant." Cassel, "Excavating Extraterritoriality: The 'Judicial Sub-Prefect' as a Prototype for the Mixed Court in Shanghai," *Late Imperial China* 24.2 (2003): 156–182, p. 175. See also Cassel's review of previous scholarship on pages 156–159.

63. For a detailed analysis of the complex politics of exclusion and nationalism associated with the Public Garden, see Robert Bickers and Jeffrey Wasserstrom, "Shanghai's 'Dogs and Chinese Not Admitted' Sign: Legend, History, and Contemporary Symbol," *The China Quarterly* 142 (1995): 444–466. For a variety of different accounts of the accessibility of the Public Garden to Chinese residents in the nineteenth century, see Ye Xiaoqing, "Shanghai before Nationalism" *East Asian History* 3 (1992), especially pp. 49–52.

64. Shih, *The Lure of the Modern*, pp. 5–12.

65. Andrew Jones, *Yellow Music: Media Culture and Colonial Modernity in the Chinese Jazz Age*.

66. Bickers, *Britain in China*, p. 13; Betta, "Marginal Westerners in Shanghai," pp. 43–45; Barbara J. Brooks, "Japanese Colonial Citizenship in Treaty Port China: The Location of Koreans and Taiwanese in the Imperial Order," in *New Frontiers*, ed. Robert Bickers and Christian Henriot: 109–124; Shih, *The Lure of the Modern*, p. 276. On the complicated experiences of African American musicians and writers in 1920s and '30s

Shanghai, see Jones, *Yellow Music,* especially pp. 1–7 and 147. For a conclusive explanation of Liu Na'ou's Taiwanese origin, see Peng, *Haishang shuo qingyu,* pp. 105–144.

67. For more detail on Leisure Garden, see chapter 1.

68. On the place of the Public Garden in twentieth-century Chinese nationalist discourse, see Bickers and Wasserstrom, "Shanghai's 'Dogs and Chinese Not Admitted' Sign." Ye Xiaoqing notes that Chinese residents were more interested in the Yangshupu Garden than in the Public Garden. "Shanghai before Nationalism," p. 51.

69. Arnold Wright and H. A. Cartwright provide a description of Zhang's Garden at the turn of the century: "In a spacious concert hall, known as 'The Arcadia,' Chinese theatricals and other entertainments are given by some of the best-known native talent and visiting troupes, and there are also cinematograph entertainments and shooting galleries. From time to time special attractions are provided, such as a balloon ascent, a good band, a pyrotechnic display, or a native procession." Wright and Cartwright, eds., *Twentieth-Century Impressions of Hong Kong, Shanghai, and Other Treaty Ports of China: Their History, People, Commerce, Industries, and Resources,* p. 690. See also Chi, *Huyou mengying,* pp. 161–163, *Shenjiang shixia shengjing tushuo,* 1.2ab, and Des Forges, "Street Talk and Alley Stories," pp. 27–29 for more on Zhang's Garden and others. For a detailed analysis of the cultural politics of these parks in late-Qing Shanghai, which nonetheless continues to a certain extent to emphasize the "Western" / "Chinese" binary, see Meng Yue, "Re-envisioning the Great Interior: Gardens and the Upper Class between the Imperial and the 'Modern,'" *Modern Chinese Literature and Culture* 14.1: 1–50. For an example of the significance of Zhang's Garden as the central place to be seen in Shanghai c. 1911, see Zamperini, "On Their Dress They Wore a Body," p. 306.

70. Cf. Wasserstrom, "Locating Old Shanghai: Having Fits about Where It Fits," in *Remaking the Chinese City: Modernity and National Identity, 1900–1950,* ed. Joseph W. Esherick, p. 210.

71. Chen and Yuan, eds., *Shanghai jindai wenxue shi,* p. 235. Zou Tao was also the author of the commentary to *Qinglou meng,* a "courtesan novel" published by Shen bao guan. *Haishang chentian ying* was serialized in the leisure paper *Qu bao* at the rate of a page each day (A Ying, *Wan Qing wenyi baokan shulüe,* p. 71; see also an advertisement in *Youxi bao* no. 363, p. 1, for *Qu bao,* which makes reference to the serialization of *Xinbian Duanchang bei* as a supplement. *Duanchang bei* (The stele of broken hearts) was an alternate title of *Haishang chentian ying.*)

72. The first nineteen chapters of *Haishang mingji sida jin'gang qishu* appeared as a supplement to *Xiaoxian bao* in the spring of 1898, and a hundred-chapter volume edition was subsequently published by Wenyi shuju (Guo Changhai, "Wu Jianren xieguo naxie changpian xiaoshuo?" *Shinmatsu shōsetsu* 17 [1994]: 32). It was soon printed in installments again in Wu Jianren's *Caifeng bao,* beginning in July of 1898. Thanks to Patrick Hanan for pointing out advertisements for the novel in *Caifeng bao* issues held in the Shanghai Library. (For the identification of Wu Jianren as one of the main editors of *Caifeng bao,* see, among others, Ma Xuexin, ed., *Shanghai wenhua yuanliu cidian,* p. 348). An advertisement for the independent volume edition of *Sida jin'gang qishu* appears in *Youxi bao* no. 380, p. 1. This novel was published under what was probably

one of Wu Jianren's many pseudonyms; Wei Shaochang, Yuan Jin, and Patrick Hanan attribute it to Wu Jianren. (Yuan, *Yuanyang hudie pai*, p. 14; Wei, "*Haishang mingji sida jin'gang qishu liang ti*" in *Shinmatsu shōsetsu* 15 [1992]: 64–69; Hanan, *Chinese Fiction of the Nineteenth and Early Twentieth Centuries*, p. 26). Guo Changhai argues that the novel could not have been written by Wu Jianren, but his reasoning is not persuasive. (Guo, "Wu Jianren xieguo naxie changpian xiaoshuo?" pp. 24–33). *Haishang mingji si da jin'gang qishu* is reproduced in volumes 15–19 of *Shinmatsu shōsetsu*.

73. A lithographically printed edition of *Huoshao Shanghai Hongmiao yanyi* is in the Zhejiang Provincial Museum; the plot is summarized in *Zhongguo tongsu xiaoshuo zongmu tiyao*, pp. 830–831.

74. See book advertisements in *Youxi bao* no. 703, p. 3, and *Youxi bao* no. 713, p. 3.

75. For example, *Haishang mingji si da jin'gang qishu* also appeared as *Si da jin'gang zhuan*, *Si da jin'gang qishu*, *Haishang qinlou chuguan yeyou zhuan*, and *Da'nao Shanghai qinlou chuguan yanyi*. *Zhongguo tongsu xiaoshuo zongmu tiyao*, p. 806.

76. *Haishang fanhua meng* appeared first in *Caifeng bao*, and later in *Xiaolin bao*, before coming out in a volume edition beginning in 1903. For rough estimates of the number of volumes printed, see Wei, *Li Boyuan yanjiu ziliao*, p. 471, and Sun Yusheng, *Tuixinglu biji*, 2.11b.

77. Written by Tian Meng, published by the Shanghai Gailiang xiaoshuo she in 1911. See Wei Shaochang, *Li Boyuan yanjiu ziliao*, p. 471; also, *Zhongguo tongsu xiaoshuo zongmu tiyao*, p. 1229.

78. By Xia Lülan. See Wei, *Li Boyuan yanjiu ziliao*, p. 471.

79. Shanghai: Gailiang xiaoshuo she, 1910.

80. Reprinted in A Ying, *Wan Qing wenxue congchao*, vol. 8.

81. Published 1911. See *Zhongguo tongsu xiaoshuo zongmu tiyao*, p. 1228.

82. By Lao Shanghai. Listed in Wei, *Li Boyuan yanjiu ziliao*, p. 471. Shoudu tushuguan has a *Haishang xin fanhua meng (chuji)* with eight chapters, by Lao Shanghai, Shanghai Huitong xinji shuju, 1909, probably the same work. *Shoudu tushuguan cang Zhongguo xiaoshuo shumu chubian*, p. 225.

83. Ōta Tatsuo, *Kaijōka retsuden*, p. 532.

84. Chen's sequel (in 36 *juan*) was titled *Xu Haishang hua liezhuan*, and is mentioned in a list of his works on page 1a of *Miwu chunxiao qu*, a collection of verses printed in *San jia qu*, 1900, held by Fudan University Library; I would like to thank Patrick Hanan for mentioning this reference to me. For a brief account of Chen Diexian's life and writings, see Chen, *The Money Demon*, trans. Patrick Hanan, pp. 1–11. The other two sequels were printed in installments: *Hou Haishang hua liezhuan* (1902) in *Suzhou baihua bao*, and *Xu Qinglou baojian* (1908) in *Baihua xiaoshuo*. (See A Ying, *Wan Qing wenyi baokan shulüe*, pp. 83–84, and *Zhongguo jindai wenxue daxi*, vol. 30, pp. 23–24 and 214–215 for more details).

85. These satires, most of which were begun anonymously and never completed, include *Shanghai zhi weixin dang* (Shanghai's reform party, 1905); *Shanghai zhi mimi* (The secrets of Shanghai, 1906); *Shanghai youcan lu* (A record of Shanghai travels,

1907), by Wu Jianren; *Shanghai kongxin da laoguan* (Fraudulent rich men of Shanghai, 1908); *Haishang fengliu meng* (A fashionable dream of Shanghai, 1910); *Haishang feng-liu xianxing ji* (An account of fashionable doings in Shanghai, 1910); *Zuijin Shanghai mimi shi* (A secret history of recent Shanghai, 1910). The narrative structure of these satires for the most part differs strikingly from other Shanghai fiction, with many fewer storylines and less sophisticated plot construction.

86. See also Yuan, *Yuanyang hudie pai,* p. 10.

87. See, for example, the prefaces to *Beijing xin fanhua meng:* the first preface concedes that Shanghai is the leading city in China (Beijing is second), and quotes from the preface to *Haishang fanhua meng* at length; the second notes *Haishang hua liezhuan* and *Haishang fanhua meng* as sources of inspiration. Similarly, *Jiuwei gui* begins with an explanation of how Suzhou differs from Shanghai (which is presumed to be the standard), and Zeng Pu was careful to explain how he wanted to go beyond *Haishang hua* when he wrote *Niehai hua.*

88. Cf. Prendergast, *Paris and the Nineteenth Century,* p. 28: "Several of the novels I shall be looking at re-write, or un-write, the already-written Paris of the novel, principally the Paris of Balzac."

89. *Xiepu chao* was written under the pen name Haishang shuomeng ren, and published in installments in *Xin Shen bao* (*Xiepu chao,* p. 1); *Renjian diyu* was serialized in *Shen bao.* Other novels set in Shanghai during this period included Zhu Shouju, *Xin Xiepu chao* (c. 1923), Bao Tianxiao's *Shanghai chunqiu* (1924), Wumu shanren's *Haishang Daguan yuan* (1924), Sun Yusheng's *Haishang ranxi lu* (1925 reprint), Ping Jinya's *Renhai chao* (1926?), *Haishang huo diyu* (1929), and *Shanghai fengyue* (1929). Other novels not included here are listed in the appendix to Des Forges, "Street Talk and Alley Stories."

90. Shih, *The Lure of the Modern,* pp. 265–266. See also Wu Fuhui, *Dushi xuanliu zhong de haipai xiaoshuo;* Yingjin Zhang, *The City in Modern Chinese Literature and Film;* Li Jin, *Haipai xiaoshuo yu dushi wenhua;* Peng, *Haishang shuo qingyu.*

Chapter 1: Rhetorics of Territory, Mixture, and Displacement

1. "I really want to write a paper on those Shanghai novels [Hsia refers specifically to *Haishang fanhua meng, Xiepu chao,* and *Shanghai chunqiu,* and elsewhere in the same piece to *Haishang hua liezhuan*]. The alternate fascination and disgust the British and French have for London and Paris respectively, must have frequently appeared in their novels." Hsia, "Novel and Romance," pp. 231–232.

2. Peter Brooks, *Reading for the Plot: Design and Intention in Narrative,* p. 43 and pp. 143–170. See also Raymond Williams, *The City and the Country;* Christopher Prendergast, *Paris and the Nineteenth Century;* Walter Benjamin, "Paris, Capital of the Nineteenth Century," in *Reflections,* pp. 146–162; Donald Fanger, *Dostoevsky and Romantic Realism: A Study of Dostoevsky in Relation to Balzac, Dickens, and Gogol.*

3. "Semicolonial" is used here in the sense suggested by Shu-mei Shih: "I choose to

use 'semicolonialism' to describe the cultural and political condition in modern China to foreground the multiple, layered, intensified, as well as incomplete and fragmentary nature of China's colonial structure. The 'semi-' here is not to denote 'half' of something, but rather the fractured, informal, and indirect character of colonialism, as well as its multilayeredness." Shih, *The Lure of the Modern*, p. 34. See also p. 35, and Jürgen Osterhammel, "Semi-Colonialism and Informal Empire in Twentieth-Century China: Towards a Framework of Analysis," in *Imperialism and After: Continuities and Discontinuities*, ed. Wolfgang J. Mommsen and Jürgen Osterhammel.

4. The exceptions usually refer to Shanghai more obliquely by naming the Huangpu River or using archaic-sounding designations like "Hujiang" or "Hubin." For more detailed discussions of urban settings in earlier Chinese vernacular fiction, see among others Jaroslav Průšek, "The Beginnings of Popular Chinese Literature: Urban Centres—the Cradle of Popular Fiction," and "Les contes chinoises du moyen âge comme source de l'histoire économique et sociale sous les dynasties des Sung et des Yüan"; Patrick Hanan, *The Chinese Vernacular Story*, pp. 60–61; Des Forges, "Street Talk and Alley Stories," pp. 73–76.

5. Hanan, "*Fengyue meng* and the Courtesan Novel."

6. See, for example, Han Bangqing, *Haishang hua liezhuan* (1894; reprint, Beijing: Renmin wenxue chubanshe, 1985), 1/1. This edition will be abbreviated in all later references as *Haishang hua*. Sun Yusheng, *Haishang fanhua meng* (Shanghai: Shanghai guji chubanshe, 1991), 1/3. This edition will be abbreviated in later references as *Fanhua meng*. Erchun jushi [Li Boyuan?], *Haitian hong xueji* (Nanchang: Jiangxi renmin chubanshe, 1989 reprint), 1/191. This edition will be abbreviated in all later references as *Haitian hong*). Bi Yihong, *Renjian diyu* (Shanghai: Shanghai guji chubanshe, 1991 reprint—this edition will be referred to in all later references as *Renjian diyu*).

7. *Xiepu chao*, 21/276; see also chapters 23, 24, and 30.

8. *Haitian hong*, 12/264, 13/268; *Fanhua meng*, 1/7–10, 5/47, 29/316, 54/595, 65/735, 74/841; Wang Tao's preface, Zou Tao, *Haishang chentian ying* (Minzu chubanshe, 1995 reprint), p. 1. This edition will be abbreviated in all later references as *Chentian ying*); *Haishang hua*, 12/98.

9. Anne Querrien, "The Metropolis and the Capital," *Zone* 1/2, pp. 219–220.

10. Zhou Zuoren and Shen Congwen initiated this critique, provoking responses from Shanghai writers like Du Heng. See Jeffrey Kinkley, *The Odyssey of Shen Congwen*, p. 194; Zhang, *The City in Modern Chinese Literature*, pp. 22–24 and 179–180; Shih, *The Lure of the Modern*, 176ff; and Lu Xun, "'Haipai' he 'jingpai,'" in *Lu Xun quanji*, vol. 6, pp. 300–304.

11. Des Forges, "Street Talk and Alley Stories," pp. 73–76. Or, to use Hill Gates's terminology, between the tributary mode of production and the petty capitalist mode of production. Gates's insistence on reading administrative activity as itself a mode of production helps to reveal the motivated character of distinctions between "haipai" and "jingpai." See *China's Motor: A Thousand Years of Petty Capitalism*, especially pp. 13–41.

12. Although Shanghai had been the site of the Jiangnan Customs Administration

since 1730, the function of the Customs Administration (to regulate overseas trade) was primarily "metropolitan." For an incisive theoretical discussion of Shanghai as a "frontier" city in comparison with the cultural center that was eighteenth- and early nineteenth-century Yangzhou, see Meng, "Re-envisioning the Great Interior" and *Shanghai and the Edges of Empires*.

13. See Yuan Xiangfu's preface to Ge, *Huyou zaji*. William Rowe writes that Hankow was "the single most important entrepôt for Ch'ing China's domestic interregional trade—a trade which I have argued was far larger than usually recognized—and it was this function which above all shaped the city's society. . . . Administratively, Hankow claimed no position whatsoever in the Ch'ing hierarchy of provincial, prefectural, and county capitals." *Hankow: Conflict and Community in a Chinese City*, p. vii.

14. Prendergast, *Paris and the Nineteenth Century*, p. 14.

15. Earlier novels which make use of some dialect expressions include *Jin Ping Mei*, *Xingshi yinyuan zhuan* (A tale of marriage destinies to awaken the world), Liren heqiu's *Mindu bieji* (An unofficial history of the Fujian region), and *Fengyue meng*.

16. "*Haishang hua liezhuan* liyan," in *Haishang hua*, prefaces, p. 1.

17. *Jindai wenxue daxi*, vol. 30, pp. 23–24, 214–215. In addition to Li Boyuan's well-known *Shijie fanhua bao*, which made partial use of Wu dialect, there were four other Shanghai dailies that used dialect more extensively: *Jishi xingle bao* (est. 1901), *Fangyan bao* (est. 1902), *Suzhou baihua bao* (est. 1902), and *Hua shijie* (1903–1910). A Ying, *Wan Qing wenyi baokan shulüe*, pp. 79, 83–85. See the introduction for information on sequels to *Haishang hua liezhuan*.

18. As Hu Shi points out, although Han did use the character *viao*, he did not use *ven* (*wu* + *ceng*), which appeared for the first time only in later fiction. Hu, "*Haishang hua liezhuan* xu," p. 585.

19. Cang Jie was the fabled inventor of the Chinese writing system.

20. Sun, *Tuixing lu biji*, 2.11ab.

21. See, among others, Hu Shi, "*Haishang hua liezhuan* xu," pp. 585–586; Zhang Ailing, *Haishang hua kai*, pp. 18–19, *Haishang hua luo*, p. 724; Huang Yanbo, "Lun *Haishang hua liezhuan* deng Wuyu xiaoshuo de lishi jiaoxun." *Liaoning daxue xuebao* 107: 53–55. Liu Fu is slightly more optimistic; while he also sees Wu dialect literature as severely restricted in audience, he suggests that literary success has little to do with the number of readers, and that eventually there will be more readers who are capable of understanding Wu dialect. Liu, "Du *Haishang hua liezhuan*," p. 604. For a more detailed discussion of Eileen Chang's "translation" of the dialogue in *Haishang hua* into Mandarin, see chapter 7.

22. A Ying, *Xiaoshuo ertan*, p. 84. For examples of Wu dialect prose-verse narratives, see Ōta Tatsuo's *Gogo danshi tōhō* (How to read Wu dialect *tanci*), Gogo kenkyū sōkan, vol. 3, 1970, and Shi Rujie, *Wuyu duben: Ming Qing Wuyu he xianzai Suzhou fangyan*. I would like to thank Tomoko Shiroyama for mentioning the latter source to me.

23. Yuan Jin's estimates of literacy rates for 1890s Shanghai (60 percent for men, 10 to 30 percent for women) are somewhat more conservative than Western observers' esti-

mates of literacy in nineteenth-century Guangzhou. Combined with Rhoads Murphey's figure of 500,000 Chinese residents in Shanghai as a whole by 1890, however, these rates yield between 160,000 and 220,000 adults with basic literacy in Shanghai alone in the last decade of the nineteenth century. By 1905 the population of Shanghai had doubled to one million. Yuan, *Yuanyang hudie pai*, p. 34; Murphey, *Shanghai: Key to Modern China*, p. 22. Lee and Nathan, "The Beginnings of Mass Culture: Journalism and Fiction in the Late Ch'ing and Beyond," p. 372. For a definition of the Wu dialect area, see S. Robert Ramsay, *The Languages of China*, fig. 6, and pp. 88–95.

24. Watt, *The Rise of the Novel: Studies in Defoe, Richardson, and Fielding*, pp. 35–36; Des Forges, "Street Talk and Alley Stories," p. 46.

25. "Translations of Extracts from the Published Newspapers 1905–1916," vol. 1, p. 38; original attributed to "Universal Gazette," August 5, 1905. In fact, as early as 1856, the missionary Martha Crawford wrote a fictional narrative that was printed in a romanized form of Shanghai dialect. See Hanan, *Chinese Fiction*, p. 75.

26. For sequels to *Haishang hua*, see the introduction. There were at least nine distinct reprint editions of *Haishang hua* in the late Qing and early Republican period (in addition to the original 1892 *Haishang qishu* serialization and 1894 Dianshi zhai volume edition), and at least three more later on in the Republican period (printed by Qinghua, Yadong, and Dada tushu hongying she). The late Qing and early Republican era reprints are as follows:

(1–4) Ōta Tatsuo notes the following four reprint editions: a Guangxu era lithographic reprint with the title *Qinglou baojian;* a 1903 lithographic reprint by Rixin shuju with the title *Haishang baihua qule yanyi* (owned by Mr. Takakura); a Guangxu era lithographic reprint with the title *Haishang kanhua ji;* and a Guangxu lithographic reprint titled *Zuixin Haishang fanhua meng* (Shanghai Liwen xuan shuzhuang). Ōta, *Kaijōka retsuden*, p. 532.

(5) The Capital Library in Beijing has a lithographic reprint published by Jiangnan shuju, 1901. *Shoudu tushuguan cang Zhongguo xiaoshuo shumu chubian*, p. 219.

(6–8) Beijing Normal University Library has three reprints from this period: a 1908 lithographic reprint from Rixin shuzhuang, a partial early Republican period lithographic reprint, and another Republican period lithographic reprint under the title *Qinglou baojian*. See *Beijing shifan daxue tushuguan zhongwen guji shumu*.

(9) *Zhongguo jindai wenxue da cidian* notes an edition titled *Haishang qinglou qiyuan* (p. 834).

27. Selected recent reprint editions of either the 1894 Dianshi zhai edition of *Haishang hua*, or the 1926 Yadong tushuguan edition, both of which have the original Wu dialect dialogue, include the following: Taipei: Tianyi chubanshe, 1974; Beijing: Renmin wenxue chubanshe, 1982 and 1985; Taipei: Guiguan, 1983 and 1985; Shanghai: Shanghai guji chubanshe, 1990 and 1994; Nanchang: Baihua zhou wenyi chubanshe, 1993; Beijing: Zhongguo xiju chubanshe, 1999; Beijing: Dazhong wenhua chubanshe, 1999.

The Eileen Chang translation version has gone through several editions at Huangguan, and has been reprinted on the mainland several times.

28. In this context, the contrast between dialect usage in texts, recordings, and films produced in Shanghai in the 1920s and '30s and those produced in Canton during the same period is instructive. For a discussion of dialect film, see Zhiwei Xiao, "Constructing a New National Culture: Film Censorship and the Issues of Cantonese Dialect, Superstition, and Sex in the Nanjing Decade."

29. See Zhang Chunfan, *Jiuwei gui*, and Li Boyuan, *Guanchang xianxing ji* (The bureaucrats), among others. After 1905, it is rare to find a *male* character speaking in Wu dialect. This correspondence between gender distinctions and dialect distinctions acquired such force that T. A. Hsia wrote in 1959 that the dialect used by men and women in *Haishang hua liezhuan* was "too effeminate." "Novel and Romance," pp. 230, 232.

30. See Peter Kornicki, "Kashihon bunka hikakukō," *Jinbun gakuhō* 57: 54–55; and for more detail on one Edo author and his works, Robert Leutner, *Shikitei Sanba and the Comic Tradition in Edo Fiction.*

31. Hsia, "Novel and Romance," p. 232. See also Hu Shi, "*Haishang hua liezhuan* xu," which refers throughout to "Suzhou tuhua," "Subai," and "Wuyu."

32. These distinctions were clear-cut already by the 1860s; see, for example Joseph Edkins, *A Vocabulary of the Shanghai Dialect*, pp. 73, 151, and Wang Tao, *Yingruan zazhi*, p. 11.

33. *Haishang hua*, passim; Miyata Ichirō, "*Kaijōka retsuden* no gengo" *Tōyō kenkyū* 73 (1985), pp. 27–36; see also Hu Mingyang's study of changes in Shanghai dialect over time, "Shanghai hua yibai nian lai de ruogan bianhua" *Zhongguo yuwen* 1978.3: 199–205.

34. See *Haitian hong*, pp. 187–189 and passim.

35. Prendergast, *Paris and the Nineteenth Century*, pp. 27–28.

36. There is one work of fiction published in the 1870s—the satire *He dian*—that does make extensive use of Wu dialect slang expressions in the narrative portion as well as in the dialogue. Unlike novels set in Shanghai, however, *He dian* does not attempt to represent the *sound* of spoken Wu dialects through the use of loan characters.

37. *Fanhua meng*, 19/198, 20/202, 29/315, 95/1091 *(Suzhou hua)*, 96/1098, and so on.

38. See, for example, the confusion between *dù* and *tú*—both *du*[13] in Wu dialect (*Fanhua meng*, 44/480), and between [Shao]'*an* and [Shao]*yu*—much closer in present-day Wu dialect than in the northern standard (*Fanhua meng*, 76/875). For the readings of these characters in present-day Shanghai dialect, see Miyata, *Shanghai go jōyō dōon jiten*, pp. 76–77, 167, 207. See also Min Jiaji et al., eds. *Jianming Wu fangyan cidian*.

39. This struggle in fact begins two decades before the first Shanghai fiction, in the world of fashion and theater; in the 1870s, "Capital-style goods" *(jinghuo)* were considered most stylish, and Peking opera had crowded *Kunqu* out of theaters, as Shanghai residents began to define themselves in contrast to the better-known metropolises of Suzhou and Yangzhou. See Dai Shadi, "Beijing shi Shanghai de chanpin ma?" in *Beijing:*

dushi xiangxiang yu wenhua jiyi, ed. Chen Pingyuan and Wang Dewei, for more on this point.

40. Gu Bo, "Shijing de huixiang," in *Beijing: dushi xiangxiang yu wenhua jiyi,* ed. Chen Pingyuan and Wang Dewei, pp. 161–162.

41. Wang Tao, *Yingruan zazhi,* p. 11; Chi, *Huyou mengying,* p. 155; Goodman, *Native Place, City, and Nation,* pp. 1, 15; *Xiepu chao,* prefaces, p. 7.

42. Querrien, "The Metropolis and the Capital," pp. 219–220.

43. See, for example, the following passage: "In this way, the character that his own labor possesses of being socially useful takes the form of the condition, that the product must not only be useful, but useful for others." Robert C. Tucker, *The Marx–Engels Reader,* p. 322.

44. For more detail on the Shanghai publishing industry and its products, see chapter 4; also, Link, *Mandarin Ducks and Butterflies;* Lee and Nathan, "The Beginnings of Mass Culture"; Des Forges, "Street Talk and Alley Stories," pp. 34–44; and Christopher Reed, *Gutenberg in Shanghai.*

45. Raymond Williams, *The Country and the City,* p. 148.

46. Perhaps the best example of this phenomenon is found in Zhang Chunfan's *Jiuwei gui,* in which Shanghai is the standard against which Suzhou is measured, even as Suzhou dialect and Suzhou courtesan culture retain their privileged status. Zhang, *Jiuwei gui,* pp. 2, 7, 11, 1009, 1010–1012, 1024. In this connection, it is also worth noting that the earliest known edition of *Fengyue meng,* a novel full of *Yangzhou* urban flavor, was not first published in that city, but rather in Shanghai in 1883, more than three decades after it was written. Hanan, "*Fengyue meng* and the Courtesan Novel," p. 346.

47. Zhu, *Xin Xiepu chao* (Shanghai guji chubanshe, 1991 reprint), prefaces, p. 4 (hereafter cited as *Xin Xiepu chao*). A slightly different claim to world-city status—based on the large number of scams perpetrated on the unwary—appears in *Shanghai zhi pianshu shijie,* p. 1a.

48. For the clearest example of the former approach, see Shih, *The Lure of the Modern;* for the latter, see Lee, *Shanghai Modern,* especially chapters 1 and 9. I use "mimicry" here in the complex sense that Homi Bhabha gives the word in "Of Mimicry and Man: The Ambivalence of Colonial Discourse," in *The Location of Culture.*

49. On the importance of Japan as a means of problematizing the China/West binary, see Shih, *The Lure of the Modern,* pp. 4–5, 16–30, 140–144, 257–265, 331–338.

50. For discussions of native-place identity, see Goodman, *Native Place, City, and Nation;* Elizabeth Perry, *Shanghai on Strike: The Politics of Chinese Labor;* and Emily Honig, *Creating Chinese Ethnicity: Subei People in Shanghai, 1850–1980.* "As is evident in the friction between the Guangdong processionists in the Jubilee and the International Settlement police, native-place organization also underlay early struggles between Chinese and foreign authorities in the city, struggles that would be retrospectively marked by developing Chinese nationalism as "Chinese" struggles against foreign imperialists. . . . Of course, at the time of the Silver Jubilee of the International Settlement [1893], these opposing positions of "Chinese" and "foreign" were only gradually crystallizing in

Chinese residents' political imaginations." Goodman, "Improvisations on a Semicolonial Theme," p. 922. See also pp. 894, 912, and 921.

On "British" identity, see Betta, "Marginal Westerners," pp. 43–45; and Bickers, *Britain in China*, pp. 13, 71–72. "Communal identity and solidarity in Britain in China, as we shall see, were located most visibly in questions of race, and the polarity between a constructed 'white' British presence and the other 'races' it encountered in China. British Asians or Eurasians muddied these waters and threatened not only that identity but that very presence" (p. 72). "'British' investment also included investment by the 'other Westerners,' namely British-protected subjects: Baghdadi Jews, Indian Parsis, Straits Settlement and Hong Kong Chinese, and Eurasians with British protection" (p. 13).

51. N. V. Gogol, "Peterburgskie zapiski 1836 goda," in *Polnoe sobranie sochinenii*, vol. 8, p. 178. Translation based in part on Fanger, *Dostoevsky and Romantic Realism*, p. 108.

52. Lotman, "Symbolic Spaces: 4. St. Petersburg," in Lotman, *Universe of the Mind: A Semiotic Theory of Culture*, p. 201.

53. Wang, *Yingruan zazhi*, p. 115; Maclellan, *The Story of Shanghai*, pp. 47–57; Murphey, *Shanghai: Key to Modern China*; Johnson, *Shanghai: From Market Town to Treaty Port*; Goodman, *Native Place, City, and Nation*; Des Forges, "Street Talk and Alley Stories," pp. 8–13; cf. Xudong Zhang, "Shanghai Nostalgia: Postrevolutionary Allegories in Wang Anyi's Literary Production in the 1990s," *positions* 8.2: 366.

54. Fanger, *Dostoevsky and Romantic Realism*, pp. 104–105. Specifically "the most abstract and intentional city in the whole round world." Dostoevsky, *Notes from the Underground*, p. 17.

55. N. V. Gogol, *Peterburgskie povesti*, p. 43.

56. See, for example, Wu Zhen's ordeal in jail in Hanshang mengren, *Fengyue meng*, chapters 23–26, 32.

57. *Haishang hua*, 1/2. Cf. Michel de Certeau's discussion of the use of the proper name as metaphor, in *The Practice of Everyday Life*, p. 104.

58. Luo Zhufeng, et al., eds. *Hanyu da cidian*, vol. 7, p. 1316; Morohashi Tetsuji, *Dai kanwa jiten*, vol. 7, p. 1086.

59. I place the word "concessions" in quotes in my translation of the title, because the original involves the use of characters that are parts of the expression *zujie*. Lu Xun was referring here to the location of his own house in one of the contested areas into which the International Settlement expanded. Lu Xun, *Qiejie ting zawen*. See also Hanchao Lu, *Beyond the Neon Lights*, pp. 368–369n101, where *qiejie* is translated as "semiconcessions."

60. According to the report "Extra-Settlement Roads 1853–1930," popular resistance to concession expansion and boundary realignments often continued long after Qing authorities had yielded to foreign pressure and agreed to them. The struggle between the Ningbo Guild and the French Concession authorities over the concession authorities' plan to build a road through the guild cemetery is discussed briefly in Perry, *Shanghai on Strike*, p. 23, and in more detail in Goodman, *Native Place, City, and Nation*, pp. 158–175. See also Goodman, *Native Place, City, and Nation*, p. 66. In some

cases, however, scholars may have overemphasized tensions between ordinary Shanghai residents and foreign settlers prior to the turn of the century. Cf. Ye Xiaoqing, "Shanghai before Nationalism."

61. Ge, *Huyou zaji* (1989 reprint), pp. 3, 12, 17–18; *Fanhua meng,* 1/10; *Dianshi zhai huabao,* Zi 3, 18.

62. For example, see the summary of the *North China Herald*'s December 25, 1858 "tour" of the southern city in Johnson, *Shanghai: From Market Town to Treaty Port,* pp. 335–338.

63. Grace Thompson Seton, *Chinese Lanterns,* p. 90. According to Jeffrey Wasserstrom, the designation of the southern city as "Chinatown" reappeared in jest in a tour guide's description of the city in 1996. Wasserstrom, "Locating Old Shanghai: Having Fits about Where It Fits," p. 193.

64. Johnson, *Shanghai: From Market Town to Treaty Port,* pp. 113–119; Shanghai tushuguan, *Lao Shanghai ditu,* pp. 17, 71.

65. The overwhelming majority of concession residents were Chinese from the earliest years forward; as early as 1893, at least 40 percent of the shares of some foreign companies were held by Chinese investors (Murphey, *Shanghai: Key to Modern China,* p. 6). "To take one example, an estimated one-third of 'British' real estate in Shanghai was actually Chinese-owned in 1926" (Bickers, *Britain in China,* p. 13). Note also that as mentioned above, the definition of "Western" in nineteenth- and early twentieth-century Shanghai includes individuals who would be understood as colonial subjects in other locations, such as Singapore, Baghdad, or Bombay.

66. *Haishang hua,* 4/30. Similarly, in *Dreams of Shanghai Splendor,* Tu Shaoxia takes refuge in his family's compound in the southern city from his creditors and the courtesans he previously patronized; Yao Jinghuan begins his life of dissipation in minor and relatively harmless fashion in teahouses around the City Temple, and only later graduates to pursuits in the concessions. *Fanhua meng,* 33/356.

67. *Fanhua meng,* 7/63. This characterization of the southern city recurs in later works; see, for example, Wu Jianren, *Ershi nian mudu zhi guai xianzhuang,* p. 2.

68. *Fanhua meng,* 70/798.

69. *Fanhua meng,* 19/189.

70. Leo Lee makes a similar point about Shanghai cultural production in the 1930s; see Lee, *Shanghai Modern,* pp. 307–312.

71. Fletcher, "Heyday of the Ch'ing Order," pp. 360–395, especially 375–385; Piper Rae Gaubatz, *Beyond the Great Wall: Urban Form and Transformation on the Chinese Frontiers,* p. 312.

72. Mayers, *Treaties between the Empire of China and Foreign Powers,* p. 1.; Cassel, "Excavating Extraterritoriality"; Ristaino, *Port of Last Resort,* pp. 5–6.

73. Julia Kristeva, *Powers of Horror: An Essay on Abjection,* pp. 4–5. Note also the emphasis on filth in the description of certain lower-ranking prostitutes (*Haishang hua,* 15/121).

74. *Fanhua meng,* 99/1136.

75. Frederic Wakeman, *Policing Shanghai 1927–1937*, p. 14 and passim.

76. For an earlier example of the convergence of what we generally consider two very different categories—technology and ritual—see Judith Boltz's discussion of the uses of gunpowder (probably a recent invention at that time) in Daoist exorcisms of the Song dynasty. Boltz, "Not by the Seal of Office Alone: New Weapons in Battles with the Supernatural," especially pp. 277–286.

77. See, for example, an illustration in *Dianshi zhai huabao* depicting the "arrest" and confinement of pigs found in the French Concession to the police station. (*Dianshi zhai huabao*, Zi 3, 18) A partial list of prohibited behavior in the concessions—including littering, setting firecrackers, carrying ducks and chickens upside-down through the streets, and so on—appears in Ge, *Huyou zaji*, p. 3.

78. Examples of the former include the limitation of police and fire surveillance under ordinary circumstances to the space within concession boundaries; for the latter, we may note the different punishments implemented by the International Settlement Mixed Court depending on the time of day—foreign consular officials presided only at specified hours. *Fanhua meng*, 98/1127.

79. Wu Fuhui, *Dushi xuanliu zhong de haipai xiaoshuo*, p. 149; Xu Xu, *Feng xiaoxiao* (The sound of the wind), pp. 14–26. This novel was first published in installments in 1943, and in a volume edition in 1944. See Zhang, *The City in Modern Chinese Literature and Film*, p. 223.

80. *Mengyou Shanghai mingji zhengfeng zhuan* (Shanghai: Guangyi shuju, after 1904), abbreviated hereafter as *Zhengfeng zhuan*. Patrick Hanan has a copy of *Mingji zhengfeng zhuan*. Ping Jinya mentions the last, published in 1900, in *Jiu Shanghai de yan, du, chang*, ed. Shanghai wenshi yanjiu guan, p. 263. The text has also been reprinted more recently under the title *Shanghai mingji zhuan*; see Hanan, "*Fengyue meng* and the Courtesan Novel," p. 349.

81. See *Zhengfeng zhuan*, 1.5b, where Sicha lu, a Yangzhou street name, remains while other place-names are changed to refer to Shanghai. There is also a slight lapse on 1.4a, where a less-than-careful substitution suggests that the walk from the concession areas to the City Temple is but a few steps.

82. Hanshang mengren, *Fengyue meng*, p. 35; *Zhengfeng zhuan*, 1.6b.

83. Hanshang mengren, *Fengyue meng*, p. 237; *Zhengfeng zhuan*, 4.2b.

84. For a thorough account of mid-Qing Yangzhou cosmopolitanism and cultural dominance, especially relative to Shanghai, see Meng Yue, "Re-envisioning the Great Interior" and Antonia Finnane, "Yangzhou's 'Mondernity': Fashion and Consumption in the Early Nineteenth Century."

85. *Fanhua meng*, 98/1127–1128. For an illustration of this kind of procession, see chapter 4 below, figure 6.

86. Wu Jianren, *Ershi nian mudu zhi guai xianzhuang*, p. 1. Cf. Milena Doleželová-Velingerová, *The Chinese Novel at the Turn of the Century*, pp. 66–67.

87. Bickers, "Shanghailanders," p. 199. For Chinese-language examples, see, among others, the preface to *Haishang qinglou tuji*. By way of contrast, see Yuan Xiangfu's 1876

preface to Ge, *Huyou zaji,* which notes the impact of trade on Western ships, but traces Shanghai's prosperity further back to the change in grain shipments earlier in the Daoguang period.

88. Johnson, *Shanghai: From Market Town to Treaty Port,* pp. 98–99. Cf. Wang, *Yingruan zazhi,* p. 98. Wang Tao also lists seven other gardens that were well-known in Daoguang, Xianfeng and Tongzhi eras, but they may have been more exclusive. *Yingruan zazhi,* pp. 38–42.

89. Shen Fu, *Fusheng liuji* (Six chapters from a floating life), 4.16b.

90. *General Description of Shanghae and its Environs Extracted from Native Authorities,* p. 164.

91. Ge, *Huyou zaji,* p. 4. See also Yu Xingmin, *Shanghai, 1862 nian,* p. 416.

92. Yao Xie, "Kuhai hang," 29b; Johnson, *Shanghai: From Market Town to Treaty Port,* p. 99.

93. Gail Hershatter, *Dangerous Pleasures,* p. 36; cf. the discussion of the changing fortunes of Also a Garden, located in the southern city, in *Fanhua meng* 19/189–191.

94. Zhang Xuesen, ed., *Yuanlin jiqu,* pp. 5–6. Cf. Wang, *Yingruan zazhi,* p. 45.

95. Ōno Mihoko, "Shanghai ni okeru gien no keisei to hatten," *Ocha no Mizu shigaku* 26–27 (1983): 51–52.

96. Lu Shi'e, *Xin Shanghai,* 19/84.

97. Susan Mann Jones, "The Ningpo *Pang* and Financial Power at Shanghai," p. 74; Johnson, *Shanghai: From Market Town to Treaty Port,* pp. 163–164; Dai An'gang, "Shanghai yu wan Qing caoyun biange," pp. 51–56; Ho Ping-ti, "The Salt Merchants of Yang-chou: A Study in Commercial Capitalism in Eighteenth-Century China," pp. 131, 138; Gong Zizhen, "Jihai liuyue chongguo Yangzhou ji," translated in *Inscribed Landscapes: Travel Writing from Imperial China,* ed. Richard Strassberg; Meng Yue, *Shanghai and the Edges of Empire,* pp. xvii–xix.

98. Maclellan, *The Story of Shanghai,* pp. 47–57; Wang, *Yingruan zazhi,* p. 115; *Youxi bao* no. 695, pp. 1–2; Murphey, *Shanghai: Key to Modern China,* pp. 10–11. On the decline of Yangzhou and Suzhou (relative to Shanghai), see Wang, *Yingruan zazhi,* p. 107.

99. Des Forges, "Street Talk and Alley Stories," pp. 17–19. For more detail, see Ōno, "Shanghai ni okeru gien no keisei to hatten," pp. 53–60, and Meng Yue, *Shanghai and the Edges of Empires,* chapter 3.

100. Poshek Fu, *Between Shanghai and Hong Kong: The Politics of Chinese Cinemas,* p. 4.

101. Ristaino, *Port of Last Resort.*

102. Ristaino, *Port of Last Resort,* pp. 5–6.

103. See, for example, the fascination with the figure of the Russian woman in so much of 1930s Shanghai fiction.

104. With the exception of a brief period in the 1860s when Shanghai residents fled from the southern city into the concession and settlement areas in fear of the Taiping Rebellion, it was not until c. 1895 that the concession and settlement areas matched the population of the rest of the city. After the concession areas stopped expanding in

1915, their share of the overall population of the urban area fell to less than one third by 1930. Murphey, *Shanghai: Key to Modern China*, p. 22.

105. Yeh, "The Life-Style of Four *Wenren*," p. 420; Zhu Weizheng, "Wan Qing Shanghai wenhua: yi zu duan lun," *Fudan xuebao* 1992.5: 43.

106. Ge, *Huyou zaji* 1989 reprint edition, prefaces, pp. 6–8. *Huyou zaji* served as an unacknowledged source for later writings about the city; it was reprinted at least twice (with revisions) in Shanghai (Ge, *Chongxiu Huyou zaji*, 1887, 1887) and once in Tokyo (Ge, *Huyou zaji*, annot. Hori Naotarō, 1878); and was translated into Japanese as *Shanghai hanjōki* (Ge, *Huyou zaji*, 1989 reprint edition, prefaces, p. 5). See also the preface to *Haishang qinglou tuji*, which suggests that this collection of illustrations of courtesans can serve as a guide for people who do not live in Shanghai.

107. Johnson, *Shanghai: From Market Town to Treaty Port*, p. 187. See also Catherine Yeh's discussion of images of exotic Westerners in lithographic illustration collections. *Shanghai Love*, pp. 316–318.

108. See Meng, "Re-envisioning the Great Interior" for an analysis of the significance of Western architecture and landscaping in Zhang's Garden, one of the best-known parks open to the public in the late nineteenth century, and Zamperini, "On Their Dress They Wore a Body," pp. 304, 307, and 318 for examples of the appropriation of "Western" styles by turn-of-the-century courtesans and women of "proper" families.

Chapter 2: From Street Names to Brand Names

1. A photograph of the English Settlement from the clock-tower of Trinity Church taken by Tomishige Rihei (1837–1922) is reproduced in Muramatsu Shin, *Shanghai: toshi to kenchiku, 1842–1949*, pp. 84–85.

2. Wang, *Yingruan zazhi*, p. 37.

3. Ge, *Huyou zaji*, pp. 19, 57. See also *Shenjiang mingsheng tushuo*, 70a; Wu, *Haishang baiyan tu*, 1.16a, reprinted in *Wu Youru huabao*; *Youxi bao* no. 60, p. 2.

4. D. Satow, *Shanghai Views No. 1* (Shanghai, before 1903), p. 25; Shanghai Views No. 3, pp. 14, 15, and 18; respectively. Satō's photography studio appears in W. E. B., *The Hotel Metropole Guide to Shanghai and environs containing all necessary informations for tourists and others*, and he is referred to as a skilled photographer in Jiancun youke, *Shanghai*, p. 7a.

5. Examples of Shanghai verse collections include Yang Guangfu's *Songnan yuefu* and Zhang Chunhua's *Hucheng suishi quge*, both reprinted in 1989 by Shanghai renmin chubanshe.

6. See, among others, Kung Tai, "Shanghai Bund," held in Tōyō bunko, Tokyo; "Panoramic View of Foreign Section of Shanghai, China," Phillips Library, Peabody Essex Museum, Salem, MA; and Muramatsu, *Shanghai: toshi to kenchiku, 1842–1949*, pp. 24–25, 72–73. See also the photo album *Shanghai*.

7. "From Yangshu pu in the north to Shiliu pu in the south, along the Huangpu

River; should one look at the gas and electric lights along the shore at night, it is indeed like a fiery dragon." *Haitian hong,* 1/191. This is the same view (from the eastern bank of the Huangpu River) taken by countless painters and photographers in the nineteenth and early twentieth centuries.

8. Writing in *Youxi bao* in 1897, Li Boyuan claims that Fourth Avenue is the most prosperous stretch of real estate in all of China. (*Youxi bao* no. 101, p. 1).

9. *Haitian hong,* 1/191.

10. *Fanhua meng,* 30/324, 64/723, 72/817, 80/917, 86–87/991ff. Similarly, Zhu Shiquan, a "wild chicken," is to be found in Daxing Alley, two blocks west of Stone Street (*Haishang hua,* chapter 27). For a discussion of this hierarchy that is drawn instead from guidebooks, newspaper articles, and memoirs, see Hershatter, *Dangerous Pleasures,* pp. 41–50.

11. *Haishang hua,* 4/28.

12. *Xiepu chao,* 22/289. In this same chapter (p. 297), Wei Wenjin moves to this alley from Burkill Road (Baike lu) because he believes being on a major street makes it easier for his concubine to cheat on him.

13. Pierre Bourdieu, *The Rules of Art,* pp. 40–43. Some examples of these movements: *Haishang hua,* 12/98; *Haishang hua,* 28/234; *Fanhua meng,* chapter 90.

14. *Haishang hua,* 31/256–257; *Fanhua meng,* 30/324, 72/817. For guidebooks of the late Qing and Republican era, see Hershatter, *Dangerous Pleasures,* p. 36.

15. Cf. "Xinzeng chongxiu Shanghai xiancheng xiang zujie dili quantu," and the list of street names and locations in *Shanghai zhinan.* Ōta Tatsuo has also consulted an 1884 map of the city in order to show where key locations in *Haishang hua* can be found. Ōta, trans., *Kaijōka retsuden,* p. 523.

16. *Haishang hua,* 3/18, 10/77–78, 24/197, and 32/270; *Fanhua meng,* 47/514, 72/824.

17. Muramatsu, *Shanghai: toshi to kenchiku,* pp. 89–95; Hanchao Lu, "Away from Nanjing Road: Small Stores and Neighborhood Life in Modern Shanghai," *Journal of Asian Studies* 54.1: 94–95.

18. *Shanghai zhanggu,* pp. 92–100; Lu, *Beyond the Neon Lights,* pp. 173, 175–176, 181–185, 277, 314.

19. *Caifeng bao* was published in Taiping Lane (off Third Avenue), *Shijie fanhua bao* was published in Yixin Alley (off Grand Avenue), and *Xiaolin bao* was published in Yingchun Lane at the turn of the century. These addresses are invariably listed on the masthead of the newspapers. In 1917 the famous Uchiyama Bookstore was established in Weisheng Alley in Hongkou. (Lu, *Beyond the Neon Lights,* p. 176).

20. "These arcades, a recent invention of industrial luxury, are glass-roofed, marble-walled passages cut through whole blocks of houses, whose owners have combined in this speculation. On either side of the passages, which draw their light from above, run the most elegant shops, so that an arcade of this kind is a city, indeed, a world in miniature." From a nineteenth-century guide to Paris, quoted in Walter Benjamin, *Reflections,* pp. 146–147.

21. *Fanhua meng,* 63/719.

22. *Haishang hua*, 1/2.

23. *Haishang hua*, 1/2.

24. Des Forges, "Building Shanghai, One Page at a Time," pp. 787–788. For a list of dates cited in *Haishang hua*, see Stephen Cheng, "*Sing-Song Girls of Shanghai* and its Narrative Methods," pp. 113–114. On the significance of chronological discrepancies in earlier fiction, see Rolston, *How to Read the Chinese Novel*, pp. 56–57 and 224; Rolston, *Traditional Chinese Fiction and Fiction Commentary*, p. 181.

25. Cf. M. M. Bakhtin's formulation of the "chronotope": "Time, as it were, thickens, takes on flesh, becomes artistically visible; likewise, space becomes charged and responsive to the movements of time, plot, and history. This intersection of axes and fusion of indicators characterizes the artistic chronotope." *The Dialogic Imagination*, p. 84.

26. *Fanhua meng*, chapters 61 through 63. See also the progress of Hong Shanqing's letter to his sister in Suzhou, *Haishang hua*, 29/238, and the unwillingness of the *Xiepu chao* narrator to go beyond the Shanghai city limits, discussed in the first chapter.

27. Bedini, *The Trail of Time: Time Measurement with Incense in East Asia*, pp. 10, 16–17, and chapters 4 and 7–9.

28. Ge, *Huyou zaji*, p. 16, 57; the first of these two references is repeated almost word for word in *Shenjiang shixia shengjing tushuo*, 1.13b.

29. See, for example, Ge, *Huyou zaji*, p. 56; Chi, *Huyou mengying*, p. 156. For a detailed theory of defamiliarization or "enstrangement" *(ostranenie)*, see Viktor Shklovsky, *Theory of Prose*, especially pp. 6–12. "In practice [poetic] language is often quite literally foreign."

30. *Chentian ying*, 2/17.

31. For an analysis of this new significance of lineage discourse, see Kai-wing Chow, *The Rise of Confucian Ritualism in Late Imperial China: Ethics, Classics, and Lineage Discourse*, especially pp. 71–128.

32. See also Des Forges, "Street Talk and Alley Stories," chapters 2 and 4, and Des Forges, "Building Shanghai, One Page at a Time," pp. 781–810, for detail on the narrative structures characteristic of Shanghai fiction.

33. Simmel, "The Metropolis and Mental Life," pp. 50–51.

34. Joshua Goldstein, "From Teahouse to Playhouse: Theaters as Social Texts in Early-Twentieth-Century China," *Journal of Asian Studies* 62.3 (2003), especially pp. 768–770.

35. E.g., the role of the opera in Tolstoy's *War and Peace,* and the theater in works by Balzac and Zola. For an example of a woman attending a theater in Beijing and drawing the attention of the audience, see Zamperini, "On Their Dress They Wore a Body," pp. 305–306.

36. For examples of men who take an interest in women after seeing them perform, see *Haishang hua*, 44/371–373; *Fanhua meng*, 4/37–39 and chapter 79; and *Haitian hong*, 1/195. Li Boyuan notes that "*tanci* halls" were particularly useful for visitors from out of town who had no other way to make a courtesan's acquaintance. By the late 1890s, prose-verse narratives were in fact performed less often in "*tanci* halls" than set

pieces from the Peking opera repertoire. (Youxi zhuren, *Haishang youxi tushuo,* 4.24b. See also Jiancun youke, *Shanghai,* (1903), p. 11a.)

37. Male to male attraction, not explicitly discussed in most Shanghai novels, plays a central role in Chen Sen's *Pinhua baojian,* a novel set in early nineteenth-century Beijing. See Carlos Rojas, "The Coin of Gender in *Pinhua baojian.*"

38. *Fanhua meng,* 88/1006–1008. A similar complaint appears several years later in Zhang Chunfan's *Jiuwei gui* in chapters 158 (pp. 1043–1044) and 160 (1052–1066). See also Hershatter, *Dangerous Pleasures,* pp. 116–118.

39. *Xiepu chao,* 15/201ff.

40. Meng Yue, *Shanghai and the Edges of Empires,* p. 102.

41. An interesting precedent to these "new productions" appeared in eighteenth-century Yangzhou, where storytellers occasionally presented narratives based on contemporary events. Lucie Borotová, "Storytelling in Yangzhou in the Eighteenth Century: *Yangzhou huafang lu,*" p. 202.

42. *Youxi bao* no. 119, p. 1; no. 448, p. 2; no. 451 pp. 1–2; no. 457, p. 2. *The Celestial Empire* also refers to these topical productions in an article on April 1, 1892 (p. 427) Spectators flocked to a show titled "Fuzhou lu," thinking that it would consist of present-day Shanghai scandals; contrary to their expectations, it was in fact based on *Sanguo zhi.*

43. *Fanhua meng,* 87–88/1003ff.

44. *Haishang hua,* 34/287. This play is a dramatization of the events of chapters 44 through 46 of *Shuihu zhuan;* see Ōta, *Kaijōka retsuden,* p. 249.

45. *Haishang hua,* 30/246.

46. See, for example, *Fanhua meng,* chapters 87–88.

47. Lu Hsun, *A Brief History of Chinese Fiction,* p. 335. Xu Qinfu, who arranged for the 1922 Qinghua reprint of *Haishang hua,* has a story which is superficially similar but in fact contradicts Lu Xun's version at a number of points. Thorough critiques of both Lu Xun and Xu Qinfu's claims appear in Hu Shi, "*Haishang hua liezhuan* xu" (pp. 572–576), and in Eileen Chang's afterword to her translation of *Haishang hua* into Mandarin (Zhang, *Haishang hua luo,* pp. 713–715).

48. Upon reflection, even Lu Xun realizes that the novel is carefully structured from the very beginning, with Zhao Erbao's fate foreshadowed in her uncle's very first mention of her. Lu Hsun, *A Brief History of Chinese Fiction,* p. 335.

49. Ōta Tatsuo discusses a variety of proposed "models" for *Haishang hua* characters in an afterword to his translation of the novel into Japanese. Ōta, *Kaijōka retsuden,* pp. 530–532. Despite Hu Shi and Lu Xun's disagreement on a number of other questions connected with *Haishang hua,* they both are impressed by its "realistic" style. Hu, "*Haishang hua liezhuan* xu," p. 574; Lu Hsun, *A Brief History of Chinese Fiction,* pp. 330–331. See also Liu Fu, "Du *Haishang hua liezhuan,*" p. 599; Wu Guifang, *Songgu mantan,* pp. 211–233.

50. Ge, *Huyou zaji,* p. 57. See also Catherine Yeh's discussion of courtesans' photographs in *Shanghai Love* (pp. 84–86), and the preface to *Haishang qinglou tuji,* in which it is suggested that for residents in other cities, looking at lithographic illustrations of these Shanghai courtesans will be "like looking at the women [themselves]."

51. *Haishang hua,* 45/380, and *Haitian hong,* 16/287–289.

52. Marston Anderson, *The Limits of Realism: Chinese Fiction in the Revolutionary Period,* pp. 9–10.

53. See Des Forges, "Street Talk and Alley Stories," pp. 178–180 for more detail on this point.

54. Lu Shi'e, *Xin Shanghai* (Shanghai guji chubanshe, 1997), 2/7–8, 12/54, 20/88–92. This edition will be referred to in later footnotes as *Xin Shanghai.*

55. See, among others, *Fanhua meng,* 18/178, 26/274, 49/534, 83/946.

56. Des Forges, "Street Talk and Alley Stories," p. 180.

57. I discuss the recursive structure of nineteenth-century courtesan novels in more detail in "From Source Texts to 'Reality Observed.'"

58. "To take a deliberately trivial example, the functions order a drink, obtain it, drink it, pay for it, constitute an obviously closed sequence, it being impossible to put anything before the order or after the payment without moving out the homogenous group *'Having a drink.'* The sequence is indeed always nameable." Barthes, "Introduction to the Structural Analysis of Narratives" (in Roland Barthes, *Image, Music, Text*), p. 101. The "deliberate" triviality of Barthes's example is necessary: in most cases, the precise outlines of a narrative sequence are subject to debate and differences of interpretation. We will return to this point in the next chapter.

59. For more detail on these links between particular types of urban spaces and specific narrative functions, see Des Forges, "Street Talk and Alley Stories," pp. 125–139.

60. Barthes, "The Reality Effect," in *The Rustle of Language,* pp. 141–148; see also Anderson, *The Limits of Realism,* p. 16–17.

61. Wang, *Fin-de-siècle Splendor,* pp. 55, 90.

62. Catherine Yeh, "The Life-style of Four *Wenren,*" p. 449; see also Yeh, *Shanghai Love.*

63. For a discussion of the logic of the roman à clef in the late Qing, see Wang, *Fin-de-siècle Splendor,* pp. 188–189.

64. Wu, *Haishang baiyan tu,* 1.15b; *Haishang hua,* 50/423; *Xiepu chao,* chapter 40. See also *Fanhua meng,* 16/159–160.

65. Even commentaries to *Dream of the Red Chamber* written by individuals with no personal knowledge of the author's family frequently make a point of identifying contradictions and inconsistencies in that novel.

66. Jonathan Spence, *The Memory Palace of Matteo Ricci,* pp. 1–23.

67. For detail on the creation of courtesan "brand-names," see Yeh, *Shanghai Love,* pp. 45, 222.

Chapter 3: Synchronized Reading

1. A similar stairway scene appears earlier in *Fengsu zhi tushuo,* 2.11b. The technical possibilities of lithography are evident if one contrasts illustrations in *Shenjiang shixia shengjing tushuo* and *Shenjiang shenjing tu,* both of which were lithographically printed, with similar scenes in *Shenjiang mingsheng tushuo,* which

is printed from woodblocks. The former show much larger crowds in much greater detail.

2. Other examples include the eighteenth-century *Wanshou tu* and *Gusu fanhua tu*. See Des Forges, "Street Talk and Alley Stories," pp. 57–58. Note the dismissive attitude taken in the renowned painters' manual *Jiezi yuan huazhuan* toward works of art that contain many figures (see Mai-mai Sze, *Mustard Seed Garden Manual of Painting*, p. 220). Ironically, the *Jiezi yuan huazhuan* was itself reprinted by Dianshi zhai, one of the earliest Shanghai lithographic presses, in 1887–1888.

3. "The institutions comprising 'the exhibitionary complex,' by contrast, were involved in the transfer of objects and bodies from the enclosed and private domains in which they had previously been displayed (but to a restricted public) into progressively more open and public arenas where, through the representations to which they were subjected, they formed vehicles for inscribing and broadcasting the messages of power (but of a different type) throughout society." Bennett, "The Exhibitionary Complex," reprinted in *Culture/Power/History*, ed. Dirks, et al., p. 124.

4. Anderson, *Imagined Communities*, pp. 22–36.

5. The word *chuancha* appears in Zhang Zhupo's commentary to *Jin Ping Mei*, where it refers to the technique of weaving together diverse plot elements. Rolston, *How to Read the Chinese Novel*, p. 234.

6. *Haishang hua*, prefaces, p. 2.

7. For a more detailed discussion of these two chapters, see Des Forges, "Building Shanghai, One Page at a Time," pp. 793–794.

8. See, for example, *Xiepu chao* (serialized 1916–1921), in which no fewer than ten narrative threads are set in motion in the first thirty chapters.

9. Zhang Peiheng, "*Haishang hua lie zhuan* yu qi yiqian de xiaoshuo," *Ming Qing xiaoshuo yanjiu* 1985.8: 328–329; Rolston, *How to Read the Chinese Novel*, p. 221.

10. For sequels to and imitations of *Shuihu zhuan* and *Honglou meng*, see Ellen Widmer, *The Margins of Utopia* and "*Honglou meng* Sequels and Their Female Readers in Nineteenth-Century China," and Keith McMahon, "Eliminating Traumatic Antinomies: Sequels to *Honglou meng*."

11. Sun, *Tuixing lu biji*, 2.11ab.

12. Sun, *Tuixing lu biji*, 2.8ab.

13. *Xin Shanghai*, 1/4.

14. See, among other examples, the mirror relationship between the story of Wu Chuyun in *Haishang fanhua meng* (chapters 61 through 63) and Jin Yuelan in *Jiuwei gui* (chapters 2 and 3), published around the same time; the courtesans Hua Xiaonong and Hua Liannong in *Haishang fanhua meng*, chapter 33, who reside in Tong*qing* Alley; a clear reference to Han Bang*qing*'s pseudonym Hua ye lian nong; the use more generally of similar alley names across textual boundaries to draw parallels between characters in different works, as discussed in the previous chapter; and the commentary to the eighth chapter of *Haitian hong xueji*, which refers to Li Shufang, a character in *Haishang hua liezhuan*, instead of Ling Shufang (*Haitian hong*, 8/238).

15. Anderson, *Imagined Communities,* pp. 35–36.

16. Cf. Kathleen Tillotson's discussion of the "close relation between author and reader" characteristic of mid-nineteenth-century British installment fiction. Tillotson, *Novels of the Eighteen Forties,* pp. 33–39.

17. Wei Shaochang, *Li Boyuan yanjiu ziliao,* p. 471.

18. In the Republican era, certain writers worked together, writing one chapter each in turn; these compositional circles soon broadened, with instances of authors starting a narrative and soliciting contributions from readers to continue it. See Link, *Mandarin Ducks and Butterflies,* p. 170; Rui Heshi, ed., *Yuanyang hudie pai wenxue ziliao,* vol. 2, 590–596; Liu Yangti, ed., *Yuanyang hudie pai zuopin xuanping,* p. 117; Haiyan Lee, "All the Feelings That Are Fit to Print."

19. By late 1898, *Youxi bao,* one paper closely associated with the publication of installment fiction, was available for purchase in twenty-four cities across China, as well as in Tokyo, as can be seen from the list of bookstores on the masthead of each issue; *Shijie fanhua bao* and other leisure papers soon followed.

20. See, for example, the contemporary critics cited in Chen Pingyuan, *Zhongguo xiaoshuo xushi moshi de zhuanbian,* pp. 280–282; Sima Xiao, "'Wo de tongshi' Zhang Henshui," *Daren* 16: 60; Link, *Mandarin Ducks and Butterflies,* pp. 180–181; and Chen and Yuan, *Shanghai jindai wenxue shi,* p. 286. For a more detailed discussion of some of these points, see Des Forges, "Building Shanghai, One Page at a Time," pp. 782–792.

21. *Haishang hua,* prefaces, p. 2.

22. "What needs to be noted, however, is that the terms from several sequences can easily be imbricated in one another: a sequence is not yet completed when already, cutting in, the first term of a new sequence may appear. Sequences move in counterpoint; functionally, the structure of narrative is fugued: thus it is that narrative at once 'holds' and 'pulls on.'" Barthes, *Image, Music, Text,* pp. 103–104, also p. 118.

23. *Haishang hua,* 3/18.

24. *Haishang hua,* 24/198.

25. *Haishang hua,* 33/275ff., 34/286–288.

26. *Haishang hua,* 54/461–462.

27. *Haishang hua,* 57/485–486.

28. Han Bangqing celebrates this very abruptness; see the above discussion of the "hidden flashes" technique.

29. Qian Xinbo, *Xieyu congtan* (chuji), preface, p. 1. For evidence of Shanghai installment fiction's popularity, see the introduction and chapter one.

30. A similar foreshadowing of an innovative mode of presentation through literary form occurs in Wei Xiuren's 1850s novel *Huayue hen* (Traces of flowers and the moon), in which the chapter-by-chapter narrative style of previous vernacular fiction is given a deeper, more ironic grounding through conscious reference to the author's own livelihood as a household tutor and occasional storyteller. This earlier case, with its more subtle thematic suggestion that we should take chapter-by-chapter presentation seriously, instead of just as an empty form, may well in turn have set the foundation for *Haishang hua liezhuan*'s own appearance in two-chapter installments. See Wei Zi'an,

Huayue hen, pp. 3–4 and 430. For the influence of *Huayue hen* on later fiction, see Yuan, *Yuanyang hudie pai.*

31. Des Forges, "Building Shanghai, One Page at a Time," pp. 786–792.

32. "The sign for this: if Mali disappears from the pages of the *New York Times* after two days of famine reportage, for months on end, readers do not for a moment imagine that Mali has disappeared or that famine has wiped out all its citizens. The novelistic format of the newspaper assures them that somewhere out there the 'character' Mali moves along quietly, awaiting its next reappearance in the plot" (Anderson, *Imagined Communities,* p. 33). A similar overlap in reading strategies is found between installment fiction and newspaper articles in Victorian England (Linda K. Hughes and Michael Lund, *The Victorian Serial,* p. 11).

33. *Youxi bao* no. 43, p. 2.

34. *Shijie fanhua bao* no. 238, p. 2.

35. *Shijie fanhua bao* no. 79, p. 3.

36. For more examples of this kind of interrupted presentation, see Yeh, *Shanghai Love,* p. 225.

37. Andrew Field, "Selling Souls in Sin City: Shanghai Singing and Dancing Hostesses in Print, Film, and Politics, 1920–1949," in *Cinema and Urban Culture in Shanghai,* ed. Yingjin Zhang, pp. 102–103.

38. Cited in Wu, *Dushi xuanliu zhong de Haipai xiaoshuo,* p. 134.

39. For *Youxi bao* circulation at the turn of the century, see Tarumoto, "Yūgi shujin sentei 'Kōshi zuikyū kasen,'" p. 18. The success of installment fiction was vital to the rise of French newspapers (Brooks, *Reading for the Plot,* pp. 147–152); Perry Link notes evidence of a similar tendency in early twentieth-century China (Link, *Mandarin Ducks and Butterflies,* pp. 12, 151).

40. See, for example, the preface to *Beijing xin fanhua meng.* The question of "addiction" to installment fiction is discussed in more detail in the next chapter.

41. Hughes and Lund, *The Victorian Serial,* p. 11; Brooks, *Reading for the Plot,* 164ff.; Link, *Mandarin Ducks and Butterflies,* p. 22. See also John Christopher Hamm, *Paper Swordsmen,* pp. 52–55 for a detailed analysis of the fictional and "non-fictional" narratives simultaneously unfolding in the pages of Hong Kong's *Xin wanbao* in early February of 1955.

42. Sun Xun and Sun Juyuan, *Zhongguo gudian xiaoshuo meixue ziliao huicui,* pp. 214–220; Rolston, *How to Read the Chinese Novel,* p. 225.

43. Alexander Des Forges, "Opium / Leisure / Shanghai: Urban Economies of Consumption," pp. 168–175; Des Forges, "Street Talk and Alley Stories," pp. 37–38.

44. Daniel Dayan, "The Tutor Code of Classical Cinema," *Film Quarterly* 28.1; for critiques and elaborations, see William Rothman, "Against 'The System of Suture,'" *Film Quarterly* 29.1; Stephen Heath, "Notes on Suture," *Screen* 18.4; and Kaja Silverman, *The Subject of Semiotics.*

45. Barthes, "Introduction to the Structural Analysis of Narratives" in *Image, Music, Text,* Genette, *Narrative Discourse: An Essay in Method,* and Brooks, *Reading for the Plot.*

46. Rolston, *How to Read the Chinese Novel,* p. 225.

47. For an analysis of a sequence of transitions, see Des Forges, "Building Shanghai," pp. 793–794.

48. See, for example, Liu Ts'un-yan's introduction to *Chinese Middlebrow Fiction from the Ch'ing and Early Republican Eras,* p. 14. Hu Shi also tends in this direction: see "*Haishang hua liezhuan* xu," pp. 574, 578.

49. *Haishang hua,* prefaces, p. 2.

50. Genette, *Narrative Discourse,* pp. 95–96, 109–110.

51. See David Rolston's discussion of the distinction between host and guest characters and the use of "shadows" *(yingzi)* to add a dimension to main characters. *Traditional Chinese Fiction and Fiction Commentary,* pp. 195–196, 198.

52. *Haishang hua,* 57/486ff.

53. *Haishang hua,* p. 3.

54. *Haitian hong,* 19/304.

55. Note especially the importance of the concept of the "main character" and the discreteness of narrative line in his resolution of certain analytical ambiguities on pages 50–51 (homodiegetic vs. heterodiegetic analepses) and pages 189–192 (external vs. internal focalization). See also the importance of fairy tales, folk narratives, myths, and stories from the Bible for Brooks, Barthes, Lévi-Strauss, and Vladimir Propp; discussion of such "fundamental" genres allows these theorists to make ahistorical and universalizing claims about narrative as a *human* practice.

56. Brooks, *Reading for the Plot,* pp. 4, 12–13, 39, 104.

57. Andrew Plaks, "Terminology and Central Concepts," in *How to Read the Chinese Novel,* ed. Rolston, p. 88. Li Yu, *Xianqing ouji,* pp. 17–18.

58. See *Fanhua meng,* chapters 58 and 60; *Haishang hua,* chapter 35.

59. "In the novel of plot, in particular, the feeling of completeness is substituted for the feeling of meaning; there would seem to be something mutually exclusive about the type of attention required for the apprehension of the various strands of the plot, and the transformational process whereby for the sentences of the individual work is substituted a sudden global feeling of a vision of life of some kind." Fredric Jameson, "Metacommentary," reprinted in *The Ideologies of Theory,* p. 8.

60. Lotman, *Universe of the Mind: A Semiotic Theory of Culture,* p. 63.

61. In a seventeenth-century commentary to the play *Xixiang ji,* Jin Shengtan wrote that if read in the right way, the play becomes the reader's own creation, with each sentence just the way that reader would want. Similarly, a later critic of *Honglou meng* asserted that he himself wrote the novel. (Rolston, *Traditional Chinese Fiction and Fiction Commentary,* p. 126). Zhang Zhupo, the most famous commentator to *Jin Ping Mei,* wrote of the novel that in order not to be deceived by it, "you must read it as though it were your own work . . . it is even better to read it as a work that is still in its early planning stages. Only if you start out with the assumption that you will have to work out every detail for yourself in order to avoid being deceived will you avoid being deceived." (Rolston, *How to Read the Chinese Novel,* p. 224.) The reader is never quite seen to reach this level of involvement in European fiction before the twentieth century,

although there was a distinct concern with his or her imagination as a productive force among English writers of installment fiction in the nineteenth century. Janice Carlisle, *The Sense of an Audience: Dickens, Thackeray, and George Eliot at Mid-Century,* p. 15.

Chapter 4: Desire Industries

1. *Haishang hua,* 64/552.

2. Scholars researching *Haitian hong* often characterize it as unfinished, because it ends in sudden fashion, apparently without bringing the story lines presented to a conclusion. On balance, however, it seems likely that *Haitian hong* was conceived of as an integral twenty-chapter unit, "complete" in its "incompleteness" whether a continuation appeared or not. Des Forges, "Street Talk and Alley Stories," pp. 109–111.

3. See Andrew Plaks, "Towards a Critical Theory of Chinese Narrative" in *Chinese Narrative: Critical and Theoretical Essays,* ed. Andrew Plaks, pp. 338–339; Plaks, *The Four Masterworks of the Ming Novel: Ssu Ta Ch'i-shu,* p. 75; and Rolston, *How to Read the Chinese Novel,* pp. 282–283, 286. In the event that the high point of the narrative did occur in the closing chapters, it was generally the case that all of the narrative threads would be neatly tied up in the process. Rolston, *How to Read the Chinese Novel,* p. 218 and *Traditional Chinese Fiction and Fiction Commentary,* pp. 136, 249, 259, 261. This emphasis on narrative closure was likely related to the aesthetics of dramatic structure advanced by contemporary critics like Li Yu. Li, *Xianqing ouji,* pp. 123–124. The best-known exception to this general tendency was Jin Shengtan's seventy-chapter version of *Shuihu zhuan.* But even though this version does end abruptly in a dream sequence, the ending is carefully positioned at precisely the point where all of the main characters have been gathered together at Liangshan, thus preserving the *da tuanyuan* climax as a logical ending point.

4. *Haishang hua,* preface, p. 1. This same phrase, "to conclude by not concluding," was also used to characterize Jin Shengtan's version of *Shuihu zhuan.* Rolston, *Traditional Chinese Fiction and Fiction Commentary,* p. 263.

5. *Fanhua meng,* 31/331–332.

6. Shanghai: Wenming shuju, 1915–1916.

7. Including at least *Shanghai shi zimei* (Ten sisters of Shanghai, Wenming shuju; advertised on the back of the 1918 Wenming shuju reprint of *Xu Haishang fanhua meng houji*), *Haishang ranxi lu* (A record of [things seen by the light of] a burning rhinoceros horn in Shanghai, Shanghai tushuguan 1925 reprint edition), and *Heimu zhong zhi heimu* (Scandals within scandals, which Catherine Yeh translates as "Dark shadows behind the scene"; Yeh, *Shanghai Love,* p. 217).

8. See the introduction, and also Des Forges, "Street Talk and Alley Stories," pp. 112–113.

9. Wang, *Fin-de-siècle Splendor,* pp. 56–58, 71–72.

10. See chapter one for a list of early reprints of *Haishang hua,* and the introduction for a list of sequels.

11. Based on the original and reprint editions discussed in chapter one alone, it is likely that more than 20,000 copies of *Haishang hua* were in circulation in the two decades after 1894. For information on Republican-era print runs for works of Lu Xun, Yu Dafu, Guo Moruo, and Mao Dun, see Chen, *Zhongguo xiaoshuo xushi moshi de zhuanbian,* p. 278 and Mao Dun, *Wo zouguo de daolu,* vol. 2, pp. 122–123; for *Niehai hua,* see A Ying, *Xiaoshuo santan,* p. 175.

12. Q. D. Leavis, *Fiction and the Reading Public,* p. 7: "This along with the information volunteered by a public librarian that many take out two or three novels by Edgar Wallace a week, and the only other books they borrow are 'Sapper's' or other 'thrillers,' suggests that the reading habit is now often a form of the drug habit." See also pp. 56, 136–137; and Patrick Brantlinger, *The Reading Lesson: The Threat of Mass Literacy in Nineteenth-Century British Fiction,* introduction. For a comparison between installment fiction and alcohol in a preface to an early twentieth-century Chinese novel, see below.

13. *Renjian diyu,* chapter 9. Several exceptions found in *Haishang fanhua meng* are noted in Des Forges, "Opium / Leisure / Shanghai," pp. 180–181. Opium does play a prominent role in several nineteenth- and twentieth-century novels that are *not* set in Shanghai; see Keith McMahon, *The Fall of the God of Money: Opium Smoking in Nineteenth-Century China,* pp. 139–169.

14. The "horse-of-intention" is often paired with the "monkey-mind" as *yima xinyuan* or *xinyuan yima,* as in the quote at the beginning of this chapter. Luo et al., eds., *Hanyu da cidian,* vol. 7, p. 641; Nakamura Hajime, *Bukkyōgo daijiten,* p. 42.

15. Huang Shiquan, *Songnan mengying lu,* p. 113; *The Celestial Empire,* August 1, 1890, p. 118; *Youxi bao* no. 66–68, passim; Chi, *Huyou mengying,* p. 160; Charles Mayne, *Notes on Tramways,* p. 1; *Youxi bao* no. 639, pp. 1–2; *Youxi bao* no. 671, p. 1.

16. *Fanhua meng,* 8/71, 75, 77. Cf. *Youxi bao* no. 654, p. 2.

17. Zhou Yuanhe, *Shanghai jiaotong hua dangnian,* pp. 42–43. For turn-of-the-century carriage routes superimposed on a period city map, see Yeh, *Shanghai Love,* p. 71.

18. Youxi zhuren, *Haishang youxi tushuo* 4.3b–4a, 7b. See also Hershatter, *Dangerous Pleasures,* p. 92 and Yeh, *Shanghai Love,* pp. 62–68.

19. *Haishang hua,* 16/123, 54/462; *Fanhua meng,* 23/235. See also illustrations in Wu Youru, *Haishang baiyan tu,* 1.19a, 1.25b, 2.12a.

20. *Fanhua meng,* 18/178; *Haitian hong,* 20/310; Yeh, *Shanghai Love,* p. 71. Cf. *Youxi bao* no. 66, p. 2.

21. Note the confrontation between actors and carriage drivers staged in *Fanhua meng* chapters 89 and 90. See also *Haitian hong,* 19/307, 20/310, Hershatter, *Dangerous Pleasures,* pp. 116–117, and Yeh, *Shanghai Love,* p. 81.

22. *Haitian hong,* 20/311.

23. *Fanhua meng,* 31/331–332.

24. Delays in Du Shaomu's planned return to Suzhou occur in chapters 8, 13, 14, 39, and so on.

25. *Fanhua meng,* 71/801–805. It turns out that the courtesan, Liu Xianxian, in fact has nothing to tell him: "Xianxian chuckled, saying 'You fell into my trap! I wanted to

trick you into coming to hold a banquet . . . I was afraid that you would not come, so I said I knew what had happened to her.' . . . Shaomu was very disappointed, then laughed at himself for being deceived by Xianxian" (p. 805).

26. "It was only that there were limitations to the format . . . there were manuscripts of several tens of thousands of words length which exhausted the size of the pages and could not be printed in full. [We] were forced by circumstance to break [these longer pieces] up and print them in successive months. Readers found fault with this. I say that in gathering together these works of ancients and moderns, one should not be limited by time, nor by space available; one should just select those worth transmitting and leave it at that." Qian, *Xieyu congtan (chuji)*, preface, p. 1.

27. Hou Zhongyi, *Zhongguo wenyan xiaoshuo cankao ziliao*, p. 597.

28. Rolston, *How to Read the Chinese Novel*, p. 225; Sun and Sun, *Zhongguo gudian xiaoshuo meixue ziliao huicui*, pp. 214–220.

29. *Beijing xin fanhua meng*; Chen, *Zhongguo xiaoshuo xushi moshi de zhuanbian*, p. 283.

30. Chen Weizhao, "Yin'guo, sekong, suming guannian yu Ming-Qing changpian xiaoshuo de xushi moshi," *Hua'nan shifan daxue xuebao* 74: 61–66; see also Wang, *Fin-de-siècle Splendor*, p. 58.

31. The exact quote (from the *Grundrisse*) is: "Production not only supplies a material for the need, but it also supplies a need for the material" (Tucker, *The Marx–Engels Reader*, p. 230).

32. Although Han himself does not mention this, the fact that there are sixty-four chapters to *Haishang hua*, as there are sixty-four hexagrams in the *Book of Changes*, provides strong evidence that the book was meant to end at this point all along.

33. Postface to *Haishang hua*, pp. 553–554. Zhang Henshui used a similar argument in his second refusal to write a sequel to *Tixiao yinyuan zhuan* (An account of marriage fates in tears and laughter), which was the best-selling novel of the 1920s and '30s (Link, *Mandarin Ducks and Butterflies*, p. 31.).

34. Rolston, *Traditional Chinese Fiction and Fiction Commentary*, p. 128.

35. *Fanhua meng*, 60/674–675.

36. See also *[Xu] Fanhua meng*, 1/1157.

37. "The writing of *Chunqiu* is none other than praise of the worthy and criticism of the unworthy, and stands as the example to ten thousand generations of rulers and officials. Fiction and drama speak of nothing other than sadness and happiness, separation and reunion, and please the hearts of those at the time who read them" (*Zhongguo lidai xiaoshuo xuba xuanzhu*, ed. Zeng Zuyin et al., p. 249). Cf. *Ming-Qing xiaoshuo xuba xuan*, ed. Dalian tushuguan cankao bu, pp. 45, 50, and Ban Gu, *Han shu*, p. 1754.

38. For a discussion of temporal shifting and the intentional integration of eighteenth-century Kaifeng with its late Ming antecedent in the eighteenth-century novel *Qilu deng* (The light at the crossroads), see Daniel Youd, "Geographies of Success and Failure in Li Lüyuan's (1707–1790) *Qilu deng*."

39. *Fanhua meng*, 63/718–719.

40. *Fanhua meng*, 71/804.

41. *Fanhua meng,* 87/1002–1003.

42. Before, actors seduced women, but now the times have changed, and it is the women—even those of "good families"—who attempt to seduce the actors; for more detail, see chapter 2.

43. *[Xu] Fanhua meng,* 1/1157; see also 61/1831.

44. *Xin Xiepu chao,* prefaces pp. 3–4.

45. Xu Jielu, *Hubin shentan lu,* p. 1.

46. Rolston, ed., *How to Read the Chinese Novel,* p. 128.

47. See, for example, Shi Zhecun's advocacy of "purely modern poetry" in 1933: "The so-called modern life includes various idiosyncratic forms: harbors lined with large steamers, factories clamoring with noise, mines burrowing deep into the earth, dancing floors playing jazz music, sky-scraping department stores, air battles, spacious race courses. . . . Even the natural scenery is different from that of earlier periods. How can the emotion such a life inspires in the poet be the same as those of the previous generation?" Shih, *The Lure of the Modern,* p. 251.

48. *Fanhua meng,* 29/316.

49. See the 1890 map of assessed property values in the English Settlement reprinted in Muramatsu, *Shanghai: toshi to kenchiku,* p. 83 and similar maps of estimated land value from 1929 and 1944 reprinted in Shanghai tushuguan, *Lao Shanghai ditu,* pp. 98–101, as well as Catherine Yeh's reconstruction of carriage routes in *Shanghai Love,* p. 81.

50. See, for example, Hu Shi, "*Haishang hua liezhuan* xu," p. 586.

51. Yeh, *Shanghai Love,* pp. 6, 82, 341–344, 365–366. For concrete examples of the significance of the leisure industry, see, among others, Yu, *Shanghai, 1862 nian,* p. 415; *Shenjiang shixia shengjing tushuo,* 2.2b; Ōno, "Shanghai ni okeru gien no keisei to hatten," pp. 56–57; Huang, *Songnan mengying lu,* pp. 117, 143; Jiancun youke, *Shanghai,* p. 10a; Youxi zhuren, *Haishang youxi tushuo,* 3.10ab.

52. Hanshang mengren, *Fengyue meng,* p. 163. See also *Xingshi yinyuan zhuan* for a description of the entertainment possibilities afforded even individuals of modest means by a pilgrimage. Glen Dudbridge, trans. "Women Pilgrims to T'ai-shan: Some Pages from a Seventeenth-Century Novel."

53. *Youxi bao* of January 7, 1899 (no. 556), pp. 1–2; *Caifeng bao* of November 18, 1899, pp. 1–2.

54. Zhang, *Jiuwei gui,* 158/1043.

55. MacCannell, *The Tourist: A New Theory of the Leisure Class,* p. 3.

56. A customs commissioner identifies the flourishing courtesan houses in the International Settlement as one of the main attractions for retired officials, those waiting for assignments, and other rich individuals who relocated to Shanghai in large numbers in the 1880s, despite high rents and taxes higher than in other cities. Cited in Rudolf Wagner, "The Role of the Foreign Community in the Chinese Public Sphere," *The China Quarterly* 142: 428–429.

57. Hershatter, *Dangerous Pleasures,* pp. 81–82, and 90. Hershatter also writes of the metal tokens issued by courtesan houses to sedan chair bearers, rickshaw pullers,

and cab drivers. "The fact that these tokens were accepted citywide in lieu of petty currency indicates just how many small commercial transactions involved the courtesan houses" (p. 95).

58. For a list of tax rates on a variety of establishments, see Jiancun youke, *Shanghai*, p. 34a. See also *Land Regulations and Bye-laws for the Foreign Settlements of Shanghai North of the Yang-king-pang;* Yu, *Shanghai, 1862 nian*, p. 422; Johnson, *Shanghai: From Market Town to Treaty Port*, p. 327. Cf. Elizabeth Remick, "Prostitution Taxes and Local State Building in Republican China," *Modern China* 29.1 (2003), which focuses on taxes on prostitution in Guangdong Province.

59. Ōno, "Shanghai ni okeru gien," p. 51; Yao Gonghe, *Shanghai xianhua*, p. 10; *Youxi bao* no. 101, p. 1; Muramatsu, *Shanghai: toshi to kenchiku*, p. 83.

60. *Travellers Guide to Shanghai*, p. 37; Yao, *Shanghai xianhua*, p. 13.

61. Issue no. 2 of *Xiaoxian bao*, excerpted in A Ying, *Wan Qing wenyi baokan shulüe*, pp. 66–67. Issue no. 62 of the *Xiaoxian bao* came out January 9, 1898, according to *Shanghai tushuguan guancang Zhongwen baozhi fukan mulu*, p. 511. This suggests that issue no. 2 dates from November 10, 1897.

62. See Stuart Blumin, "George G. Foster and the Emerging Metropolis," in *New York by Gas-Light and Other Urban Sketches*, ed. Stuart Blumin, 11ff.

63. For a detailed history of the great publishing families in Ming and Qing Shanghai, see Yang Zhenfang, "Shanghai Yuan Ming Qing shiqi zhuming de chuban jia," *Chuban shiliao* 1992.3: 68–74, 20.

64. *Shenjiang shixia shengjing tushuo*, 1.15a; see also 1.19b–20a. Most prominent among these were the Jiangzuo shulin, Saoye shanfang, Wenrui lou, and Qianqing tang.

65. Reed, *Gutenberg in Shanghai*, pp. 88–127. By 1889, lithographic publishers were putting woodblock publishing houses out of business. (pp. 98–102). See also Zhu Lianbao, "Jiefang qian Shanghai shudian, chubanshe yinxiang ji (9)," *Chuban shiliao* 1987.4: 104; Song Yuanfang, "Zhongguo jindai chuban da shi ji," *Chuban shiliao* 1990.1, p. 140; Link, *Mandarin Ducks and Butterflies*, p. 81; A Ying, *Xiaoshuo santan*, 126ff.

66. Reed, *Gutenberg in Shanghai*, pp. 128–160.

67. Yuan, *Yuanyang hudie pai*, p. 34.

68. Reed, *Gutenberg in Shangai*, p. 207; Rey Chow, *Woman and Chinese Modernity: The Politics of Reading between West and East*, p. 38.

69. Hatano Tarō, "Chūgoku shōsetsu gikyoku yōgo kenkyū nōto" (12) in *Chūgoku kankei ronsetsu shiryō* 1969.2a, pp. 500–505 and "Chūgoku shōsetsu gikyoku yōgo kenkyū nōto" (14) in *Chūgoku kankei ronsetsu shiryō* 1974.2b, pp. 330–334; Song, "Zhongguo jindai chuban da shiji," p. 140.

70. Roswell Britton, *The Chinese Periodical Press 1800–1912*, p. 69; Song, "Zhongguo jindai chuban da shiji," pp. 140–141; Jonathan Hay, "Painters and Publishing in Late Nineteenth-Century Shanghai."

71. Dianshi zhai published a lithographic edition of the *Kangxi zidian* in 1882. According to Zhang Jinglu, the press sold a total of more than 100,000 copies of this dictionary, probably an unprecedented number of copies for a single edition of any

book (Zhang Jinglu, *Zhongguo jindai chuban shiliao,* vol. 1, illustration page 27). See also Link, *Mandarin Ducks and Butterflies,* p. 82, and Bao Tianxiao, *Chuanying lou huiyi lu,* pp. 41–42.

72. Chen, *Zhongguo xiaoshuo xushi moshi de zhuanbian,* p. 17. Kang Youwei later reiterated this point in an attempt to encourage Liang Qichao to write *Xin Zhongguo weilai ji.* See A Ying, ed., *Wan Qing wenxue congchao,* vol. 2, p. 311.

73. "Starting with the decade of the 1880s, new editions of the *Honglou meng* with commentary appeared at a stupendous pace. This decade saw the large-scale introduction and use of modern printing techniques like lithography and metallic moveable type, with Shanghai as the center of activity." Rolston, *How to Read the Chinese Novel,* p. 320; see also pp. 316–320 and 477–478, and Yi Su, *Honglou meng shulu,* 56ff. *Fengyue meng* and *Fusheng liuji* were printed as part of the *Shenbao guan congshu,* as were *Qinglou meng* (Dream of the courtesans' quarters), *Huifang lu* (A record of flowers illustrated), and *He dian* (What's the reference?). Other novels first printed in Guangxu-era Shanghai include *Yesou puyan* (A humble rustic's idle words) (Song, "Zhongguo jindai chuban da shiji," p. 140); and *Qixia wuyi* (Seven heroes and the righteous five) (Ping Buqing, *Xiawai junxie,* pp. 650–651). See also A Ying's index of a wide variety of high-quality lithographic reprint editions of novels from this period. The great majority of these editions were printed in Shanghai; only one out of forty-eight can be said with certainty to have been published elsewhere. *Xiaoshuo santan,* pp. 126–141.

74. Siao-chen Hu, "Literary *Tanci:* A Woman's Tradition of Narrative in Verse"; A Ying, *Xiaoshuo santan,* pp. 47–102 and *Xiaoshuo ertan,* pp. 73, 80–81, 86. See also Chen Tongxun's 1857 assessment of the genre in Qiu Xinru, *Bi sheng hua,* preface, p. 1.

75. See Hu Shiying, *Tanci baojuan mulu.* This catalog of prose-verse narratives lists only one *tanci* edition printed in Shanghai before 1875, but over the next two decades, nearly half of the *tanci* listed were printed in Shanghai, and since many of the other *tanci* listed give no publisher or city of publication, it is possible that Shanghai's true share of the national market was in fact significantly larger. For an account of an early entrepreneur who produced cheap leisure reading see Ping Jinya, "Shanghai chuban jie suowen," p. 220.

76. By 1889 they were distributed through twenty major regional centers as far away from Shanghai as Yunnan. Zhang, *Zhongguo jindai chuban shiliao,* vol. 1, illustration p. 24.

77. Britton, *The Chinese Periodical Press,* p. 85; Ping Jinya, "Shanghai chuban jie suowen," p. 222.

78. *Youxi bao* no. 49, 54.

79. Britton, *The Chinese Periodical Press,* p. 96; A Ying, *Wan Qing wenyi baokan shulüe,* 53ff. See also Link, *Mandarin Ducks and Butterflies,* pp. 141–142, and *Youxi bao* masthead, August 1897. For a listing of the cities in which *Youxi bao* was available in 1898, see, for example, no. 443 masthead.

80. Tarumoto Teruo, "Yūgi shujin sentei 'Kōshi zuikyū kasen,'" p. 18; Zhou Shou-

juan notes a special edition in 1897 with a print run of 5,000, followed immediately by a second run of 3,000, on the occasion of a "flower-list election." Hershatter, *Dangerous Pleasures*, p. 167.

81. A Ying, *Wan Qing wenyi baokan shulüe,* p. 55. Song, "Zhongguo jindai chuban da shiji," p. 143. Zhu Junzhou, "Qingmo Minchu qizhong hanjian wenyi baokan gouchen," *Chuban shiliao* 1992.4: 130–141.

82. Bao, *Chuanying lou huiyi lu,* p. 446; Chen Pingyuan, *Zhongguo xiaoshuo xushi moshi de zhuanbian,* p. 270; Song, "Zhongguo jindai chuban da shiji," p. 142.

83. Han Bangqing worked as an editor at *Shen bao* (Hu Shi, "*Haishang hua liezhuan* xu," p. 568); the newspaper connections of other authors of Shanghai fiction are detailed in chapter 3.

84. For a map showing the expansion of the Settlement and Concession areas over time, see Chen and Zhang, *Shanghai jindai jianzhu shi gao,* p. 3.

85. Des Forges, "Opium / Leisure / Shanghai," p. 177. See McMahon, *The Fall of the God of Money,* pp. 105–138 and 193–215, for an annotated translation and extensive analysis of *Yanhua.*

86. Des Forges, "Opium / Leisure / Shanghai," pp. 168, 171–182. See also Meng Yue's discussion of the concept of *yin* (excess, depravity) in the Shanghai context in chapter 3 of *Shanghai and the Edges of Empires.*

87. See Plaks, *The Four Masterworks of the Ming Novel,* pp. 82–83.

88. "Just as they reached the corner of Stone Street, they suddenly saw a carriage flying towards them; in the blink of an eye it was close at hand. When Xianglan glanced over, she saw that it was Canny Old A Kang's carriage, carrying Hua Yu and a man whom she couldn't see clearly. Xianglan quickly stood up and called to A You, 'Quick, turn around and chase A Kang's carriage!' A You assented, and taking up the reins pulled back sharply, immediately wheeling around. Xianglan's young horse could really run, and when A You gave it two strokes of the whip, the horse's blood was up; extending its neck, with four hooves flying, it went forward like a whirlwind. Canny Old A Kang never imagined that someone would want to charge his carriage, but suddenly he heard hooves clattering, and when he turned his head to look, Xianglan's carriage was no more than a few yards away. Hua Yu yelled from inside the carriage: 'Quickly, A Kang! Xianglan is trying to run into our carriage!'" (*Haitian hong,* 20/311).

89. This story is reprinted in Shi Zhecun, *Bomu de wunü,* pp. 202–216. Note especially the repeated references to the heat, and the secluded location where the story comes to a crisis. See also Lee, *Shanghai Modern,* pp. 184–185.

90. *Haitian hong,* 20/312.

91. Zhang Chunhua, *Hucheng suishi quge;* passim; see also Goodman, *Native Place, City, and Nation,* 93ff, for an analysis of Yulanpen gatherings and processions as means for sojourners in Shanghai to articulate their native-place identities. Cf. discussions of twentieth-century processions and ritual circulations in Steven Sangren, *History and Magical Power in a Chinese Community,* especially pp. 61–92, and Kenneth Dean, *Taoist Ritual and Popular Cults of Southeast China.* Parades were also a favorite activity of

European settlers in Shanghai. Bickers, "Shanghailanders," p. 197, and Goodman, "Improvisations on a Semicolonial Theme."

92. *Fanhua meng*, 98/1127–1128.

Chapter 5: Brokers, Authors, "Shanghai People"

1. Characters in Shanghai fiction often use opium and are occasionally presented as addicts, but it is rare that addiction is discussed at length, or serves any real narrative significance. Contrast this with the obsessive attention to the subjectivity of the opium addict and his or her travails in the nineteenth-century fiction analyzed by Keith McMahon in *The Fall of the God of Money* (pp. 139–174), the significance of opium consumption in guidebooks and travel accounts (Des Forges, "Opium / Leisure / Shanghai"), or the frequency with which "the opium addict" appears as a stock type in both Chinese and Western photographs of Shanghai individuals in the late nineteenth and early twentieth centuries.

2. As David Wang points out, these encounters often take place in courtesan houses. Wang, *Fin-de-siècle Splendor*, p. 55.

3. Des Forges, "Street Talk and Alley Stories," pp. 145–146, and "Building Shanghai, One Page at a Time," pp. 793–794.

4. *Haishang hua*, 12/97.

5. Zeng Pu, *Niehai hua*, pp. 9–14.

6. See Yen-p'ing Hao, *The Comprador in Nineteenth-Century China: Bridge Between East and West* for a thorough account of the development of the comprador system and the importance of compradors as agents of economic development and social change.

7. Lu, *Beyond the Neon Lights*, p. 56.

8. For a brief account of the central role of brokers and mediators in common business dealings in nineteenth-century Shanghai, see Sybille van der Sprenkel, "Urban Social Control," in *The City in Late Imperial China*, ed. G. W. Skinner, pp. 619–623. See also Perry, *Shanghai on Strike*, p. 22, Lu, *Beyond the Neon Lights*, pp. 160–167, and Yeh, *Shanghai Love*, p. 105.

9. Luo, et al., *Hanyu da cidian*, vol. 1, pp. 1071–1072; Morohashi, *Daikanwa jiten*, vol. 1, p. 591.

10. On the importance of Japan as a third term between "China" and "the West," see Shih, *The Lure of the Modern*, pp. 4–5, 140–144. On the significance of Cantonese sojourners in Shanghai, especially in the nineteenth century, see Goodman, *Native Place, City, and Nation*, pp. 72–81, 111–117, 238.

11. Zhang, *Haishang hua luo*, p. 709.

12. David Rolston makes a similar claim with respect to Ximen Qing, Song Jiang, and Jia Baoyu in novels of the late Ming and early to mid-Qing, calling them "central characters" around which narrative is organized (Rolston, *Traditional Chinese Fiction and Fiction Commentary*, pp. 195–197). But while these characters may differ from the protagonists of most eighteenth- and nineteenth-century European novels, they do go

through significant experiences and developments over the course of their respective narratives; as such, Hong Shanqing in fact proves a better example of this concept than characters in earlier fiction.

13. Song, "Zhongguo jindai chuban da shiji," p. 140; Jones, *Yellow Music;* Hao, *The Comprador in Nineteenth-Century China;* Lee, *Shanghai Modern,* 52–63, 120–150; Meng Yue, *Shanghai and the Edges of Empires,* pp. 31–61.

14. On the intermediary position of educated individuals more generally, see Yeh, "The Life-Style of Four *Wenren*," pp. 421–422.

15. Link, *Mandarin Ducks and Butterflies,* pp. 20–22 and passim; Chow, *Woman and Chinese Modernity,* pp. 34–84.

16. Yuan Jin contrasts Bao Tianxiao's pioneering uses of "foreign" literary techniques in the early Republican period with his "close adherence to the requirements of the *zhanghui* format" in the later *Shanghai chunqiu.* Yuan, *Yuanyang hudie pai,* p. 132.

17. See *Xiepu chao,* first and fourth prefaces (pp. 4, 7); *Renjian diyu,* prefaces, p. 12; Ping Jinya, *Renhai chao,* first and second prefaces (pp. 3–4); and for *Haishang huo diyu,* see Mark Elvin, "Tales of *Shen* and *Xin*: Body-Person and Heart-Mind in China during the Last 150 Years," p. 291.

18. See Qu Qiubai's assessment of the new vernacular, cited in Link, *Mandarin Ducks and Butterflies,* p. 19.

19. Mao Dun, *Huaxiazi,* pp. 135–136.

20. Des Forges, "From Source Texts to 'Reality Observed'" and Hanan, *Chinese Fiction,* pp. 9–32.

21. *Xin Shanghai,* 1/4.

22. Hay, "Painters and Publishing in Late Nineteenth-Century Shanghai," pp. 173–175.

23. Hockx, "Playing the Field: Aspects of Chinese Literary Life in the 1920s," in *The Literary Field of Twentieth-Century China,* ed. Michel Hockx.

24. See the comments of literary critics writing in the first decade of the twentieth century cited in Chen, *Zhongguo xiaoshuo xushi moshi de zhuanbian,* p. 281.

25. Yuan, *Yuanyang hudie pai,* p. 89. Cf. Dian Gong's comments on the status of professional writers in the early twentieth century in *Shi bao,* reprinted in *Haishang hua,* pp. 614–616.

26. See *Xin Shanghai,* 7/29, 29/133ff. Note also the figure of Qian Menghua, a newspaperman who has written a new novel *(xin xiaoshuo)*: this transgression of the boundary that the narrator is so eager to have observed leads to Qian Menghua's present reduced circumstances, in which he writes advertising copy for a drug company. *Xin Shanghai,* 17/75–76.

27. *Xin Shanghai,* 42/194; 60/278–279. See also Fan Boqun's preface to Bao Tianxiao's *Shanghai chunqiu,* pp. 12–13 and Hanan, *Chinese Fiction of the Nineteenth and Early Twentieth Centuries,* pp. 167–168.

28. *Xin Shanghai,* 1/4.

29. For a detailed discussion of the care with which the narrative structure of Shanghai fiction is usually put together, see Des Forges, "Building Shanghai, One Page

at a Time," pp. 786–792. See also Yuan Jin's comparison of *Xiepu chao* and *Guangling chao* (*Yuanyang hudie pai*, p. 128), and Hu Shi's comments on the narrative structure of *Haishang hua liezhuan*, including a direct comparison between its structure and that of *Jiuwei gui* and *Guanchang xianxing ji*. "*Haishang hua liezhuan* xu," pp. 578–579, 597. To take a few narrative threads from the early chapters in *The Huangpu Tides* as an example, it could well have been the case that individual anecdotes heard from friends or drawn from the newspapers inspired certain twists and turns of some of the narrative lines, like A having an affair with B at the Inspiring Benevolence Hospital, C squeezing out his nephew to take D as a concubine, E and F's wife having an affair; G persuading H to have an affair with J; but the aesthetic of Shanghai installment fiction rests precisely in the way A is the concubine of C's friend, and a companion of C's daughter, J is a colleague of B's, H is recently married to E, E and F having their dispute settled by C, and so on, knitting apparently disparate lines into a coherent system.

30. Link, *Mandarin Ducks and Butterflies*, p. 153. For an account of the importance of the new copyright law from the point of view of the publishers, and the subsequent formation of the Shanghai Booksellers' Guild, see Reed, *Gutenberg in Shanghai*.

31. Link, *Mandarin Ducks and Butterflies*, pp. 149–150.

32. Link, *Mandarin Ducks and Butterflies*, pp. 154–155.

33. *Xiepu chao*, prefaces, p. 5.

34. See, for example, the intense negotiations surrounding Huang Cuifeng's departure from the courtesan house where she used to work in *Haishang hua*, chapter 49. For more detail on the balance of power between courtesan or prostitute and madam drawn from the historical record, see Hershatter, *Dangerous Pleasures*, pp. 34, 74, and 69–180, passim.

35. Yeh, "The Life-Style of Four *Wenren*," pp. 432–433; Yeh, "Reinventing Ritual"; Widmer, "Inflecting Gender."

36. Keith McMahon makes a related point — that male customers are in search of a courtesan that they will not be able to leave — in his analysis of the balance of power between genders in *Haishang hua liezhuan*. "Fleecing the Male Customer."

37. Gary G. Hamilton and Chi-kong Lai, "Consumerism without Capitalism: Consumption and Brand Names in Late Imperial China."

38. *Fanhua meng*, 71/804. Cf. Hershatter, *Dangerous Pleasures*, pp. 84–85.

39. For the use and "abuse" of the names of well-known authors, see Link, *Mandarin Ducks and Butterflies*, 149ff.

40. *Shanghai fengsu suoji*, quoted in Wu, *Dushi xuanliu zhong de haipai xiaoshuo*, pp. 102–103.

41. "You can see that no matter what province, city, or county a person comes from, in less than a year after his or her arrival in Shanghai, he or she will be transformed by Shanghai's customs and habits, transformed into a Shanghai person." Canghai ke, "Shanghai guancha tan," quoted in Wu, *Dushi xuanliu zhong de haipai xiaoshuo*, p. 102; See also *Xin Shanghai*, 1/1, and Lu, *Beyond the Neon Lights*, pp. 15, 48.

42. Lu, *Beyond the Neon Lights*; see especially 308ff.

43. Wu, *Dushi xuanliu zhong de haipai xiaoshuo,* pp. 20–59.

44. See the discussion of *xiao shimin* in Link, *Mandarin Ducks and Butterflies,* pp. 5, 189–190; Yeh, "Progressive Journalism and Shanghai's Petty Urbanites"; Lu, *Beyond the Neon Lights,* pp. 61–64; and Haiyan Lee, "All the Feelings That Are Fit to Print." The kinds of texts *xiao shimin* were supposed to read included "Mandarin Duck and Butterfly" fiction and periodicals like *Shenghuo* (Life).

45. Cf. Yuri Lotman's discussion of the image of an ideal readership contained within each text. *Universe of the Mind,* p. 63

46. Courtesans who were not from Suzhou were known to work hard to learn Suzhou dialect in order to move up the hierarchy. Goodman, *Native Place, City, and Nation,* p. 25.

47. Rolston, *How to Read the Chinese Novel,* p. 224, and *Traditional Chinese Fiction and Fiction Commentary,* p. 126.

48. Between 1885 and 1950, the proportion of Shanghai residents who were nonnatives fluctuated between 70 and 85 percent. Zou Yiren, *Jiu Shanghai renkou bianqian de yanjiu,* 112ff.

49. See Honig, *Creating Chinese Ethnicity;* Perry, *Shanghai on Strike;* Goodman, *Native Place, City, and Nation* and "Variations on a Semicolonial Theme"; Wasserstrom, "Locating Old Shanghai."

50. Honig, *Creating Chinese Ethnicity.* While Honig's history of people who came to Shanghai from the area that would eventually be defined as "Subei" starts in the middle of the nineteenth century, it is worth noting that the formation of a specifically pejorative discourse about "Subei people" does not seem to begin until the very last years of the Qing and the early years of the Republic.

51. Goodman, *Native Place, City, and Nation,* p. 27.

52. McDaniel, "'Jumping the Dragon Gate': Storytellers and the Creation of the Shanghai Identity," *Modern China* 27.4: 484–507; Ye Kaidi, "Cong shijiu shiji Shanghai ditu kan dui chengshi weilai dingyi de zhengduo zhan," *Zhongguo xueshu* 1.3: 88–121; Reed, *Gutenberg in Shanghai;* Lee, *Shanghai Modern.*

Chapter 6: Marxists and Modern Girls

1. See Link, *Mandarin Ducks and Butterflies,* p. 17; Chow, *Woman and Chinese Modernity,* pp. 41–43; Wei Shaochang, ed., *Yuanyang hudie pai yanjiu ziliao,* vol. 1, pp. 2–120; and Fan Boqun et al., eds., *Yuanyang hudie pai wenxue ziliao,* pp. 726–897.

2. See, for example, Jaroslav Průšek, *Three Sketches of Chinese Literature,* pp. 36–37; C. T. Hsia, *A History of Modern Chinese Fiction, 1917–1957,* pp. 155–158; Wang, *Fictional Realism: Mao Dun, Lao She, Shen Congwen,* pp. 59–66, 87; and Anderson, *The Limits of Realism: Chinese Fiction in the Revolutionary Period,* pp. 145–151.

3. Translation adapted with slight modifications from Mao Dun, *Midnight,* p. 9. Italics added to words in English in the original.

4. See, for example, Yang Guangfu, *Songnan yuefu* [1796], p. 172; Yao Xie's hand-

written *ci* cycle "Kuhai hang" (Sailing on a sea of suffering), dating from the 1840s; as well as most Shanghai texts since then.

5. Anderson, *The Limits of Realism,* p. 148.

6. Jaroslav Průšek refers to this shifting focus in *Ziye* as the "method of letting the strands of the story drop before they have worked themselves out" in *Three Sketches of Chinese Literature,* p. 26. But what Průšek fails to explain is that strands of the story drop only temporarily, and then are taken up again, even though none is ever truly completed.

7. Mao Dun, *Wo zouguo de daolu,* vol. 2, p. 121.

8. Wang, *Fictional Realism,* p. 32; Průšek, *Three Sketches of Chinese Literature,* pp. 10–11; Mao Dun, *Wo zouguo de daolu,* vol. 2, pp. 112–113.

9. Mao Dun, *Ziye* (Chengdu: Sichuan renmin chubanshe, 1982 reprint as volume one of *Mao Dun xuanji*), chapter 1, pp. 3, 8, 9, and so on. This edition will hereafter be referred to as *Ziye.* As Leo Lee points out in his discussion of modernist writing of the same period, these commodities are presented not as elements of purely "realist" description, but rather as symbols indexing a certain type of fast, wealthy, urban culture. See Li Oufan, "Zhongguo xiandai xiaoshuo de xianqu zhe" *Lien-ho wen-hsüeh* 3.12, 12.

10. Marián Gálik summarizes Mao Dun's assessment of *Haishang hua* (together with works like *Honglou meng* and *Shuihu zhuan*): "These literary works can undoubtedly afford excellent material to sociologists interested in the study of social life of past ages. All of them may be termed 'great works,' but as far as 'creative methods' are concerned, there is little in them that could be utilized." Gálik, *Mao Tun and Modern Chinese Literary Criticism,* p. 126. The original appears in slightly more detail in "Women you shenme yichan?" in Mao Dun, *Huaxiazi,* p. 137.

11. See, for example, his essay "Ziran zhuyi yu Zhongguo xiandai xiaoshuo," published in *Xiaoshuo yuebao* in July of 1922, reprinted in *Mao Dun zhuanji,* pp. 976–991.

12. See "About *Midnight,*" in Mao Dun, *Midnight.*

13. Anderson, *The Limits of Realism,* pp. 9–11.

14. See Marián Gálik, *Milestones in Sino-Western Literary Confrontation (1898–1979),* pp. 74–75, and Wang, *Fictional Realism,* p. 70.

15. Gálik, *Mao Tun and Modern Chinese Literary Criticism;* Wang, *Fictional Realism,* p. 70.

16. Gálik, "Mao Tun's *Midnight:* Creative Confrontation with Zola, Tolstoy, Wertherism, and Nordic Mythology," in Gálik, *Milestones,* pp. 73–99.

17. Mao Dun, *Wo zouguo de daolu,* vol. 2, pp. 116–117.

18. *Ziye* was published under the pseudonym Taomo guanzhu; Gálik reads this as a transliteration of Thrym, a Norse figure, but Mao Dun's later explication is that this was an indirect reference to his leftist leanings (*Wo zouguo de daolu,* vol. 2, p. 113). Gálik also reads the working title, *Xiyang* or "Twilight," as a reference to the "Twilight of the Gods," but Mao Dun gives two other unrelated explanations for it.

19. For a discussion of continuities between short fiction of the May Fourth era and earlier fiction in Chinese, see Diana Granat, "Literary Continuity in the New Chinese Short Story: A Study Based on the 'Hsiao-shuo yüeh-pao' (Short Story Magazine)."

20. *Ziye,* 9/246; 17/454ff.

21. *Xiepu chao,* 35/481.

22. See Liu Yuying's view of the stock market in *Ziye,* 11/297ff.

23. *Fanhua meng,* chapters 75 and 91–92.

24. *Ziye,* 8/203–206.

25. Zhang, *Jiuwei gui,* p. 1043.

26. *Haitian hong,* 6/222–223. See also *Caifeng bao,* November 18, 1899, pp. 1–2, and *Youxi bao,* January 7, 1899, pp. 1–2.

27. Hershatter, *Dangerous Pleasures,* pp. 77–78. *Haishang hua* 26/210.

28. *Haishang hua,* 12/98; *Fanhua meng,* 13/131, 14/133–134.

29. Another illustration of women leaving the silk filature where they work appears in Wu, "Haishang baiyan tu" 1.15a (early 1890s). See also *The Celestial Empire,* April 24, 1896, p. 421; *Youxi bao* no. 94, p. 2; *Youxi bao* no. 709, pp. 1–2; Ye, "Shanghai before Nationalism," p. 39; and Perry, *Shanghai on Strike,* pp. 49, 60 for references to nineteenth-century women working in factories. A female factory worker appears briefly in *Fanhua meng,* but she is a minor character, of interest to the narrator primarily for the affair that she conducts with her cousin's lover.

30. Průšek, *Three Sketches of Chinese Literature,* p. 35; Zhang, *The City in Modern Chinese Literature and Film,* p. 134. Cf. Marston Anderson's elaboration of a disjunction between Mao Dun's "urge for comprehensiveness" and his difficulties with scale and closure in *The Limits of Realism,* pp. 127–131, 146–148.

31. Mao Dun, "Dushi wenxue," pp. 421–423.

32. See chapter 4; also, Des Forges, "Opium / Leisure / Shanghai."

33. For an account of the development of the domestic machine manufacturing industry, with particular attention to the role of the Shanghai publishing boom in the 1920s and '30s, see Reed, *Gutenberg in Shanghai,* pp. 128–160.

34. See Shen, "Ziran zhuyi yu Zhongguo xiandai xiaoshuo," reprinted in *Mao Dun zhuanji* and Zheng Zhenduo, "Xiaoxian?" (first published in *Wenxue xunkan* in 1921; reprinted in Wei Shaochang ed., *Yuanyang hudie pai yanjiu ziliao,* pp. 58–59), among others.

35. *Ziye,* 9/228.

36. Attention to this kind of parallelism separated by long stretches of the text is central to Qing commentaries to the canonical works of long vernacular fiction. See, for example, Rolston, *How to Read the Chinese Novel,* pp. 188, 191.

37. Xu Qinfu, *Hujiang fengyue zhuan,* 1/1; *Shanghai chunqiu,* preface, p. 1.

38. See also Des Forges, "Street Talk and Alley Stories," pp. 116–160.

39. Li, "Zhongguo xiandai xiaoshuo de xianqu zhe," pp. 8, 14.

40. Li, "Zhongguo xiandai xiaoshuo de xianqu zhe"; Yan Jiayan, "Xin ganjue pai zhuyao zuojia"; Shu-mei Shih, "Gender, Race, and Semicolonialism"; Shih, *The Lure of the Modern;* Wu, *Dushi xuanliu zhong de haipai xiaoshuo;* Zhang, *The City in Modern Chinese Literature and Film;* Fruehauf, "Urban Exoticism in Modern and Contemporary Chinese Literature"; Li, *Haipai xiaoshuo yu xiandai dushi wenhua;* Peng, *Haishang shuo qingyu.*

41. See, for example, Zhang, *The City in Modern Chinese Literature and Film*, pp. 117–118, 132–133.

42. Wu, *Dushi xuanliu zhong de haipai xiaoshuo*, p. 17; see also the introduction, p. 3; chapter one passim; and p. 30. Note that when Wu Fuhui does acknowledge some connection across this "modern / premodern" divide—in his discussion of the influence of "the past" on Mu Shiying, for example—it is "old rural / familial culture" as a totality that has the power to inspire the "modern" writer, never individual texts from an earlier period. Wu, *Dushi xuanliu zhong de haipai xiaoshuo*, p. 162.

43. Shih, "Gender, Race, and Semicolonialism," pp. 947–954. Shih perceptively identifies the constructed image of a "traditional" exotic woman in the European texts as the primary object of critique by Liu Na'ou and other Shanghai modernists, but she invokes a similar image of oppressive (Chinese) tradition at several key points: "his desire for her can never be in the traditional form of 'possessing' her sexuality" (p. 949); and references to "patriarchal morality" (p. 950) and "feudal structures" (p. 953), among others.

44. See Zhang, *The City in Modern Chinese Literature and Film*, pp. 22–24.

45. Wu, *Dushi xuanliu zhong de haipai xiaoshuo*, p. 134.

46. Zhang Ailing, "Yi Hu Shizhi," reprinted in *Zhang kan*, pp. 142–145, 153–154; Zhu, *Xiepu chao*, prefaces p. 3. The other six favorites were *Honglou meng, Xingshi yinyuan zhuan, Lao Can youji, Er Ma, Lihun,* and *Richu.*

47. Wu, *Dushi xuanliu zhong de haipai xiaoshuo*, p. 82ff.

48. Zhang, *The City in Modern Chinese Literature and Film*, pp. 157, 164.

49. Shih, "Gender, Race, and Semicolonialism," pp. 943–945; see also Wu, *Dushi xuanliu zhong de haipai xiaoshuo*, pp. 25–26, 146, 152.

50. UFA was the one of the largest film production consortiums in Europe in this period, and during the 1920s rivaled Hollywood in its dominance of the international market. Zhang Zhen notes the significance of UFA to Shi Zhecun's story "At the Paris Cinema." Zhang, *An Amorous History of the Silver Screen*, pp. 85, 370.

51. Wu, *Dushi xuanliu zhong de haipai xiaoshuo*, pp. 106, 110, 150–152; Zhang, *The City in Modern Chinese Literature and Film*, pp. 157ff., 164. As David Wang has pointed out, there are also important resonances between certain of the dissipated young men in New Sensationist fiction and the playboy Zhang Qiugu of *Jiuwei gui*. Wang, *Fin-de-siècle Splendor*, pp. 88–89.

52. Wu, *Dushi xuanliu zhong de haipai xiaoshuo*, pp. 30, 106, 111, 117–118, 155; Zhang, *The City in Modern Chinese Literature and Film*, pp. 159–160. Jianmei Liu notes that "it is impossible to find a clear-cut distinction between so-called high modernism and low culture in the Shanghai school literature." *Revolution Plus Love: Literary History, Women's Bodies, and Thematic Repetition in Twentieth-Century Chinese Fiction*, p. 137.

53. Wu, *Dushi xuanliu zhong de haipai xiaoshuo*, pp. 33, 124ff. One of the best examples of ironization of the newspaper form is Mu Shiying's "Benbu xinwenlan bianjishi li yi zha fei gao shang de gushi" (A story from an article draft abandoned in the editorial office of a newspaper in this city), in Mu, *Shanghai de hubuwu*, pp. 145–159.

54. Wu, *Dushi xuanliu zhong de haipai xiaoshuo*, pp. 46, 93.

55. This figure is ubiquitous in short urban fiction of the period. Li, "Zhongguo xiandai xiaoshuo de xianqu zhe," p. 11; Wu, *Dushi xuanliu zhong de haipai xiaoshuo*, p. 185; Shih, "Gender, Race, and Semicolonialism," p. 949. For one use of the phrase *jindai de chanwu* to refer to a woman, see Liu Na'ou, *Dushi fengjing xian*, p. 7.

56. Translated in Zhang, *The City in Modern Chinese Literature and Film*, p. 168. For the sports car simile, see Shih, *The Lure of the Modern*, p. 268, and Ye Lingfeng, "Liuxing xing ganmao" (A contagious cold; reprinted in Wu Huanzhang, *Haipai xiaoshuo jingpin*), p. 40.

57. Liu Na'ou, "Liangge shijian de bu ganzheng zhe" (Two who weren't in tune with time) in *Dushi fengjing xian*, p. 104. See also Shih, *The Lure of the Modern*, pp. 294–295 for an analysis of this passage.

58. Zhang, *The City in Modern Chinese Literature and Film*, pp. 171, 174–175. See also Wu, *Dushi xuanliu zhong de haipai xiaoshuo*, pp. 175–176.

59. Shih, "Gender, Race, and Semicolonialism," pp. 935, 947–951.

60. "Reqing zhi gu" appears in Liu Na'ou's *Dushi fengjing xian*. For a partial plot summary and discussion of *Haishang huo diyu*, see Elvin, "Tales of *Shen* and *Xin*."

61. The first two appear in *Fanhua meng*; the latter two in *Haishang hua*.

62. "As a matter of fact, the image of 'woman as fugitive' seems so fitting to the precarious sense of urban flow and circulation that it has almost become part of a new perception in the modern city: elusive woman, like fluid time, is no longer fixable in the era of modernity. By contrast, in the context of the traditional city, women—especially prostitutes—are always fixed in a defined space and ready to service male adventurers, as depicted in Chinese urban narratives at the turn of the century." Zhang, *The City in Modern Chinese Literature and Film*, p. 185. See also Shih, *The Lure of the Modern*, pp. 294–297.

63. To list just a few examples: *Haishang hua*, chapters 13 and 14; *Haitian hong*, chapters 3–5, 17–19; *Fanhua meng*, chapters 14, 20–21.

64. This trap appears with relative frequency in Shanghai novels from the 1890s forward. One of the better examples is in *Xin Shanghai*, 10/44–12/53, where the term "immortal's leap" itself is cited. See also Zhang, *Jiuwei gui*, pp. 154, 157, and Hershatter, *Dangerous Pleasures*, pp. 140–141.

65. Hu Ying, *Tales of Translation: Composing the New Woman in China, 1898–1918*, pp. 5–8.

66. The "product of modern times" in Liu Na'ou's "Youxi" (Game) has a "Hellenic" nose (Liu, *Dushi fengjing xian*, p. 7); Rongzi declares a preference for the work of Paul Morand, Yokomitsu Riichi, and Sinclair Lewis in Mu Shiying's "Bei dangzuo xiaoqianpin de nanzi." See also Li, "Zhongguo xiandai xiaoshuo de xianqu zhe," p. 11, Shih, *The Lure of the Modern*, pp. 292, 298, and Peng, *Haishang shuo qingyu*, pp. 66–71. The politics involved in the appropriation of "Western" physical features are too complex to treat at length here; for a discussion of the issue in detail, see Terry Kawashima, "Seeing Faces, Making Races: Visual Readings and Appropriations in the Construction of 'Race,'" *Meridians: feminism, race, trans-nationalism* 3.1 (2002): 161–190.

67. Wu, *Dushi xuanliu zhong de haipai xiaoshuo*, pp. 186–189. Yingjin Zhang also

notes "traditional-style" women in Mu Shiying's "Gongmu" (Cemetery), as well as in the stories of Shi Zhecun and the poetry of Dai Wangshu. Zhang, *The City in Modern Chinese Literature and Film,* 167ff.

68. Liu, *Dushi fengjing xian,* pp. 70, 73, 76, 81–82, 93, etc.

69. Ye, "Liuxing xing ganmao," in Wu, *Haipai xiaoshuo jingpin,* pp. 43–44.

70. See for, example, the recurring use of the word "weekend" in Liu Na'ou's "Fengjing" (Scenery). Liu, *Dushi fengjing xian,* pp. 21–33.

71. Shih, "Gender, Race, and Semicolonialism," pp. 934, 936.

72. Shih, "Gender, Race, and Semicolonialism," p. 942.

73. Yan, "Xin ganjue pai zhuyao zuojia," p. 15. Leo Lee notes that Shi Zhecun said that while he himself wrote about Shanghai, Liu Na'ou was "actually" writing about Tokyo. "Zhongguo xiandai xiaoshuo de xianqu zhe," p. 14. For detail on Liu Na'ou's background, see Peng, *Haishang shuo qingyu.*

74. Shih, *The Lure of the Modern,* p. 285. See also Li, "Zhongguo xiandai wenxue de 'tuifei' ji zuojia," *Tang-tai* 93, p. 32. Japanese usages are scattered throughout *Dushi fengjing xian,* ranging from unusual phrasings to specific words like *getsuyōbi* for "Monday." Liu, *Dushi fengjing xian,* p. 21.

75. Wu, *Dushi xuanliu zhong de haipai xiaoshuo,* p. 108.

76. Shih, "Gender, Race, and Semicolonialism," p. 934.

77. Yao, *Shanghai xianhua,* p. 18.

78. Yu, *Shanghai, 1862 nian,* p. 429; Wu, *Dushi xuanliu zhong de haipai xiaoshuo,* 49ff. (note the citation here of an English-language guidebook to Shanghai printed in 1912 that emphasizes the importance of "pidgin English"); Lu, *Beyond the Neon Lights,* p. 56. There are also numerous Yangjing bang English entries in Yan Meisun, *Shanghai suyu da cidian,* pp. 6, 16, 30, 41, and so on. See Zhang, *An Amorous History of the Silver Screen,* chapter 2, for a more general discussion of Yangjing bang as a form of vernacular central to early twentieth-century Shanghai cultural production.

79. Shi Zhecun's story "Si xizi de shengyi" (Lucky Four's business) is a rare exception to this rule, including a few dialect words and Shanghai slang in a narrative about a rickshaw puller. Shi, *Bomu de wunü,* pp. 302–316; Lee, *Shanghai Modern,* p. 184.

80. On fiction written in romanized Shanghai dialect, see Hanan, *Chinese Fiction,* p. 75. For the use of Chinese characters to transcribe Yangjing bang English, see Wu, *Dushi xuanliu zhong de haipai xiaoshuo,* pp. 49–50 and Yao, *Shanghai xianhua,* p. 19. For the use of a syllabic system to write in Yangjing bang English, see Yao, *Shanghai xianhua,* p. 18 and Yu, *Shanghai, 1862 nian,* p. 429.

81. Shih, *The Lure of the Modern,* pp. 231–233, 343.

82. See, for example, Shi Zhecun's "Meiyu zhi xi," in which the protagonist walks home from the office even though it is raining; his route is described in careful detail. This story is reprinted in *Bomu de wunü,* pp. 206–217.

83. Zhang, *The City in Modern Chinese Literature and Film,* p. 158.

84. Des Forges, "Opium / Leisure / Shanghai."

85. Shi, *Bomu de wunü,* p. 221. This translation is based on Shi Zhecun, *One Rainy Evening,* p. 25, with extensive modifications.

86. Similar narrative dynamics are central to the first half of Shi's "Si xizi de sheng-yi," for example. Shi, *Bomu de wunü*, pp. 302–316.

87. Liu, *Dushi fengjing xian*, p. 99; Shi, *Bomu de wunü*, p. 216.

88. Cf. Hana Wirth-Nesher's conclusions regarding twentieth-century European and American fiction: "The private self in conflict with a public world, a self bent on carving out a suitable private enclave, is replaced by a self that both constructs and is constructed by the cityscape. At times the plot itself unfolds as a sequence of perceptions of place, of actual movement through the cityscape and 'readings' of the urban environment." Wirth-Nesher, *City Codes: Reading the Modern Urban Novel*, p. 21. Conversely, Walter Benjamin found the arcades of Paris to exemplify the interior structure of bourgeois consciousness: "The covered shopping arcades of the nineteenth century were Benjamin's central image because they were the precise material replica of the internal consciousness, or rather, the unconsciousness of the dreaming collective. All of the errors of bourgeois consciousness could be found there (commodity fetishism, reification, the world as 'inwardness'), as well as (in fashion, prostitution, gambling) all of its utopian dreams." Susan Buck-Morss, *The Dialectics of Seeing: Walter Benjamin and the Arcades Project*, p. 39.

89. See, for example, the opening portions of Huang, *Songnan mengying lu* (1883) and Chi, *Huyou mengying* (1893).

90. *Fanhua meng*, chapter 1; *Haitian hong*, chapter 20; *Haishang chentian ying*, chapter 2; *Haishang hua*, chapters 1 and 64.

91. Mu Shiying, "Shanghai de hubuwu," in Wu, *Haipai xiaoshuo jingpin*, p. 535.

92. Li, "Zhongguo xiandai xiaoshuo de xianqu zhe," p. 13.

93. Zhang, *The City in Modern Chinese Literature and Film*, pp. 162–163.

94. Wu, *Haipai xiaoshuo jingpin*, p. 526.

95. Note the similarities between this "tour" (conducted for the reader's benefit?) and the sightseeing trip in the early chapters of Lu, *Xin Shanghai* (1909).

96. Wu, *Haipai xiaoshuo jingpin*, p. 532.

97. See Paul de Man's discussion of this question in "Literary History and Literary Modernity."

98. Fruehauf, "Urban Exoticism in Modern and Contemporary Chinese Literature," p. 156.

Chapter 7: Lineages of the Contemporary and the Nostalgic

* T. A. Hsia, "Novel and Romance: Hsia Tsi-an on Chinese Popular Literature," trans. Dennis Hu, *Chinese Literature: Essays, Articles, Reviews* 2.2: 231–232.

1. Svetlana Boym, *The Future of Nostalgia*, p. xvi.

2. *Hujiang fengyue zhuan*'s dialect usage also differs from novels like *Guanchang xianxing ji* and *Jiuwei gui*, in which courtesans speak in Wu dialect but men never do.

3. Liu, "Du *Haishang hua liezhuan*," p. 604; see Chang-tai Hung, *Going to the People:*

Chinese Intellectuals and Folk Literature, 1918–1937, for more detail on Liu Fu's interest in the "folk," especially pp. 33–40.

4. Hu, "*Haishang hua lie zhuan* xu," pp. 587–588.

5. Zhang, *Haishang hua kai,* pp. 18–19.

6. Zhang, *Haishang hua luo,* p. 724.

7. Zhang, *Haishang hua luo,* p. 713.

8. For more detail on sequels to *Haishang hua,* see the introduction; for details on reprint editions and the popularity of the novel in comparison with some of the better-known fiction of the early twentieth century, see chapters 1 and 4 above.

9. Des Forges, "From Source Texts to 'Reality Observed.'"

10. Wei, *Huayue hen,* pp. 4, 430.

11. Wumu shanren, *Haishang Daguan yuan,* prefaces pp. 1–4. Cf. Ristaino, *Port of Last Resort,* p. 22 and Chiara Betta, "The Rise of Silas Aaron Hardoon (1851–1931) as Shanghai's Major Individual Landowner," *Sino-Judaica: Occasional Papers of the Sino-Judaic Institute* 2: 1–40.

12. Yu Yingshi, *Honglou meng de liangge shijie,* pp. 35–59 and 221–256.

13. Hershatter, *Dangerous Pleasures,* pp. 8–9, 18, 42–43.

14. *Haishang hua,* chapter 9; *Fanhua meng,* chapters 89–90.

15. *Fanhua meng,* 73/836–838.

16. Meng, "Re-envisioning the Great Interior," pp. 29–37.

17. See, for example, the construction of the garden in opposition to the "marketplace" in texts like *Changwu zhi.* Clunas, *Fruitful Sites: Garden Culture in Ming Dynasty China,* pp. 168–169.

18. *Fanhua meng,* 100/1147.

19. *Fanhua meng,* 7/63. Others include Caojia du and Shuiyun xiang.

20. *Fanhua meng,* 19/189–191.

21. Similarly, Yu Yingshi remarks of *Dream of the Red Chamber* that "we become aware of the author's desire to inform us at all times that the ideal world in the novel was actually erected on the foundation of a real world that harbored the greatest vice. He wanted us to bear in mind that in fact the greatest purity was born of the greatest impurity" (Yu, *Honglou meng de liangge shijie,* pp. 237–238).

22. There are twelve courtesans for the "Qunfang pu" (Catalog of assorted fragrances) compiled in Qi Yunsou's garden, a clear reference back to the grouping of girls and women in *Honglou meng* into sets of twelve (*Haishang hua,* 53/450–451).

23. *Haishang hua,* 47/401.

24. See, for example, Liu Fu's "Du *Haishang hua liezhuan,*" especially pp. 600–602.

25. *Haishang hua,* pp. 346, 361, 369, 380–381, and 428; also 52/438ff.

26. Meng, "Re-envisioning the Great Interior."

27. Chang's chapter 38 contains edited versions of 38 and 39 from the original; 39 contains 40 and part of 41; 40 contains part of 41 and 42; 48 includes 50 and 51; 57 includes 60 and 61. See Zhang Ailing, *Haishang hua kai* pp. 19–20, and *Haishang hua luo.*

28. "[T]he structural changes made in this translation, in the form of deletion and minor rewriting, are mostly based on choices made by Eileen Chang." Hung, "Afterword," in Eileen Chang and Eva Hung, trans., *The Sing-Song Girls of Shanghai*, p. 531.

29. Eva Hung explains the aim of her afterword in the following words: "The sing-song house, with its special rules and rituals, was a familiar scene to the author Han Bangqing and his contemporary readers, but to twentieth-century readers used to an ever-quickening pace of life, it is part of an alien and distant past. Though readers of the novel in translation are shielded from the problem of dialect, they are at least as unfamiliar with the novel's world. I hope that my essay 'The World of the Shanghai Courtesans' will bridge some of the knowledge gaps." Hung, "Afterword," in Chang and Hung, *The Sing-Song Girls of Shanghai*, p. 530.

30. T. A. Hsia includes *Xiepu chao* in a list of "Shanghai novels" in "Novel and Romance," p. 231.

31. See Wei Shaochang's preface to *Xiepu chao* (prefaces, p. 3).

32. *Xiepu chao,* prefaces, p. 5.

33. *Xiepu chao,* prefaces, p. 6.

34. Literally, distinguish between the Zi and the Sheng, two rivers in Shandong Province that flow together (Luo, et al., eds., *Hanyu da cidian,* vol. 5, p. 1438).

35. *Xiepu chao,* prefaces, p. 6.

36. The first 52 chapters of *Guangling chao* were printed between 1909 and 1911 in a Hankou newspaper; between 1914 and 1919, these chapters were reprinted and an additional 28 chapters were added in installments in two Shanghai newspapers. The final volume edition ran to 100 chapters. (Yuan, *Yuanyang hudie pai,* p. 73). On the relationship between *Fengyue meng* and early Shanghai fiction, see chapter 1 of this book, and also Hanan, "*Fengyue meng* and the Courtesan Novel."

37. See prefaces four and five and the author's introduction to *Renjian diyu,* prefaces pp. 8–9, 13; the author's introduction to Bao Tianxiao, *Shanghai chunqiu* (preface, p. 1); and also Mark Elvin, "Tales of *Shen* and *Xin*," p. 303.

38. Hershatter, *Dangerous Pleasures,* pp. 11, 20, 37.

39. For more on "the Thirties" *(sanshi niandai)* as a privileged object of Shanghai recollection in the 1990s, see Hanchao Lu, "Nostalgia for the Future: The Resurgence of an Alienated Culture in China," *Pacific Affairs* 75.2.

40. Wakeman, *Policing Shanghai 1927–1937,* p. 10; Zhang Zhongli, ed., *Jindai Shanghai chengshi yanjiu,* pp. 1105–1107; Poshek Fu, *Between Shanghai and Hong Kong,* p. 32. Advertisements for movie showings appear frequently in leisure papers like *Youxi bao* and *Xiaolin bao* at the turn of the century.

41. Braester, "Shanghai's Economy of the Spectacle," especially pp. 50–55; Zhang, *The City in Modern Chinese Literature and Film;* Shih, *The Lure of the Modern,* pp. 269, 288; Li Jin, *Haipai xiaoshuo yu xiandai dushi wenhua,* especially pp. 141–180. On Shanghai film more generally, see Zhang, *An Amorous History of the Silver Screen.*

42. Zhang, *An Amorous History of the Silver Screen,* p. 208.

43. For a more detailed discussion of changes of movie showing and changes in

audience behavior in the 1910s and 1920s, see Chen Jianhua, "From Teahouse to Movie Theater: Zhou Shoujuan as an Early Chinese Moviegoer," unpublished paper.

44. *Fanhua meng,* chapter 59.

45. See, among others, the reactions included in Zhu Tianwen [Chu T'ien-wen], *Jishang zhi meng: "Haishang hua" dianying quan jilu,* pp. 14, p. 65; Xu Gang, "Shijue de cangshan yu fanyi," Jintian 52(2001): 254–265; and Ke Dexi [Nicholas Kaldis], "Fan yuwang shi de dongfang qingdiao: lüeshu Hou Xiaoxian de 'Haishang hua,'" *Jintian* 52 (2001): 266–272.

46. It should be noted that even if Hou Hsiao-hsien's plan to shoot two or three brief outdoor scenes on location had been realized, these short intervals would not in and of themselves have opened up the film to any great extent. See Zhu, *Jishang zhi meng,* p. 145 and Michael Berry, "Words and Images: A Conversation with Hou Hsiao-hsien and Chu T'ien-wen," *positions* 11.3 (2003): 676–716, 693–694.

47. Even the soundtrack of the movie testifies to this dampening of the spirits of the narrative: much of the action unfolds to low mournful music that is rather generic in character; the one instance in which we are presented with music intended to be recognizably "Chinese" or Shanghai-specific consists of a sung *tanci.* But this is yet another "betrayal." Wu dialect *tanci* from Suzhou were certainly an important part of a courtesan's repertoire in the mid-nineteenth century, but by the 1890s, this kind of singing was considered too delicate and insufficiently stimulating, and had yielded in most cases to the singing of more "vital" and "up-to-date" set pieces from Peking opera. Aficionados of the female voice note this transition as early as the 1880s, remarking on it with disgust. Youxi zhuren, *Haishang youxi tushuo,* 4.24b; Jiancun youke, *Shanghai,* p. 11a.

48. Berry, "Words and Images," pp. 691–692; Chu T'ien-wen makes a point of acknowledging Eileen Chang's postface to the translated version of *Haishang hua* as the source for her own brief "Background to the film" (Yingpian de beijing). Zhu, *Jishang zhi meng,* pp. 10–11. Cf. Ke, "Fan yuwang shi de dongfang qingdiao," p. 267, and Xu Gang's discussion of Eileen Chang's decision to translate "Haishang hua" as "Sing-song Girls of Shanghai," in "Shijue de cangshan yu fanyi."

49. Barbara Johnson, "Taking Fidelity Philosophically," in *Difference in Translation,* ed. Joseph F. Graham.

50. Xu, "Shijue de cangshan yu fanyi," p. 258.

51. On the paradoxical use of an overload of nostalgic detail to weaken the force of exoticist desire, see Ke, "Fan yuwang shi de dongfang qingdiao," especially 268–269.

52. This text is particularly appropriate given the number of "translations" Han Bangqing's novel has inspired: into Japanese in the late 1960s, into Mandarin by Eileen Chang in the 1970s, and into English, again by Eileen Chang and Eva Hung.

53. "Fragments of a vessel which are to be glued together must match one another in the smallest details, although they need not be like one another. In the same way a translation, instead of resembling the meaning of the original, must lovingly and in detail incorporate the original's mode of signification, thus making both the original and the translation recognizable as fragments of a greater language, just as fragments are part of a vessel." Benjamin, *Illuminations,* p. 78.

54. On the relative height of the camera angle, see Zhu, *Jishang zhi meng,* p. 75. Although he is talking about a *movie* camera, not a *surveillance* camera, Hou's own comments do raise the question of the place of "mechanized vision" in the film. See Xu, "Shijue de cangshan yu fanyi," pp. 261–262.

55. Sergei Eisenstein, "The Cinematographic Principle and the Ideogram," in Eisenstein, *Film Form: Essays in Film Theory,* pp. 40–41.

56. See, for example, the narrator's explanation of his reasons for writing *Haitian hong* (1/191).

Epilogue: Shanghai 2000

1. Zhang, "Shanghai Nostalgia," p. 355.

2. Abbas, "Cosmopolitan De-scriptions: Shanghai and Hong Kong," p. 780; Boym, *The Future of Nostalgia,* introduction. See also Huang, *Walking between Slums and Skyscrapers,* chapter 8.

3. For a discussion of cafés and restaurants, see Lu, "Nostalgia for the Future."

4. Ron Gluckman and Crystyl Mo, "Lights, Culture, Action," *Asiaweek,* March 30, 2001, pp. 50–51; see also Lu, "Nostalgia for the Future," p. 175.

5. Cf. Yang, "Mass Media and Transnational Subjectivity in Shanghai."

6. Jiani, *Yuedu haipai nü; Dangdai Zhongguo guangbo dianshi tai baijuan congshu: Shanghai Dongfang guangbo diantai juan,* pp. 48–49; Shanghai Zhengda yanjiusuo, *Xin Shanghairen.*

7. Despite the general consensus that new arrivals in Shanghai can make it as Shanghai people if they try hard enough, there are a few more nuanced inquiries into the presuppositions necessary for and the effects resulting from this discourse of transformation. See, for example, Cao Jinqing, "Fangfa yu gushi: wo xinmu zhong de 'Shanghairen,'" in *Xin Shanghairen* (ed. Shanghai Zhengda yanjiusuo, pp. 96–107).

8. Wang Xiaoming, "Jiushi niandai Zhongguo de xin yishi xingtai: cong guanyu 'chenggong renshi' de shenhua shuoqi"; see also Huang, *Walking between Slums and Skyscrapers,* pp. 109–110.

9. Huang, *Walking between Slums and Skyscrapers,* pp. 109–112.

10. Lu, "Nostalgia for the Future," pp. 172–173.

11. Shih, *The Lure of the Modern,* p. ix.

12. Hsia, "Novel and Romance," pp. 231–232.

13. Xu Xixian and Xu Jianrong, *Baibian Shanghai.*

14. Gilles Deleuze and Félix Guattari, *Anti-Oedipus,* p. 36.

15. Zhang, "Shanghai Nostalgia," pp. 385–386.

16. "While Shanghai continued to be the major industrial center creating wealth for the whole nation, urban cosmopolitan cultural life saw a radical curtailment when, in the new ethos of revolutionary asceticism, it came to be labeled a decadent 'bourgeois culture.' With tight fiscal and political control by the center, the city focused on heavy

industry rather than cultural production." Yang, "Mass Media and Transnational Sub-jectivity," p. 290.

17. There are a variety of analyses of the transfer of Shanghai cultural produc-tion to Hong Kong in the 1950s, including Lee, *Shanghai Modern,* pp. 324–341; Fu, *Between Shanghai and Hong Kong;* Abbas, "Cosmopolitan De-scriptions: Shanghai and Hong Kong"; and Audrey Yue, "'In the Mood for Love': Intersections of Hong Kong Mo-dernity," but surprisingly little attention to the shift in "high culture" production from Shanghai to Beijing during this same period.

Character Glossary

Names and titles listed in the bibliography are not included in this glossary.

A Jin　阿金

A Kang　阿康

A Su　阿素

A You　阿有

Aiwenyi lu　愛文義路

"Ala Szahaenin"　阿拉上海人

baihua　白話

Baihua Alley　百花里

baihua xiaoshuo　白話小說

Baike lu　白克路

Baoshan jie　寶善街

baozhang xiaoshuo　報章小說

"Bei dangzuo xiaoqianpin de nanzi"　被當作消遣品的男子

Beijing fanhua meng　北京繁華夢

Beijing xilu　北京西路

Beijing xin fanhua meng　北京新繁華夢

beimian wenzi　背面文字

"Benbu xinwenlan bianjishi li yi zha fei gao shang de gushi"　本埠新聞欄編輯室裡一札廢稿上的故事

Bi Yihong　畢倚虹

biaoji　標記

biji　筆記

bin　賓

bu jie er jie　不結而結

Caifeng bao　采風報

cainü　才女

Cang Jie　倉頡

Canghai ke　滄海客

cangshan　藏閃

Cao Xueqin　曹雪芹

Caojia du　曹家渡

ceng　曾

changsan/zasae　長三

Chen Sen　陳森

Chen Tongxun　陳同勛

Chen Xiaoyun　陳小雲

Chengdu　成都

chenggong renshi　成功人士

chengli　城裡

chuancha cangshan zhi fa　穿插藏閃之法

Chuanxin jie　穿心街

Chunqiu　春秋

Da malu　大馬路

da tuanyuan　大團圓

da xiaoshuo jia　大小說家

Daguan yuan　大觀園

Da'nao Shanghai qinlou chuguan yanyi　大鬧上海秦樓楚館演義

Dangui yuan　丹桂園

Daoguang　道光

Daxing Alley　大興里

Deng Zitong　鄧子通

Dianshi zhai　點石齋

dù　杜

Du Shaomu　杜少牧

Du Sujuan　杜素娟

Duan Qianqing　段情卿

East Hexing Alley　東合興里

East Shangren Alley　東尚仁里

Edo　江戶

er fangdong　二房東

Er Ma　二馬

fanben　翻本

fang　坊

Fangyan bao　方言報

Fanwangdu　梵王渡

Feng Yunqing　馮雲卿
"Fengjing"　風景
Foshan　佛山
Fujian lu　福建路
Fusheng liuji　浮生六記
Fuzhou lu　福州路
Gao Xianglan　高湘蘭
getsuyōbi　月曜日
Gong Zizhen　龔自珍
"Gongmu"　公墓
Gongyang Alley　公陽里
Guanchang xianxing ji　官場現行記
Guangling chao　廣陵潮
Guangxu　光緒
Guangzhou　廣州
guanjian　關鍵
Guiguan　桂冠
Gujin tushu jicheng　古今圖書集成
Guo Moruo　郭沫若
Guowen bao　國聞報
Gusu fanhua tu　姑蘇繁華圖
haipai　海派
"'Haipai' he 'jingpai'"　「海派」和
　「京派」
Haishang baihua qule yanyi　海上白話
　趣樂演義
Haishang fanhua zhaoxi　海上繁華
　朝夕
Haishang fengliu xianxing ji　海上風流
　現行記
Haishang fengliu zhuan　海上風流傳
"*Haishang hua liezhuan* liyan"　海上
　花列傳例言
Haishang huo diyu　海上活地獄
Haishang kanhua ji　海上看花記
Haishang mingji si da jin'gang qishu
　海上名妓四大金剛奇書
Haishang qinglou qiyuan　海上青樓
　奇緣
Haishang qinglou tuji　海上青樓圖集
Haishang qinlou chuguan yeyou zhuan
　海上秦樓楚館冶遊傳
Haishang qishu　海上奇書
Haishang ranxi lu　海上燃犀錄

haishang xiaoshuo　海上小說
Hangzhou　杭州
Hankou　漢口
Hantong　罕通
hao　號
He dian　何典
Heimu zhong zhi heimu　黑幕中之
　黑幕
Hong Baobao　紅寶寶
Hong Shanqing　洪善卿
Hongkou　虹口
Honglou meng　紅樓夢
Hou Haishang hua liezhuan　後海上花
　列傳
Hu bao　滬報
Hu Baoyu　胡寶玉
hua　華
Hua Haohao　花好好
Hua Liannong　花憐儂
Hua shijie　花世界
Hua Xiaonong　花笑儂
Hua ye lian nong　花也憐儂
huagao　畫稿
Huaihai lu　淮海路
huajie　華界
Huang Cuifeng　黃翠鳳
Huangpu　黃浦
Huaxing Lane　華興坊
huayang jiaojie　華洋交界
huayanjian/hu'igei　花煙間
Hubin　滬濱
huiguan　會館
Hujiang　滬江
Hunan　湖南
Huoshao Shanghai Hongmiao yanyi
　火燒上海紅廟演義
Jia Baoyu　賈寶玉
Jia Fengchen　賈逢辰
Jiang Youchun　蔣又春
Jiangnan　江南
Jiangnan shuju　江南書局
Jiangzuo shulin　江左書林
jie [territory]　界
jie [to serve as intermediary]　介

jie er bu jie 結而不結

Jieziyuan huazhuan 芥子園畫傳

"Jihai liuyue chongguo Yangzhou ji"
  己亥六月重過揚州記

Jiliang suo 濟良所

Jin Ping Mei 金瓶梅

Jin Shengtan 金聖歎

Jin Wenqing 金雯青

Jin Yuelan 金月蘭

Jin Zifu 金子富

jindai de chanwu 近代的產物

Jing Yingzhi 經營之

Jing'an Temple 靜安寺

Jingbao 晶報

Jingdezhen 景德鎮

jinghuo 京貨

jingpai 京派

jingshen 精神

"Jinsuo ji" 金鎖記

Jishi xingle bao 及時行樂報

jiu wenxue 舊文學

Jiu'an Alley 久安里

Kade lu 卡德路

Kaifeng 開封

Kang Youwei 康有為

Kangxi zidian 康熙字典

Kuang Er 匡二

kunqu 崑曲

Kyoto 京都

Lao Can youji 老殘遊記

li 里

Li Heting 李鶴汀

Li Meibo 李梅伯

Li Shifu 李實夫

Li Shufang 李漱芳

Li Tianbao 李天葆

Liang Qichao 梁啟超

"Liangge shijian de bu ganzheng zhe"
  兩個時間的不感症者

Liangshan 梁山

Lihun 離婚

lilong 里弄

Ling Shufang 凌漱芳

Liu Xianxian 柳纖纖

Liu Yuying 劉玉英

liudong renkou 流動人口

"Liuxing xing ganmao" 流行性感冒

Liwen xuan shuzhuang 理文軒書莊

Lou Shiyi 樓適夷

Lu Xiaoting 陸小庭

Lu Xiubao 陸秀寶

"Lun xiaoshuo yu qunzhi zhi guanxi"
  論小說與群治之關係

mang 忙

mangzhong zhi xianbi 忙中之閒筆

Manpan lu 蔓盤路

mao'er xi 髦兒戲

Master Lai 賴公子

"Meiyu zhi xi" 梅雨之夕

Mengyou Shanghai zhengfeng zhuan
  夢遊上海爭風傳

ming 名

Mingji zhengfeng zhuan 名妓爭風傳

Miss Xiao 沈小小姐

'*mma* 無麼

'*mpe* 無撥

Ms. Shao 邵氏

Ms. Xue 薛氏

Mu Shiying 穆時英

Mudan ting 牡丹亭

Naitō Konan 內藤湖南

Nanjing lu 南京路

Nanjing xilu 南京西路

Ni Junren 倪俊人

Nianzai fanhua meng 廿載繁華夢

Nicheng qiao 泥城橋

Ningbo 寧波

Ningguo 寧國

'*nælig;* 耐

'*nong* 儂

Pan 潘

Pan Shao'an 潘少安

Peiwen yunfu 佩文韻府

piaojie 嫖界

piaojie zhinan 嫖界指南

pingdan er jin ziran 平淡而近自然

Pinhua baojian 品花寶鑒

Pudong 浦東

Qi Yunsou　齊韻叟

Qian Menghua　錢夢花

Qian Ruhai　錢如海

Qian Shouyu　錢守愚

Qianqing tang　千頃堂

qianze xiaoshuo　譴責小說

Qilu deng　歧路燈

"Qingcheng zhi lian"　傾城之戀

Qinghe Lane　清和坊

Qinghua　清華

Qinghua shuju　清華書局

qingjing zhi di　清淨之地

Qinglou baojian　青樓寶鑒

Qinglou meng　青樓夢

Qingming shanghe tu　清明上河圖

Qixia wuyi　七俠五義

Qizai fanhua meng　七載繁華夢

Qu bao　趣報

Qu Qiubai　瞿秋白

Qunfang pu　群芳譜

Qunyu Lane　群玉坊

rao　繞

Renhai chao　人海潮

"Reqing zhi gu"　熱情之骨

Richu　日出

Rixin shuju　日新書局

Rixin shuzhuang　日新書莊

Rongguo　榮國

Rongzi　蓉子

Rulin waishi　儒林外史

Sanguo zhi　三國志

sanshi niandai　三十年代

Saoye shanfang　掃葉山房

Shanghai chunqiu　上海春秋

"Shanghai de hubuwu"　上海的狐步舞

"Shanghai fengsu suoji"　上海風俗瑣記

"Shanghai guancha tan"　上海觀察談

Shanghai kongxin da laoguan　上海空心大老官

Shanghai kuangxiang qu　上海狂想曲

Shanghai shi zimei　上海十姊妹

Shanghai youcan lu　上海遊驂錄

Shanghai zhi mimi　上海之秘密

Shanghai zhi weixin dang　上海之維新黨

shangjie　商界

Shao'an　少安

Shaoxing　紹興

Shaoyu　少愚

shehui zhi hua　社會之花

shen　身

Shen bao　申報

Shen Congwen　沈從文

Shen Xiaohong　沈小紅

Shen Yifan　沈一帆

Shen yuan　申園

Sheng chunü de ganqing　聖處女的感情

Shenghuo　生活

Shengping lou　升平樓

Shi bao　時報

Shi lu　石路

Shi Ruisheng　施瑞生

Shi Tianran　史天然

shikumen　石庫門

Shiliu pu　十六舖

Shimen erlu　石門二路

shin kankaku ha　新感覺派

shuchang　書場

Shuihu houzhuan　水滸後傳

Shuihu zhuan　水滸傳

Si da jin'gang　四大金剛

Si da jin'gang qishu　四大金剛奇書

Si da jin'gang zhuan　四大金剛傳

Si malu　四馬路

Sicha lu　思岔路

Sichuan lu　四川路

Songjiang　松江

su　俗

Su Guanxiang　蘇冠香

Subai　蘇白

Subei　蘇北

Sun Sulan　孫素蘭

Suren　蘇人

Suzhou baihua bao　蘇州白話報

Suzhou fanhua meng　蘇州繁華夢

Suzhou hua　蘇州話
Suzhou tubai　蘇州土白
Szahaenin　上海人
Taiping　太平
Taiping Lane　太平坊
tanci　彈詞
Tang Xiao'an　湯嘯菴
Tang Zhizhai　湯質齋
Tao Yufu　陶玉甫
Taomo guanzhu　逃墨館主
tebie shangbiao　特別商標
Third Master Shi　史三公子
Tianjin　天津
tigang　提綱
Tomishige Rihei　冨重利平
Tong'an Alley　同安里
Tongqing Alley　同慶里
Tongzhi　同治
tú　屠
Tu Shaoxia　屠少霞
Uchiyama Bookstore　內山書店
ven　齣
viao　勦
wailai　外來
Wang Liansheng　王蓮生
Wang Tao　王韜
Wangjia ku　王家庫
Wangping jie　望平街
Wanshou tu　萬壽圖
Wei Xiaxian　衛霞仙
Wen Miaoxiang　聞妙香
wenming　文明
Wenrui lou　文瑞樓
Wenxue xunkan　文學旬刊
wenzi　文字
West Huifang Alley　西薈芳里
"Women you shenme yichan?"　我們
　　有甚麼遺產？
wu　勿
Wu　吳
Wu Chuyun　巫楚雲
Wu Sunfu　吳蓀甫
Wu Zhen　吳珍
Wugui lieche　無軌列車

Wushuang　無雙
Wuxi　無錫
Wuyu　吳語
Xiamen　廈門
xian　閒
Xiandai　現代
Xiangchun Alley　祥春里
xianhua　閒話
xianren tiao　仙人跳
xianzi　閒字
Xiao Liu'er　小柳兒
xiao shimin　小市民
xiaobao　小報
Xiaolin bao　笑林報
xiaoshuo　小說
xiaoshuo jie　小說界
Xiaoshuo yuebao　小說月報
xiaoxian　消閒
Xiaoxian bao　消閒報
xiaxie xiaoshuo　狹邪小說
Xie You'an　謝幼安
xieshi　寫實
Ximen Qing　西門慶
Xin fanhua meng　新繁華夢
xin ganjue pai　新感覺派
Xin Shen bao　新申報
xin wenxue　新文學
Xin Wutai　新舞台
xin xiaoshuo　新小說
Xin Zhongguo weilai ji　新中國未來記
Xinbian Duanchang bei　新編斷腸碑
Xingshi yinyuan zhuan　醒世因緣傳
Xinjiang ribao　新疆日報
Xintiandi　新天地
xinxi　新戲
xinyuan yima　心猿意馬
Xinzha　新閘
Xixiang ji　西廂記
Xiyang　夕陽
Xiyou bu　西遊補
Xiyou ji　西遊記
Xizang lu　西藏路
Xu Junmu　徐君牧
Xu Qinglou baojian　續青樓寶鑒

Xu Xingyun　許行雲
Xu Xu　徐訏
Xu yuan　徐園
Xu Zhenya　徐枕亞
xuanlü　旋律
xunbu　巡捕
xunli　巡禮
Yadong tushuguan　亞東圖書館
Yan Huasheng　顏華生
Yan Ruyu　顏如玉
yang　洋
Yang Feita　楊妃榻
yangchang caizi　洋場才子
Yanghang jie　洋行街
yangjie　洋界
Yangjing bang　洋涇浜
Yangshu pu　楊樹浦
Yangzhou　揚州
Yanhua　煙話
yao　要
Yao Jinghuan　姚景桓
Yao Wenjun　姚文君
yao'er/yo'ni　么二
Ye Lingfeng　葉靈鳳
ye mache　夜馬車
yeji/'iaji　野雞
Yeshi yuan　也是園
Yesou puyan　野叟曝言
Yeyou Xin malu　冶遊新馬路
"Yi Hu Shizhi"　憶胡適之
yiguan　夷館
yima xinyuan　意馬心猿
yin　淫
Yingchun Lane　迎春坊
Yingguo huiguan　英國會館
"Yinglun de wu"　英倫的霧
"Yingpian de beijing"　影片的背景
yingzi　影子
Yokomitsu Riichi　橫光利一
"Youxi"　遊戲
Yu Dafu　郁達夫
Yu Qie　予且
Yu yuan　豫園
yuan　園

Yuan Xiangfu　袁翔甫
Yulanpen　盂蘭盆
Yuli hun　玉梨魂
za　雜
"Zai Bali da xiyuan"　在巴黎大戲院
zai falü shang　在法律上
Zhang Ailing quanji　張愛玲全集
Zhang Henshui　張恨水
Zhang Huizhen　張蕙貞
Zhang Qiugu　張秋谷
Zhang Xiaocun　張小村
Zhang Xinzhi　張新之
Zhang Xiuying　張秀英
Zhang yuan　張園
Zhang Zhupo　張竹坡
zhanghui　章回
Zhao Botao　趙伯韜
Zhao Erbao　趙二寶
Zhao Puzhai　趙樸齋
Zhaofu Alley　兆富里
Zhaogui Alley　兆貴里
Zhendan daxue　震旦大學
Zhenjiang　鎮江
Zhongguo xiaoshuo shiliao congshu
　　中國小說史料叢書
zhongshiji sheng chunü　中世紀聖處女
Zhou Leshan　周樂山
Zhou Shoujuan　周瘦鵑
Zhou Shuangyu　周雙玉
Zhou Shuangzhu　周雙珠
Zhoufu lianhuan zhi　州府連環誌
Zhouli　周禮
zhu　主
Zhu Shiquan　諸十全
Zhu Shuren　朱淑人
zhu'nao　主腦
Zhuang Lifu　莊荔甫
Zhuxian　朱仙
zongzhi　宗旨
Zuijin Shanghai mimi shi　最近上海
　　秘密史
Zuixin Haishang fanhua meng　最新
　　海上繁華夢
zujie　租界

Bibliography

A Ying 阿英 [Qian Xingcun 錢杏村], ed. *Wan Qing wenxue congchao* 晚清文學叢鈔. Volumes 2 and 8. Beijing: Zhonghua shuju, 1960.

———. *Wan Qing wenyi baokan shulüe* 晚清文藝報刊述略. Shanghai: Gudian wenxue chubanshe, 1958.

———. *Wan Qing xiaoshuo shi* 晚清小說史. 1980 revised edition. Reprint, Beijing: Renmin wenxue chubanshe, 1991.

———. *Xiaoshuo ertan* 小說二談. Shanghai: Gudian wenxue chubanshe, 1958.

———. *Xiaoshuo santan* 小說三談. Reprint, Shanghai guji chubanshe, 1979.

Abbas, Ackbar. "Cosmopolitan De-scriptions: Shanghai and Hong Kong." *Public Culture* 12.3 (2000): 769–786.

Adorno, Theodor. *The Culture Industry: Selected Essays on Mass Culture.* Edited by J. M. Bernstein. London: Routledge, 1991.

Altick, Richard. *The English Common Reader: A Social History of the Mass Reading Public, 1800–1900.* Chicago: University of Chicago Press, 1957.

Anderson, Benedict. *Imagined Communities: Reflections on the Origin and Spread of Nationalism.* Revised edition. New York: Verso, 1991.

Anderson, Marston. *The Limits of Realism: Chinese Fiction in the Revolutionary Period.* Berkeley: University of California Press, 1990.

Bakhtin, Mikhail Mikhailovich. *The Dialogic Imagination.* Translated and edited by Michael Holquist and Caryl Emerson. Austin: University of Texas Press, 1981.

Ban Gu 班固. *Han shu* 漢書. Reprint, Beijing: Zhonghua shuju, 1962.

Bao Tianxiao 包天笑. *Chuanying lou huiyi lu* 釧影樓回憶錄. Reprinted as vols. 48.1 and 48.2 in *Jindai Zhongguo shiliao congkan xubian* 近代中國史料叢刊續編. Wenhai chubanshe youxian gongsi, [1974].

———. *Shanghai chunqiu* 上海春秋. 1924. Reprint, Guilin: Lijiang chubanshe, 1987.

Barlow, Tani E. "Colonialism's Career in Postwar China Studies." In *Formations of Colonial Modernity in East Asia*, edited by Tani Barlow, 373–411. Durham: Duke University Press, 1997.

Barthes, Roland. *Image, Music, Text.* Translated by Stephen Heath. New York: Hill and Wang, 1977.

———. *The Rustle of Language.* Translated by Richard Howard. New York: Hill and Wang, 1996.

Bedini, Silvio. *The Trail of Time: Time Measurement with Incense in East Asia.* Cambridge: Cambridge University Press, 1994.

Béguin, Albert. *Balzac visionnaire: propositions.* Geneva: Skira, 1946.

Beijing shifan daxue tushuguan zhongwen guji shumu 北京師範大學圖書館中文古籍書目. Beijing shifan daxue tushuguan, 1983.

Beijing xin fanhua meng 北京新繁華夢. Shanghai: Gailiang xiaoshuo she, 1910. Gest Library, Princeton University.

Benjamin, Walter. *Illuminations.* Translated by Harry Zohn. New York: Schocken Books, 1969.

———. *Reflections.* Translated by Edmund Jephcott; edited by Peter Demetz. New York: Schocken Books, 1986.

Bennett, Tony. "The Exhibitionary Complex." In *Culture/Power/History: A Reader in Contemporary Social Theory,* edited by Nicholas B. Dirks, Geoff Eley, and Sherry B. Ortner. Princeton: Princeton University Press, 1994.

Berry, Michael. "Words and Images: A Conversation with Hou Hsiao-hsien and Chu T'ien-wen." *positions* 11.3 (2003): 676–716.

Betta, Chiara. "Marginal Westerners in Shanghai: The Baghdadi Jewish Community, 1845–1931." In *New Frontiers: Imperialism's New Communities in East Asia, 1842–1953,* edited by Robert Bickers and Christian Henriot, 38–54. Manchester: Manchester University Press, 2000.

———. "The Rise of Silas Aaron Hardoon (1851–1931) as Shanghai's Major Individual Landowner." *Sino-Judaica: Occasional Papers of the Sino-Judaic Institute* 2: 1–40.

Bhabha, Homi. *The Location of Culture.* London: Routledge, 1994.

Bi Yihong 畢倚虹, and Bao Tianxiao 包天笑. *Renjian diyu* 人間地獄. 1922–1924. Reprint, Beijing: Jinghua chubanshe, 1994.

———. *Renjian diyu* 人間地獄. 1922–1924. Reprint, Shanghai guji chubanshe, 1991.

Bickers, Robert. *Britain in China: Community, Culture, and Colonialism, 1900–1949.* Manchester: Manchester University Press, 1999.

———. "Shanghailanders: The Formation and Identity of the British Settler Community in Shanghai, 1843–1937." *Past and Present* no. 159 (May 1998): 161–211.

Bickers, Robert, and Christian Henriot, eds. *New Frontiers: Imperialism's New Communities in East Asia, 1842–1953.* Manchester: Manchester University Press, 2000.

Bickers, Robert, and Jeffrey Wasserstrom. "Shanghai's 'Dogs and Chinese Not Admitted' Sign: Legend, History, and Contemporary Symbol." *The China Quarterly* no. 142 (1995): 444–466.

Blumin, Stuart. "George G. Foster and the Emerging Metropolis." In *New York by Gas-Light and Other Urban Sketches,* by George Foster. Edited and with an introduction by Stuart M. Blumin. Berkeley: University of California Press, 1990.

Boltz, Judith. "Not by the Seal of Office Alone: New Weapons in Battles with the

Supernatural." In *Religion and Society in T'ang and Sung China*, edited by Patricia Buckley Ebrey and Peter Gregory, 241–305. Honolulu: University of Hawai'i Press, 1993.

Borotová, Lucie. "Storytelling in Yangzhou in the Eighteenth Century: *Yangzhou huafang lu.*" In *The Eternal Storyteller: Oral Literature in Modern China*, edited by Vibeke Børdahl, 197–209. Surrey: Curzon, 1999.

Bourdieu, Pierre. *The Rules of Art*. Translated by Susan Emanuel. Stanford: Stanford University Press, 1996.

Boym, Svetlana. *The Future of Nostalgia*. New York: Basic Books, 2001.

Braester, Yomi. "Shanghai's Economy of the Spectacle: The Shanghai Race Club in Liu Na'ou's and Mu Shiying's Stories." *Modern Chinese Literature* 9 (1995): 39–58.

Brantlinger, Patrick. *The Reading Lesson: The Threat of Mass Literacy in Nineteenth-Century British Fiction*. Bloomington: Indiana University Press, 1998.

Britton, Roswell. *The Chinese Periodical Press: 1800–1912*. Shanghai: Kelly & Walsh, 1933.

Brokaw, Cynthia J. "Commercial Publishing in Late Imperial China: The Zou and Ma Family Businesses of Sibao, Fujian." *Late Imperial China* 17.1 (1996): 49–92.

Brook, Timothy. *The Confusions of Pleasure: Commerce and Culture in Ming China*. Berkeley: University of California Press, 1998.

Brooks, Barbara J. "Japanese Colonial Citizenship in Treaty Port China: The Location of Koreans and Taiwanese in the Imperial Order." In *New Frontiers: Imperialism's New Communities in East Asia, 1842–1953*, edited by Robert Bickers and Christian Henriot, 109–124. Manchester: Manchester University Press, 2000.

Brooks, Jeffrey. *When Russia Learned to Read: Literacy and Popular Literature, 1861–1917*. Princeton: Princeton University Press, 1985.

Brooks, Peter. *Reading for the Plot: Design and Intention in Narrative*. Reprint, Cambridge, MA: Harvard University Press, 1992.

Buck-Morss, Susan. *The Dialectics of Seeing: Walter Benjamin and the Arcades Project*. Cambridge, MA: MIT Press, 1989.

Caifeng bao 采風報. Shanghai, 1898–? Shanghai Library.

Cao Jinqing 曹錦清. "Fangfa yu gushi: wo xin mu zhong de 'Shanghairen'" 方法與故事: 我心目中的「上海人」. In *Xin Shanghairen* 新上海, edited by Shanghai Zhengda yanjiusuo 上海證大研究所, 96–107. Hong Kong: Sanlian shudian, 2003.

Carlisle, Janice. *The Sense of an Audience: Dickens, Thackeray, and George Eliot at Mid-Century*. Athens: University of Georgia Press, 1981.

Cassel, Pär. "Excavating Extraterritoriality: The 'Judicial Sub-Prefect' as a Prototype for the Mixed Court in Shanghai." *Late Imperial China* 24.2 (2003): 156–182.

Celestial Empire, The. Shanghai: Offices of "The Celestial Empire" and "Shanghai

Mercury." Weekly, 1877?–1896? Partial run in the New England Depository Library.

Certeau, Michel de. *The Practice of Everyday Life*. Translated by Steven F. Rendall. Berkeley: University of California Press, 1984.

Chang, Eileen [Zhang Ailing], and Eva Hung, trans. *Sing-Song Girls of Shanghai*. New York: Columbia University Press, 2005.

Chen Bohai 陳伯海, and Yuan Jin 袁進, eds. *Shanghai jindai wenxue shi* 上海近代文學史. Shanghai renmin chubanshe, 1993.

Chen Congzhou 陳從周, and Zhang Ming 章明, eds. *Shanghai jindai jianzhu shi gao* 上海近代建築史稿. Shanghai: Sanlian shudian, 1988.

Chen Diexian 陳蝶仙. *Miwu chunxiao qu* 靡蕪春曉曲. Printed in *San jia qu* 三家曲. 1900 preface. Fudan University Library.

———. *The Money Demon*. Translated by Patrick Hanan. Honolulu: University of Hawai'i Press, 1999.

Chen, Jianhua. "From Teahouse to Movie Theater: Zhou Shoujuan as an Early Chinese Moviegoer." Unpublished paper.

Chen Pingyuan 陳平原. *Zhongguo xiaoshuo xushi moshi de zhuanbian* 中國小說敘事模式的轉變. Shanghai renmin chubanshe, 1988.

Chen Weizhao 陳維昭. "Yin'guo, sekong, suming guannian yu Ming-Qing changpian xiaoshuo de xushi moshi" 因果，色空，宿命觀念與明清長篇小說的敘事模式. *Hua'nan shifan daxue xuebao* 74 (October 1989): 61–66.

Cheng, Stephen. "*Sing-Song Girls of Shanghai* and its Narrative Methods." In *Chinese Middlebrow Fiction from the Ch'ing and Early Republican Eras*, edited by Liu Ts'un-yan. Hong Kong: Chinese University Press, 1984.

Chi Zhicheng 池志澂. *Huyou mengying* 滬遊夢影. 1893. Reprint, Shanghai guji chubanshe, 1989.

Chia, Lucille. *Printing for Profit: The Commercial Publishers of Jianyang, Fujian (11th to 17th Centuries)*. Cambridge, MA: Harvard University Asia Center, 2002.

Chinese Repository. Volume 4. Canton, 1835.

Chow, Kai-wing. *The Rise of Confucian Ritualism in Late Imperial China: Ethics, Classics, and Lineage Discourse*. Stanford: Stanford University Press, 1994.

———. "Writing for Success: Printing, Examinations, and Intellectual Change in Late Ming China." *Late Imperial China* 17.1 (1996): 120–157.

Chow, Rey. *Woman and Chinese Modernity: The Politics of Reading Between West and East*. Minneapolis: University of Minnesota Press, 1991.

Clifford, Nicholas. *The Spoilt Children of Empire: Westerners in Shanghai and the Chinese Revolution of the 1920s*. Hanover: Middlebury College Press, 1991.

Clunas, Craig. *Fruitful Sites: Garden Culture in Ming Dynasty China*. Durham: Duke University Press, 1996.

Dai An'gang 戴鞍鋼. "Shanghai yu wan Qing caoyun biange" 上海與晚清漕運變革. In *Shanghai yanjiu luncong* 2, 51–56. Shanghai shehui kexue yuan chubanshe, 1989.

Dai Shadi 戴沙迪 [Alexander Des Forges]. "Beijing shi Shanghai de chanpin ma?"

北京是上海的產品嗎? In *Beijing: dushi xiangxiang yu wenhua jiyi* 北京：都市想像與文化記憶, edited by Chen Pingyuan 陳平原 and Wang Dewei 王德威, 234–238. Beijing: Beijing daxue chubanshe, 2005.

Dalian tushuguan cankao bu 大連圖書館參考部. *Ming-Qing xiaoshuo xuba xuan* 明清小說序跋選. Shenyang: Chunfeng wenyi chubanshe, 1983.

Dangdai Zhongguo guangbo dianshi tai baijuan congshu: Shanghai Dongfang guangbo diantai juan 當代中國廣播電視台百卷叢書：上海東方廣播電台卷. Edited by Shanghai Dongfang guangbo diantai juan bianweihui 上海東方廣播電台卷編委會. Beijing: Zhongguo guangbo dianshi chubanshe, 1997.

Dayan, Daniel. "The Tutor Code in Classical Cinema." *Film Quarterly* 28.1 (1974): 22–31.

De Man, Paul. "Literary History and Literary Modernity." In *Blindness and Insight: Essays in the Rhetoric of Contemporary Criticism*. 2d edition, 142–145. Minneapolis: University of Minnesota Press, 1983.

Dean, Kenneth. *Taoist Ritual and Popular Cults of Southeast China.* Princeton: Princeton University Press, 1993.

Debray, Régis. *Media Manifestos.* Translated by Eric Rauth. London: Verso, 1996.

Deleuze, Gilles, and Félix Guattari. *Anti-Oedipus: Capitalism and Schizophrenia.* Translated by Robert Hurley, Mark Seem, and Helen R. Lane. Minneapolis: University of Minnesota Press, 1983.

Denton, Kirk, ed. *Modern Chinese Literary Thought: Writings on Literature, 1893–1945.* Stanford: Stanford University Press, 1996.

Des Forges, Alexander. "Building Shanghai, One Page at a Time: The Aesthetics of Installment Fiction at the Turn of the Century." *Journal of Asian Studies* 62.3 (2003): 781–810.

———. "From Source Texts to 'Reality Observed': The Creation of the 'Author' in Nineteenth-Century Chinese Vernacular Fiction." *Chinese Literature: Essays, Articles, Reviews* 22 (2000): 67–84.

———. "Opium / Leisure / Shanghai: Urban Economies of Consumption." In *Opium Regimes: China, Britain, and Japan, 1839–1952*, edited by Timothy Brook and Bob Wakabayashi, 167–185. Berkeley: University of California Press, 2000.

———. "The Rhetorics of Modernity and the Logics of the Fetish." In *Contested Modernities in Chinese Literature*, edited by Charles Laughlin, 17–31. New York: Palgrave, 2005.

———. "Street Talk and Alley Stories: Tangled Narratives of Shanghai from 'Lives of Shanghai Flowers' (1892) to 'Midnight' (1933)." Ph.D. dissertation, Princeton University, 1998.

Dianshi zhai huabao 點石齋畫報. Shanghai: Dianshi zhai, 1884–1898.

Doleželová-Velingerová, Milena, ed. *The Chinese Novel at the Turn of the Century.* Toronto: University of Toronto Press, 1980.

Dostoevsky, Fyodor. *Notes from the Underground.* Translated by Jessie Coulson. Harmondsworth: Penguin, 1972.

Dudbridge, Glen. "Women Pilgrims to T'ai-Shan: Some Pages from a Seventeenth-Century Novel." In *Pilgrims and Sacred Sites in China*, edited by Susan Naquin and Chün-fang Yü, 39–64. Berkeley: University of California Press, 1992.

Edkins, Joseph. *A Vocabulary of the Shanghai Dialect.* Shanghai: Presbyterian Mission Press, 1869.

Eisenstein, Sergei. *Film Form: Essays in Film Theory.* San Diego: Harcourt Inc., [1949].

Elvin, Mark. "Tales of *Shen* and *Xin*: Body-Person and Heart-Mind in China during the last 150 Years." In *Zone* 4 (Fragments for a History of the Human Body, part 2), 266–349. Cambridge, MA: MIT Press, 1989.

Erchun jushi 二春居士 [Li Boyuan 李伯元?]. *Haitian hong xueji* 海天鴻雪記. 1899. Reprinted in *Zhongguo jindai xiaoshuo daxi* 中國近代小說大系 vol. 10, 181–314. Nanchang: Jiangxi renmin chubanshe, 1989.

"Extra-Settlement Roads 1853–1930." Typed report most likely prepared for the Shanghai Municipal Council. Shanghai, 1930. Shanghai Municipal Archives.

Fan Boqun et al., eds. *Yuanyang hudie pai wenxue ziliao.* Fuzhou: Fujian renmin chubanshe, 1984.

Fanger, Donald. *Dostoevsky and Romantic Realism: A Study of Dostoevsky in Relation to Balzac, Dickens, and Gogol.* Chicago: University of Chicago Press, 1967.

Faubion, James, ed. *Michel Foucault: Aesthetics, Method, Epistemology.* New York: The New Press, 1998.

Field, Andrew. "Selling Souls in Sin City: Shanghai Singing and Dancing Hostesses in Print, Film, and Politics, 1920–1949." In *Cinema and Urban Culture in Shanghai, 1922–1943*, edited by Yingjin Zhang, 99–127. Stanford: Stanford University Press, 1999.

Finnane, Antonia. "Yangzhou's 'Mondernity': Fashion and Consumption in the Early Nineteenth Century." *positions* 11.2 (2003): 395–425.

Fletcher, Joseph. "The Heyday of the Ch'ing Order in Mongolia, Sinkiang, and Tibet." In *The Cambridge History of China*, edited by Denis Twitchett and John K. Fairbank, vol. 10, 351–408. New York: Cambridge University Press, 1978.

Fruehauf, Heinrich. "Urban Exoticism in Modern and Contemporary Chinese Literature." In *From May Fourth to June Fourth: Fiction and Film in Twentieth-Century China*, edited by Ellen Widmer and David Der-wei Wang, 133–164. Cambridge, MA: Harvard University Press, 1993.

Fu, Poshek. *Between Shanghai and Hong Kong: The Politics of Chinese Cinemas.* Stanford: Stanford University Press, 2003.

Gálik, Marián. *Mao Tun and Modern Chinese Literary Criticism.* Wiesbaden: Franz Steiner Verlag, 1969.

———. *Milestones in Sino-Western Literary Confrontation (1898–1979).* Wiesbaden: Otto Harrassowitz, 1986.

Gates, Hill. *China's Motor: A Thousand Years of Petty Capitalism.* Ithaca: Cornell University Press, 1996.

Gaubatz, Piper Rae. *Beyond the Great Wall: Urban Form and Transformation on the Chinese Frontiers.* Stanford: Stanford University Press, 1996.

Ge Yuanxu 葛元煦. *Chongxiu Huyou zaji* 重修滬遊雜記. 1887. Shanghai Library.

———. *Huyou zaji* 滬遊雜記. 1876. Reprint, Shanghai guji chubanshe, 1989.

———. *Huyou zaji* 滬遊雜記. With punctuation by Hori Naotarō 堀直太郎. Tokyo, 1878. National Diet Library, Tokyo.

General Description of Shanghae and its Environs Extracted from Native Authorities. Shanghai: The Mission Press, 1850. Widener Library, Harvard University.

Genette, Gérard. *Narrative Discourse: An Essay in Method.* Translated by Jane E. Lewin. Ithaca: Cornell University Press, 1980.

Gluckman, Ron, and Crystyl Mo. "Lights, Culture, Action." *Asiaweek.* March 30, 2001.

Gogol, N. V. *Peterburgskie povesti.* St. Petersburg: Lenizdat, 1995 reprint.

———. *Polnoe sobranie sochinenii.* Leningrad: Izdatel'stvo Akademii Nauk, 1952.

Goldstein, Joshua. "From Teahouse to Playhouse: Theaters as Social Texts in Early-Twentieth-Century China." *Journal of Asian Studies* 62.3 (2003): 753–780.

Goodman, Bryna. "Improvisations on a Semicolonial Theme, or, How to Read Multiethnic Participation in the 1893 Shanghai Jubilee." *Journal of Asian Studies* 59.4 (2000): 889–926.

———. *Native Place, City, and Nation: Regional Networks and Identities in Shanghai, 1853–1937.* Berkeley: University of California Press, 1995.

Granat, Diana. "Literary Continuity in the New Chinese Short Story: A Study Based on the 'Hsiao-shuo yüeh-pao' (Short Story Magazine)." Ph.D. dissertation, University of Pennsylvania, 1980.

Groppe, Alison. "Not Made in China: Inventing Local Identities in Contemporary Malaysian Chinese Fiction." Ph.D. dissertation, Harvard University, 2006.

Gu Bo 古柏 [Paize Keulemans]. "Shijing de huixiang" 市井的回響. In *Beijing: dushi xiangxiang yu wenhua jiyi* 北京：都市想像與文化記憶, edited by Chen Pingyuan 陳平原 and Wang Dewei 王德威, 156–169. Beijing: Beijing daxue chubanshe, 2005.

Guo Changhai 郭長海. "Wu Jianren xieguo naxie changpian xiaoshuo?" 吳趼人寫過哪些長篇小說? *Shinmatsu shōsetsu* 17 (1994): 24–33.

Guo Yanli 郭延禮. *Zhongguo jindai wenxue fazhan shi* 中國近代文學發展史. Jinan: Shandong jiaoyu chubanshe, 1990.

Gutzlaff, Karl. "Journal of a Residence in Siam, and of a Voyage along the Coast of China to Mantchou Tartary." In *The Chinese Repository* 2nd edition, vol. 1. Canton, 1832.

Haishang qinglou tuji 海上青樓圖集. Shanghai, 1892. Fudan University Library.

Hamilton, Gary G., and Chi-kong Lai. "Consumerism without Capitalism: Consumption and Brand Names in Late Imperial China." In *The Social Econ-*

omy of Consumption, edited by Henry J. Rutz and Benjamin S. Orlove, 253–279. Lanham: University Press of America, 1989.

Hamm, John Christopher. *Paper Swordsmen: Jin Yong and the Modern Martial Arts Novel*. Honolulu: University of Hawai'i Press, 2005.

Han Bangqing 韓邦慶. *Haishang hua liezhuan* 海上花列傳. Shanghai: Dianshi zhai, 1894. Fudan University Library.

———. *Haishang hua liezhuan* 海上花列傳. 1894 lithographic edition. Reprint, Beijing: Renmin wenxue chubanshe, 1982, 1985.

———. *Haishang hua liezhuan* 海上花列傳. 1926 Yadong tushuguan typeset edition. Reprint, Taipei: Guiguan tushu gufen youxian gongsi, 1983, 1985.

Hanan, Patrick. *Chinese Fiction of the Nineteenth and Early Twentieth Centuries*. New York: Columbia University Press, 2004.

———. *The Chinese Vernacular Story*. Cambridge, MA: Harvard University Press, 1981.

———. "*Fengyue meng* and the Courtesan Novel." *Harvard Journal of Asiatic Studies* 58.2 (1998): 345–372.

Hanshang mengren 邗上蒙人. *Fengyue meng* 風月夢. 1848 preface. Reprint, Taipei: Hanyuan wenhua, 1993.

Hao, Yen-p'ing. *The Comprador in Nineteenth-Century China: Bridge Between East and West*. Cambridge, MA: Harvard University Press, 1970.

Hatano Tarō 波多野太郎. "Chūgoku shōsetsu gikyoku yōgo kenkyū nōto" 中國小說戲曲用語研究ノート (12). In *Chūgoku kankei ronsetsu shiryō*, vol. 2a, 500–505. Tokyo: Chūgoku kankei ronsetsu shiryō hozonkai, 1969.

———. "Chūgoku shōsetsu gikyoku yōgo kenkyū nōto" 中國小說戲曲用語研究ノート (14). In *Chūgoku kankei ronsetsu shiryō*, vol. 2b, 330–334. Tokyo: Chūgoku kankei ronsetsu shiryō hozonkai, 1974.

Hay, Jonathan. "Painters and Publishing in Late Nineteenth-Century Shanghai." In *Art at the Close of China's Empire*, edited by Chou Ju-hsi, 134–188. Tempe: Arizona State University Phoebus Occasional Papers in Art History, 1998.

Heath, Stephen. "Notes on Suture." *Screen* 18.4 (1977): 48–75.

Hershatter, Gail. *Dangerous Pleasures: Prostitution and Modernity in Twentieth-Century Shanghai*. Berkeley: University of California Press, 1997.

Ho, Ping-ti. "The Salt Merchants of Yang-chou: A Study in Commercial Capitalism in Eighteenth-Century China." *Harvard Journal of Asiatic Studies* 17 (1954): 130–168.

Hockx, Michel. "Playing the Field: Aspects of Chinese Literary Life in the 1920s." In *The Literary Field of Twentieth-Century China*, edited by Michel Hockx, 61–78. Honolulu: University of Hawai'i Press, 1999.

Honig, Emily. *Creating Chinese Ethnicity: Subei People in Shanghai, 1850–1980*. New Haven: Yale University Press, 1992.

Hou Zhongyi 侯忠義, ed. *Zhongguo wenyan xiaoshuo cankao ziliao* 中國文言小說參考資料. Beijing daxue chubanshe, 1985.

dited by Joseph F. Graham, 142–148. Ithaca: Cornell University Press, 985.

1, Linda Cooke. *Shanghai: From Market Town to Treaty Port, 1074–1858.* tanford: Stanford University Press, 1995.

Andrew F. *Yellow Music: Media Culture and Colonial Modernity in the Chiese Jazz Age.* Durham: Duke University Press, 2001.

iusan Mann. "The Ningpo *Pang* and Financial Power at Shanghai." In *The Chinese City Between Two Worlds*, edited by Mark Elvin and G. William ikinner. Stanford: Stanford University Press, 1974.

iima, Terry. "Seeing Faces, Making Races: Visual Readings and Appropriaions in the Construction of 'Race.'" *Meridians: feminism, race, transiationalism* 3.1 (2002): 161–190.

i 柯德席 [Nicholas Kaldis]. "Fan yuwang shi de dongfang qingdiao: lüeshu Hou Xiaoxian de 'Haishang hua'" 反欲望式的東方情調: 略述侯孝賢的「海上花」. *Jintian* 52 (2001): 266–272.

7, Jeffrey C. *The Odyssey of Shen Congwen.* Stanford: Stanford University Press, 1987.

orothy. *Teachers of the Inner Chambers: Women and Culture in Seventeenth-Century China.* Stanford: Stanford University Press, 1994.

ki, Peter. "Kashihon bunka hikaku kō" 貸本文化比較考. *Jinbun gakuhō* 57 1984): 37–57.

a, Julia. *Powers of Horror: An Essay on Abjection.* Translated by Leon S. Roudiez. New York: Columbia University Press, 1982.

Tai. "Shanghai Bund." [Panoramic photographs of the Shanghai Bund] N.p., n.d. Tōyō bunko, Tokyo.

egulations and bye-laws for the foreign settlements of Shanghai north of the Yang-king-pang. Shanghai: F & C Walsh, 1870. Phillips Library, Salem, MA.

Q. D. *Fiction and the Reading Public.* 1932. Reissued, London: Chatto & Windus, 1965.

aiyan. "All the Feelings That Are Fit to Print: The Community of Sentiment and the Literary Public Sphere in China, 1900–1918." *Modern China* 27.3 (2001): 291–327.

eo Ou-fan. *Shanghai Modern: The Flowering of a New Urban Culture in China, 1930–1945.* Cambridge, MA: Harvard University Press, 1999.

eo Ou-fan, and Andrew Nathan. "The Beginnings of Mass Culture: Journalism and Fiction in the Late Ch'ing and Beyond." In *Popular Culture in Late Imperial China*, edited by David Johnson, Andrew J. Nathan, and Evelyn S. Rawski, 360–395. Berkeley: University of California Press, 1985.

er, Robert. *Shikitei Sanba and the Comic Tradition in Edo Fiction.* Cambridge, MA: Harvard Council on East Asian Studies Publications, 1985.

李今. *Haipai xiaoshuo yu xiandai dushi wenhua* 海派小說與現代都市文化. Hefei: Anhui jiaoyu chubanshe, 2000.

fan 李歐梵 [Leo Ou-fan Lee]. "Zhongguo xiandai wenxue de 'tuifei' ji zuojia" 中國現代文學的「頹廢」及作家. *Tang-tai* 93 (January 1994): 22–47.

Hsia, C. T. *A History of Modern Chinese Fiction,* ┆
⠀⠀University Press, 1961.

Hsia, T. A. "Novel and Romance: Hsia Tsi-an on ┆
⠀⠀Translated by Dennis Hu. *Chinese Literature:*
⠀⠀2.2: 224–236.

Hu Mingyang 胡明揚. "Shanghai hua yibai nian lai d ┆
⠀⠀百年來的若干變化. *Zhongguo yuwen* 1978.3: 1┆

Hu Shi 胡適. "*Haishang hua liezhuan* xu" 「海上ㄱ┆
⠀⠀in *Haishang hua liezhuan,* by Han Bangqing,
⠀⠀1985.

———. "Wushi nian lai Zhongguo zhi wenxue" 五十
⠀⠀printed in *Hu Shi zuopin ji,* vol. 8. Taipei: Yuan

Hu Shiying 胡士瑩. *Tanci baojuan mulu* 彈詞寶卷目錄
⠀⠀chubanshe, 1957.

Hu, Siao-chen. "Literary *Tanci*: A Woman's Traditi
⠀⠀Ph.D. dissertation, Harvard University, 1994.

Hu Ying. *Tales of Translation: Composing the New W*
⠀⠀Stanford: Stanford University Press, 2000.

Huang Lin 黃霖. *Jindai wenxue piping shi* 近代文學排
⠀⠀guji chubanshe, 1993.

Huang Shiquan 黃式權. *Songnan mengying lu* 淞南夢影
⠀⠀hai guji chubanshe, 1989.

Huang, Tsung-yi Michelle. *Walking Between Slums a*
⠀⠀*Open Space in Hong Kong, Tokyo, and Shanghai*
⠀⠀University Press, 2004.

Huang Yanbo 黃岩柏. "Lun *Haishang hua liezhuan* der
⠀⠀jiaoxun" 論「海上花列傳」等吳語小說的歷史教訓
⠀⠀107 (January 1991): 53–55.

Hughes, Linda K., and Michael Lund. *The Victorian Seri*
⠀⠀sity Press of Virginia, 1991.

Hung, Chang-tai. *Going to the People: Chinese Intellec*
⠀⠀*1918–1937.* Cambridge, MA: Harvard Council on
⠀⠀cations, 1985.

Jameson, Fredric. *The Ideologies of Theory: Essays 1971–*
⠀⠀versity of Minnesota Press, 1988.

———. *The Political Unconscious: Narrative as a Socia*
⠀⠀Cornell University Press, 1981.

Jauss, Hans Robert. *Toward an Aesthetic of Reception.*
⠀⠀Bahti. Minneapolis: University of Minnesota Press,

Jiancun youke 劍村遊客. *Shanghai* 上海. N.p., 1903. Shan

Jiani 佳妮. *Yuedu haipai nü* 悅讀海派女. Xiamen: Xia
⠀⠀2005.

Johnson, Barbara. "Taking Fidelity Philosophically." In *I*

————. "Zhongguo xiandai xiaoshuo de xianqu zhe" 中國現代小說的先驅者. *Lien-ho wen-hsüeh* 3.12: 8–14.

Li Yu 李漁. *Xianqing ouji* 閒情偶寄. Annotated by Li Zhongshi 李忠實. Tianjin guji chubanshe, 1996.

Link, Perry. *Mandarin Ducks and Butterflies: Popular Fiction in Early Twentieth-Century Chinese Cities.* Berkeley: University of California Press, 1981.

Liren heqiu 里人何求. *Mindu bieji* 閩都別記. Reprint, [Fuzhou]: Fujian renmin chubanshe, 1987.

Liu Fu 劉復. "Du *Haishang hua liezhuan*" 讀「海上花列傳」. 1926. Reprinted in *Haishang hua liezhuan*, by Han Bangqing, 589–605. Taipei: Guiguan, 1986.

Liu, Jianmei. *Revolution Plus Love: Literary History, Women's Bodies, and Thematic Repetition in Twentieth-Century Chinese Fiction.* Honolulu: University of Hawai'i Press, 2003.

Liu Na'ou 劉吶鷗. *Dushi fengjing xian* 都市風景線 [*Scène*]. Shanghai: Shuimo shudian, 1930.

Liu, Ts'un-yan. "Introduction." In *Chinese Middlebrow Fiction from the Ch'ing and Early Republican Eras*, edited by Liu Ts'un-yan. Hong Kong: Chinese University Press, 1984.

Liu Yangti 劉揚體, ed. *Yuanyang hudie pai zuopin xuanping* 鴛鴦蝴蝶派作品選評. Chengdu: Sichuan wenyi chubanshe, 1987.

Lotman, Yuri M. *Universe of the Mind: A Semiotic Theory of Culture.* Translated by Ann Shukman. Bloomington: Indiana University Press, 1990.

Lu, Hanchao. "Away from Nanjing Road: Small Stores and Neighborhood Life in Modern Shanghai." *Journal of Asian Studies* 54.1 (1995): 92–123.

————. *Beyond the Neon Lights: Everyday Shanghai in the Early Twentieth Century.* Berkeley: University of California Press, 1999.

————. "Nostalgia for the Future: The Resurgence of an Alienated Culture in China." *Pacific Affairs* 75.2 (2002): 169–186.

Lu Hsun [Lu Xun]. *A Brief History of Chinese Fiction.* Translated by Yang Hsien-yi and Gladys Yang. Beijing: Foreign Languages Press, 1976.

Lu Shi'e 陸士諤. *Xin Shanghai* 新上海. 1909. Reprint, Shanghai guji chubanshe, 1997.

Lu Xun 鲁迅. *Lu Xun quanji* 鲁迅全集. Volume 6. Beijing: Renmin wenxue chubanshe, 1973.

————. *Qiejie ting zawen* 且介停雜文. Reprint, Tianjin renmin chubanshe, 1999.

————. *Zhongguo xiaoshuo shi lüe* 中國小說史略. Reprint, Shanghai: Beixin shuju, 1932.

Luo Zhufeng 羅竹風, et al., eds. *Hanyu da cidian* 漢語大詞典. Shanghai cishu chubanshe, 1987–1994.

Ma Xuexin 馬學新 et al., eds. *Shanghai wenhua yuanliu cidian* 上海文化源流辭典. Shanghai shehui kexue yuan chubanshe, 1992.

MacCannell, Dean. *The Tourist: A New Theory of the Leisure Class.* Revised edition, New York: Schocken Books, 1989.

Maclellan, J. W. *The Story of Shanghai: From the Opening of the Port to Foreign Trade.* Shanghai: North-China Herald Office, 1889.

Mao Dun 茅盾 [Shen Yanbing 沈雁冰]. "Dushi wenxue" 都市文學. In *Mao Dun quanji* 茅盾全集, vol. 19, 421–423. Beijing: Renmin wenxue chubanshe, 1991.

———. *Huaxiazi* 話匣子. Liangyou tushu gongsi, 1944.

———. *Mao Dun zhuanji* 茅盾專集. Fujian renmin chubanshe, 1983.

———. *Midnight.* Translated by Xu Mengxiong. Beijing: Foreign Languages Press, 1957.

———. *Wo zouguo de daolu* 我走過的道路. Volume 2. Beijing: Renmin wenxue chubanshe, 1984.

———. *Ziye* 子夜. 1933. Reprinted as volume one of *Mao Dun xuanji* 茅盾選集, Chengdu: Sichuan renmin chubanshe, 1982.

Markovits, Claude. "Indian Communities in China, c. 1842–1949." In *New Frontiers: Imperialism's New Communities in East Asia, 1842–1953*, edited by Robert Bickers and Christian Henriot, 55–74. Manchester: Manchester University Press, 2000.

Mayers, William Frederick, ed. *Treaties between the Empire of China and Foreign Powers.* 1877. Reprint, Taipei: Ch'eng-wen Publishing Company, 1966.

Mayne, Charles. *Notes on Tramways.* Shanghai, 1895. Shanghai Municipal Archives.

McDaniel, Laura. "'Jumping the Dragon Gate': Storytellers and the Creation of the Shanghai Identity." *Modern China* 27.4 (2001): 484–507.

McMahon, Keith. "Eliminating Traumatic Antinomies: Sequels to *Honglou meng.*" In *Snake's Legs: Sequels, Continuations, Rewritings, and Chinese Fiction*, edited by Martin W. Huang, 98–115. Honolulu: University of Hawai'i Press, 2004.

———. *The Fall of the God of Money: Opium Smoking in Nineteenth-Century China.* Lanham: Rowman & Littlefield, 2002.

———. "Fleecing the Male Customer in Shanghai Brothels of the 1890s." *Late Imperial China* 23.2 (2002): 1–32.

Meng, Yue. "Re-envisioning the Great Interior: Gardens and the Upper Class between the Imperial and the 'Modern.'" *Modern Chinese Literature and Culture* 14.1 (2002): 1–50.

———. *Shanghai and the Edges of Empires.* Minneapolis: University of Minnesota Press, 2006.

Mengyou Shanghai mingji zhengfeng zhuan 夢遊上海名妓爭風傳. Shanghai: Guangyi shuju, after 1904. Harvard-Yenching Library.

Min Jiaji 閔家驥, Fan Xiao 范曉, Zhu Chuan 朱川, and Zhang Songyue 張嵩岳, eds. *Jianming Wu fangyan cidian* 簡明吳方言詞典. Shanghai cishu chubanshe, 1986.

Miyata Ichirō 宮田一郎. "*Kaijōka retsuden* hōgen shigo kaishaku"「海上花列傳」方言詞語解釋. *Kyoto Gaidai kenkyū ronsō* 32 (1988): 418–479.

———. "*Kaijōka retsuden* no gengo"「海上花列傳」の言語. *Tōyō kenkyū* 73 (1985).

———, ed. *Shanghai go jōyō dōon jiten* 上海語常用同音字典. Tokyo: Kōseikan, 1988.

Morohashi Tetsuji 諸橋轍次, ed. *Dai kanwa jiten* 大漢和辭典. Reprint, Tokyo: Taishūkan shoten, 1971.

Mu Shiying 穆時英. *Shanghai de hubuwu* 上海的狐步舞. Beijing: Jingji ribao chubanshe, 2002.

Muramatsu Shin 村松伸. *Shanghai: toshi to kenchiku, 1842–1949* 上海：都市と建築. Tokyo: Parco shuppankyoku, 1991.

Murphey, Rhoads. *Shanghai: Key to Modern China*. Cambridge, MA: Harvard University Press, 1953.

Nakamura Hajime 中村元. *Bukkyōgo daijiten* 佛教語大辭典. Compact edition. Tokyo: Tokyo shoseki kabushiki gaisha, 1981.

Ōno Mihoko 大野美穂子. "Shanghai ni okeru gien no keisei to hatten" 上海に於ける戲院の形成と發展. *Ocha no Mizu shigaku* 26–27 (1983): 50–70.

Orchard, John E. "Shanghai." *The Geographical Review* 26.1 (1936): 1–31.

Osterhammel, Jürgen. "Semi-Colonialism and Informal Empire in Twentieth-Century China: Towards a Framework of Analysis." In *Imperialism and After: Continuities and Discontinuities*, edited by Wolfgang J. Mommsen and Jürgen Osterhammel, 290–314. London: Allen & Unwin, 1986.

Ōta Tatsuo 太田辰夫. *Gogo danshi tōhō* 吳語彈詞讀法. Gogo kenkyū sōkan, no. 3, 1970.

———. *Kaijōka retsuden* 海上花列伝. 1969. Reprint, Tokyo: Heibonsha, 1994.

———. *Kaiten kō sekki: Gogo shukō* 海天鴻雪記：吳語注稿. Gogo kenkyū sōkan no. 2, 1970.

"Panoramic View of Foreign Section of Shanghai, China." Phillips Library, Peabody Essex Museum, Salem, MA.

Peng Hsiao-yen 彭小妍. *Haishang shuo qingyu: cong Zhang Ziping dao Liu Na'ou* 海上說情慾：從張資平到劉吶鷗. Taipei: Zhongyang yanjiu yuan wenzhe yanjiusuo, 2001.

Perry, Elizabeth. *Shanghai on Strike: The Politics of Chinese Labor*. Stanford: Stanford University Press, 1993.

Ping Buqing 平步青. *Xiawai junxie* 霞外捃屑. Reprint, Shanghai guji chubanshe, 1982.

Ping Jinya 平襟亞. *Renhai chao* 人海潮. Reprint, Shanghai guji chubanshe, 1991.

———. "Shanghai chuban jie suowen" 上海出版界瑣聞. In *Shanghai difang shi ziliao* 4, 218–244. Shanghai shehui kexue yuan chubanshe, 1986.

Plaks, Andrew. *The Four Masterworks of the Ming Novel: Ssu Ta Ch'i-shu*. Princeton: Princeton University Press, 1987.

———. "Terminology and Central Concepts." In *How to Read the Chinese Novel*, edited by David Rolston, 75–123. Princeton: Princeton University Press, 1990.

———. "Towards a Critical Theory of Chinese Narrative." In *Chinese Narrative: Critical and Theoretical Essays*, edited by Andrew Plaks, 309–352. Princeton: Princeton University Press, 1977.

Prendergast, Christopher. *Paris and the Nineteenth Century*. London: Blackwell, 1992.

Průšek, Jaroslav. "The Beginnings of Popular Chinese Literature: Urban Centres—The Cradle of Popular Fiction." In *Chinese History and Literature*, 396–448. Prague, Academia, 1970.

———. "Les contes chinois du moyen âge comme source de l'histoire économique et sociale sous les dynasties des Sung et des Yüan." In *Chinese History and Literature*, 467–494. Prague: Academia, 1970.

———. *Three Sketches of Chinese Literature*. Prague: The Oriental Institute in Academia, 1969.

Qian Xinbo 錢忻伯, ed. *Xieyu congtan* 屑玉叢譚. In *Shenbao guan congshu*. Shanghai: Shen bao guan, 1878.

Qiu Xinru 邱心如. *Bi sheng hua* 筆生花. 1894. Reprint, Henan: Zhongzhou guji, 1984.

Querrien, Anne. "The Metropolis and the Capital." *Zone* 1/2, 218–221. Cambridge, MA: MIT Press, 1986.

Ramsay, S. Robert. *The Languages of China*. Princeton: Princeton University Press, 1987.

Rawski, Evelyn Sakakida. *Education and Popular Literacy in Ch'ing China*. Ann Arbor: University of Michigan Press, 1979.

Reed, Christopher. *Gutenberg in Shanghai: Chinese Print Capitalism, 1876–1937*. Vancouver: University of British Columbia Press, 2004.

Remick, Elizabeth. "Prostitution Taxes and Local State Building in Republican China." *Modern China* 29.1 (2003): 38–70.

Ristaino, Marcia Reynders. *Port of Last Resort: The Diaspora Communities of Shanghai*. Stanford: Stanford University Press, 2001.

Rojas, Carlos. "The Coin of Gender in *Pinhua baojian*." In *Dynastic Crisis and Cultural Innovation: From the Late Ming to the Late Qing and Beyond*, edited by David Der-wei Wang and Shang Wei, 297–324. Cambridge, MA: Harvard University Asia Center, 2005.

Rolston, David, ed. *How to Read the Chinese Novel*. Princeton: Princeton University Press, 1990.

———. *Traditional Chinese Fiction and Fiction Commentary: Reading and Writing between the Lines*. Stanford: Stanford University Press, 1997.

Rothman, William. "Against 'The System of Suture.'" *Film Quarterly* 29.1 (1975): 45–50.

Rowe, William T. *Hankow: Conflict and Continuity in a Chinese City, 1796–1895*. Stanford: Stanford University Press, 1989.

Rui Heshi 芮和師, ed. *Yuanyang hudie pai wenxue ziliao* 鴛鴦蝴蝶派文學資料. [Fuzhou]: Fujian renmin chubanshe, 1984.

Sangren, Steven. *History and Magical Power in a Chinese Community*. Stanford: Stanford University Press, 1987.

Satow, D. [Satō Denkichi]. *Shanghai Views*. Nos. 1–5 [Five albums of turn-of-the-century photos]. Shanghai, before 1903.

Seton, Grace Thompson. *Chinese Lanterns.* New York: Dodd, Mead & Co., 1924.

Shahar, Meir. *Crazy Ji: Chinese Religion and Popular Literature.* Cambridge, MA: Harvard University Asia Center, 1998.

Shanghai. [Photo album]. Shanghai: Max Nössler & Co., c. 1904. Tōyō bunko, Tokyo.

Shanghai tushuguan 上海圖書館. *Lao Shanghai ditu* 老上海地圖. Shanghai: Shanghai huabao chubanshe, 2001.

Shanghai tushuguan guancang Zhongwen baozhi fukan mulu 上海圖書館館藏中文報紙附刊目錄. Shanghai tushuguan, 1985.

Shanghai wenshi yanjiu guan 上海文史研究館, ed. *Jiu Shanghai de yan, du, chang* 舊上海的煙，賭，倡. Reprint, Hong Kong: Zhongyuan chubanshe, 1990.

Shanghai zhanggu 上海掌故. Shanghai wenhua chubanshe, 1982.

Shanghai Zhengda yanjiusuo 上海證大研究所, ed. *Xin Shanghairen* 新上海人. Hong Kong: Sanlian shudian, 2003.

Shanghai zhi pianshu shijie 上海之騙術世界. Shanghai: Saoye shanfang, 1924. Shanghai Library.

Shanghai zhinan 上海指南. Shanghai: Shangwu yinshuguan, 1909.

Shen bao 申報. Shanghai: Shen bao guan.

Shen bao guan congshu 申報館叢書. Shanghai: Shen bao guan, 1878–?

Shen bao guan shumu 申報館書目. Shanghai: Shen bao guan, 1877. Fudan University Library.

Shen Fu 沈復. *Fusheng liuji* 浮生六記. Shanghai: Shen bao guan, 1877.

Shen Yanbing 沈雁冰 [Mao Dun 茅盾]. "Ziran zhuyi yu Zhongguo xiandai xiaoshuo" 自然主義與中國現代小說. 1922. Reprinted in *Mao Dun zhuanji* 茅盾專集, 976–991. [Fuzhou]: Fujian renmin chubanshe, 1983.

Shenjiang mingsheng tushuo 申江名勝圖說. Shanghai: Haishang rouyun guan, 1884.

Shenjiang shengjing tu 申江勝景圖. Shanghai: Dianshi zhai, 1884.

Shenjiang shixia shengjing tushuo 申江時下勝景圖說. 1894. Reprinted in *Guoli Beijing daxue Zhongguo minsu xuehui minsu congshu* 國立北京大學民俗學會民俗叢書, vol. 78. Taipei: Dongfang wenhua shuju, 1972.

Shi Rujie 石汝杰. *Wuyu duben: Ming Qing Wuyu he xiandai Suzhou fangyan* 吳語讀本：明清吳語和現代蘇州方言. Tokyo: Kohbun, 1996.

Shi Zhecun 施蟄存. *Bomu de wunü* 薄暮的舞女. Zhongguo huaqiao chubanshe, 1997.

———. *One Rainy Evening.* Beijing: Chinese Literature Press, 1994.

Shih, Shu-mei. "Gender, Race, and Semicolonialism: Liu Na'ou's Urban Shanghai Landscape." *Journal of Asian Studies* 55.4 (1996): 934–956.

———. *The Lure of the Modern: Writing Modernism in Semicolonial China, 1917–1937.* Berkeley: University of California Press, 2001.

Shklovsky, Viktor. *Theory of Prose.* Translated by Benjamin Sher. Elmwood Park: Dalkey Archive Press, 1990.

Shoudu tushuguan cang Zhongguo xiaoshuo shumu chubian 首都圖書館藏中國小說書目初編. Beijing: Shoudu tushuguan, 1960.

Silverman, Kaja. *The Subject of Semiotics*. New York: Oxford University Press, 1983.

Sima Xiao 司馬小. "'Wo de tongshi' Zhang Henshui" 「我的同事」張恨水. *Daren* 16 (1971): 60–62.

Simmel, Georg. "The Metropolis and Mental Life." Translated by Kurt Wolff. Reprinted in *Classic Essays on the Culture of Cities*, edited by Richard Sennett, 47–60. New York: Appleton–Century–Crofts, 1969.

Song Yuanfang 宋原放. "Zhongguo jindai chuban da shiji" 中國近代出版大事記. *Chuban shiliao* 1990, no. 1: 136–154.

Spence, Jonathan. *The Memory Palace of Matteo Ricci*. London: Faber and Faber Limited, 1985.

Strassberg, Richard E., ed. *Inscribed Landscapes: Travel Writing from Imperial China*. Berkeley: University of California Press, 1994.

Sun Xun 孫遜, and Sun Juyuan 孫菊園, eds. *Zhongguo gudian xiaoshuo meixue ziliao huicui* 中國古典小說美學資料匯粹. Shanghai guji chubanshe, 1991.

Sun Yusheng 孫玉聲 [Sun Jiazhen 孫家振]. *Haishang fanhua meng* 海上繁華夢. 1898–1906. Reprint, including *Xu Haishang fanhua meng*, Shanghai guji chubanshe, 1991.

———. *Haishang ranxi lu* 海上燃犀錄. Shanghai tushuguan, 1925 reprint.

———. *Tuixing lu biji* 退醒廬筆記. Reprinted in *Jindai Zhongguo shiliao congkan* no. 80. Taipei: Wenhai chubanshe, 1972.

———. *Xiuxiang Haishang fanhua meng xinshu chuji, erji* 繡像海上繁華夢新書初集，二集. Shanghai: Xiaolin baoguan, 1903. Fudan University Library.

———. *Xu Haishang fanhua meng* 續海上繁華夢. 1915–1916. Reprinted in *Haishang fanhua meng*, Shanghai guji chubanshe, 1991.

Sze, Mai-mai, trans. and ed. *The Mustard Seed Garden Manual of Painting: Chieh Tzu Yüan Hua Chuan, 1679–1701*. Princeton: Princeton University Press, 1977.

Tarumoto Teruo 樽本照雄. "Yūgi shujin sentei 'Kōshi zuikyū kasen'" 遊戲主人選定「庚子蕊宮花選」. *Shinmatsu shōsetsu kenkyū* 5 (1981): 15–25.

Tillotson, Kathleen. *Novels of the Eighteen Forties*. London: Oxford University Press, 1954.

"Translations of Extracts from the Published Newspapers 1905–1916." Volume 1. Shanghai Municipal Archives, no. W1-0-501.

Travellers Guide to China. Shanghai and its Vicinity. Shanghai: China Advertising Co., 1909. Tōyō bunko, Tokyo.

Tucker, Robert C., ed., *The Marx–Engels Reader*. Second edition. London: W. W. Norton, 1978.

van der Sprenkel, Sybille. "Urban Social Control." In *The City in Late Imperial China*, edited by G. William Skinner, 609–632. Stanford: Stanford University Press, 1977.

W. E. B. *The Hotel Metropole Guide to Shanghai and environs containing all necessary informations for tourists and others*. Shanghai: Oriental Press, 1903.

Wagner, Rudolf. "The Role of the Foreign Community in the Chinese Public Sphere." *The China Quarterly* 142 (1995): 423–443.

Wakeman, Frederic E. Jr. *Policing Shanghai 1927–1937*. Berkeley: University of California Press, 1995.

Wang Anyi 王安憶. *Xunzhao Shanghai* 尋找上海. Shanghai: Xuelin chubanshe, 2001.

Wang, David Der-wei. *Fictional Realism: Mao Dun, Lao She, Shen Congwen*. New York: Columbia University Press, 1992.

———. *Fin-de-siècle Splendor: Repressed Modernities of Late Qing Fiction, 1848–1911*. Stanford: Stanford University Press, 1997.

Wang Tao 王韜. *Yingruan zazhi* 瀛壖雜誌. 1875. Reprint, Shanghai guji chubanshe, 1989.

Wang Xiaoming 王曉明. "Jiushi niandai Zhongguo de xin yishi xingtai: cong guanyu 'chenggong renshi' de shenhua shuoqi" 九十年代中國的新意識形態：從關於「成功人士」的神話說起. Unpublished paper.

Wasserstrom, Jeffrey N. "Locating Old Shanghai: Having Fits about Where It Fits." In *Remaking the Chinese City: Modernity and National Identity, 1900–1950*, edited by Joseph W. Esherick, 192–210. Honolulu: University of Hawai'i Press, 2000.

Watt, Ian. *The Rise of the Novel: Studies in Defoe, Richardson, and Fielding*. Berkeley: University of California Press, 1957.

Wei Shaochang 魏紹昌. "*Haishang mingji sida jin'gang qishu* liang ti"「海上名妓四大金剛奇書」兩題. *Shinmatsu shōsetsu* 15 (1992): 64–69.

———. "*Haitian hong xueji* de zuozhe wenti"「海天鴻雪記」的作者問題. *Henan daxue xuebao*, 1991, no. 2: 61–63.

———, ed. *Li Boyuan yanjiu ziliao* 李伯元研究資料. Shanghai guji chubanshe, 1980.

———, ed. *Niehai hua ziliao* 孽海花資料. Beijing: Zhonghua shuju, 1962.

———, ed. *Yuanyang hudie pai yanjiu ziliao* 鴛鴦蝴蝶派研究資料. Shanghai wenyi chubanshe, 1984.

Wei Zi'an 魏子安 [Wei Xiuren 魏秀仁]. *Huayue hen* 花月痕. Reprint, Beijing: Renmin wenxue chubanshe, 1982.

Widmer, Ellen. "*Honglou meng* Sequels and Their Female Readers in Nineteenth-Century China." In *Snake's Legs: Sequels, Continuations, Rewritings, and Chinese Fiction*, edited by Martin W. Huang, 116–142. Honolulu: University of Hawai'i Press, 2004.

———. "The Huanduzhai of Hangzhou and Suzhou: A Study in Seventeenth-Century Publishing." *Harvard Journal of Asiatic Studies* 36 (1996): 77–122.

———. "Inflecting Gender: Zhan Kai/Siqi Zhai's 'New Novels' and Courtesan Sketches." *Nannü* 6.1 (2004): 136–168.

———. *The Margins of Utopia:* Shui-hu hou-chuan *and the Literature of Ming Loyalism*. Cambridge, MA: Harvard Council on East Asian Studies Publications, 1987.

Williams, Raymond. *The Country and the City.* London: Oxford University Press, 1973.

———. *Marxism and Literature.* London: Oxford University Press, 1977.

Wirth-Nesher, Hana. *City Codes: Reading the Modern Urban Novel.* Cambridge: Cambridge University Press, 1996.

Wright, Arnold, and Cartwright, H. A., eds. *Twentieth-Century Impressions of Hong Kong, Shanghai, and Other Treaty Ports of China: Their History, People, Commerce, Industries, and Resources.* London: Lloyd's Greater Britain Publishing Company, Ltd., 1908. Kyoto University Institute of Humanities Library.

Wu Fuhui 吳福輝. *Dushi xuanliu zhong de haipai xiaoshuo* 都市漩流中的海派小說. [Changsha]: Hunan jiaoyu chubanshe, 1995.

Wu Guifang 吳貴芳. *Songgu mantan* 淞故漫談. Shanghai renmin chubanshe, 1991.

Wu Huanzhang 吳歡章, ed. *Haipai xiaoshuo jingpin* 海派小說精品. Revised edition. Shanghai: Fudan daxue chubanshe, 1996.

Wu Jianren 吳趼人. *Ershi nian mudu zhi guai xianzhuang* 二十年目睹之怪現狀. Reprinted as volume 5 of *Zhongguo jindai wenxue daxi.* Shanghai shudian.

———. *Haishang mingji si da jingang qishu* 海上名妓四大金剛奇書. Shanghai: Wenyi shuju, 1898. Photoreprint in *Shinmatsu shōsetsu* 15, 17, 18, and 19.

Wu Youru 吳友如. *Fengsu zhi tushuo* 風俗誌圖說. Reprinted in *Wu Youru hua bao* 吳友如畫寶. Shanghai: Wenrui lou, 1925.

———. *Haishang baiyan tu* 海上百艷圖. Reprinted in *Wu Youru hua bao* 吳友如畫寶 [1908]. Shanghai guji chubanshe, 1983.

Wumu shanren 烏目山人. *Haishang Daguan yuan* 海上大觀園. 1924. Reprint, Shanghai guji chubanshe, 1991.

Xiao, Zhiwei. "Constructing a New National Culture: Film Censorship and the Issues of Cantonese Dialect, Superstition, and Sex in the Nanjing Decade." In *Cinema and Urban Culture in Shanghai, 1922–1943,* edited by Yingjin Zhang, 183–199. Stanford: Stanford University Press, 1999.

Xinji Haishang qinglou tuji 新輯海上青樓圖集. Shanghai, 1895.

"Xinzeng chongxiu Shanghai xiancheng xiang zujie dili quantu" 新增重修上海縣城廂租界地理全圖. Shanghai: Zhaoji wucai shi yinshuju, 1895. Photograph courtesy of Wei Shaochang.

Xu Gang 徐剛. "Shijue de cangshan yu fanyi—cong xiaoshuo *Haishang hua liezhuan* dao Hou Xiaoxian de dianying *Haishang hua*" 視覺的藏閃與翻譯—從小說「海上花列傳」到侯孝賢的電影「海上花」. *Jintian* 52 (2001): 254–265.

Xu Jielu 徐絜廬. *Hubin shentan lu* 滬濱神探錄. 1927–1928. Reprint, Shanghai guji chubanshe, 1991.

Xu Qinfu 許廑父. *Hujiang fengyue zhuan* 滬江風月傳. Shanghai: Qinghua shuju, 1921.

Xu Xiaotian 許嘯天. *Shanghai fengyue* 上海風月. 1929. Reprint, Yangzhou: Jiangsu guangling guji keyin she, 1998.

Xu Xixian 徐喜先, and Xu Jianrong 徐建榮. *Baibian Shanghai* 百變上海. Shanghai renmin meishu chubanshe, 2005.

Xu Xu 徐訏. *Feng xiaoxiao* 風蕭蕭. Reprint, Hong Kong: Wuxing ji shubao she, 1964.

Yan Jiayan 嚴家炎. "Xin ganjue pai zhuyao zuojia" 新感覺派主要作家. *Lien-ho wen-hsüeh* 3.12: 15–19.

Yan Meisun, ed. *Shanghai suyu da cidian* 上海俗語大詞典. Reprint, Shanghai: Yunxuan chubanbu, 1924.

Yang Guangfu 楊光輔. *Songnan yuefu* 淞南樂府. 1796. Reprint, Shanghai: Shanghai guji chubanshe, 1989.

Yang, Mayfair Mei-hui. "Mass Media and Transnational Subjectivity in Shanghai: Notes on (Re)Cosmopolitanism in a Chinese Metropolis." In *Ungrounded Empires: The Cultural Politics of Chinese Transnationalism*, edited by Aihwa Ong and Donald Nonini, 287–319. London: Routledge, 1997.

Yang Zhenfang 楊振方. "Shanghai Yuan Ming Qing shiqi zhuming de chuban jia" 上海元明清時期著名的出版家. *Chuban shiliao* 1992.3: 68–74, 20.

Yao Gonghe 姚公鶴. *Shanghai xianhua* 上海閒話. Reprint, Shanghai guji chubanshe, 1989.

Yao Xie 姚燮. "Kuhai hang" 苦海航. Manuscript, 1848 postface. Suzhou University Library.

Ye, Kaidi 葉凱蒂 [Catherine Yeh]. "Cong shijiu shiji Shanghai ditu kan dui chengshi weilai dingyi de zhengduo zhan" 從十九世紀上海地圖看對城市未來定義的爭奪戰. *Zhongguo xueshu* 1, no. 3 (2000): 88–121.

Ye, Xiaoqing. "Shanghai before Nationalism." *East Asian History* 3 (1992): 33–52.

Yeh, Catherine. "Creating the Urban Beauty: The Shanghai Courtesan in Late Qing Illustrations." In *Writing Materiality in China: Essays in Honor of Patrick Hanan*, edited by Judith Zeitlin and Lydia Liu, 397–447. Cambridge, MA: Harvard University Asia Center, 2003.

———. "The Life-style of Four *Wenren* in Late Qing Shanghai." *Harvard Journal of Asiatic Studies* 57.2 (1997): 419–470.

———. "Reinventing Ritual: Late Qing Handbooks on Proper Customer Behavior in Shanghai Courtesan Houses." *Late Imperial China* 19.2 (1998): 1–63.

———. *Shanghai Love: Courtesans, Intellectuals, and Entertainment Culture, 1850–1910*. Seattle: University of Washington Press, 2006.

Yeh, Wen-hsin. "Progressive Journalism and Shanghai's Petty Urbanites: Zou Taofen and the Shenghuo Enterprise, 1926–1945." In *Shanghai Sojourners*, edited by Frederic E. Wakeman, Jr. and Wen-hsin Yeh, 186–238. Berkeley: University of California Press, 1992.

Yi Su 一粟, ed. *Honglou meng shulu* 紅樓夢書錄. Revised edition. Shanghai guji chubanshe, 1981.

Youd, Daniel. "Geographies of Success and Failure in Li Lüyuan's (1707–1790) *Qilu deng*." Paper presented at the 1999 Association for Asian Studies annual meeting.

Youxi bao 遊戲報. Shanghai: Youxi baoshe, 1897–[1910?].

Youxi zhuren 遊戲主人 [Li Boyuan 李伯元]. *Haishang youxi tushuo* 海上遊戲圖說. Shanghai: Youxi baoshe, 1898.

Yu Da 俞達. *Qinglou meng* 青樓夢. Shanghai: Shen bao guan 1878.

Yu Xingmin 于醒民. *Shanghai, 1862 nian* 上海，1862年. Shanghai renmin chubanshe, 1991.

Yu Yingshi 余英時. *Honglou meng de liangge shijie* 紅樓夢的兩個世界. Shanghai shehui kexue yuan chubanshe, 2002.

Yuan Jin 袁進. *Yuanyang hudie pai* 鴛鴦蝴蝶派. Shanghai shudian, 1994.

———. *Zhongguo wenxue guannian de jindai biange* 中國文學觀念的近代變革. Shanghai shehui kexue yuan chubanshe, 1996.

Yue, Audrey. "'In the Mood for Love': Intersections of Hong Kong Modernity." In *Chinese Films in Focus: 25 New Takes*, edited by Chris Berry, 128–136. London: British Film Institute, 2003.

Zamperini, Paola. "On Their Dress They Wore a Body: Fashion and Identity in Late Qing Shanghai." *positions* 11.2 (2003): 301–330.

Zeng Pu 曾樸. *Niehai hua* 孽海花. Revised edition. Shanghai guji chubanshe, 1979.

———. "Xiugai hou yao shuo de jiju hua" 修改後要說的幾句話. 1934. Reprinted in *Niehai hua ziliao* 孽海花資料, edited by Wei Shaochang. Beijing: Zhonghua shuju, 1962.

Zeng Zuyin 曾祖蔭, et al., eds. *Zhongguo lidai xiaoshuo xuba xuanzhu* 中國歷代小說序跋選注. Hubei: Changjiang wenyi chubanshe, 1982.

Zhang Ailing 張愛玲 [Eileen Chang] trans. *Haishang hua kai; Haishang hua luo* 海上花開；海上花落. 2 volumes. Taipei: Huangguan, 1983. Reprint, 1995.

———. *Zhang kan* 張看. Reprint, Taipei: Huangguan, 1995.

Zhang Chunfan 張春帆. *Jiuwei gui* 九尾龜. 1906–1911. Reprinted in *Zhongguo jindai xiaoshuo daxi* 中國近代小說大系. Nanchang: Jiangxi renmin chubanshe, 1989.

Zhang Chunhua 張春華. *Hucheng suishi quge* 滬城歲事衢歌. 1839. Reprint, Shanghai guji chubanshe, 1989.

Zhang Jinglu 張靜廬, ed. *Zhongguo jindai chuban shiliao* 中國近代出版史料. 2 volumes. Beijing: Zhonghua shuju, 1957.

Zhang Peiheng 張培恆. "*Haishang hua liezhuan* yu qi yiqian de xiaoshuo"「海上花列傳」與其以前的小說. *Ming Qing xiaoshuo yanjiu* 1985.8: 325–334.

Zhang, Xudong. "Shanghai Nostalgia: Postrevolutionary Allegories in Wang Anyi's Literary Production in the 1990s." *positions* 8.2 (2000): 349–388.

Zhang Xuesen 張學森, ed. *Yuanlin jiqu* 園林記趣. Shanghai huabao chubanshe, 1991.

Zhang, Yingjin. *The City in Modern Chinese Literature and Film: Configurations of Space, Time, and Gender*. Stanford: Stanford University Press, 1996.

Zhang, Zhen. *An Amorous History of the Silver Screen: Shanghai Cinema, 1896–1937*. Chicago: University of Chicago Press, 2005.

Zheng Zhenduo 鄭振鐸. "Xiaoxian?" 消閒. Reprinted in *Yuanyang hudie pai yan-*

jiu ziliao 鴛鴦蝴蝶派研究資料, edited by Wei Shaochang 魏紹昌, 58–59. Volume 1. Shanghai wenyi chubanshe, 1984.

Zhang Zhongli 張仲禮, ed. *Jindai Shanghai chengshi yanjiu* 近代上海城市研究. Shanghai renmin chubanshe, 1990.

Zhongguo jindai wenxue da cidian 中國近代文學大詞典. Hefei: Huangshan shushe, 1995.

Zhongguo jindai wenxue daxi 中國近代文學大系. Shanghai shudian, 1996.

Zhongguo tongsu xiaoshuo zongmu tiyao 中國通俗小說總目提要. Beijing: Zhongguo wenlian chuban gongsi, 1990.

Zhou Yuanhe 周源和. *Shanghai jiaotong hua dangnian* 上海交通話當年. Shanghai: Huadong shifan daxue chubanshe, 1992.

Zhu Junzhou 祝均宙. "Qingmo Minchu qizhong hanjian wenyi baokan gouchen" 清末民初七種罕見文藝報刊鉤沉. *Chuban shiliao* 1992.4: 130–141.

Zhu Lianbao 朱聯保. "Jiefang qian Shanghai shudian, chubanshe yinxiang ji (9)" 解放前上海書店，出版社印象記. *Chuban shiliao* 1987.4: 104–105.

Zhu Shouju 朱瘦菊 [Haishang shuomeng ren 海上說夢人]. *Xiepu chao* 歇浦潮. 1916–1921. Reprint, Shanghai guji chubanshe, 1991.

———. *Xin Xiepu chao* 新歇浦潮. 1922–? Reprint, Shanghai guji chubanshe, 1991.

Zhu Tianwen 朱天文 [Chu Tien-wen]. *Jishang zhi meng: "Haishang hua" dianying quan jilu* 極上之夢：「海上花」電影全紀錄. Taipei: Yuanliu chubanshe, 1998.

Zhu Weizheng 朱維錚. "Wan Qing Shanghai wenhua: yi zu duan lun" 晚清上海文化：一組短論. *Fudan xuebao* 1992.5.

Zou Tao 鄒弢. *Haishang chentian ying* 海上塵天影. Reprint, Beijing: Minzu chubanshe, 1995.

Zou Yiren 鄒依仁. *Jiu Shanghai renkou bianqian de yanjiu* 舊上海人口變遷的研究. Shanghai renmin chubanshe, 1980.

Index

Abbas, Ackbar, 180

aesthetic of interruption, 80–92, 101; and desire for continuity, 182–183; in fiction, contrasted with film, 177; and modernist stream-of-consciousness writing, 155–156; and Shanghai's "recovery" of past glory, 183. *See also* frustration

"Ala Szahaenin" (We Shanghai people), 181

alleys *(lilong)*, 30; linking different narratives together, 70; as a mode of urban development, 60; and referentiality, 63; significance of, 58–59, 70–71; and structure of Shanghai fiction, 62–63; as a system of relations, 59, 62–63, 70

Also a Garden (Yeshi yuan), 42, 167

Anderson, Benedict, 6, 75, 78–79, 83

Anderson, Marston, 133, 135

Arcadia Hall, 84

Aurora University (Zhendan daxue), 151

author, professional, 121–125

automobiles. *See* carriage-riding

Balzac, Honoré de, 29, 89; and *Comédie humaine,* 95

Bao Tianxiao, 24, 119, 132. See also *Renjian diyu*

Barthes, Roland, 68–69, 87

base and superstructure: critique of the distinction between, 5–6, 138–140. *See also* consumption

"Bei dangzuo xiaoqianpin de nanzi" (Men taken as leisure items), 148

Beijing, 23, 52, 77, 108; as cultural center, 31, 39, 183

Beijing fanhua meng (Dreams of Beijing splendor), 23

Beijing xin fanhua meng (New dreams of Beijing splendor), 23, 99

Benjamin, Walter, 60, 178–179, 232n88

Berlin, 63, 144

Bi Yihong, 24. See also *Renjian diyu*

Boym, Svetlana, 160, 180

brand names, 72, 105, 125; "Shanghai" as, 1, 180–182

Britain, 14, 42

brokers and intermediaries, 114–121; authors as, 118–121. *See also* Shanghai

Brooks, Peter, 89

Bubbling Well Road (Nanjing xilu), 97, 133, 141, 167

Bund, the, 1, 57, 61, 97, 141

Caifeng bao (Selected rumors daily), 78, 105

Cang Jie, 33, 161

Canghai ke, 225n41

cangshan (hidden flashes). See *chuancha cangshan zhi fa*

Canton. *See* Guangzhou

Cao Xueqin, 33. See also *Honglou meng*

carriage drivers, 97, 111, 125

carriage-riding, 82; and excess of desire, 110–113; as leisure activity, 96–98; and property value, 105; and speed, 133, 148, 175. *See also* carriage drivers; circulation

Chang, Eileen (Zhang Ailing), 147, 180; interest in Shanghai fiction, 4, 24, 144; Mandarin translation of *Haishang hua liezhuan,* 117, 163–164, 169

Chen Diexian, 23

chenggong renshi (successful individual), 181–182

Cadres and Corruption: The Organizational Involution of the Chinese Communist Party, by Xiaobo Lü. Stanford University Press, 2000.

Japan's Imperial Diplomacy: Consuls, Treaty Ports, and War with China, 1895–1938, by Barbara Brooks. Honolulu: University of Hawai'i Press, 2000.

China's Retreat from Equality: Income Distribution and Economic Transition, ed. Carl Riskin, Zhao Renwei, Li Shi. Armonk, NY: M.E. Sharpe, 2000.

Nation, Governance, and Modernity: Canton, 1900–1927, by Michael T. W. Tsin. Stanford University Press, 1999.

Assembled in Japan: Electrical Goods and the Making of the Japanese Consumer, by Simon Partner. Berkeley: University of California Press, 1999.

Civilization and Monsters: Spirits of Modernity in Meiji Japan, by Gerald Figal. Durham, NC: Duke University Press, 1999.

The Logic of Japanese Politics: Leaders, Institutions, and the Limits of Change, by Gerald L. Curtis. New York: Columbia University Press, 1999.

Contesting Citizenship in Urban China: Peasant Migrants, the State and Logic of the Market, by Dorothy Solinger. Berkeley: University of California Press, 1999.

About the Author

Alexander Des Forges is assistant professor of Chinese in the
Department of Modern Languages and the Program in East Asian
Studies at the University of Massachusetts, Boston. He received
a Ph.D. in Chinese literature from Princeton University and has
published a number of articles on Shanghai culture and modern
Chinese literature. This is his first book.

Production Notes for Des Forges / *Mediasphere Shanghai*
Jacket design by Santos Barbasa Jr.
Text design by Paul Herr with text in Minion and display
    in Bernhard Modern
Composition by Santos Barbasa Jr.
Printing and binding by The Maple-Vail Book Manufacturing Group
Printed on 60 lb. Maple-Vail White Offset, 440 ppi